FLORIDA STATE
UNIVERSITY LIBRARIES

JUN 0 1 2001

TALLAHASSEE, FLORIDA

BACKBENCH DEBATE WITHIN THE CONSERVATIVE
PARTY AND ITS INFLUENCE ON BRITISH FOREIGN
POLICY, 1948–57

Backbench Debate within the Conservative Party and its Influence on British Foreign Policy, 1948–57

Sue Onslow

DA
589.8
.O57
1997

 First published in Great Britain 1997 by
MACMILLAN PRESS LTD
Houndmills, Basingstoke, Hampshire RG21 6XS and London
Companies and representatives throughout the world

A catalogue record for this book is available from the British Library.

ISBN 0-333-65637-7

 First published in the United States of America 1997 by
ST. MARTIN'S PRESS, INC.,
Scholarly and Reference Division,
175 Fifth Avenue, New York, N.Y. 10010

ISBN 0-312-16471-8

Library of Congress Cataloging-in-Publication Data
Onslow, Sue, 1958–
Backbench debate within the Conservative Party and its influence
on British foreign policy, 1948–57 / Sue Onslow.
p. cm.
Includes bibliographical references (p.   ) and index.
ISBN 0-312-16471-8 (cloth)
1. Great Britain—Foreign relations—1945–   2. Conservatism—Great
Britain—History—20th century.   3. Conservative Party (Great
Britain)   4. World politics—1945–1955.   I. Title.
DA589.8.057   1996
327.41'009'045—dc20   96-28389
                                                      CIP

© Sue Onslow 1997
All rights reserved. No reproduction, copy or transmission of this publication may be made without written permission.

No paragraph of this publication may be reproduced, copied or transmitted save with written permission or in accordance with the provisions of the Copyright, Designs and Patents Act 1988, or under the terms of any licence permitting limited copying issued by the Copyright Licensing Agency, 90 Tottenham Court Road, London W1P 9HE.

Any person who does any unauthorised act in relation to this publication may be liable to criminal prosecution and civil claims for damages.

The author has asserted her right to be identified as the author of this work in accordance with the Copyright, Designs and Patents Act 1988.

This book is printed on paper suitable for recycling and made from fully managed and sustained forest sources.

10 9 8 7 6 5 4 3 2 1
06 05 04 03 02 01 00 99 98 97

Printed in Great Britain by
The Ipswich Book Company Ltd
Ipswich, Suffolk

Contents

Acknowledgements	vi
Abbreviations	ix
Key Dates	x
1 Introduction: Conservative backbenchers and political influence	1
2 Conservative attitudes to European integration	12
3 The Conservative Party and Europe: in opposition 1948–50	33
4 The waiting room of power: 1950–51	55
5 The Conservatives and Europe: the pragmatism of power 1951–57	78
6 The genesis of the Suez Group and the Anti-Suez Group	107
7 The Conservative Party and the Middle East: 1948–51	128
8 The Conservatives in power: Egypt and the Sudan 1951–53	151
9 Negotiating the withdrawal from the Suez Canal Zone base: 1953–54	166
10 The Conservative Party and the Middle East: 1955–57	188
11 Conclusion	222
Notes	236
Appendices	291
Bibliography	299
Index	309

Acknowledgements

In preparing this book I owe a great debt of thanks to the late Dr Roger Bullen of the London School of Economics, whose encouragement to continue my PhD thesis research through the vicissitudes of moving and early motherhood was invaluable. I would also like to thank my supervisor, Professor Donald Watt, for his considerable insight and gentle guidance; John Barnes, for his untiring support and advice, and Dr Robert Boyce at the London School of Economics; also Dr John Ramsden of Queen Mary's College, London. My special thanks go to Dr David Butler, a fellow at Nuffield College, Oxford.

I am indebted to the efficiency and courtesy of the staff at the British Library of Political and Economic Science at the London School of Economics; the London Library; the British Library; Dr Martin Moore and his colleagues at the Bodleian Library, Oxford; the House of Lords' archives; the Churchill Archives Centre, Churchill College, Cambridge, the Staff at the Brotherton Library, University of Leeds, and the Archivist at the Library of the University of Birmingham, the Public Records Office in Kew and the Newspaper Library in Colindale.

I would like to thank Curtis Brown Group Ltd on behalf of the estate of the late Sir Winston S. Churchill for permission to quote from Sir Winston's papers, held at the Churchill Archive Centre, Churchill College, Cambridge (copyright © Winston S. Churchill). I am most grateful for Lady Avon's permission to consult and quote from the Avon papers, which are kept at the library of the University of Birmingham.

I am also grateful for the permission of Sir Nicholas Hedworth Williamson and the Keeper of Archives at the Churchill Archives Centre, Churchill College, Cambridge to consult Lord Hailes' papers; Julian Sandys for his agreement to consult and quote extracts from his father's papers held in the Churchill Archives Centre; the Master and Fellows of Trinity College, Cambridge for permission to use extracts from Lord Layton's papers; and the Director of Conservative Policy Centre for permission to use material from the Conservative Party Archive at the Bodleian.

I would like to thank Mrs Chowdrahay-Best for her permission

Acknowledgements

to consult Lady Juliet Rhys-Williams' papers, held at the British Library of Political and Economic Science at the London School of Economics; the Earl of Woolton for his kind permission to use quotations from his father's papers, the first Earl of Woolton, at the Bodleian Library, Oxford; and Miss Lisl Biggs-Davison for letting me look at her father's papers at the House of Lords' archive. I am also grateful to the family of the late Lord Gridley for their permission to quote from Sir Arnold Gridley's letter to Duncan Sandys of October 1949.

Lady Legge-Bourke kindly let me consult her husband, Sir Harry Legge-Bourke's press cuttings and his private papers (held at the Brotherton Library at the University of Leeds) and her warm support was most welcome. I am also grateful to her son Captain William Legge-Bourke for his friendly tolerance when I arrived to look at his father's newspaper clippings at what must have seemed like an ungodly hour on New Year's morning.

I would like particularly to thank Nigel Nicolson for his good-humoured interest and shrewd comments, on top of the loan of private correspondence relating to the Suez crisis; Lord and Lady Sandwich for allowing me to look through Viscount Hinchingbrooke's papers and press lettings at Mapperton, for their hospitality and not least for their suggestion which allowed me a blissfully solitary walk on a frosty January evening through their sunken garden; Major Hugo Waterhouse for his kindness and hospitality; and Paul Williams who tolerated endless questions and lent me his private Suez papers twice.

I had the great advantage of warm support from a considerable number of former parliamentarians, journalists and Conservative party officials, who were all generous with their time. My particular thanks go to Lord Amery, Lord Aldington, Sir John Astor, John Baldock, Sir Reginald Bennett, Sir Richard Body, Lord Boyd-Carpenter, Sir Bernard Braine, Sir Paul Bryan, Lord Carr, Sir Robin Chichester-Clark, Sir Frederick Corfield, Sir Geoffrey Cox, Sir Douglas Dodds-Parker, Sir Edward du Cann, Lord Deedes, Lord Eccles, Lord Healey, Sir Edward Heath, Aubrey Jones, Sir Anthony Kershaw, Lord Lauderdale, Sir Gilbert Longden, Sir Anthony Nutting, Lord Orr-Ewing, Enoch Powell, Sir David Price, Sir Robert Rhodes James, Sir Julian Ridsdale, Lord Rippon, Wilfred Sendall, Lord Thomas and Sir Richard Thompson. I was also fortunate to receive the generous cooperation of Miss Ursula Branston, Arthur Gavshon, Lord Glendevon, Lord Colyton, Somerset de Chair, Lord Fraser of Kilmorack, Lord Margadale, Sir Charles Mott-Radclyffe, Sir Godfrey Nicholson and his daughter, Mrs Luce, Lord Nugent, Lord Thorneycroft and Lord Watkinson.

Dr Stuart Ball of the University of Leicester was also very helpful in letting me look at his transcript of Sir Cuthbert Headlam's diary. Dr Anthony Seldon, Director of St Dunstan's College, allowed me to make use of the transcripts of interviews he conducted with Sir Hugh Lucas-Tooth, Sir Kenneth Thompson, Lord Garner, Sir John Arbuthnot, Sir John Ward, Sir Ashley Clarke, Sir Frank Roberts, Lord Strang, Lord Butler, Lord Clitheroe, Sir William Hayter, Lord Sherfield, Sir Christopher Soames, John Foster, Lord Tranmire, Lord Thorneycroft, Sir Eric Bertoud, Lord Rhyl, Lord Duncan-Sandys, Lord Gladwyn, Sir Hubert Ashton, Sir John Coulson, and Allan Noble which form part of an oral history archive at present in the keeping of John Barnes; and the transcripts of his interviews with Lord Boyle, Viscount Muirshiel and Lord Carr in the British Oral Archive of Political History at the London School of Economics. I was also fortunate to attend a fascinating series of lectures given by Professor Wm Roger Louis of the Austin University, Texas, on Eden and the Suez crisis at the London School of Economics in 1992.

Finally, I need to thank my father, Sir Cranley Onslow, for his inspiration, humour and political acumen; and my mother, Lady June Onslow, along with Mrs Dorothy Grey and Mrs Susanna Bevan without whose help I could not have persevered. But my greatest debt is to my long-suffering husband, Bart and our small children, Claerwen and Kit who rapidly learnt when they could and could not touch the precious computer.

Abbreviations

ANZUS	Australia/New Zealand/United States
BOAPAH	British Oral Archive of Political and Administrative History
C&L	Conservative and Liberal
ECSC	European Coal and Steel Community
EDC	European Defence Community
EEC	European Economic Community
EFTA	European Free Trade Area
ELEC	European League for Economic Cooperation
EPC	European Political Community
EPU	European Payments Union
EURATOM	European Atomic Energy Ageney
FAC	Foreign Affairs Committee
HC Deb	Parliamentary Debates (Hansard) Fifth Series. House of Commons Official Report
HL Deb	Parliamentary Debates (Hansard) Fifth Series. House of Lords Official Report
LSE	London School of Economics
MES-C	Middle East Sub-committee
NATO	North Atlantic Treaty Organization
NL&C	National Liberal and Conservative
OEEC	Organization for European Economic Cooperation
PPS	Parliamentary Private Secretary
UEM	United Europe Movement
UNO	United Nations Organization
WEU	West European Union

Key Dates

19 September 1946	Churchill's speech 'Let Europe Unite', University of Zurich
3 December 1946	United Europe Committee formed
14 May 1947	Inaugural meeting of the United Europe Movement at the Royal Albert Hall
5 June 1947	Secretary of State Marshall's Harvard speech
21 February 1948	Communist *coup* in Prague
15 March 1948	Treaty of Brussels
7–10 May 1948	Congress at the Hague
15 May 1948	Palestine mandate surrendered
24 June 1948	Berlin blockade begins
4 April 1949	North Atlantic Treaty signed
19–20 April 1949	ELEC Westminster Economic Conference
5 May 1949	Statute of Westminster creating the Consultative Assembly and the Committee of Ministers
10 August 1949	Inaugural meeting of the Consultative Assembly of the Council of Europe in Strasbourg Churchill calls for German admission
23 February 1950	British General Election: Labour Government majority reduced to 6
30 March 1950	West Germany formally invited to join Council of Europe
9 May 1950	Schuman Plan proposed
25 June 1950	North Korean invasion of South Korea
14 August 1950	Churchill calls for a European Army in the Consultative Assembly of the Council of Europe
15 August 1950	Macmillan-Eccles Plan proposed in the Consultative Assembly
12 September 1950	NAT meeting in New York: American pressure for West German rearmament

Key Dates

24 October 1950	Pleven Plan unveiled
1 October 1951	Decision to evacuate British personnel from Abadan
8 October 1951	Egyptian unilateral abrogation of 1936 Anglo-Egyptian treaty, and 1899 treaty for the condominium of the Sudan
25 October 1951	British General Election: Conservative Government's majority 17
28 November 1951	Maxwell Fyfe speech in Strasbourg vs Eden at NAT meeting in Rome
20 March 1952	Eden Plan
23 July 1952	*Coup d'etat* against King Farouk of Egypt
25 July 1952	ECSC ratification complete
12 February 1953	Anglo-Egyptian agreement on the future independence of the Sudan
5 March 1953	Death of Stalin
April-October 1953	Eden absent through illness
23 June 1953	Churchill's stroke
2 December 1953	Bermuda conference
11 December 1953	British association with European Coal and Steel Community
27 July 1954	Heads of Agreement on Suez Canal Base agreement initialled
30 August 1954	European Defence Community defeated on a procedural vote in the French National Assembly
3 October 1954	Agreement on West German rearmament within NATO via the enlargement of WEU
19 October 1954	Anglo-Egyptian treaty on the Suez Canal Base signed
4 April 1955	Britain joins Baghdad Pact (already signed by Iraq and Turkey)
5 April 1955	Churchill resigns as Prime Minister
26 May 1955	British General Election: Conservative Government's majority 60
5 June 1955	Messina conference
27 September 1955	Czech-Egyptian arms deal

11 November 1955	British decision to withdraw from the Spaak Committee deliberations
1 March 1956	General Sir John Glubb dismissed as commander of the Arab Legion
9 March 1956	Archbishop Makarios deported to the Seychelles
25 May 1956	Venice Conference: Spaak Committee report by the Six
13 July 1956	Last British troops withdrawn from Suez Canal Zone
17 July 1956	British Cabinet decision not to finance Aswan Dam
19 July 1956	Eisenhower Administration withdrawal of offer of finance for Aswan Dam
26 July 1956	Nasser announces nationalization of Suez Canal Company
2 August 1956	British Government recalls reservists
14 August 1956	18-Power London Conference convened to discuss internationalisation of Suez Canal
4 September 1956	Dulles' Suez Canal Users Association proposed (endorsed by British Cabinet 11 September 1956)
19 September 1956	Suez Canal Users' Conference convened in London
2 October 1956	Selwyn Lloyd arrives in New York for negotiations on the Suez Canal at the UNO
12–13 October 1956	Conservative party conference at Llandudno. Free trade area plan outlined by Macmillan
14 October 1956	General Challe's and Gazier's meeting with Eden
29 October 1956	Israeli attack on Egypt
30 October 1956	Anglo-French ultimatum to Egypt and Israel
31 October 1956	British bombing of Egyptian airfields
4 November 1956	Russian troops invade Hungary
5 November 1956	Anglo-French assault on Port Said
6 November 1956	Ceasefire announced

8 November 1956	Critical vote of confidence in the House of Commons
23 November 1956	Eden leaves for Jamaica
26 November 1956	Macmillan announces intention to seek a free trade area within OEEC
3 December 1956	British withdrawal from Port Said announced
14 December 1956	Eden returns to Britain
10 January 1957	Eden's resignation. Harold Macmillan becomes Prime Minister
25 March 1957	Treaty of Rome signed
29 March 1957	Archbishop Makarios released. Lord Salisbury resigns.
9 April 1957	Suez Canal reopens to shipping
13 May 1957	Macmillan announces British vessels may use Suez Canal
15 May 1957	First British H-bomb exploded
1 January 1958	European Economic Community formally created without Britain
8 October 1959	British General Election: Conservative Government's majority 100
21 November 1959	EFTA of the Seven signed.

1 Introduction: Conservative backbenchers and political influence

Are backbenchers[1] mere 'cannon fodder' for the division lobbies? In 1990 it seemed Margaret Thatcher had committed the cardinal error of assuming that her supremacy in Cabinet was 'the bottom line', forgetting that she was ultimately answerable to the party in the House of Commons. But the Conservative party has always operated in a more sophisticated fashion than a simple model of Tory leaders outlining policy to their uncomplaining supporters. Certainly, the initiative and ultimate policy-making decisions do rest with the leadership. But these decisions have to reflect the pulse of opinion within the Tory ranks; otherwise, dissent ferments to the point of open criticism and erodes the leadership's ability to carry the party forward. Mainstream Conservatives would concur that while it is not their role to *make* policy, 'we are failing in our duty if we do not help *form* it'.[2]

This is not to say the motley collection of backbench groups which have always existed within the 'broad church'[3] of the Conservative party tamely accept their role as *shapers* of policy rather than *makers* of policy. 'The leaven within the lump' will try to seize the leadership's attention, as well as to attempt to drum up support within the central mass to endorse their arguments. But there is a limit to which the leadership will yield: thus, in this 'constructive tension'[4] between the Conservative front and backbenches, there is a decided element of bluff and counter-bluff.

So, a point for political scientists, interested in sustaining generalizations about power within political parties: this need for constant management of the parliamentary party was just as applicable in the late 1940s and 1950s as today. The Whips' office (and to a lesser degree ministerial Parliamentary Private

Secretaries – in that there were many fewer of them) played the same role as highly effective lines of communication between the back and front benches.[5] Their main tasks were communication, management and persuasion.[6] The disciplinary role of No. 12 Downing Street[7] is now grossly over-exaggerated – witness Michael Dobbs' sly appeal to popular prejudice in choosing to call Francis Urquart's Chief Whip 'Tim Stamper'.[8] In reality, it was – and is – very much a 'two-way linkage'.[9] Much depended, however, on the style of the Chief Whip. In addition, just as in the 1990s, there were a number of important criteria which governed backbenchers' attempts to exert influence, individually or collectively: the political experience of the individual MP; the size of the backbench revolt relative to the government's majority; and the unity of the Cabinet.

The influence of personality was also important, which is frequently discounted, but the pattern of personal likes and dislikes was woven into the very fabric of political debate.[10] There were also the opportunities for MPs to appeal to, or manipulate, opinion outside the Chamber: support for a cause in the House of Lords, in the press, in the party in the country (constituency associations), or at the Party conference, and general public opinion could be crucial in promoting a particular line.

Historians are more interested in policy outcomes. Most concentrate on the role of the political and civil service élite when dealing with Britain's emerging relationship with Europe[11] and her forced detachment from the Middle East after World War II. But Conservative backbench opinion proved to be a vital ingredient and between 1948 and 1957 there developed discernible backbench groups who held decided views on these issues and who exercised a significant influence: the Conservative Europeanists,[12] the Suez Group and – in the 1956 Suez crisis – the Anti-Suez Group.[13]

As this influence upon the party leadership was usually exerted in informal ways, in party committees and behind the scenes, the political setting of the 1940s and 1950s was important: the character of the House of Commons, the forms of public debate inside and outside Westminster and the nature and structure of the Conservative party. The Tory party of the 1945 Parliament was much smaller than before the War;[14] in addition, one third of Conservative MPs were newcomers.

The Whips' Office under James Stuart[15] and Patrick Buchan-Hepburn,[16] then widely regarded as a home for retired army officers,[17] persisted in its pre-war opinion of the party as a superior regiment and sought to impose military discipline on the backbench troops; this, together with the experience of public school[18] and war service (reinforced by the continued practice of addressing MPs by their war-time rank[19]), did instill in the party generally a certain discipline and sense of order.[20] But the newfound freedom, and indeed irresponsibility, of opposition was compounded by a greater tendency to political independence as the election of a considerable number of independent-minded MPs,[21] whose war-time service rendered them less inclined to obey the dictates of No. 12 Downing Street, combined with the continued presence of older MPs who regarded their constituencies as personal fiefs.[22]

The 1950 election saw the passing of a political generation. The intake of 92 new Conservatives included grammar school Tories and industrialists with different connections and allegiances. These capable young MPs were increasingly less beholden to the aristocratic families who had formerly controlled seats and were more inclined to question the wisdom and judgment of their leaders who had made their political reputations before the War, expecting the government to earn the loyalty of its supporters.[23] This new influx, combined with the reappearance of some 1930s stalwarts at Westminster, such as Captain Charles Waterhouse and Sir Herbert Williams, dashed the Whips' hopes that the incoming Conservative government's small majority of 17 would militate against too public an expression of discontent. Despite the political changing of the guard in 1950, 'this was still the world of the magic circle':[24] contacts and friendships formed at school, university, through the regiment or other wartime experiences continued to play a vital part. The tradition of Tory political families continued, as did the attitude among some members that the best way to address a problem was a quiet word with the Minister, who was probably a family friend, in the box at Ascot or in the pavilion at Lords.[25] There continued, too, for many an 'old fashioned' view of politics, underscored by a sense of public service. The Conservative backbenches contained many 'knights of the shires',[26] who entertained no sense of ambition beyond serving their constituents and their country to the best of their ability

– from the backbenches (for example, John Morrison, Anthony Hurd, Guy Lloyd, Air Commodore, Arthur Vere Harvey, Charles Mott-Radclyffe and Major Harry Legge-Bourke).[27] These knights formed 'the ballast of the party'. To describe them as 'backwoods men' would be a considerable injustice: instinctively conservative and wary of rapid change, they were men of principle and independent thought, but whose loyalty to the party was unswerving. For them, the greatest length to which their opposition to Government policy would go was their studied absence from Westminster despite the imposition of a three-line whip.[28]

The House of Commons in the late 1940s and 1950s provided the supreme forum for political debate. With television in its infancy (as well as limited in its political coverage by the 14 Day rule[29]), political debate outside Westminster was conducted largely on the hustings, in public meetings in constituencies, and in the press. MPs had far more contact with the general public and many older MPs deplored the introduction of 'surgeries'.[30] There was greater attendance at public meetings, and down in his constituency fastness – away from the control of Central Office – an MP was likely to be more forthright 'on the stump' than at Westminster. Here the importance of the local and provincial press was significant, since the public relied upon the radio and the printed word for information and MPs' speeches were syndicated around the country in a manner no longer seen.

The press generally was very focused on Parliament and Parliamentary reporting was extensive, but the need for outside employment or independent wealth to supplement a meagre parliamentary salary[31] meant that full-time Conservative MPs were rare. Attendance at debates was poor, except on important occasions or when the Member wished to speak.[32] Those who could fill the Chamber were few: on the annunciator the names Churchill, Bevan, Boothby or William (Will 'Y') Darling, described as 'the licensed jester of the backbenches',[33] could rouse MPs from their roosts in the smoking rooms or the bar, but 'most people beat it to the Tea Room as soon as the Minister sat down'.[34] This made good attendance at a debate worthy of comment.

The different pattern of attendance was underscored by the lack of office facilities in the Palace of Westminster. 'Only the very grand had offices there';[35] more often an MP would use one of the communal rooms, or indeed the committee corridor, to dictate correspondence to a secretary. In the 1950 Parliament during the Conservative war of attrition against the knife-edge Labour majority of six, marathon all-night sittings and snap divisions obliged many young MPs to sleep where they could find a convenient bench.[36] In addition, the relationship between backbenchers and ministers was very much less structured. Although the reversal of Conservative fortunes in 1945 induced greater contact and sense of *camaraderie* between senior and junior MPs, there remained a discernible divide between the political generations. This generation gap, underlined by wartime and opposition experience, became even more apparent when the Conservatives returned to office in 1951.[37]

All of this made the private forums of debate very important.[38] It reinforced the importance of party backbench committees[39] as a primary source of information and augmented the influence of opinions expressed there. As discussion in these committees was confidential,[40] it was possible to have uninhibited exchanges of view in a way impossible on the floor of the House.[41] The considerable influence exercised by these backbench committees over their front bench[42] was enhanced by the very fact it was discreet. With a Whip and the relevant minister's PPS[43] in attendance, these committees 'were very much a two-way street: we heard the Government view ahead of the backbenches, and we got to the Government what the party had in mind'.[44]

Relatively few in number, the most important official Conservative backbench committee was the 1922 Committee,[45] followed by those which shadowed the three great offices of state: Foreign Affairs, Treasury and Home Affairs. These committees met regularly; others, for example the Defence Committee, were convened only to discuss specific issues when they arose. The Smoking Room, supplemented by the Members' Dining Room,[46] was the other chosen venue for Conservative MPs to meet, gossip and exchange views. Opinion was divided over which venue formed the powerhouse of debate. The social animals or the intriguers had a decided preference for the former, whereas the more patrician MPs placed the emphasis upon the latter.

There were also important unofficial (that is, non-elective) Conservative backbench groups which offered vital links in the web of backbench influence. Although Churchill directed that the Tory Reform Group be wound up in 1945, and decreed that there should be no more such political cliques as they dissipated the energies of the party, the Progress Trust[47] continued to meet throughout these years. Originally formed in 1943 as a 'libertarian' counterweight to the Tory Reform Group which was advocating the implementation of the Beveridge Report, the Trust subsequently evolved from a bulwark of the Conservative *laissez faire* tradition in social policy into a forum to protect Conservative principles.[48] In essence, the Trust represented the persistence of a pre-war view of the ideal political arrangement – paternalistic and strictly hierarchical. Its continued existence was indicative of the political influence it wielded and the value placed upon its work by Tory leaders.

The Trust was highly organized and possessed its own sources of information. Membership was selective, limited to approximately 20 MPs, and was considered a very great honour.[49] It met weekly, the chairman had immediate access to the Chief Whip's Office and to No. 10 whenever he so wished, and the monthly dinner invitations to Cabinet Ministers were not to be ignored.[50] Its organization was extremely discreet and deliberately so, in the firm belief that private influence was the most effective way for a backbench group to convey its views to the party leadership. This was very much in keeping with the attitude to all private debate within the party's backbench committees. The Progress Trust's members' highly discreet influence ensured the continuation of the Tory party as a class organization,[51] despite its more progressive public face.

The Progress Trust was composed not just of Tory grandees; its members were also MPs of considerable independence and acknowledged political influence, holding other important backbench positions, including on the 1922 Committee executive.[52] By the late 1940s many MPs had come to regard the Progress Trust, even more than the 1922 Committee, as the backbone of the Tory party; indeed, in the mid-1950s the Trust became the unofficial backbench cabal,[53] setting the tone for the party's other official backbench committees. The success of the Progress Trust behind the scenes in influencing the agenda and tone of political debate within the party obviated the need to publicize such views. So political commentators who asserted that the claim of sustained 'right-wing' influence on the Conservative party was hollow[54] completely missed the point.

In addition to the other more informal regular backbench gatherings such as the NAAFI (No Aims Ambitions Fractional Interest) Club, a jocular dining club,[55] the 5,000 Acre Club (a telling reflection of the extensive landed interests of some Conservative MPs) and each political generation's own dining club, there existed other important backbench ginger groups: the Suez Group; One Nation (formed in 1950);[56] a backbench ginger group fiercely critical of Butler's economic policy in the 1950s, which was led by Ralph Assheton and Captain Charles Waterhouse; an informal group whose main aim was the introduction of commercial television and whose success gave a considerable fillip to other pressure groups;[57] a faction led by Gerald Nabarro and Colonel Claude Lancaster which harried the Conservative Government on fuel and power; and Lord Hinchingbrooke, from his position as Chairman of the backbench Transport Committee, led backbench pressure for a change in transport policy.

All in all, the Conservative leadership, in opposition and in government, was a good deal more sensitive towards their backbenchers than is generally acknowledged.[58] Admittedly, foreign policy involves almost no legislation and Parliament is normally only required to endorse or register disapproval of the Government's line. And obviously, Conservative backbench opinion was only one factor in a Conservative government's formulation and management of foreign policy: Conservative Central Office, the pro- and anti-Tory press, opinion in the constituencies and the City all played a part. However, although direct backbench influence on government decisions may have been rare, indirect backbench influence was a constant factor – on the terms on which foreign policy was debated, advocated and defended. Professional civil servants in the Foreign Office were very conscious of the political scene in which ministers had to operate. This contribution to the 'atmosphere of contentment or disillusion' – serving as a check on policy makers by helping to set the parameters within which the Government was obliged to manoeuvre – was probably more significant than backbench input into policy formulation.

Then there is the matter of partisan influence. In normal circumstances, Conservative backbench opinion on foreign policy issues had no impact on the Labour front bench. Conversely, Labour backbench opinion had precious little bearing on Conservative thought[59] – if anything, attempts to coordinate cross-party cooperation on an issue were regarded with intense suspicion by the opposing party.[60] However, opposition opinion was important from the point of view of political tactics. Any Labour political divisions would raise Conservative morale, fuelling the desire to exploit the weakness of the other side. Similarly, the Labour party was keenly aware that a dissident Conservative faction offered the opportunity of defeating a Tory government – particularly if the government's majority was slim: all depended upon the resolution of the rebels and their willingness to see the Government fall. Therefore cross-party cooperation was normally minimal and confined to non-political issues. This made Winston Churchill's all-party United Europe Committee and the all-party parliamentary committee's campaign to promote European unity in the 1945 Parliament all the more extraordinary. No such cross-party deviation occurred, for example, on Middle Eastern issues.

From the point of view of political practice, a study of the Conservative Europeanists, the Suez Group and Anti-Suez Group offers an interesting contrast between the influence on the formation and presentation of British foreign policy exercised by a tendency[61], a well-organized faction[62], and an *ad hoc* pressure group; and the reaction of the Conservative party machine to these groups' activities. Some might argue that these groupings, which differed markedly in their organization, the public perception of the calibre of their membership and their approach, were symptomatic of a more basic division of Conservative philosophy; that is, the Europeanists and the Anti-Suez Group, and the Suez Group as an expression of the progressive and the reactionary wings of the party. However, the party in the decade after the War defies attempts to identify such fundamental divisions. There was no permanent right-wing opposition and the party fractured according to specific issues.[63] At best, a broad generalization can be made about the type of MP likely to be an adherent to each group; certainly, Conservative views on the merits of maintaining and extending imperial preference, and strong undercurrents of hostility towards America and the new United Nations Organization[64] – what was seen as unnecessary British subservience to her wartime ally and a preference of a system of 'spheres of influence' which appeared to have functioned more satisfactorily – had an important bearing upon backbench divisions over European integration and British policy in the Middle East. But there are important exceptions to each group's membership, and for some apparent imperial stalwarts securing a strong Commonwealth/Europe grouping was the natural obverse of the visceral Conservative reluctance to see the world ruled by the United States.

The Suez Group has suffered from the image of the Tory 'old guard' trumpeting one of the last hurrahs of Empire. Political appearances can be extremely deceptive, and the power of official party propaganda very pervasive: in reality, those who sought to influence the leadership to adopt a more robust stance to defend British power and prestige in the Middle East occupied crucial positions within the web of backbench influence and were adept at manipulating the climate of debate. As one former Conservative Chief Whip once remarked to another: 'It is not so easy to deal with a party of backroom boys as with a party of backwoods boys'.[65]

The internal Conservative struggle over the best means to maintain British paramountcy in the Middle East has no modern-day parallel. That said, the Suez Group's fundamental importance lies in 'the continuum it represents within the Tory party':[66] the discernible thread which runs through the party's internal struggle over Tariff Reform in 1903–11 and 1921–3; opposition to Indian independence in the 1930s; opposition to the Yalta agreement of 1945; opposition to withdrawal from Palestine in 1948, and Abadan, the Sudan and Egypt in the 1950s; opposition to government policy on Cyprus in the mid-1950s; and Rhodesia in the 1960s. The unifying theme is 'Britain and Empire', and Britain's corresponding global role. Ironically, at the time some staunch imperialists also favoured closer links with Europe, spurred by their conviction that the Empire and Europe could form a formidable economic bloc which would free Britain from American tutelage and the domination of the mighty dollar. This also appeared to offer British leadership of an alternative political power bloc in a world divided between the two superpowers.

However, this reactionary refrain has had an important and enduring impact on Conservative attitudes to the emerging European institutions, manifest in Tory opposition to British entry into the European Economic Community in 1962, the anti-Marketeers of the 1970s, the anti-Maastricht rebels and Conservative Euro-sceptics in the 1990s – precisely because British involvement in European integration appears to presuppose a choice between the Continent and Britain in the wider world. To Tory opponents, past and present, British involvement in European federation smacks of 'dwindling into a wife'[67], rather than offering (as it does, for example, to the French) the attraction of wielding greater influence in the international arena as a leading part of a powerful European federation. Washington's encouragement of European political federation merely served to fan the fires of Tory anti-American feeling.

The historical parallels between the current Tory civil war over Europe and Conservative resistance to European integration in the late 1940s and 1950s are quite startling. The following words were written in 1954: 'The isolationists, which still persist in both major parties, are inclined to assert that Britain has been dragged into this European venture by the machinations of unscrupulous continental politicians. They ought to realize that the whole early inspiration and driving force for the European movement came from this country', specifically from Duncan Sandys and Winston Churchill.[68] Forty years on, there are two important differences in tactics and alternative power-political groupings: (i) Churchill deliberately acted through a cross-party body and resisted his lieutenants' attempts to make Europe a partisan issue; and (ii) in the decade after the War, Britain at the head of the Empire and emerging Commonwealth, or indeed Atlantic Union (a combination of Britain, Canada and the United States), appeared a practical economic and political option compared to seemingly nebulous notions of Europe revived and united. Now, (i) the political parties cannot resist the temptation to make Europe a party issue (although Labour is just as riven as the Tories) and (ii) no such potential alternative power-bloc exists. Just as in the late 1940s and 1950s, the European federalists continue to set the pace of debate, fuelled by Chancellor Kohl's fear that the existing European institutions dare not stand still in the uncertain post-Cold War world: Germany revived and reunited still needs to be contained to be saved from her darker self, now perhaps more than ever. John Major's ideas of a 'Europe of Nations' are rejected, while Conservative hardline opponents of closer political links with Europe appear to offer only 'Little England'. Britain's imperial history, the abiding memory of victory in World War II, her island geography and the relative ease of Britain's decolonizing experience still conspire to prevent a public revaluation of the harsh realities of Britain's position. Meanwhile, this country continues to take advantage of the benefits of Franco-German rapprochement – political and economic stability in Europe – whilst bewailing the cost.

2 Conservative attitudes to European integration

Conservative views on Europe in the late 1940s should not be seen though the prism of later Conservative antagonisms towards the Continent. Although at the time no hard and fast divisions in attitudes to European integration were apparent to the active participants, Conservatives could be divided into three general categories. Composition of these groups tended to shift according to the international climate, and as the debate became focused upon specific proposals.

The Europeanists were those vocal MPs who favoured closer British cooperation with Europe, ranging from Churchill's preference for British sponsorship and support (stopping short of actual membership) to those who were keen to see British participation in European confederal arrangements. The group included MPs whose membership of organizations favouring more 'extreme' measures (for example, Federal Union and World Government) indicated their enthusiasm for close links with Europe to prevent a future war, rather than any desire for British political federation with Europe. 'No Conservative favoured a federal Europe.'[1] Between those who urged a more positive approach and those who remained distinctly suspicious, sat the majority of Conservatives who were ambivalent about the lure of Europe. The Sceptics were convinced that Britain had far more pressing global concerns, or harboured strong doubts about the implications of closer association with the Continent which, it was feared, might jeopardize Britain's historic ties with the Empire and Commonwealth. This was 'a section of the party'[2] rather than an active pressure group, whose feelings were aroused only on specific issues or particular occasions, moving the fulcrum of opinion within the party. The small group of anti-Europeans became deeply opposed to closer ties with the Continent. Most appear to have regarded their Continental neighbours as degenerate, second-rate foreigners.[3] Although these chauvinist sentiments did not apply to all anti-Europeans, these MPs shared a deep-seated antipathy towards any moves which might limit Britain's freedom of action and prejudice her future; they were also all staunch supporters of imperial preference.

THE EUROPEANISTS

In the immediate post-war period the question of Europe was inextricably linked to the question of security.[4] The bedrock concern was that there should never again be war between the European nations – specifically France and Germany – and, as the shadow of Russia fell across the Continent, that Europe must unite to protect herself against this threat. Thus there was an overwhelming sense that this cause, which also restored a sense of self-worth to the defeated nations of the Continent, was highly laudable. Although the press might imply the 'Strasbourgers' formed an identifiable faction, the Europeanists did not represent a united bloc within Parliament. Advocacy of closer links with Europe was left to individual, often well-placed Conservative backbenchers and, unlike the Suez Group's cause, there was support from the Labour benches and from outside domestic and international organizations.[5] Approximately 60 Conservative MPs favoured an active approach towards European integration. There was a hard core: 'a personal Churchill clique, (dating) back to anti-appeasement',[6] which included Winston Churchill, Duncan Sandys,[7] Robert Boothby and Harold Macmillan. Beyond this lay two outer concentric circles of MPs[8] whose enthusiasm for Europe fluctuated between 1946 and 1949. There were the 'enthusiasts for some form of closer union'[9] who ably supported Churchill's 'clique';[10] although these MPs were sensitive towards potentially conflicting obligations of Empire and Europe,[11] they were confident that the problems could be bridged.[12] Beyond these MPs, there existed a wider circle of interested observers: 'the pro-Commonwealthers'[13] who, while accepting that closer unspecified links with Europe were an excellent idea, were determined that 'nothing should be done which might adversely affect the Commonwealth and Empire, particularly to the advantage of Continentals'.[14]

In any discussion of the Conservatives and Europe in the 1940s the principal figure is Churchill. Without his leadership and inspiration, the cause of Europe would never have acquired its political momentum, nor would the Conservative party have come to be closely identified with Europe in the public's mind, however mistakenly. To a great extent, the political vacuum in post-war Europe lent itself overwhelmingly to the European ideal, which found wide appeal across the political spectrum. The European countries were in a state of misery and collapse.[15] America appeared to be repeating its disastrous retreat into isolation (despite membership of the newly formed UNO) just as the Russian barbarian seemed poised to ravish the prostrate European nations that lay outside Soviet control. And Britain appeared to be the Continent's natural leader: 'the sole European victor [who, although] she had suffered materially ... by comparison with the other countries in Europe [was] still relatively rich and her commerce and industry were largely intact.'[16]

From the outset Churchill was a key player. Long before the War he had pondered the notion of European Union. At the time of the Briand Plan (1929–30) Churchill wrote an article published in *the Saturday Evening Post* (a popular American magazine, which admittedly did not enjoy a wide readership in Britain), setting out his views on British association with such an entity: 'We are with Europe but not of it. We are linked but not comprised. We are interested, associated but not absorbed.' He repeated the strand of these thoughts on European integration on various occasions in the succeeding years[17] and returned again to the idea in speeches immediately after the War.[18] Thus his speech entitled 'Let Europe Arise', delivered at the University of Zurich on 19 September 1946, stemmed largely from a long-held conviction, augmented by his desire to promote lasting peace[19] and his concern that if European civilization was to save itself from Russian encroachment it had to do so by its own efforts. This speech, which was widely reported, was a logical progression from his address at Fulton, Missouri, six months earlier, when he had warned of an iron curtain descending across Europe from Stettin to Trieste.

Motives of political calculation and personal vanity almost certainly also featured in Churchill's decision to act as leader of the United Europe Movement (UEM) in early 1947. Churchill enjoyed 'an unrivalled position as the war leader who had helped to save Europe'.[20] He was an intuitive politician *par excellence* and sensed the emotional attraction of the phoenix rising from Europe's ashes. He also appreciated the practicalities. The domestic political scene offered little scope for him to play world statesman – and after all those years of supreme power Churchill had little interest in being leader of the Opposition.[21] But a united Europe held out a potential solution to Franco-German antagonism, it would offer hope and encouragement to the East European countries under Russia's yoke[22] and, perhaps best of all, it presented a weapon with which to beat Labour at Westminster.[23] Labour's later accusations that Churchill's campaign was merely a publicity stunt, motivated solely by political opportunism,[24] probably contained an element of truth.

Once persuaded by Sandys to act as Chairman of the UEM, Churchill threw his considerable energies into 'the crusade . . . of forming a united Europe'.[25] He remained 'a man of empire who believed in the comity of nations'.[26] Britain should provide moral support and intellectual leadership for a United Europe, but would stay, of necessity, outside the emerging institutions. This country was to provide the vital link with America and, because of her Empire, with Africa, Asia and the Pacific basin.[27] He was to make a virtue of his lack of a clear plan on how European integration was to be achieved, claiming that his task was to provide the vision; it was for others to fill in the details.

Churchill did not share the federalists' conviction of the need for European political federation for its own sake. However, free from the constraints of office he and his pro-European supporters fell into the trap of trying to offer all things to all men. Intent on 'forcing the European pace on the Europeans, Churchill aimed his speeches at a world audience',[28] recognizing the need to attract a broad spectrum of support from existing organizations for the UEM. His own preference for generalizations – and keen political sense that specific details might prove unattractive (or indeed unpalatable) to the British electorate – reinforced an inherent contradiction in his vision towards European unity, which 'he never resolved, either intellectually or emotionally'.[29] In Zurich Churchill spoke of Britain's 'benevolent association' with a United States of Europe, implying that Britain's position as head of the Commonwealth precluded ordinary membership. However, his speech at the Royal Albert Hall on 14 May 1947 (to mark the inauguration of the UEM) referred to Britain as a member of a European family and having to play her full part; he added that although the Commonwealth would have to support such an association he saw no reason why the Dominions would not do so – thus implying Britain's active participation. Not unnaturally, Continental enthusiasts read more into Churchill's declarations than he had intended while those worried about the implications were increasingly concerned.

Churchill's decision to adopt the cause of Europe was influenced by three Conservatives: Leo Amery, Duncan Sandys and Robert Boothby. No longer an MP but still very much an elder Tory statesman, Amery had long held coherent views of Europe's place in an expanded imperial economic structure – ideas which his son, Julian, absorbed and argued with intellectual conviction and vigour. Amery knew well the pre-war Continental pro-European politicians, such as Count Richard Coudenhove-Kalergi,[30] and had attended conferences on the topic in the 1930s. A political ally of Churchill from the days of his opposition to appeasement, Amery persuaded Churchill to come to lunch to meet Coudenhove-Kalergi in early 1939; this meeting prompted Churchill to publish an article in *The Evening Standard* on the importance of a united Europe.[31] In the summer of 1946 Amery sent Churchill the text of his speech to the London University on the subject of European integration, and came to believe that this was the origin of Churchill's call in Zurich.[32] It was certainly a contributory factor.

Amery was involved from the outset in Churchill's pro-Europe venture. Not only did he urge Churchill to pursue the idea,[33] Amery's contacts with Coudenhove-Kalergi became very important as the latter was busy reviving his pre-war organization and was keen that Churchill should preside at his forthcoming Congress.[34] Julian Amery was staying with Coudenhove-Kalergi in Gstaad when a telegram arrived from Churchill: 'I remember you have a European movement and I am thinking of starting one. I would like to combine. Please send all details.'[35] Julian Amery returned to London fully briefed, and reported accordingly at Churchill's lunch part on 30 September 1946 , attended by Leo Amery, Sandys and Boothby.[36]

Amery's position as 'head of the imperial preference boys'[37] was of crucial importance to his involvement with the UEM:

'Churchill was very conscious that the imperial wing of the party might be very unhappy; to make [Amery] vice-chairman was seen as an answer to any criticism that the European movement was not anti-Empire.'[38] This tactic did not bear fruit: Amery's leadership of the imperial wing was to diminish the force of his message, as '90% of these imperial stalwarts were anti-European'.[39] Until his death in 1955, Amery remained an impassioned supporter of European unity. He was convinced that at all costs Britain must avoid a return to a 'balkanized' Europe where small states looked to outside patrons for support in their squabbles, 'while the outside patrons will consciously or unconsciously tend to foment their quarrels'. Only a European Commonwealth could 'hold its own with Russia and figure... as one of the real world powers'.[40] He also saw Europe as the opportunity to revive the Conservative party's electoral fortunes – hoping to use the idea as a creed to attract the working classes.[41]

Amery and Sandys shared the conviction that 'the only hope of keeping Germany with us is to hold out the prospect of playing a real part in a united Europe rather than as an annex of Bolshevism'.[42] At Churchill's prompting, throughout the summer of 1946 Sandys had been in close touch with Coudenhove-Kalergi and the latter's attempts to revive his pre-war pan-Europe organization. Churchill himself had been reluctant to become involved in such moves, on account of the overtly anti-Russian bent of Coudenhove-Kalergi's concept,[43] and there may also have been an element in Churchill's thinking of giving a tiresome and ambitious son-in-law something to do.[44]

Sandys was crucial in persuading Churchill to adopt the cause of Europe, first by encouraging Churchill to use his forthcoming speech in Zurich as the occasion to issue a clarion call to the free nations of Europe;[45] and, after this speech (which he had helped to draft[46]), by organizing a committee to promote the United Europe idea.[47] Despite Churchill's own initial reluctance to follow up this address with an organized campaign, by late September he yielded to Sandys' pleas to chair the new organization, provided this did not amount to 'anything more than signing letters and acting as the figurehead'.[48]

Officially only the general Secretary of Churchill's United Europe Committee (formally established in January 1947),

Sandys was to play the decisive role in maintaining the momentum unleashed by Churchill.[49] Out of Parliament until 1950, he devoted his prodigious energy and tenacity to the issue, seeking to provide the 'nuts and bolts' to Churchill's grand design. From the outset he was keen to enlist all sections of the Conservative party for the nascent movement, as well as recruiting Labour and Liberal support. Accordingly, he approached known Conservative supporters of European integration (Boothby and Macmillan), and senior Tories who commanded influence and respect within the party: Harry Crookshank, Lord Cranborne,[50] Walter Elliot, Geoffrey Lloyd and Oliver Stanley. Significantly, Eden was not initially canvassed. Sandys appreciated the need to enlist Eden's support but he certainly did not crave Eden's involvement. Sandys harboured a deep resentment of Eden, by now Churchill's acknowledged heir, which dated from the 1930s[51] and which Sandys did nothing to hide. 'It became a sort of feud within the Tory party.'[52]

While acting as Churchill's liaison officer with the emerging European movement, to a large extent Sandys was left to his own devices. His working techniques were legion: 'the man was a steam roller – he would grind away in first gear and nothing could stand in his path'[53] and his influence considerable; for example, Churchill sent Sandys the text of the speech he intended to make at the UEM inaugural meeting: 'Sandys did not like Churchill's speech, and wrote his own version, which he sent back to Winston. Churchill did not like that, and rang Sandys up asking for the original. Sandys said he was very sorry, but he had torn it up. As there was no common copy, Churchill had to make Sandys' speech, with such changes as he could make.'[54]

Sandys also used his relationship with Churchill as an umbrella for his activities on the Continent. Armed with letters of introduction from Churchill, few Continental politicians refused to see him.[55] When the International Committee for a United Europe was established in December 1947, Sandys became its chairman. He deliberately sought to exploit the organizations and contacts of existing groups favouring European integration – including those promoting political federation. Sandys himself favoured more modest cooperation between governments but recognized that Continental support for the campaign was vital, and that the federalists could deliver one of the few multinational groupings. Accordingly, Churchill's committee contained four representatives of Federal Union.[56] Sandys also enlisted supporters of World Government, on the basis that 'European unity should be pursued as the immediate practical step and that any idea of World Government is a project for the more distant future'.[57] Sandys thus decided to attend the preliminary meeting of parliamentary delegates held in Gstaad in July 1947, the forerunner to the Continental federalists' conference convened in Montreux the following month.[58] Although Sandys only attended the Montreux congress as an observer, he spoke at a public meeting at the Palais des Sports; and after talking to Joseph Retinger[59] 'the whole of one night', the two men decided to join forces to organize a large-scale Congress of Europe,[60] 'from which all else flowed'.[61]

The third major influence upon Churchill came from Robert Boothby who had been a supporter of ideas of European integration since the 1920s.[62] Aware of the Continental appeal of a revived Europe through his contacts with the Free French in the 1940s, he had called for the creation of a United States of Europe in his despatches from the San Francisco conference in 1945,[63] and acted as secretary to the *ad hoc* all-party parliamentary committee which drafted the Early Day Motion (EDM) of 16 March 1948 calling for Western Union; in February 1949 he was elected co-Vice President of the reconstituted all-party group. Boothby repeatedly expressed his ardent conviction of the need for economic, political and cultural integration in Western Europe,[64] on the grounds that Western democracies were too small to survive as independent political and economic units flanked by America and Russia.

Boothby was an extremely gifted, able, but flawed politician. 'It was said that at his christening, the good fairies had given him every gift – except the ability to distinguish right from wrong.'[65] One of the most outspoken Conservatives of his generation since his election to Parliament in 1924, and a former *protégé* of Churchill, he was asked to join Churchill's European venture at the outset. However, he never regained Churchill's total confidence which he had enjoyed before the War.[66] Boothby remained tainted by the 'Czech gold scandal' of the early 1940s[67] as an undercurrent of mistrust persisted within the Conservative party about 'what could be in it for Boothby'.

One of the few MPs able to rouse his colleagues from their roosts in the smoking rooms or the bar with the appearance of his name on the annunciator, his speeches attracted comment but not respect. 'He had the character that when he made a speech in the Commons, you could be sure that the applause he got came from the Opposition benches.'[68] In a sense, he was the Conservatives' Richard Crossman, with whom he was great friends. He was disliked intensely by establishment Tories: James Stuart, the Tory Chief Whip until 1948, loathed him.[69] Thus although Boothby held sincere and articulate views on British ties with the Continent, persistent questions about his integrity undermined the force of his message. He was appreciated as a very convivial companion, but was regarded as 'a thoroughly bad man!'.[70]

Other senior Conservative supporters of Churchill's Europe campaign included Harold Macmillan, David Maxwell Fyfe, Peter Thorneycroft, Walter Elliot and David Eccles. Another supporter of Churchill in 1938 and 1940, Macmillan too had long given thought to European integration.[71] Macmillan was among the senior Tories invited to the UEM's inaugural meeting in May 1947, and was later included on the General Committee. Macmillan became an active member of the British Committee of ELEC and by 1949 he had taken on the important and influential position of chairman of the UEM's East European committee.

In these years, Macmillan was still as much in the political wilderness as he had been before the War, despite his wartime position as Resident Minister in North Africa. He was not so cynical a politician for political opportunism to be his only motive[72] for joining forces with the Europeanists, but the glamorous appeal of the crusade, and the not inconsiderable element of eschewing the forlorn political landscape at home,[73] combined with his desire to pour himself into politics to compensate for the wasteland of his personal life. To his credit, Macmillan was a sincere admirer of Jean Monnet, and his greatest nightmare was a revived rearmed Germany without Britain's counterweight in the European Defence Community[74] – or even worse a revived Germany unshackled to the West leaning towards Russia (the spectre of Rapallo[75]). He had coherent views on the necessity to harness the Ruhr industries to the economies of the West, which he repeatedly voiced inside and outside Westminster. Europe became the new focus for his idealism, but his enthusiasm for this newfound cause came to appear to some of his colleagues as 'boundless and excessive'[76]: on 17 August 1949 he went so far as to table an amendment in the Consultative Assembly calling for the Committee of Ministers to be an executive authority with supranational powers.

A former Attorney-General and Prosecutor at the Nuremberg War Crimes Trials, Maxwell Fyfe attended the first meeting of Churchill's committee on 3 December 1946 and was invited to join the managing committee of the UEM at the beginning of 1947. Unlike Macmillan, Sandys and Boothby, Maxwell Fyfe had not supported Churchill in his opposition to appeasement before the War; some of Maxwell Fyfe's colleagues ascribed his fervour for Europe as an attempt to atone for his stance in 1938.[77] Immensely hard-working and determined, in the period between the Congress of the Hague of 1948, and the convention of the Consultative Assembly of the Council of Europe in 1949, Maxwell Fyfe devoted 'considerable study to a European Convention of Human Rights', serving as one of the *rapporteurs* to the International Judicial Section established by the European Movement, which set about preparing a draft Convention.[78] Significantly, Maxwell Fyfe also 'did not get on with Eden'.[79] Walter Elliot was invited by Leo Amery to join Churchill's movement in late 1946. Elliot's political position was somewhat anomalous: tipped in the 1930s as a potential leader of the party,[80] his political confidence had been shattered by Munich; and although he was acknowledged as a senior and very popular politician after the War[81] and a powerful force for moderation, he never fulfilled the promise of his early political career.

David Eccles and Peter Thorneycroft also became members of Churchill's committee. Eccles' undoubted ability was unfortunately marred by his arrogant manner[82] which had earned him the nickname 'Smartyboots' in the party.[83] Nor was Eccles a Smoking Room man which might have mitigated this fault in his critics' eyes. His parliamentary impact was inhibited by his inability to make political friends,[84] and unfortunately he spoke less well in the House than he did in private.[85] Concentrating on the economic aspects of European union, through his active membership of the British Committee of ELEC, Eccles saw the argument for European union as fundamentally one of security: the chance to avert renewed Franco-German hostility, and to defend Europe against Russia's advance.[86] Thorneycroft, a barrister and former officer in the Royal Artillery elected to Parliament in 1938, had been co-founder of the Tory Reform Group in 1942 with Lord Hinchingbrooke. He was the first of the defeated Tory candidates in 1945 to find his way back into the House of Commons at a by-election. Thorneycroft also served on the British Committee of ELEC, and as the moving spirit behind the Conservative policy pamphlet '*Design for Freedom*' in 1947 and a number of similar documents, helped to mould Conservative policy in the Opposition years.

Of the second-tier backbenchers Sir Peter MacDonald and Peter Roberts were the most important. Chairman of the Conservative party Imperial Affairs Committee, as well as a founder member of the all-party parliamentary committee on European union and later Vice-President of the reconstituted all-party group, MacDonald was very much an old-world Tory. He was an ardent supporter of imperial preference and a prime example of those who envisaged the union of economic blocs together with their colonial empires. By his own admission,[87] MacDonald was sceptical about European federation and Britain's participation in any such moves, but he was impressed by the enthusiasm on the Continent. All depended on what shape the policy took: if this required the surrender of British sovereignty, then he was against joining such an organization. Like MacDonald, Roberts was originally involved (as Secretary) in Ronald Mackay's British Group of European Parliamentary Union (EPU). Considerable tension developed within this committee between Mackay's band of federalists and those Conservatives and National Liberals who favoured a looser British association with Europe. Roberts resigned from the British Group of EPU in December 1948 and, when the autonomous all-party parliamentary group was established up in February 1949, Roberts was elected Honorary Secretary.

Among the Conservative Europeanists, just as within the European Movement as a whole, differences existed over Britain's relationship with the Continent. These lay at the very heart of the Movement. Churchill might speak of Britain being part of the European family, but this was always in the context of his vision of the 'three interlocking circles'; Britain's relationships with America and her Commonwealth and Empire precluded placing the greatest emphasis on Western Europe. Sandys, on the other hand, was more swayed than Churchill by the arguments of Monnet and Spaak. Also Sandys had come to feel, with the end of the British Raj in India, that the days of the Empire were numbered; he was fearful that if Britain allied with America she would be too subordinate to exercise any influence. In his opinion, Britain was no longer a great power and union with Europe offered the only feasible alternative. He envisaged union with Europe based on the Marshall Plan, with economic integration leading to military integration;[88] thus he conceived of the vital necessity of British membership of a European community – something which Churchill did not endorse. There were also marked differences of opinion in the economic sphere. Eccles favoured a *laissez faire* approach along the lines of the General Agreement on Trade and Tariffs (GATT), whereas Boothby advocated welding together Europe and the overseas territories into a coherent economic bloc.

The need to gloss over these political and economic divisions contributed to the confusion over the precise meaning of such phrases as European union, European unity, European federation, European integration. With the benefit of hindsight this seems an inherently flawed approach, but at the time the method provided the necessary cloak for European integration to move forward. Churchill was aware that Conservative Europeanists were in danger of voicing high-sounding phrases which merely wished away difficulties.[89] However, out of office, the Conservatives 'could give the appearance of being all things to all men, and the very fact of being in opposition, encouraged opposition to the Government's policy regardless of content'.[90]

In addition, in the early years, very few people had a clear idea of the means and the ends, save for the federalists who saw European integration as the halfway house towards their utopia of world government. Churchill himself repeatedly refused to be drawn, in public or in private, on what he meant by a United States of Europe on the grounds that '[we] are not making a machine, we are growing a living plant, and we must wait and see until we understand what this plant turns out to be'.[91] Unfortunately, this ambiguity, proved a two-edged sword as, not unnaturally, Churchill's imprecision, together with the apparent endorsement by the Conservative party through the presence of leading Tories on the United Europe Committee (Boothby, Maxwell Fyfe, Oliver Stanley, Leo Amery, Sandys and Ernest Brown), fostered the belief among British and Continental federalists that they only had to wait until Churchill was returned to power for Britain to become a full member of a united Europe. Nice distinctions between 'European unity' and 'European union' were lost, too, on the bulk of the British public. The link between the Tory party and European integration was reinforced in the public's imagination when the National Executive of the Labour Party forbade any of its members to have anything to do with Churchill's United Europe Committee.

This unintentional but occasionally deliberate obfuscation aroused the antagonism of the Labour party from the start;[92] Churchill protested that the UEM did not aspire to compete with the Government in any way but was merely designed to foster 'moral, cultural, sentimental and social unities and affinities through Europe',[93] but he was accused of seeking to make 'political capital out of what is fundamentally a non-party ideal'.[94] Labour felt that if Churchill really wished to use his unique position in Europe, he should have resigned the leadership of the Opposition and raised himself above party political considerations.

THE SCEPTICS

In the late 1940s Conservative support for closer British ties with Europe ebbed and flowed.[95] The great majority of party politicians had no idea of European unity before 1946.[96] In the run up to the Congress of the Hague in May 1948 many were borne along on the pro-Europe tide but their enthusiasm was not very well thought out[97] and there also was an element of 'jumping on the political bandwagon'.[98] Overall, 'the motive force of Tory opinion in this period [on Europe was] more a function of the views of one man – Churchill – and less of a conscious party reappraisal.'[99] Conservative enthusiasm waned as Churchill and his fellow Europeanists persisted in statements that were long on eloquence but short on substance, and frequently seemed to commit the party to a drastic departure from its traditional approach to Europe. 'Feelings ranged from dislike to suspicion to wariness'[100] with 'doubts crystalliz(ing) a bit at the Hague Conference'.[101] However, these reservations never led to the formation of a Conservative centrist group to counter Churchill and the Europeanists.

Eden was the most prominent Tory agnostic. Throughout the late 1940s he was noticeably restrained in his comments on closer association with Europe. 'Although his war papers talked much of European union, by the end of the War he had come to the conclusion that we were broke, Europe was even broker, and our only hope was to be with the Americans.'[102] Eden was not crudely 'anti-European', being acutely aware of the need, and the desirability, for harmonious relations with the Continent. Nor was he oblivious to the advantages of some sort of European economic integration. On several occasions after the War he called on the Labour Government to take steps to secure closer economic cooperation with 'our Western neighbours, and in particular with France'.[103] This remained firmly in the context of intergovernmental cooperation. He approved of the development of the Organization for European Economic Cooperation (OEEC) as 'wholly compatible with the progressive development of trade which we all want to see within the Empire'.[104] There was a logical progression from this approval of intergovernmental economic cooperation to his arguments that Britain should accept the French invitation for discussions on the Schuman Plan in 1950.

Throughout Eden remained a convinced 'Concert of Europe man'. 'A product of his political generation',[105] he shared with Churchill the goal of close and harmonious relations between European states, and also the vision of Britain at the centre of the 'three interlocking circles'.[106] The difference between them lay in their use of 'emotion':[107] 'Eden's temperament could not have been more different from Churchill's. They both broadly agreed with Britain not being part of Europe [but] they had a different approach to Europe.'[108] Eden, although a consummate diplomat, was not a man of vision;[109] he concentrated more on tactics, and he shared with the Foreign Office[110] an innate distaste for the sentimental underpinning of the European movement. He remained in close touch with Foreign Office officials,[111] both because of his war-time role and because it was clear that if the Conservatives were re-elected he would again be Foreign Secretary. His personal prejudice was thereby reinforced by the civil servants. Unlike Churchill, and in particular Sandys, who saw the emotional yearning for European integration as the essential fuel for their cause, the practical Eden regarded such sentiments as clouding the issue. He had no time for such distractions.

Eden, and other more thoughtful Conservatives also realized Bevin's stance on Europe was more in tune with the British electorate. The British moves towards Europe – the Brussels Pact, the European Recovery Programme leading to the creation of the intergovernmental OEEC, and then the NATO negotiations prompted by the 1948 Berlin crisis – appeared far more satisfactory and of more concrete benefit[112] than the more nebulous ideas of European political cooperation. They also wished to support the Foreign Secretary's policy to ensure that isolationist 'Third Force' arguments of the Labour left would not prevail.

Eden's vanity, it seems, was also involved. He was the other acknowledged foreign affairs expert on the Conservative benches, yet 'Churchill was getting all the applause, all the glamour for his leadership of Europe'.[113] He came to see Churchill's conduct in the Council of Europe as a 'party stunt', devoid of any political meaning.[114] Jealous of his position within the party,[115] Eden was quick to react to any perceived slight. Churchill's refusal to have a shadow cabinet *per se*[116] – relying instead on a group of senior parliamentary colleagues who were called upon to speak in the House on a variety of topics[117] – did nothing for Eden's *amour propre*. 'It was almost automatic that if there was a foreign affairs debate, Eden was chosen to lead unless Churchill wanted to do so himself; [but] no one had a prescriptive right – therefore Eden had to [work to] maintain his supremacy in foreign affairs. This played a part in it.'[118]

Sandys' attempt to soothe Eden's potentially ruffled feelings, by recommending Churchill extend a personal invitation to Eden to attend the UEM's inaugural meeting at the Royal Albert Hall,[119] did not extend to a concerted campaign to recruit Eden. (As they admitted, Boothby and Sandys later saw this as a fundamental mistake.) The hostility of key active Europeanists to Eden was heartily reciprocated. 'I think he was impatient of Sandys, Macmillan and Boothby, who did not hold him in high regard either. There were mutters that Eden had not really been anti-appeasement before the War.'[120] For political and personal reasons, Eden was deeply suspicious of the behaviour of those who surrounded Churchill, whom he regarded as potential rivals for the crown, and preferred to distance himself from his ebullient leader's pronouncements. However, his appearance at the Hague Congress conferred upon the proceedings the official stamp of party approval and confirmed the public impression the Conservative front ranks were united on the issue.

Eden's distaste for the pro-Europe policy pursued by Churchill undoubtedly made the older, more empire-minded Tory backbenchers pause for thought. In addition, other members of Churchill's front bench were noticeably reticent on the subject of Europe. R.A. ('RAB') Butler and Oliver Stanley spoke in increasingly qualified terms. A month after Churchill's speech in Zurich, Butler had urged greater economic cooperation with Europe,[121] and opened the foreign policy debate in early May 1948 with the words 'there must be even more urgency in pursuing this desirable aim'; however, he came to see Churchill's European crusade as an electoral liability.[122] Similarly, Stanley spoke in support of European union at the inaugural meeting of the UEM and was a member of the United Europe Committee; he, too, shared Eden's prejudices[123] and his statements became increasingly more restrained. Their front bench colleagues (Ralph Assheton, Patrick Buchan-Hepburn, Harry Crookshank, Oliver Lyttleton, William Morrison, James Stuart and Henry Willink) were pointedly subdued or silent. The leading Tories in the House of Lords, Salisbury and Woolton, were also notably cautious.

The majority of Conservatives[124] echoed Eden's view that 'the whole European "thing" was insubstantial'.[125] For some of these MPs, their personal support for Churchill was ambivalent. Although Churchill and his supporters had ruthlessly weeded out party opponents in the candidate selection process, aided by the failure of many former Chamberlain men to be re-elected in 1945, an 'anti-Churchill' rump remained after the War.[126] Of the Sceptics, 35 had supported Neville Chamberlain in 1940, and only two supported Churchill (Drewe and Winterton). There was an attempt to oust Churchill as party leader in 1947,[127] and renewed rumblings against his leadership following the Conservatives' defeat in the South Hammersmith by-election in February 1949.[128] However, in the main, dissatisfaction against his leadership was confined to private grumbles that 'the Old Boy is past it', not active intriguing to replace him.[129]

The Sceptics tended to be of an older political generation who wanted to rescue Europe from her post-war impotence, and to help unite the Continent under British leadership, by association with the British Commonwealth. Thus when Attlee stated, 'Western Europe cannot live by itself as an economic unit ... hence the desire for wider integration with Africa and other overseas territories and with the great Western democracies and with our own Dominions',[130] he was voicing the Sceptics' creed for relations with Europe. They favoured Bevin's gradualist, intergovernmental approach, 'rather than ... some kind of dramatic meeting with a concrete plan where probably all the difficulties of the plan would come out most clearly and all the details would cause dissension ... Union of Europe is a fruitful idea [but] we must be careful not to think that it is something exclusive, and something that excludes the rest of the world.'[131]

Sandys' political antennae were acutely sensitive to this unease, *vide* his recommendation that all senior Conservatives should be invited to the UEM's inaugural meeting, specifically to avoid any feelings of exclusion or pique.[132] He alerted Churchill to the 'feeling among Conservative backbenchers that they have not sufficiently been taken into your confidence about your United Europe Movement and ... in consequence [there is] a danger they may become hostile to it',[133] and suggested Churchill should address the 1922 Committee in the near future to 'endeavour to secure their good will and support'. These efforts to assuage internal dissent were not entirely successful as the Sceptics' underlying anxiety over Churchill's European posturing did not abate.

There remained on both sides of the House a profound feeling that the value of British institutions had been reconfirmed by their survival in the crucible of war, together with a realization that Britain's salvation in the recent conflict had lain with two non-European nations, Russia and America. There persisted, too, the feeling that twice in the past fifty years Britain had become deeply embroiled in the Continent, and 'each time it had had disagreeable results'.[134] These MPs' recent service experience reinforced the Conservative party's tradition of colonial connections. The continuing conviction that the British Empire and emerging Commonwealth was the mainstay of Britain's great power status, and that this unit had a viable future, provided a powerful counterweight to the lure of Europe. Therefore, it was felt, Britain should not ally herself too closely with the Continent.

THE ANTI-EUROPEANS

As the euphoria created by Churchill's ringing rhetoric in Zurich subsided and calm reflection reasserted itself, so too did deep unease at the public utterances by some on the Tory front bench. Eden's obvious reservations and the silence from other respected senior Conservatives confirmed many Tories in their gut feeling that their leader's attachment to European integration was woefully misplaced. Among a small section of the party[135] this disquiet hardened into a deep-seated antipathy towards European federation, with or without Britain.[136] These MPs developed a hearty dislike of the Council of Europe[137] on the grounds that it was an international pressure group;[138] but it was not until the Conservatives forced a debate on Labour's refusal to attend the Paris talks on the Schuman Plan that parliamentary opposition to European integration came into the open.

Although the date of entry into Parliament is not an infallible guide to backbenchers' attitudes towards Europe, the anti-Europeans tended to be among the longer-serving MPs, and were all stalwart supporters of the Empire, for whom Britain's imperial record was a source of considerable pride and achievement. They favoured increasing collaboration with the Commonwealth because this would not restrict Britain's freedom of action, and heartily endorsed the view that every time Britain became entangled with Europe, the result was disagreeable.[139] They were therefore determined that Britain should retain her historic aloofness from the Continent. This was not a large group, and these MPs' hostility rarely emerged in debate or at question time. More usually they confined their criticism to party committees or discreet words to the Whips.

This does not mean that their convictions were not deeply held.

The influence of the right-wing press was apparent: Anthony Marlowe was the son of Thomas Marlowe, former editor of *The Daily Mail*; Max Aitken was Beaverbrook's son, and Beverley Baxter, another Canadian and journalist for the Beaverbrook stable, was a crony. Despite his membership of Churchill's personal wartime clique, Beaverbrook vehemently opposed the Tory leader's crusade, even going to the lengths of directing his newspapers to avoid any coverage of the issue in the 1950s. Kenneth Pickthorn's acerbic tongue and sarcastic manner was not to every one's taste; an intellectual and former Cambridge don who was once described by Oliver Stanley as 'God's gift to Socialism',[140] he was strictly a 'Concert of Europe' Conservative and once stormed out of a Conservative backbench committee discussion on Europe, 'complaining that the smell of *paté de foie gras*, and clink of glasses was making him feel nauseous'.[141]

Part of the problem was Churchill, who was evidently not a Tory.[142] True to his Liberal roots, Churchill remained an advocate of free trade – in marked contrast to the Conservative advocates of maintaining and extending imperial preference; and Baxter, Mellor and Marlowe had supported Chamberlain in 1940. In addition, 'nobody outside of (Churchill's) intimate circle knew what he thought about Europe ... To the backbenches it simply seemed that he was saying that Europe was a good thing and should set itself up on better lines than before, and that the Empire was a good thing and should continue to be such. How he proposed to reconcile the two was unclear.'[143] This lack of clarity – vital if Churchill and Sandys were to carry the motley collection of European politicians along with their crusade – alienated the anti-Europeans, unused perhaps to the apparent chicanery that accompanies diplomatic negotiations.

A discernible thread of anti-American feeling united these anti-Europeans; there was also a noticeable anti-UNO flavour in their views. They were strongly suspicious of American encouragement for European union. Did America see Britain as a second-class nation, in the same category as the prostrate and morally bankrupt nations of Western Europe? The idea that Britain was no longer a power of the first rank, and fit only to be, as Bevin once expressed it, 'a cog in the European wheel' was deeply insulting. It seemed that America was trying to hurry European integration to provide the excuse for another retreat into 'splendid isolation' – a concern these MPs shared with Bevin and the Foreign Office. The anti-Europeans were consistently opposed to what they regarded as American economic imperialism, voting against Bretton Woods and the US loan in 1945,[144] and served notice again that they opposed American sponsorship of closer ties with the Continent by voting against Marshall Aid in 1948.[145] It was feared that the creation of a United States of Europe was also part of America's plan through the GATT to create global free trade without, of course, America lowering its own high tariff walls; Marshall Aid was thus seen as Europe under American tutelage. Washington's determination to reshape the global economy through the Bretton Woods System and the GATT was fundamentally inimical to the continuation of the sterling area and imperial preference – nothing less than a challenge to Britain's status as a great power, at the political and economic head of the Empire and Commonwealth.

This idea of Empire was 'still the main religion of the Tory party'.[146] In marked contrast to the opportunities offered by the Empire and Commonwealth, to these Tories

> Europe was a basket case. Not to put too fine a point on it, the French were regarded with contempt after their abject performance in 1940 and during the Vichy years. The Germans were regarded with intense dislike, though not with the bitter hatred which I remember after World War I ... The Italians had run away pitiably in North Africa and had been panicked by a couple of British cruisers into sinking their own fleet, through sheer incompetence ... Charming people, but no one took them seriously ... There was not much else. But the Empire, all told, had come up trumps in a tight corner, [although] nobody actually said all this in public. It is difficult to realize today just how powerful [the Empire] was, in the national mind and particularly in Conservative thinking, right up to the early Sixties. Many of us thought ... that the concept could be revived and indeed could take on a new and greater dimension in the form of the Commonwealth. This would give Britain a part more in

keeping with her post-war capabilities, would give free rein to the political aspirations of the Colonial Empire and the Dominions, and would give us a distinctive position in the modern geopolitical scene. It was attractive from every point of view.[147]

These MPs did not share Macmillan's recurrent fear of Germany dominating a United Europe. As the 1940s progressed, there was a growing Conservative awareness of a revival of German economic competition in British overseas markets, but 'Germany looked altogether too decrepit still to be thought of as a threat, and the Germans of those days were distressingly apologetic'.[148] As for the notion of a Communist United Europe: 'certainly the Communist threat in Europe, particularly in France and Italy, was perceived as being much more substantial than it really was, [but] I doubt whether [this] idea crossed the horizon at any time.'[149] Europe 'did not appear to many people to require much thought! ... They saw it as a straight case of either [Europe] or [Empire]. If that were so, there was no doubt which it should be'.[150] Insofar as they considered the issue at all, faced with the idea of Europe uniting without Britain, these diehards entertained the historic feeling that a Europe united without Britain was a danger to this country and Britain should therefore try to prevent it happening.[151]

Thus, from the start there were internal Conservative tensions on the preferred approach to 'Europe', between the enthusiasts, the pro-Commonwealthers, the Sceptics and the 'out-and-out antis'.[152] So long as it appeared that the Conservatives would not have to take 'Europe' seriously, these remained mere undercurrents of opinion. However, when faced with the reality of Europe in 1950 (in the shape of the Schuman Plan and the European Defence Community), the Conservative party was forced to confront the issue. Then 'came the divergence on principle'.[153]

3 The Conservative Party and Europe: in opposition 1948–50

In January 1948, following the breakdown of the Conference of Foreign Ministers the previous month, the Foreign Secretary, Ernest Bevin signalled that he was more favourably disposed towards ideas of European integration circulating on the Continent.[1] Bevin hoped that, by organizing a Western European system,

> backed by the power of the Commonwealth and the Americas, it should be possible to develop our own power and influence to equal that of the United States of America and the USSR... by giving a spiritual lead now we should be able to carry out our task in a way which will show clearly that we are not subservient to the US or the Soviet Union.[2]

Further evidence of Bevin's determination to forge closer links with Europe came with negotiations with the French and the Benelux countries which culminated in the Brussels Treaty in March 1948. In negotiating this treaty, the Labour Government was 'consciously borrowing some of the ideas of the [Continental] Federalists...; that there should be a Parliament, for instance, and that it should cope with all kinds of social and economic matters which would not normally be in a Treaty ... short of accepting their actual supranational element which ... was not acceptable to Great Britain'.[3] These were, of course, also the ideas to which Churchill was giving such prominence.

Although Bevin's move towards Europe was welcomed by the Conservative Europeanists, they remained impatient at the Government's caution in seizing the lead in Europe.[4] The Continental federalists too were disappointed by the Brussels Treaty, which was only integrated on the military side.[5] Using his contacts with the federalists, Sandys successfully tapped Continental despair of the British Government joining some kind of federal Europe;[6] together with Joseph Retinger, he lobbied so effectively that the 'counter show'[7] at the Hague was organized under Churchill's leadership, which met to form a real European entity and unity. Whatever the Foreign Office in London might think,[8] Churchill was not a dupe in the federalists' plans: he and Sandys fully realized the federalists' aims but were intent on channelling their energy and drive, as well as the power of their organization, towards this exciting new concept. Both also felt that to specify too rigid a form for future European relations would be counter-productive: the critical factor was to harness the emotional appeal of the Idea. Bevin's initiative in intergovernment cooperation was thus sidetracked and overshadowed by the glamour of Churchill and the excitement his campaign generated on the Continent.

With the Communist *coup* in Prague in February 1948 providing further stimulus to discussion on West European integration, the Conservative Europeanists contributed significantly to the momentum of Churchill's campaign. Against the background of Sandys' 'persistence and perseverance'[9] in the International Committee of the Movement for European Unity,[10] on 16 March 1948 Boothby, MacDonald, Roberts, and the Labour MPs Shawcross, Mackay and Hale sponsored an EDM calling for Western Union, which stated

> that in the opinion of this House, steps should now be taken in consultation with other members of the British Commonwealth to create in Western Europe a political union strong enough to save European democracy and the values of Western civilization, and a trading area large enough, with the Colonial territories, to enable its component parts to achieve economic recovery and stability.

The motion went on to call for a 'long-term policy designed to bring forthwith a Council of Western Europe consisting of representatives of the governments of the 16 participating countries in the European Recovery Programme, and Western Germany, to lay down the lines of common action'; it ended by calling for a constituent assembly to be formed to frame a constitution for a democratic federation of Europe with 'defined powers with respect to ... external affairs, defence, currency, customs and the planning and production, trade, power and transport'. This EDM was 'not without importance', as it put in specific terms an aspect of foreign policy 'which has not been put in concrete terms before [and] represents quite an advance as it has brought together many different points of view'.[11] It was a fairly radical document for any Tory to sign; but despite the strong federalist tone, thanks to the efforts of Conservative and Labour sponsors, over the following weeks[12] this EDM was signed by approximately 200 MPs, over 60 of whom were Conservatives. The sheer number of signatures – gathered in the Easter recess – reflected the interest and support for Europe being generated by the forthcoming Congress.

These Conservatives form an interesting cross-section of political generations and outlooks. The list contained the independent souls, such as Martin Lindsay, and inveterate members of ginger groups (Ian Orr-Ewing and Arthur Vere Harvey); newcomers to the European idea and those, such as Quintin Hogg, who had given the matter considerable thought. Approximately half were first elected to Parliament in 1945 and youth was prominently represented. However, pre-war MPs were also conspicuous.[13] Of the older Tories, some were inveterate supporters of Churchill; others had supported Neville Chamberlain in the Munich crisis and in May 1940.[14] The list also included MPs[15] who were later to have second thoughts about the wisdom of closer economic and political ties with Europe; their signatures were symptomatic of the prevailing Conservative optimism that a way could be found to reconcile the old loyalties of Empire and the new obligations of Europe, using imperial preference to integrate the two trading systems. Conservative concern at the possible diminution of national sovereignty and reluctance to distance Britain from the Commonwealth, her historic source of strength, was already surfacing. Five[16] of those who signed the EDM later endorsed an amendment sponsored by Major Harry Legge-Bourke, which stressed 'agreement' rather than mere 'consultation' with the Commonwealth. Ralph Glyn signed the second amendment to the Western Union EDM, put forward by the Labour MP Richard Stokes, which accepted cooperation with Europe, but rejected federation.

MPs of all parties felt it was particulary important to have a debate on European integration before the Hague Congress.[17] Despite its unwillingness to grant parliamentary time to this,[18] not least because of a suspicion on the Labour backbenches 'about anything that can get such strong support from our opponents',[19] the Government was obliged to bow to intense parliamentary pressure, orchestrated through Mackay's all-party group. The group's Conservative officers, Boothby, Roberts and MacDonald played a prominent part, helping to arrange the names of members wishing to speak, and coordinating and assisting in the preparation of speeches.[20] Churchill himself remained determinedly aloof,[21] seeking instead to counter government criticism that his was a one-man crusade by demonstrating the widespread backbench support for the topic.

The EDM on Western Union was debated during the second day of the foreign policy debate on 5 May, an unusual mark of attention for a backbench motion. In the main Conservatives showed themselves enthusiasts for membership of a European association or integration with Europe,[22] but sought refuge in generalities which deliberately avoided examination of Britain's exact role in a united Europe. With the example of Churchill's grandiloquent phrases[23] before them, there was little incentive for the Europeanists to grasp the nettle. Boothby alone disdained such obfuscation, elaborating his arguments for the need for a planned European economy combined with the development and regional and federation of European colonial territories. Calling on the Government to make plain its real intentions towards Europe, he argued passionately for a positive union, supported by the British Commonwealth and the United States and not just for immediate political or economic ends, which he felt would fail, or for defensive ends, which would lead to war.[24]

Despite the Europeanists' success in helping to generate parliamentary interest in European union which influenced Bevin and the Foreign Office in their negotiations on the Brussels Treaty, the Labour Government was not persuaded into accepting the available vehicle for Europe before the Congress at the Hague. However, thanks in large part to the Conservative Europeanists, the Government increasingly was on the defensive: coming immediately before the Hague meeting, the cross-party support for the EDM on Western Union had a considerable impact upon Continental politicians 'where people generally doubt whether British support for any real form of European federation is quite genuine'.[25] The National Executive Committee's instruction to Labour MPs to stay away from the Congress appeared motivated by pique. It also left the stage free for Churchill.

The Conservative Europeanists had not won their colleagues' wholehearted approval. As enthusiasm for European integration surged within the party, Eden publicly endorsed Bevin's cautious approach[26] – implicitly rebuking his more enthusiastic colleagues and determined to discourage those Labour backbenchers who pinned their hopes on European political union forming the bulwark of Europe's defences. In his view, ultimately Britain's security lay with America – an uncomfortable, indeed unpalatable, truth for some Tory and Labour MPs alike. Intent on preserving a facade of unity with Churchill, Eden chose his words with care. He wanted 'the closest and most effective collaboration, economic, political and cultural, with all the free nations of Europe,' but '[that] collaboration can take any of a number of forms... Some people speak of a united Europe and others again speak of a union of the nations of Western Europe. In my judgement, each and all of these objectives can be reconciled.'[27] His reservations emerged again in the debate on Western Union, when he again made association with Europe conditional upon the Empire and tried to temper the Europeanists' enthusiasms by reminding them of Britain's global responsibilities which ruled out any exclusive association with Europe.

Eden's scarcely coded public criticism echoed private Conservative misgivings which surfaced in committee.[28] A 'considerable portion' of the party 'was doubtful and even anxious about [the] movement' on the grounds that it might prejudice Britain's position as head of the Commonwealth and Empire.[29] The EDM was criticized as appearing to 'jump all the fences at once', and tending to by-pass ministerial responsibility in international affairs.[30] MPs were reminded that the League of Nations had shown the dangers of embarking on grandiose schemes before the foundations had been properly laid.[31]

Before his departure for the Hague Churchill was made aware of these hesitations about his role as leader of the UEM, and was sufficiently concerned to make an unusual appearance before the Foreign Affairs Committee in mid-April 1948. He implicitly acknowledged that the party was not united with his qualifications, 'the Conservative party *as a whole*[32] welcomed the *broad*[33] aims of his and other movements'. But he rebuffed private criticisms of unofficial 'European' action (clearly aimed at Sandys), stating that he was content to leave individuals to work out their actions as they pleased. Once more Churchill stressed his vision of the growth of Europe as providing an opportunity for Britain to resume on a new plane her moral leadership in world affairs, repeating his view that Britain's cultural and political inheritance, together with her geographic position, placed her as the natural focus for developments in Europe.[34]

THE CONGRESS AT THE HAGUE

Until the Congress at the Hague (held on 7–10 May 1948), the average Tory paid no attention to ideas of European unity.[35] Britain's own troubles, although considerably less severe economically, politically and spiritually than those endured by the Continental countries, were sufficiently absorbing that 'the ordinary Tory did not have a clue'.[36] The Congress at the Hague changed that dramatically: although many Conservatives still only had the haziest idea of what was being proposed, the topic attracted enormous attention,[37] and to a great extent unreasoned support.[38]

The Congress was a resounding success. Organized by the whole European movement, it was attended by 730 delegates, including several former Prime Ministers, 29 former foreign ministers and several ministers in office. A strong Conservative delegation attended, but it was not numerous.[39] These delegates enjoyed themselves immensely:[40] the opportunity of being entertained by friends, with the chance to renew old friendships and make new ones underlined the fun and spectacle of the occasion; the venue offered a marked contrast to a joyless Britain, where all seemed grey, arid and regulated.[41] Eden also attended, more out of a sense of duty than any enthusiasm for the cause,[42] and his presence, despite the contingent of 41 Labour MPs who had defied 'Bevin's diktat',[43] reinforced the impression that the Conservative party favoured the emerging European cause, whereas the Labour party did not.

'The guidelines of what was later done over the next twenty or so years to achieve various measures of European Unity were in fact first laid down at the Hague in Resolutions and Declarations.'[44] The central figure was Churchill,[45] the main speaker, placing himself at the head of the European unity movement which was endorsed by so many Continental leaders and politicians. Conservatives played important roles in the conference committees: Maxwell Fyfe, who 'wanted to say something on human rights',[46] joined the cultural committee; Manningham-Buller acted as chairman of the steering committee of the Political Committee, which considered the draft political resolution. Behind the scenes, Sandys played a vital part through his key position as chairman of the International Committee of the Movements for European Unity and he fought hard to resist Continental efforts to promote resolutions favouring a supranational approach to unity.

It was mainly as a result of Sandys' prodigious energies that there emerged from the Congress 'a movement for something more extensive than the Brussels Treaty organization'.[47] Together with Paul-Henri Spaak (former Prime Minister and Foreign Minister of Belgium) and Retinger, he lobbied with such effect[48] that the most spectacular of the Hague resolutions was achieved – the creation of a new European institution, a parliamentary assembly.[49] His efforts were backed by the Conservative Europeanists at home who continued to harry the Government. The Tory members of the all-party group endorsed the committee's proposal to put down a motion asking for the convening of a European assembly, deliberately coinciding[50] with efforts to secure the tabling of similar motions in other European parliaments. Support for this motion was widely canvassed. The highly public manner in which Churchill and his UEM committee chose to put before Attlee the results of the Hague Congress and its main proposals was a deliberate reproof: the theatre of their procession from the House of Commons to Downing Street[51] undoubtedly appealed to Churchill's sense of mischief, but also conveyed the sense of frustration and dissatisfaction felt by pro-European politicians at Labour's reaction to Continental events.

Behind the scenes Conservative MPs were increasingly agitated. The improvement in the party's fortunes[52] together with the more concrete forms of intergovernmental organization which were developing (such as the OEEC), encouraged a restrained approach to Europe. Sandys hoped to secure the party's official blessing on Churchill's United Europe policy and accordingly drafted a resolution for consideration at the autumn party conference. Sandys was well aware of the opposition of the Chairman of the Executive of the National Union, Sir Herbert Williams[53] and 'his friends', fully supported by the Beaverbrook press, but felt a frank discussion would be beneficial. Although he amended his draft resolution at Amery and Eden's suggestions (to stress Britain's enduring links with the Empire and Commonwealth), Churchill vetoed the idea, convinced it would be 'a mistake' and merely reveal a great rift in party opinion;[54] promoting the idea of Europe should remain an all-party effort.

Even the enthusiasts had been concerned by the division at the Hague between those who favoured a confederal Europe and the majority who wanted to press ahead with federal arrangements.[55] Although great care had been paid to the wording of the various articles to bridge the gap,[56] they realized if the Conservative party intended to stay inside European Parliamentary Union, which was heavily involved on the side of federation, it would have to work very hard to control that view. The emotional appeal of a United Europe concealed the stark fact that people at large had simply no understanding of 'what sovereignty involved, nor how the status of the British parliament might be affected'.[57] The pervading backbench desire was for an urgent clarification of policy – it is revealing of the confusion within the Tory ranks that Butler thought it necessary to state *his* understanding of Churchill's conception – and leading Tories appreciated the electoral necessity of sustaining a positive party line, 'which could be used by members, speakers and candidates'.[58] The party, which appeared to be giving a coherent and positive lead on Europe, could not afford a split on so major an issue.[59] On one point the Conservatives were united: the Empire was not to be by-passed.

For the Labour Government the outcome of the Hague, with the final resolution calling for the establishment of a European Assembly, was a disagreeable surprise. Human emotions and frailties entered the political picture: 'Bevin, the Foreign Office and the Government regarded the Hague as simple grandstanding by Churchill to compensate for the loss of the British General Election!'[60] 'He probably thought Churchill was taking advantage of his reputation to push ideas that had not been fully worked out, and on which he, Ernie, would have had some suggestions to make... There was a certain jealousy [and] irritation at Churchill's intervention in the field of Foreign Affairs.'[61]

Bevin's objections went beyond the personal level. At the outset 'he appreciated very clearly the need to bring France and Germany into a state of mutual understanding and cooperation',[62] but he regarded any movement which promoted the unification of the whole of Europe but which excluded the USSR as 'dangerously provocative'.[63] Heartily opposed to any proposals for a European federation, or a European assembly with a mandate to prepare a federal constitution for Europe,[64] Bevin argued Britain's efforts 'should be confined to negotiations between West European governments... any alternative movement might, like the old League of Nations, get out of hand if it did not become positively harmful'.[65] There was the danger that communists and fellow travellers would exploit the assembly as a sounding board for their ideas and to foment trouble;[66] 'anything that needed to be done for European unity could surely be better done by governments working through ministers, ambassadors, and officials'.[67]

Bevin's obduracy was wholeheartedly backed by other leading Labour politicians: Attlee shared Bevin's belief in the folly of an independent assembly, particularly in view of 'the delicacy of the European situation'.[68] Stafford Cripps was generally hostile to the European idea;[69] Aneurin Bevan was suspicious of Churchill's motives;[70] and Hugh Dalton shared the general Socialist belief that the liberties and prosperities of Europe were only safe in Socialist hands.[71] Key Foreign Office and Treasury advisers were equally critical,[72] particularly of a movement whose chief characteristic seemed to be anti-Bolshevism.[73]

Throughout the remainder of 1948 the Labour Government's consistent drive was to dilute the supranational idea in Europe[74] which emerged from the Hague. Bevin's tactics were to delay while appearing to be constructive.[75] This was borne out on both the political and economic fronts. He was determined that Britain 'shouldn't go into any kind of federal thing'.[76] But under pressure from the Brussels Pact allies (in particular the Belgian and French governments, acting at Sandys' instigation[77]), supported by Conservative lobbying at home and abroad and deputations from his own backbenches,[78] Bevin was obliged to alter his 'negative attitude' and to acquiesce in the establishment of a European assembly[79] – ' "this talking shop in

Strasbourg".'[80] Labour's acceptance of the Council of Europe encouraged the optimists to hope that the Government would do everything to make the assembly a success. The pessimists feared that Labour's acceptance,[81] only to 'allow the plan to fade out in failure or neglect would be a disaster for Europe and a fatal blow to British post-war policy'.[82] They recognized[83] Bevin's insistence on the pre-eminence of the intergovernmental Council of Ministers as a deliberate wrecking move.[84]

The pressure on Britain to be associated with Europe economically had been gathering in 1947 and 1948 through the discussions surrounding a Customs Union, paralleled by the political and military aspects of the Treaty of Brussels negotiations. Bevin and Cripps[85] regarded the Customs Union idea as inimical to the sterling area, Britain's Commonwealth interests and her world position, and had successfully deflected these pressures into the creation of the OEEC. Signs that the British Government's suspicion of organizations outside national government control was hardening into outright hostility appeared when the nomination of Paul-Henri Spaak (a keen federalist) to the Chairmanship of the OEEC was vetoed.[86]

Churchill's vision and enthusiasm continued to exceed what Bevin and the Foreign Office considered desirable or practicable politics.[87] Convinced that 'entanglement' with Europe would inevitably inhibit severely Britain's own efforts to recoup after the War, politically and economically,[88] the Foreign Office's guiding principle remained that Britain should not become more involved in Europe than America was prepared to be, for fear that 'if we became involved in the purely European grouping, they were more likely to pull out'[89] which would leave Britain with the worst of both worlds. The corollary of this anxiety meant that Labour's policy towards Europe throughout this period was directed at combatting the 'endemic US disposition to isolationism'[90] through opposition to anything that detracted from intergovernmental links with the Continent.

Through his support and position as the figurehead of the European Movement, Churchill was running a powerful 'unofficial' foreign policy.[91] Thanks to his leadership and Sandys' efforts in the International Committee, there developed the parallel channel of Europe[92], encouraging the Europeans to direct their energies into the formation of the Council of Europe, rather than West European Union, to achieve their desired goal of supranationality. Churchill shared the Foreign Office's view of the vital necessity of American support in the emerging Cold War. The fundamental difference between them lay in Churchill's conviction of the necessity of Britain 'being there' in Europe to give direction whereas Bevin and the Foreign Office remained convinced that it was a distraction to the main thrust of their intergovernmental efforts through the OEEC and NATO.

By the beginning of 1949 Labour was fighting a determined rear-guard action, harassed at home by Churchill and the Conservative Europeanists[93], from within their own party (led by Mackay), and from abroad by the Americans and Europeans. Bevin did not attempt to wrest back the initiative by trying to build up the economic and social side of the Brussels Treaty organization.[94] His determination to persevere[95] with his concept of a West European intergovernmental organization, in which America was fully involved,[96] meant that in comparison to Continental enthusiasm for the Council of Europe the Labour Government appeared the odd man out. The Europeans (and that meant predominantly the federalists), supported by Churchill and Conservative Europeanists, were defining the debate; the fact that Western Union, the OEEC, and NATO (especially after 1952) were served by integrated machinery was obscured.

With an election increasingly in the air,[97] Tory doubts about Churchill's and his fellow Europeanists' behaviour were hardening, convinced that these posed a potential embarrassment to a future Conservative government. Senior Tories and Labour MPs alike feared that the Council of Europe would be 'ruined by Churchill's over-enthusiastic espousal of Federation';[98] and Eden certainly endorsed Bevin's view that foreign policy pronouncements were the prerogative of the Foreign Secretary.[99] The Conservative Europeanists themselves were also having second thoughts about the direction in which the federalists were heading. Tensions within the British Group of EPU became irreconcilable at the Interlaken conference in September 1948; the five Conservative delegates were 'not prepared to accept any immediate transfer of sovereignty to a European Parliament or a European political authority... If European union is to come about, as it must, it is not going to be assisted by fanatical federalists or constitution-mongers.'[100]

On 10 February 1949 a new all-party group was constituted, marking its formal withdrawal from EPU, with more moderate aims.

Conservative reservations were reflected in the change in tone of the second cross-party EDM on Western Union, put down on 23 February 1949. Boothby, MacDonald (Vice Chairmen) and Roberts (Hon. Secretary) were among the sponsors of this motion which welcomed the steps taken by the signatories of the Brussels Pact to establish a Council of Europe and expressed their opinion that British representation should reflect the relative strengths of the political parties in the House of Commons. No further mention was made of creating a democratic federation of Europe, with defined powers over external affairs, currency, customs and trade, as the ultimate goal. The 1948 EDM had envisaged a constituent assembly specifically framing a constitution for such a federation; the new motion did not specify the desirable role of the Council of Europe. Altogether it was a far more moderate declaration of Britain's association with Europe.

Fifty-three of the 130 signatures came from the Conservative party and their allies. The 24 new Tory signatures were of an older political generation, with the emphasis firmly on British links with her Empire and Commonwealth, rather than any new forms of association with Europe. The extraordinary inclusion of Sir Arnold Gridley's name on the order paper conveyed the official endorsement of the party backbenches upon this more moderate stance: in normal circumstances, the chairmen of the 1922 Committee were not given to signing backbench motions. Of the other additional signatories, Brendan Bracken was a Churchill intimate, but one who did not approve of his leader's activities on Europe;[101] Victor Raikes had supported Churchill on India in the 1930s; and Patrick Hannon had signed Legge-Bourke's amendment which sought to curtail possible British enthusiasm. In addition, nine of those signing had supported Chamberlain in 1940.[102] Admittedly, 27 of those who had supported the 1948 EDM did not sign the second motion, but given the manner in which signatures for EDMs are collected in Westminster, nothing sinister can necessarily be read into the absence of their names; however, it is interesting to note that Allan Noble was Eden's PPS, and

Walter Fletcher and Edward Carson took a robust imperialist stance on foreign affairs in the 1950s.

In late February 1949 the European Movement organized another meeting in Brussels, on a more limited scale to the Hague. This conference was chiefly devoted to matters of organization and to define the immediate programme of propaganda. Macmillan contributed to the plans formulated there, on the basis of the 'growing enthusiasm for the European idea' he had encountered on his recent lecture tour of Germany and Italy;[103] Sandys did 'most of the drafting'[104] of the British position. A major achievement of this conference, in which Maxwell Fyfe also played an extremely important part, was the drafting of a Charter for Human Rights, together with the recommendation for the creation of a European Court. At this conference the clear division was increasingly apparent between the formal, theoretical French and Belgian view – that if governments could be induced to sign a Treaty obliging them to cooperate, this would compel them to bring their economies and societies into line with one another and finally to arrive at political unity – and the pragmatic British and Scandinavian view. The British Conservatives argued that until progress had been made with the harmonization of the various European economies and the integration of society there was no chance that political unity could be achieved; a premature Treaty would break down in practice. This fundamental difference of opinion remained unresolved and was to wreck the Council of Europe.[105]

Two months later the Westminster Conference, devoted to economic and financial matters, was convened under the auspices of ELEC. A number of distinguished economists, both outside and inside the European Movement, attended. The chief questions addressed were currency convertibility, European payments, the organization of basic industries (what was to become the European Coal and Steel Community) and the refugee problem. Both these conferences were preliminaries to the long-awaited convention of the Council of Europe; however, they received scant attention in the press. The post-war shortage of newsprint was largely responsible, but political correspondents recognized that such topics did not sell newspapers. Similarly, these conference recommendations, with the exception of the Charter of Human Rights,[106] fell upon stony ground in Whitehall. Despite the Conservative Europeanists continuing campaign, in Parliament[107] and outside through such organizations as the British Committee of ELEC, urging the Government to take a more favourable attitude towards Europe, Labour's enmity remained entrenched.

THE ASSEMBLY OF THE COUNCIL OF EUROPE

The Statute of the Council of Europe was signed in London on 5 May 1949 and the inaugural meeting of the Consultative Assembly began on 10 August 1949. The Conservative members of the British delegation were Churchill, Macmillan, Maxwell Fyfe, Boothby, Eccles, and Sir Ronald Ross (representing the Ulster Unionists), with John Foster and Lord Birkenhead as the Conservative 'substitutes'.

In Strasbourg the Conservative delegates held the stage, in marked contrast to their position in Westminster. Of course, as 'the war leader who had helped to save Europe',[108] Churchill enjoyed an unrivalled position. The Consultative Assembly contained most of the leading figures of Free Europe[109] who 'would only listen to the Conservatives because of Churchill ... it was rather awkward for Labour because they were the Government and enjoyed a large majority'.[110] Churchill was not content just to play world statesman; to the consternation of his colleagues,[111] he rapidly assumed the role of party politician[112] and shared the general 'childish delight' among Tory delegates in a forum in which they could beat Labour.

As far as the Continental delegates were concerned, the Conservative delegates made a valued contribution to the proceedings.[113] Maxwell Fyfe served on the committee of fifteen 'to examine and interpret' the Assembly's remit, and was elected chairman of the Legal Committee.[114] He made the issue of human rights his special work in the Assembly, calling in the main meeting on 19 August 1948 for a convention setting out 'basic personal rights, to be acknowledged by all governments, and a minimum standard of democratic conduct for all members'. The matter was referred to the Legal Committee, which drafted the Convention of Human Rights, designed to provide 'a moral basis for the activities of the Council', with machinery in the form of a Commission on Human Rights and an International Court.

Macmillan and Eccles served on the political and economic committees respectively. Boothby's work on the Committee of General Affairs, to which questions on political authority were referred, was particularly important because of its work on federalist demands for the creation of a political authority without delay; in the search for a compromise formula, the idea of a 'confederation of Western Europe' emerged.[115] As at the Hague Congress, Sandys' position on the International Committee greatly augmented the Conservative delegates' ascendancy. 'Since a very large number of the members of the Assembly were well known to him, [Sandys] exercised much influence behind the scenes, in addition to acting as Chief of Staff to Churchill'.[116]

In addition to Maxwell Fyfe's work on the Convention of Human Rights, Churchill and his fellow Conservative delegates made a lasting and positive contribution in their advocacy and support for the admission of the West Germans,[117] representing the return of the pariah to the diplomatic fold. In the debate on 16–17 August on Europe's political future, in an abrupt change of tack from party political animal, Churchill 'rose to an altogether different plane,' giving a speech which though long awaited, 'must have been to the majority of those present a disappointment'.[118] Acutely aware that Germany was the most immediate of Europe's problems, and that with the intensification of the Cold War in Europe the spectre of a revived and remilitarized Germany was already rearing its head only four years after the defeat of Hitler, Churchill made the question of Germany the main and almost sole theme of his speech, 'shocking some and almost bullying others'[119] by his insistent 'Where are the Germans?'. Only Churchill could have done this: his question caused initial deep offence among those delegates from former occupied lands, but the validity of his message was recognized by even the most reluctant.

Thanks to Churchill's initiative and Macmillan's subsequent work in the political committee, at the end of the meeting the Assembly passed a final resolution for the discussion of the admission of new members to the Council of Europe – in other words, the whole German question. Before the delegates left Strasbourg a standing committee was created, empowered to deal with the Committee of Ministers. Maxwell Fyfe was selected as a member; as a former Nuremburg prosecutor his advocacy that the 'new West German state should be brought back into the comity of nations... had some effect. Yet the main inspiration was Winston's original vision and continuing pressure for the practical content of his slogan "Europe Unite".'[120] At Westminster, Bevin expressed his willingness to try and get matters agreed as soon as possible.[121] On 30 March 1950 a formal invitation was extended to the West German Government.

There were, however, limits to the influence of Conservative delegates, who played such a prominent part in the first Assembly's proceedings. The Labour Government did not regard their contribution as benign. Churchill '*was* the spirit of Europe',[122] but he – rather than the elected Labour Government – also symbolized Britain in the eyes of the Continentals. Churchill's party-political behaviour at Strasbourg infuriated Labour delegates and Government alike[123] and served to reinforce the conviction that the Council of Europe was embarrassing[124], practically useless and potentially dangerous.[125] Many on the left of the Labour party had been attracted to a united Western Europe on anti-American grounds, but the predominance of right-wing Christian Democrats at the Consultative Assembly served to dampen their enthusiasm.[126]

Despite impassioned speeches, the Conservative Europeanists failed to convince Attlee and Bevin that 'Europeanism' offered a viable alternative to the Government's pursuit of 'Atlanticism'. The Labour Government in the Committee of Ministers, apart from the establishment of the European Court and the Convention on Human Rights and the inclusion of the West Germans, studiously ignored or vetoed the bulk of the Assembly's resolutions.[127] Nor did the Conservative Europeanists persuade the bulk of their colleagues that the emerging links with Europe were complementary to, or even could strengthen, ties with Empire and Commonwealth. Churchill's awareness of abiding Conservative doubts that Britain's position as head of the Empire and Commonwealth might be prejudiced, had not inhibited him in any way at the Consultative Assembly, although these thoughts were certainly in the minds of his Strasbourg colleagues;[128] Eden, the most 'conspicuous absentee' from Strasbourg,[129] shared the growing Conservative consternation over the direction Churchill and his cohorts appeared to be taking the party.[130] Their presence and behaviour at the Consultative Assembly appeared counter-productive because it closely identified the Tories with the federal ideas.[131]

The issue came to a head at the party conference in the autumn of 1949. At previous party conferences, including the 1946 conference following Churchill's Zurich speech, Europe had been viewed in conjunction with America and the Commonwealth; that Europe had been considered at all was due solely to Churchill's and other senior Conservatives' prominent roles in European organizations and committees. Now, for the first time since Churchill's rousing cry 'Let Europe Unite', Europe became an issue in its own right, thanks to Sandys' determination to put down a resolution on the issue which was mirrored by Conservative undercurrents of dissent.

Gridley, the Chairman of the 1922 Committee, was moved to write to Sandys urging him to modify the wording of his resolution. Gridley warned:

> At the last meeting of the 1922 Committee hopes were expressed that every effort should be made to avoid any risk of divided views on the United Europe resolution at the forthcoming Party Conference ... It is felt that no risk should be run in attempting to commit the Conference to any detailed plan of action before the Party in the House has had a full opportunity of discussion thereon.

Pointing out that there was to be a general meeting of the Foreign and Imperial Affairs Committees shortly after Parliament reassembled, Gridley continued, 'It would be disastrous if anything happened at the Conference which might divide the Party at a time when complete unity is essential in the face of the coming General Election'. He included a stark instruction that Sandys was not to say anything in his resolution which 'might give rise to controversy or difference of view'.[132] Gridley clearly feared Sandys was poised to do this.

This was an extraordinary intervention by the most powerful chairman of the official backbench committees, and spoke volumes for the private backbench representations made to Gridley. The Europeanists still only comprised about 60 MPs, out of a total complement of 213 Conservatives. Some of those initially swept along by the ringing words of 1948 were having second thoughts on the emerging form of 'Europe': what did the motion passed at Strasbourg mean when it called for the Council of Europe to become a political authority with limited but definite powers? What of the resolutions passed in the French and Italian Parliaments that the Council of Europe should become as soon as possible an elected Parliament? Gridley was not in the same league as later Chairmen of the 1922 (such as John Morrison), and his position on the backbenches was overshadowed by more illustrious names. Nevertheless, coming from the leader of the party's 'praetorian guard' whose job it was to represent backbench views to the party leader, these comments carried considerable weight. They were also an implicit criticism of Churchill: Gridley was far more aware of Conservative hesitations[133] than Churchill who, despite the grumbles of discontent at his absences from the House of Commons, remained an aloof figure.

Not only were the knights of the shires alarmed at the thought of Sandys going full steam ahead on Europe, hand-in-glove with European federalists. Attempts to present a coherent approach to Europe had encountered two difficulties: (i) Conservative enthusiasts spoke in different tongues on economic and political matters;[134] and (ii) the process continued to evolve; therefore the obvious solution was to refrain from a definite line of policy. As a tactic, this 'fudge' had the merit of avoiding alienating Conservative sceptics and unbelievers at home, but raised Continental expectations which could not be fulfilled.

Sandys moved swiftly to defuse Conservative criticism about the implications of closer union by sending Gridley a copy of the speech he intended to make at the conference. Still hopeful of evolving a political structure of Europe out of the Council of Europe, Sandys was careful to ensure that the text of his resolution, which welcomed the creation of the Council of Europe and supported measures for closer European unity as consistent with the unity of Empire, had Churchill's and Macmillan's prior approval, and Leo Amery's support which was very important for the imperial wing of the party. His decision to enlist Macmillan reflected the growing influence of the latter's ideas on Europe upon Churchill, who had been impressed by Macmillan's intervention in Conservative front bench discussions on Empire–European policy for the election.

Both realized the impact a coherent approach could have on the Liberal party and the electorate as a whole.[135] Sandys also recruited Eccles and John Foster, asking Foster to second the general resolution at the conference. The resolution was passed, no small thanks to the careful selection of speakers from the floor in support of the motion.

By the end of 1949 Conservative advocates of closer links with Europe were fighting on three fronts:

(1) *Within the European Movement against the federalists*: at the Executive meeting in Paris on 16 December 1949, Boothby, MacDonald and Layton sought to tone down the aggressive federalist approach advocated by representatives of France, Italy and Holland. On the International Committee, Sandys was still trying to straddle the growing gulf between the two camps, seeking a compromise between those who advocated evolution and the exponents of a contractual method.[136]

(2) *Within their own party*: the Sceptics and the Anti-Europeanists had not been won over, clearly demonstrated by the first formal backbench discussion in the Foreign Affairs Committee on the implications of the Council of Europe in early November.[137] Several MPs raised their concern 'not so much at the content ... as the form' of the Assembly, fearful that although Conservative delegates were not supposed to be representatives of their party, the image of these MPs in cahoots with Continental politicians who were all espousing European federation, gave the impression that the Conservative party endorsed British membership. Alarmed by what was seen as excessive exuberance for European unity expressed by some Conservative delegates[138], there was a general desire to move away from 'a private army'.[139] It was conceded that Conservative delegates had avoided any pitfalls at the first session of the Consultative Assembly, and 'had not committed the party to anything undesirable';[140] the less charitable felt this was more by luck than good judgement. The whole idea was moving too fast and the instability of European governments (France leapt to mind) demonstrated 'that this was not the moment to jump all the way'.[141] The Sceptics wanted a coherent, restrained

Conservative party view, 'expressed through consultation before meetings of the Council of Europe'.[142] This should be done as discreetly as possible; Conservative grandees were keen to avoid signs of dissension on Europe unity to prevent adverse election propaganda.[143] At Eden's suggestion, a joint subcommittee of the Foreign Affairs, Finance and Imperial Affairs Committees was established to deal with matters arising from the Council of Europe, under Macmillan's chairmanship.[144] The issue that gave particular concern was preference policy, the touchstone of Empire. In August 1949, Conservative delegates at Strasbourg had voted for a resolution calling for the creation of an economic union of free Europe which would include 'the abolition by stages of restrictions on the movement of men, money and goods'.[145] Although the message from the Dominions at the recent Commonwealth Relations Conference was that short of federation, there was general support for European unity,[146] there remained concern that a customs union might cut across the preference system and might alienate the newly independent subcontinental countries. Too close links with France and Holland might also identify Britain with their 'outdated colonial systems' and any formal session of sovereignty might affect India's foreign policy 'in a way undesirable to us'.[147] The Europeanists moved swiftly to soothe their colleagues' ruffled feelings, implying the Conservative delegates' role at Strasbourg would change if the party was in power,[148] and acknowledging the need to harmonize the claims of Europe and Empire in the economic sphere.[149] They stressed Britain's first duty remained to its Empire and the sterling area,[150] and sought to allay fears of an attack on imperial preference by reassuring their colleagues that no more had been done at Strasbourg 'than to recommend to the Committee of Ministers calling of a conference to discuss freeing of trade in sterling area and Western Europe'.[151] All were aware that the party 'would be utterly opposed to any formal federation of Europe'.[152]

(3) *Against the Labour Government*, implacably opposed to their brand of Europeanism, Foreign Office officials, none of whom had any notion of British participation,[153] and

Treasury bureaucrats. All continued to misjudge the intensity of the mood in Europe.[154] Labour sought to play down the importance of the discussions at Strasbourg; Herbert Morrison, as Leader of the House, refused repeated Conservative requests to consider the outcome of the Strasbourg meeting as the topic of a separate debate in the autumn of 1949, despite support from his own side.[155] Frustrated at the behaviour of the unelected Consultative Assembly, Bevin determinedly stressed the importance of the Committee of Ministers, saying pointedly in the Foreign Affairs Debate on 17 November 1949, 'I am sure . . . [the] committee of ministers will prove vital to the unity of Europe. They represent their governments . . . The Assembly . . . has a different function to perform. The ministers, themselves, being responsible representatives of their governments will from time to time have matters referred to them on which decision have to be taken.'[156]

Thanks to Churchill's public endorsement, and the work of key Tories behind the scenes, the Conservative Europeanists had given great impetus to the ideal of European integration and had achieved a remarkable influence over Britain's relations with Europe, building upon support for European unity from the Continent, America and Monnet's friends in London. Bevin had been obliged to react to their efforts, even if this was in annoyance rather than swayed by persuasive argument. By late 1949 it appeared that the Council of Europe was the principal means by which European unity and the creation of a political authority could be achieved, rather than the intergovernmental approach of the Brussels Pact.

Churchill had 'set the pace for thought and action for integration with Europe by virtue of his status as a world statesman.'[157] But although the Conservative Europeanists had helped 'hijack' the debate, their success in promoting a more positive approach to Europe had decided limits. Despite some remarkable concessions, Bevin persisted in his Atlanticist approach to relations with Europe; in fact the Foreign Secretary's determination to pursue closer European cooperation through intergovernmental agencies was probably strengthened by the Conservatives' campaign. Nor had the Conservative Europeanists convinced the majority of their parliamentary colleagues, the party in the country nor British public opinion generally. The Labour Government was indeed more in tune with the British electorate on this matter. Given the diversity of opinion within the European movement and the fact that European integration was an evolving, messy process, the only route open to the Conservative leadership was deliberately to avoid a definite stand. With the advent of the Schuman Plan in 1950, however, the Conservatives could no longer seek refuge in obfuscation.

4 The waiting room of power: 1950-51

The effect of the general election in February 1950 upon Conservative attitudes was paradoxical: the changing of the political guard in this 'new Model Parliament'[1] altered the balance within the Conservative party on Europe. These younger MPs were more inclined to look favourably on Britain taking the lead in Europe. Some saw a united Europe principally as a defence against the Soviet Union; others appreciated the economic advantages the concept offered – the chance to combine the Empire and sterling area with Europe to create a formidable trading bloc; and there were those Tories, such as Henry Hopkinson[2] and Hamilton Kerr, who viewed the moves towards European unity as desirable in their own right.

Power seemed within the Conservatives' grasp as Labour's working majority was slashed to six, which on paper offered greater opportunities for exerting pressure on the Government to shift its stance on European integration. However, as their party moved closer to power – and another election seemed imminent – the Conservative Europeanists' stance was modified, stemming from a renewed sense of responsibility and doubts about the electoral wisdom of enthusiasm for Europe. Macmillan was now stressing that although Britain could not isolate herself from Europe, the Empire 'must always have first preference'.[3] Boothby's ardour was also cooling: at the beginning of 1950 he called for the creation of European Political Authority with 'limited competence but defined powers' which, if it was to have any reality, must include Britain and Germany.[4] As the year wore on, he came to share concerns about the direction in which French supranationalism appeared to be taking the debate.

Moreover, Conservatives remained divided as to the best way to link Western Germany with the free nations of Europe. Churchill continued to call for Germany within a united and free Europe, urging very strongly that everything possible should be done to encourage and promote Franco-German reconciliation as an approach to unity, or even perhaps some form of union; but he resisted 'attempts to draw up precise and rigid constitutions . . . too soon, or in a hurry'.[5] Some Tories, such as Macmillan and Eccles felt that as Germany still needed to be contained for the future security of Europe, Britain should be a full partner of whatever arrangements emerged to counter what was seen as inevitable German domination. Others felt Britain's imperial position posed an insurmountable barrier to full participation of any such arrangements. There was also the perennial problem of German reunification (and the spectre of German revanchism), with many politicians arguing that Western Germany needed to be anchored firmly in the Western camp before any such proposals could be considered.

Within three months of the election the Conservatives were confronted with the Schuman Plan, designed to control West Germany's coal and steel production. The subject matter was not new: in the mid-1940s Conservatives had contributed to discussions on the topic, principally in organizations such as the British Committee of ELEC, but there had not been widespread consideration of the implications within the Tory party; for example, the 1947 Conservative industrial policy statement virtually ignored Europe, and concentrated almost exclusively on the Commonwealth and colonies.[6] By the end of the decade this had changed. Thanks to Marshall Aid, Western Germany was experiencing a remarkable economic revival, reflected in Conservative backbench questions on the re-emergence of the threat of German exports to the British overseas market.[7] Although the country was still under Allied control, this industrial recovery stimulated the debate over the future of the Ruhr industries, in the past the foundation of the German war machine.

Before the advent of the Schuman Plan, Conservative spokesmen had called on the Government to study the political and economic implications of possible integration of Europe's heavy industry. Eden publicly had supported the argument for closer collaboration between the Ruhr and its competing industries in both France, Belgium and Luxembourg,[8] and had advocated integrating the heavy industry of Europe as a whole. In addition, the Conservative Research Department's paper on the internal framework of the Ruhr had been circulated by the policy committee of the Parliamentary party in January 1949, and was subsequently submitted to Sir Andrew Duncan (of the British Iron and Steel Federation) for private comment. Macmillan, who had raised the matter in general terms in the House of Commons,[9] worked with Thorneycroft, Eccles, and Lady Tweedsmuir in the British Committee of ELEC in discussions on ideas of international control of the Ruhr's iron and steel industries. These discussions led to consideration of a report on European coal and steel industries at the Westminster Economic Conference in April 1949.

There was a widespread Conservative belief that a return to 'cut-throat international competition based on free nondiscriminatory multilateral trade' would be a return to economic anarchy. Although not all pro-European Tories endorsed the view that the future lay with creation of larger economic blocs, with the Empire and Western Europe as a natural bloc and a potentially powerful counterpoint to the American economic leviathan, those who favoured increased European economic cooperation were concerned that a Western economic bloc which excluded Britain would sabotage the sterling area. And despite concerted attacks on the preferential trading system from the United States, the Empire was still very much a going concern.

CONSERVATIVES AND THE SCHUMAN PLAN

The issue of European integration came to a critical point for the Conservatives when the French Foreign Minister, Robert Schuman, issued an invitation to the British Government to attend talks on Jean Monnet's proposal for a European Coal and Steel Community (ECSC) in May 1950.[10]

Given Churchill's leadership of the UEM and Eden's presence at the Hague congress, there was a general anticipation that the Conservative leadership would applaud the French initiative. The Conservative Europeanists saw the need for a swift and positive response: otherwise their party would lay itself open to the Labour charge of hypocrisy. However, the immediate Conservative reaction to Schuman's proposals was muted: it was not until 19 May – 10 days after Schuman's invitation to the Labour Government – that Churchill welcomed the Schuman Plan as an important and effective step in preventing another war between France and Germany. In a heavily qualified statement, not the wholehearted endorsement desired by the enthusiastic Europeanists, he welcomed 'the Schuman proposal cordially in principle but we must nevertheless consider carefully the way in which Britain can participate most effectively in such a larger grouping of European industry. We must be careful it does not carry with it a lowering of British wages and standards of life and labour. We must, I feel, assert the principle of levelling up, not of levelling down.'[11] The uncomfortable reality of European integration was at last raising its head, forcing Churchill to take a specific stand on the issue – something he had successfully avoided hitherto.

Although there was widespread Tory indignation at French behaviour – first in springing the idea on Britain, then presenting an ultimatum[12] – compounded by a marked aversion to being bound in advance,[13] Conservative politicians recognized and appreciated the motivation of the French plan as 'primarily an invention to resolve the dilemma of Germany rearmed'. If the German army was not reconstituted, Western Europe would be at the mercy of Russia; if it was, France would again be at Germany's mercy. But if the steel industries of the two countries were merged, it would be impossible to make war.[14]

The problem was the manner proposed for integration. Although Britain had accepted supranational functional institutions in two World Wars (these had, of course, been for a limited duration), Churchill's own preference remained British sponsorship of Europe, short of actual membership; his fellow Europeanists favoured closer cooperation, but along intergovernmental lines. Schuman's initiative was specifically a supranational scheme. This principle had bedevilled Sandys' attempts in the International Committee in 1949 and 1950 to reconcile the British preference for collaboration short of a surrender of sovereignty, with the Continental desire for a more radical approach. With the Schuman Plan on the table, such a dichotomy of opinion could no longer be concealed.

Conservative divisions on the Schuman Plan meant that the party was loath to declare its stance. No record remains of the Foreign Affairs Committee meetings at this time, but former MPs recall that most discussion on the issue took place in the Smoking Room, or the Dining Room.

It tended to be divided into those who had a firm opinion one way or the other, who discussed mainly amongst themselves. In other words, they reinforced one another in their preconceived opinions. There were many members for whom the whole thing was slightly unreal and difficult to understand: it did not correspond at all with the political world in which they lived. There was more informed discussion outside of Parliament than within it, conducted through the Press and in various groups and movements. I think my view [on the Schuman Plan] was quite widely held. Most serious thinkers would have admitted that some dilution of sovereignty was necessary if we were to have the advantages of togetherness... The "French" view in so far as it deserved that name, was seen by me and I suspect by many others as a rainbow affair. There were out-and-out Federalists in France and in politics but they were not by any means a majority, and it was obvious then as it is today that the French would never accept supranationality if it really inconvenienced them. The political future therefore looked fluid rather than rigid.[15]

In marked contrast to the view that British participation was vital 'to push the outcome our way',[16] those Conservatives who did not have the advantages of the Strasbourg experience judged the issue in strictly national terms.[17] In addition, political memories were still raw from the recent parliamentary battle over the nationalization of Britain's own iron and steel industries. Opposition to the Schuman Plan ranged across the Conservative political generations. Many older MPs were annoyed at the Europeans who 'were always keen to know on which side of the fence the Tories would land',[18] which echoed the Labour Government's own preference for an empirical approach *vs* the French desire for a theoretical framework. Some Conservatives disliked the proposed economic arrangement on principle: the Schuman Plan was 'trying to make an honest woman of a cartel'.[19] It would be far better if European heavy industry continued under private enterprise.

However, the political implications of Jean Monnet's functional proposal were of supreme importance. The Schuman Plan was not limited to an arrangement governing coal and steel: it was a commitment to federate Europe. As such, it was unacceptable and, it was felt, would be unacceptable to the

British people. Bolstered by their knowledge that 'the British steel industry were against it, as were the French steel industry',[20] others argued 'the common unity implicit in the Schuman Plan was an artificial aspiration'.[21]

Thus, the Schuman Plan was seen as a slippery slope: once Britain had set foot upon it and subordinated two key industries, 'it would [be] inevitable that we are entering on the path of political integration as well'.[22] There were powerful emotional arguments involved: it seemed a case of either Empire or Europe, and 'if the Conservative party is now to take a further deep plunge into Europe, it must not be surprised if the countries of the Commonwealth are not prepared indefinitely to tag along like a gaggle of Strasbourg geese'.[23] In addition, 'many backbench Tories felt they were choosing between France and the USA. Looking back to the War, America had been a more secure and satisfactory ally than France.'[24]

Within the small group of Churchill's intimates there were also 'important differences on the immediate problem and the general approach to vital issues'.[25] The Conservative party could no longer disclaim responsibility as it had been able to do between 1945 and 1950, and this sense of responsibility was felt by both the Conservative front and back benches.[26] Churchill was deeply and publicly committed to the principles of the UEM. Although Eden had 'not taken an active part',[27] nevertheless he fully realized the immense opportunities either for success or failure in restoring Europe's strength and had publicly advocated economic integration with Europe. In contrast, others on the Conservative front bench were 'definitely opposed to the surrender of sovereignty'[28] (undoubtedly Crookshank), or saw practical disadvantages for British industry. British steel was the most efficient in Europe, and this country was producing better and cheaper coal than her European rivals, with a readily available market overseas. What therefore could be gained by exchanging the present system? Another faction which included Macmillan and Eccles, felt that no matter the difficulties and dangers, the greatest danger would be if the European industry was remodelled without a British contribution even at the talks.

Keen to seize the political initiative,[29] the Conservative Europeanists on the middle benches swiftly undertook a series of manoeuvres to counteract their colleagues' reluctance.

Macmillan used a constituency speech on 17 May 1950 to urge a positive British response.[30] The British Committee of ELEC (whose Conservative Parliamentary members included Julian Amery,[31] Eccles, Macmillan, Thorneycroft and Lady Tweedsmuir) similarly urged:

> The Schuman proposals to create a European steel and coal organization as one of the foundations of a new Europe may prove to be as momentous as General Marshall's offer at Harvard... It is not enough to applaud it... [The Schuman Plan's] political and economic implications are of great importance, but the details remain to be worked out. It is therefore very much in Britain's interest that we should take an active part in its elaboration from the beginning... We cannot turn our back on Europe at this critical moment.[32]

Beaverbrook issued a broadside on behalf of the Tory imperialist anti-European wing the following day when this letter was violently, and predictably, attacked in *The Daily Express*; this at least had the merit of airing the debate.

Boothby followed up the Europeanists' opening salvo with a letter written from Paris, describing the 'prevailing [French] impatience... with the timidity and insular selfishness of British foreign policy [which] is widespread... We might have led the movement for European union and moulded it according to our desires. We have chosen instead to obstruct it at every turn. What is now quite certain is that we cannot stop it. If we continue upon our present course we shall find ourselves in a position of total isolation.'[33] The same day speaking to a group of industrialists in London, Macmillan referred to the possible consequences of failure of the Schuman plan: Europe could never revert to the situation which existed before the proposal was made. If the plan was not successful, the situation created might be the turning point. It would create one of two hideous results – either people would lose confidence in Western Europe as a whole, or the plan would operate under a Germany not controlled by Britain, or America, a Germany of the wrong kind. Britain might see a German Schuman Plan in the next five years which might be akin to a Ribbentrop-Stalin pact.[34] (This persistent fear was to colour Macmillan's attitude towards Eden's treatment of European Defence Community (EDC) in the 1950s.)

For these Conservative Europeanists there was a vital principle at stake in the Schuman Plan: it was nothing less than British leadership of Europe. They recognized the Plan as a bid by the French,[35] with America's blessing, to direct emerging European institutions down the desired federal path, preventing the British (Conservative and Labour alike) from merely relying on the genuine European wish to ensure British participation to limit the scope of the relationship. Thus it was imperative that Britain attend the forthcoming talks in Paris to direct the emerging institution down acceptable intergovernmental channels to protect British and Commonwealth interests.

Despite the Government's reluctance to participate in the talks – manifest in its resistance to repeated Conservative calls for an early debate on the Schuman Plan on the grounds that British suggestions were being held in reserve until the Paris talks had had 'a fair run' – the Europeanists did not give up hope of swaying the debate in their favour. In a long letter to *The Times*, Eccles accused the Government of harbouring ideas of national sovereignty that were out of step with the Continent. He did not believe that Britain should urge member states of the Council of Europe by themselves to form close political federation for 'full federation is unwise', but added that Europe felt the need for piecemeal pooling of sovereignty. He was critical of France's methods of negotiating, 'but there is still time to take her hand and good reasons why we should'. He rebuffed Labour's arguments: the Schuman Plan could be used as a means of extending the areas of full employment; the Commonwealth would welcome British participation as it offered a stable market for produce in expanding prosperity of Europe; imperial preference could be maintained as was made clear at the Strasbourg meeting in December 1949; unless German competition was rationalized it would create future problems and the danger of a steel glut as soon as supply overtook demand. As for the strategic problem of German dominance in Europe, the Schuman Plan would make sure, if ever there was another war, that France and Germany would be on the same side: 'But on which side? How can we tell unless we are members of the Plan?'[36]

Much to the Conservative Europeanists' consternation, Churchill did not seize the heaven-sent opportunity to wrong-foot the Government, even when Attlee's polite refusal to attend the Paris talks on 13 June 1950 coincided with the publication of Labour's National Executive Committee's pamphlet on European unity, laying Labour wide open to accusations of clumsiness and ineptitude. Churchill's reluctance compared markedly with Eden's determination that Schuman's overture should not be ignored. Concerned that Britain would miss a critical chance to help resolve Franco-German antagonism, his declaration to Anthony Nutting that 'it was madness to turn down the idea as Bevin had done'[37] was a logical progression from his earlier arguments for closer economic cooperation in Europe and his coherent views on the future of the Ruhr industries.

However, Eden had no time for the political goal evident in Schuman's proposal; he believed that Britain could successfully direct negotiations down inter-governmental channels which would benefit all concerned. At a Young Conservatives rally in Yorkshire, he set out very clearly his alternative view of British association with Europe: 'We have many times made clear that in any conflict of friendship or interest the British Commonwealth and Empire will always come first. We say this not merely out of loyalty or affection, but because we know it is as the heart and centre of the Commonwealth family that we can make our fullest contribution to promote our own prosperity and the peace of the world ... But while these convictions must always have first place in our minds, we should still have confidence to be able to play a full and constructive part in world affairs in Europe and elsewhere.'[38]

Alarmed that his party was still undecided on its position,[39] and fearful that his colleagues might not reach an effective decision or even might support the Government's line, Macmillan sent an urgent minute to Churchill urging participation in the forthcoming discussions along the lines of those accepted by the Dutch (reserving the right to go back on its prior acceptance of the general principles of supranationality if, in the course of negotiations, it proved impossible to translate these into practice). 'It is now widely reported that the British Government will make an immense [and probably successful] effort to reopen negotiations ... in that event, it is absolutely vital that this should come about as a result of pressure from the Tory party and from you.' He further exhorted his leader, 'You started united Europe... This is the first supreme test... you cannot let down all in Europe'.[40]

Pleading with Churchill to put down a motion as soon as possible, he backed his argument with a description of a meeting of Conservative MPs (probably the Foreign Affairs Committee, although no record remains of the proceedings) which had taken place on 19 June 1950. Approximately 80 MPs had attended, and of the speakers, about two-thirds had been in favour of the Schuman Plan, and 'only two or three against... Some of those who have special knowledge of the industries concerned had given their support... The overwhelming majority that the party should take a lead and a motion should be tabled.'[41]

Not surprisingly, Macmillan was putting a heavy gloss on Tory attitudes to the Schuman Plan. The two-thirds of those present were not necessarily in favour of a supranational organization. Although Macmillan pointedly referred to the positive attitude desired by the younger element, this was by no means universal. The views of some 200 Conservatives who had not attended the meeting were still open to question. Undaunted, Macmillan pressed ahead. With Boothby (who was currently in Paris) his most likely informant, Macmillan craftily appealed to Churchill's vanity, reporting that the British Embassy in Paris was spreading rumours that Churchill, under influence of his advisers and fearful of losing votes, was preparing to retreat on the whole concept of a united Europe now that practical decisions were being made. Macmillan then sent Churchill a draft motion urging the use of the Dutch model. Boothby also wrote to Churchill exhorting him to provide 'the leadership for which the Western world is now praying'.[42]

Under these pressures Churchill finally made up his mind and was 'followed with differing degrees of enthusiasm by all his colleagues and the party as a whole'.[43] True to his apolitical nature, Churchill enlisted the support of the Liberals. Clement Davies, the Liberal leader, initially wanted the motion to be worded differently and in stronger language, but at once agreed with Churchill on the overriding need to coordinate the attack on the Government. The joint EDM, deliberately framed to attract the widest possible cross-party support, pressed the Government to take part in the Paris negotiations while reserving freedom of action if the plan proved impractical. As *The Times* noted, the wording carefully refrained from committing its supporters to endorsing wholeheartedly the Schuman Plan.

Churchill, whose slow reaction to Schuman's proposal reflected his own ambivalence, had undoubtedly realised that a great many Tories would not be able to stomach open Conservative support for the Schuman Plan. The careful attention to the preparation of the Conservative case in the party's briefs on the topic was clearly aimed at discounting internal as well as external criticism. A concerted effort was made to discount the argument that Conservatives were using the Schuman Plan merely as a stick with which to beat the Government. Ursula Branston, the author of these briefs from the Conservative Research Department, argued:

> We went a long way towards supranational bodies in the economic sphere through the Marshall Plan and the OEEC, and in the military sphere through NATO. If we want to dictate terms – better still if we want to be in a position where we do not need to dictate terms on which European integration can move towards gradually – we have to lead, not follow.[44]

The party briefs also sought assiduously to disarm Labour's claim that Conservative support for the Schuman Plan was incompatible with opposition to iron and steel nationalization: the Schuman Plan would be a change in general policy, not ownership and the basis of management of Britain's coal and steel industries. The political consideration for Britain was the 'disequilibrium which would be set up in the whole European structure if the Franco-German relationship was to develop apart from the UK'. The political separation, if it crystallized, might easily extend to separation in matters of defence as well as economics. 'The vital factor is Germany rather than France. If Germany obtains a dominant role, it might not be revived militarism as much as an artificial bid for neutrality which would paralyse the French – with disastrous consequences. For our own sakes as well as Western solidarity, we have to be an active participant.'[45]

The Conservative and Liberal motion successfully raised the political temperature at Westminster and 'the Schuman Plan debate was the most important thus far in the session'.[46] This was not solely because of the united Opposition attack on the Government. The press had picked up Conservative backbench misgivings that the Government might be right and Churchill and Eden were marching too far ahead of the party's traditional policies.[47] Conservative sceptics were very concerned at the implications of Churchill's motion. For them, if Churchill supported the view that it was a choice between winning the Cold War by subordinating national sovereignty and forfeiting national sovereignty by losing the Cold War, he would signal a great departure in Conservative and national policy.[48]

The bulk of the party was in a dilemma:[49] Churchill's motion was either a deft parliamentary manoeuvre to put the Government at a disadvantage, or by implication a new and important policy declaration by Her Majesty's Opposition. Privately many Tories felt that the Dutch analogy was misleading since the Dutch were prepared to accept a federal solution if it could be found to be practicable; thus the EDM seemed to imply the Government should have accepted Schuman's prior condition. This would indeed have been a startling departure from traditional Tory policy towards Europe as it would mean that the Conservatives accepted a supranational authority as the first principle, subject only to being shown this was practicable – an acceptance which would come as a great surprise to Tory voters. Alarmed and irritated that some of their colleagues seemed 'to have become more European than the Europeans',[50] dissenting Conservatives appreciated Labour's riposte that after vehemently opposing the nationalization of British iron and steel, the Tories were apparently implying their willingness to 'run half-way across Europe' to give away control to a body outside British control. Like Labour, the Conservative party as a whole had no intention of handing over commanding heights of British industry to outside control. At the time Britain was producing half the coal and one third of the steel produced in Western Europe: there appeared therefore little immediate apparent benefit. Many Conservatives privately accepted Labour's argument that Tories would not have accepted the French invitation had they been in power and presented with the same condition of attendance. Conservative party managers hoped to deflect this criticism with the counter accusation that the Schuman Plan arose from 'a most maladroit handling of foreign affairs and it is nothing more than a diplomatic disaster that Britain was absent from Paris'.[51] But, recognizing the valid charge of hypocrisy, most Tories stayed quiet.[52]

The debate itself began under a cloud; although the majority was 'inclined to play down the significance of the events in Korea, their minds kept wandering in a Far Easterly direction'.[53] The debate was conducted on two levels.[54] The first issue was the basis on which talks should have been conducted. There were clear arguments against the charge that the Government should have gone to Paris, with the Dutch reservation: it was against British diplomatic tradition to tie the Government's hand beforehand; and the feeling was widespread that it would be wrong to take a step that might reduce, rather than enhance, the chances of agreement in Europe on the principles of the Schuman Plan. On the second, broader, issue of sovereignty there was a divide. Whereas some Conservatives might rationally admit that every treaty involved the relinquishment of some aspect of sovereignty, there remained a fundamental reluctance on both sides of the House to place such vital British interests under foreign control. There was also the employment aspect.

It was therefore not surprising that the Conservatives concentrated on the issue of Labour's refusal to attend the Paris negotiations. The Labour benches were very aware of the Conservative predicament.

> The only real difference between us and the Conservatives – and Churchill made a superb speech in the House – was that Churchill thought we should be in the negotiations and be perfectly free to say, 'We're not having it', or 'We're not going to join it', whereas Attlee and Bevin said, 'No, let them have the negotiations and we'll look and see what they produce at the end of the day, and then we'll decide and see whether there is any relationship we can have with it'.[55]

Despite some initial speculation that the Government would be beaten in the vote on the Schuman Plan,[56] and whether there would then be an immediate General Election,[57] the Government's confidence that it could command its usual small majority was not misplaced. The Opposition were 15 short in the first division: five Conservatives were absent through illness, and six Tories[58] ostentatiously abstained on a three-line whip, although they voted with their party in the second division of the night. These six MPs represented 'the other wing of the Conservative party who believe... that any supranational authority must be totalitarian if it is successful and chaotic if it is not, and in any event Britain will be robbed of her nationhood and her powers of defence'.[59] It is interesting that all six later opposed Eden on his Egypt policy.

The revolt was 'fairly spontaneous, not a formal conspiracy ... a result of informal chats in the Members' lobby and elsewhere'.[60] Only Legge-Bourke had drawn attention to himself in the debate; the national newspapers were agreed that apart from the leading protagonists, his speech calling for outright rejection of the Plan had caused the greatest stir.[61] While not all Tories necessarily agreed with what Legge-Bourke said – at one point he called for the winding up of the UNO – his sincerity and courage commanded respect.[62] The other dissenters 'gave their leaders no warning. None of them protested at the various secret meetings held that week. Those who did toed the party line of the day.'[63] Politically, the most remarkable rebel was Enoch Powell, 'intellectually and morally one of the outstanding backbenchers on either side'.[64] Vere Harvey's opposition seems surprising, given his endorsement of British support of European union in the all-party parliamentary committee in the late 1940s. For him, the supranational nature of Schuman's proposal was undoubtedly the sticking point.

Unluckily for these rebels, that same evening the Government announced their position on the two-day old Korean War, so their rebellion was largely ignored in Westminster, although it attracted considerable press attention,[65] and enjoyed outright support in the right-wing press:[66] Beaverbrook lost no time in 'leaping back into the political arena to vocalize the section of the Tory party which regarded the French proposals as tantamount to the destruction of British economic links with the Commonwealth'.[67]

The Labour Government's decision not to attend the Paris talks had been made at a rump Cabinet meeting,[68] with some important absences: Bevin was ill; both Attlee and Cripps were away on holiday. Neither returned for the meeting – implying the matter was not to be taken very seriously.[69] Nor had the Commonwealth been consulted. The Government saw no need to 'initiate any action or ideas which would embarrass

Schuman'[70] following the Schuman Plan debate. The British Government's decision reflected British attitudes and national self-perceptions at the time.[71] The virtual ultimatum from Schuman had given the impression 'that Schuman did not want us in ... [and] feeling was terribly high about the manner in which it was done.'[72] Foreign Office advice remained 'Western Europe with the United Kingdom was not strong enough to stand alone. A wider grouping ... was essential if the Western democracies were to be secured' and continued to stress the 'essential importance of our relationship with the United States'.[73] Roger Makins, described as 'the most influential official at the time',[74] occupied a key position as Economic Deputy Under-Secretary and represented a powerful counterweight to those within the Foreign Office (such as Kenneth Younger) who would have liked to have taken a more positive approach.

THE MACMILLAN-ECCLES PLAN

'Unhappy and dissatisfied with the outcome of the Schuman Plan vote', which they refused to accept as the last word,[75] the Conservative Europeanists decided to use the opportunity of the next Consultative Assembly in Strasbourg in August 1950 to propose a compromise, since they recognized legitimate objections to the Schuman Plan as it currently stood.[76] They felt that the British Government's objections to surrendering national sovereignty would be shared by other European governments, especially Holland and Belgium, when details of the plan became known. They were also banking on French fears of handing her weak and obsolete industry to German control without a British counterweight; they underestimated French determination in this regard.

As a result of hard work and assistance from organizations such as ELEC, on 15 August 1950 the Macmillan-Eccles Plan was put forward in the Consultative Assembly. It was not presented as a cut-and-dried plan, but in the belief that 'they are the kind of proposals which a British government could and ought to have put forward at least as a basis of discussion'.[77] Its main purpose, set out in the formal resolution, was to 'meet British fears without injury to the main feature of the [Schuman] Plan'.[78] In other words, it was designed to meet

British fears of putting a vital industry in the hands of foreign bureaucrats. Macmillan felt this preserved 'some tenable position for Britain', and (significantly) his own party.

The new Plan differed from the Schuman original in broad areas: the experts coordinating the iron and steel industries were to be responsible to a Committee of Ministers, and thus the link with the respective member Parliaments would be maintained. Secondly, the basic social, economic and strategic interests of each country would be safeguarded from encroachment by experts. Finally, any member could withdraw at three months' notice. The imperial preference system should not be jeopardized as far as British exports to the Commonwealth were concerned, and the authority would have only advisory powers *vis-à-vis* capital investment in Britain. Other clauses sought to protect wage standards and bargaining; the voting powers of members of the authority should be in proportion to the production and consumption of coal and steel in the member countries. Since the British coal and steel industry occupied a pre-eminent position in Europe, this was a blatant tactic to ensure British supremacy in decision making. Finally British association and signature to any such treaty was to be subject to the ratification of Parliament.[79]

Significantly these proposals did not have their Conservative colleagues' wholehearted approval. Of the informal shadow cabinet, Macmillan noted Lyttleton approved, whereas Churchill was only 'fairly satisfied'. In his autobiography, Macmillan explained this away with the argument that the authors preferred Churchill not to put his name to this paper, as he had not had time to consult his Shadow Cabinet. 'It was also felt that Churchill should stay out of detailed controversy', even if he should give his general blessing.[80] Eden had been more forthcoming. In discussions with Macmillan, he expressed his opinion that this contribution was beneficial from Europe's and the Conservative party's point of view.

The authors of the revised plan realized that a federal plan would not be acceptable to the British electorate, which was a crucial consideration since an election seemed imminent. The Macmillan-Eccles Plan was designed as a compromise between the French and British positions, but also to reassert British leadership of Europe. It foundered upon Monnet's determination that the British would not sabotage his carefully laid schemes to tie the German and French economies tightly together. 'As a consequence of the immediate and continuing favourable responses the Europeans and the Americans made to the Schuman proposals, Britain lost the more or less controlling influence it had managed to exercise until then over the evolving character and extent of European unity.'[81] In the debate on the Schuman Plan in the Assembly, although Macmillan's speech was well received, Paul Reynaud argued that as the agreement on the Schuman Plan would be signed in four weeks nothing further could be done, and appealed to Macmillan to withdraw his amendment.[82]

Macmillan held a press conference immediately after the vote on the Schuman Plan in Strasbourg, and remarked, 'Of course I know that all this is only small beer and no one at home takes the slightest interest!' Behind the apparent self-deprecation, he was obviously bitter that his campaign had achieved such limited success. His Strasbourg colleague, Lord Birkenhead ruefully commented that the delegates of the Council of Europe had the feeling that they were at the hub of the universe in Strasbourg, and it had been a chastening and salutary experience on his return to Westminster to discover his political friends felt he had been buried in oblivion. This impression was attributed partly to the 'famine in newsprint' but he 'could not escape the conclusion that many regarded the Council of Europe as a polyglot debating society... merely duplicating the functions of NATO, the Brussels Treaty and OEEC'.[83]

The scant attention paid by the British press to the Strasbourgers' tactics was critical. *Crossbencher* applauded the 'farsighted men,' such as Legge-Bourke; whereas 'those slap-happy Schumanites, Boothby, Eccles and Macmillan' were blamed for laying the Tories open to Herbert Morrison's 'devastating argument',[84] which did real damage to their cause against the nationalization of iron and steel. 'The Tories have promised that if they are returned at the next election they will denationalize steel. This too is not enough. They must promise not to internationalize it.'

The Macmillan-Eccles Plan had no impact whatsoever on the British domestic scene. Although Churchill and Eden lent their qualified support, for many Tories embarrassing the Government on the issue no longer held the same political attraction.

The British Government remained determinedly aloof from the Paris discussions.[85] Labour's studied disdain of the Strasbourg Assembly continued, seen in the Government's reluctance to grant parliamentary time to consideration of the Strasbourg resolutions: such discussion should come out of time allotted to the Opposition. The Strasbourg resolutions were finally debated on 13 November 1950 against the background of the Pleven Plan. Labour, stung by Tory accusations of sloth and ineptitude, returned to the theme that Conservatives had carried national political controversy to Strasbourg,[86] with the accusations of semi-sabotage. Monnet's determination to contain the Ruhr industries in a supranational structure sealed the Macmillan-Eccles Plan's fate.

There was small consolation for the Conservative delegates to Strasbourg. In May 1951, there took place the last stage of discussions at the Consultative Assembly on the Schuman Plan, which considered the report of the Committee and the appropriate resolution. According to Macmillan, although it was tragic that the British Government had refused to join the initial talks, 'my colleagues and I could take some satisfaction in the final form of the Schuman Plan, since the Higher Authority although still supranational, was not supreme'.[87]

EUROPEAN DEFENCE

Long before the outbreak of the Korean War, Conservative politicians had argued for the rearmament of Western Germany within the Western camp. Widespread anxiety about a Communist invasion of Western Germany – the Soviet Union and its satellites already enjoyed an overwhelming superiority in numbers of troops, tanks and divisions in central Europe – had been fuelled with the news of Russia's arming the East German 'police'. Churchill raised the topic in the Foreign Affairs debate on 28 March 1950,[88] and Julian Amery chose the subject for his maiden speech in the same debate:[89] in their view, Europe must be convinced that Britain would come to its aid. Eden preferred to stress the Atlantic Pact (signed April 1949) as the preferred vehicle for a German contribution to Western defence.[90]

But for the Labour party, and indeed for many Conservatives, the prospect of a revived German High Command and possible resurgence of Prussian militarism was deeply repugnant. It was still only five years since Hitler's defeat. The Conservative Europeanists' were the targets of accusations of advocating German rearmament when there was no pressing need. Bevin was determined to resist such calls, declaring firmly that 'all of us are against' the rearming of Germany.[91]

The outbreak of the Korean War in June 1950 heightened existing fears of the Russian military threat to Western Europe. There was a strong feeling among the Europeanists that the Council of Europe was entitled to, and should, discuss defence – an area which the Committee of Ministers jealously guarded as their prescriptive right. Undaunted, Churchill seized international attention with his demand in August 1950 at the second Assembly in Strasbourg for the immediate creation of a European army under a unified command with a single Defence Minister. As with other aspects of his European 'policy', Churchill had no well-defined plan; the details were to be provided by his worker bees, in particular Sandys. Insofar as Churchill had conceived the structure of such an organization, he imagined something akin to the Allied Command of World War II. 'His purpose was to throw out general ideas and give impetus towards movements already at work. It was for others to find detailed solutions.' But as Churchill commented, there was a method in his approach: 'I am sure it would be a mistake to get involved in details. The Council of Europe can never at this stage in affairs deal with problems that belong to executive governments. It may point the way and give inspiration.'[92]

Although this did not enjoy the same success as Churchill's earlier suggestions and Churchill and his fellow Europeanists were not successful in persuading Bevin of the merits of the idea, it was thanks to the Conservative leader that the idea of German rearmament through a European army entered international debate. America had indicated in the first NATO staff meetings in 1949 that she did not intend to commit any further ground troops to Europe. Washington's change of position in September 1950 was conditional upon the rearming of Western Germany: this increase in American troops in Europe was temporary until 12 German divisions had been raised and ready to take up their position. Intent on satisfying American demands, yet determined to contain its former foe, the French Foreign Minister Réné Pleven outlined his proposal for a European Defence Community (known as the Pleven Plan) to the French National Assembly in October 1950. The Pleven Plan was an extension of Monnet's supranational ideas for the control of West Germany, with its proposals for the integration of national armies at the lowest possible level. Pleven acknowledged that his ideas were based on Churchill's plan presented to the Council of Europe earlier that summer.[93]

The Conservative Europeanists were dismayed however with the French version of Churchill's original idea; it made military nonsense and bore no relation to Churchill's original concept of a revived Grand Alliance. Churchill himself disliked the Pleven Plan intensely, describing the proposed army as a 'sludgy amalgam'.[94] Faced with the direction Europe was now taking, combined with the potent influence of Churchill who now evinced less interest in Europe, most of the Conservative Europeanists began to blow 'hot and cold' towards Europe. Sandys persisted, asking the Labour Government to reconsider its opposition to a European army.[95] In February 1951, he undertook a personal initiative, sending a compromise plan for a European army to ministers of governments taking part in the forthcoming conference in Paris. Sandys was currently the *rapporteur* for the European Army for the European Assembly, but he stressed, somewhat ingenuously, to each recipient that he was acting in a private capacity. His proposal was for the creation of a European army by progressive stages, arguing that arrangements would be confined to practical military cooperation without any political and constitutional implications. Hopefully this would enable all West European countries, including Britain, to participate in the second stage. Sandys envisaged that those nations who wished to conclude 'a closer and more defensive union would together set up the necessary European political institutions on the lines of the Pleven Plan, or any other agreed basis'.[96] This attempt at a functional, intergovernmental halfway house failed to satisfy French fears, and Sandys' initiative came to nought.

The internal Tory debate over the solution to the German problem continued between, on the one hand, those who saw the need to incorporate Germany into the Western defence system required allaying the fears of the French (the Eden thesis) and on the other, those who argued that the extravagant French proposals for European rearmament were doomed to failure, and should be allowed to fail, providing Britain with the opportunity to suggest a practical alternative – the Macmillan thesis; Macmillan felt the Pleven Plan was more likely to soothe the French than to frighten the Russians.[97] Those who were vehemently anti-European, such as Sir Herbert Williams and Legge-Bourke, were firmly opposed to the EDC,[98] stressing a preference for joint command (on NATO lines) for Europe's defence.

The Labour Government only very reluctantly acquiesced in the notion of German rearmament upon the insistence of the Americans. But the Labour Government had no intention of participating in the French compromise, and steadfastly refused to participate in discussions about the form the European Army should take. However, Churchill's support for Labour's foreign policy generally was 'a powerful reinforcement' for Attlee and Bevin in their decision to support German rearmament against the wishes of most of their Cabinet colleagues. The Prime Minister and Foreign Secretary knew they could rely upon Churchill (despite continuing reluctance inside the Foreign Office and the Parliamentary Labour Party) to bring the Conservatives to support the policy and make it bipartisan.[99]

EUROPE AND THE COMMONWEALTH

The Conservative delegates to the Strasbourg Assembly also achieved another minor but not insignificant triumph in securing the invitation to Commonwealth parliamentarians to attend the Assembly's proceedings. The Conservative delegates were constantly mindful of the tensions within their party on the issues of Europe and Empire and the instinctive mistrust of the Continent in Britain.[100] The instigators of the invitation to Commonwealth politicians clearly wanted to widen Commonwealth involvement in British links with Europe. 'As long as we are the only members of the Commonwealth present at Strasbourg, we are bound to keep looking over our shoulders to make sure that we are not getting out of step with Commonwealth opinion. But it is difficult to give a lead when you are looking over your shoulder, especially in an Assembly where decisions have to be taken quickly and there is not always time to refer back.' It was hoped that if there were representatives of Commonwealth opinion with them – not officials but politicians who could give broad guidance at every stage – then they would have the confidence to take decisions 'and run the risk that leadership demands'.[101] In May 1951 the European Assembly, on this initiative of the British delegates, issued an invitation to Commonwealth governments to be represented at Strasbourg by official observers. The following month an Empire Commonwealth conference met to consider methods of establishing closer economic relations between Western Europe and the British Dominions.

The influence wielded by the Conservative Europeanists in 1950 and 1951 was less potent than in the previous Parliament but their achievements were far from negligible. The Labour Government was forced to account for its negative stance towards the Schuman Plan; in the opinion of one junior Labour Minister, Churchill's 'Why not be there?' was devastating.[102] The Macmillan-Eccles Plan did help influence the final structure of the European Coal and Steel Community, albeit it in a minor way. Their greatest success lay in Churchill's public advocacy of a West German contribution to West European defence through the creation of a European Army, which considerably influenced the Pleven Plan.

The Conservative Europeanists' contribution to international debate was, in the eyes of their Continental colleagues in Strasbourg, of great importance. Outside that forum they dwindled in significance. The Attlee Government remained resolutely hostile to the Council of Europe proceedings. Not only had there developed a lamentable confusion between official and personal views expressed there,[103] the Consultative Assembly grossly exceeded its brief. The British Government further sought to undermine any legitimacy of discussion in Strasbourg by refusing to send a senior government minister for the 1951 session.

Nor had the Conservative Europeanists won over their colleagues. In May 1950 the Conservatives were faced with an uncomfortable issue which obliged them to examine – for some probably for the first time – what exactly they had envisaged when supporting general sentiments of European cooperation; the partisan process of government provided a convenient escape route for those who could not stomach the Schuman Plan's ultimate federalist aim. It was indeed 'the moment of truth'.[104] Once German rearmament became the political issue of the decade, the manifest ambivalence of the Tory Sceptics about the form 'Europe' was taking was increasingly shared by their more enthusiastic Conservative colleagues. Thereafter the difference between the Labour Government and the Conservative Europeanists lay in the question of emphasis and tone, not substance. And again it was the impression of Churchill's titanic personality upon his party that was the crucial factor: when he 'reined in' on Europe, so did his supporters.[105]

5 The Conservatives and Europe: the pragmatism of power 1951–57

THE TRIUMPH OF EDEN: 1951–55

With Churchill's return to Downing Street in October 1951, Continental federalists had high hopes of a substantial shift in Britain's attitudes towards European integration. They were encouraged by the presence of leading Europeanists within the Government; Sandys, Eccles and Thorneycroft were ministers, and Macmillan and Maxwell Fyfe held Cabinet posts.[1] Maxwell Fyfe was appointed to lead a strong delegation to Strasbourg and a further fillip came in the week before the Assembly's meetings when, 'despite strong opposition from the Foreign Office', Churchill appointed Boothby to represent the Conservatives, and by implication the Government, in a debate in Strasbourg between members of Congress and a delegation from the Consultative Assembly.[2]

Although the Conservative delegates[3] concurred with their Government that the Pleven Plan was quite unsuitable,[4] accepting the powerful strategic arguments against British involvement, they were keen that there should be a marked change in tone. They assured the Strasbourg Assembly that the new Conservative Government would give more encouragement to the Council of Europe: although Britain could not belong exclusively to any one grouping – considerations of defence,[5] Commonwealth ties and the economic implications of the sterling area precluded British participation in a purely European community – Britain might be the lynch pin between a wider Atlantic community and 'European arrangements on a supranational basis'.[6]

They were swiftly disillusioned. 'Maxwell Fyfe spoke in the morning in Strasbourg. The big guns [Winston, Macmillan] were sitting in Whitehall, but Maxwell Fyfe was acting with full Cabinet authority.'[7] Although the wording of his statement was carefully cautious, Maxwell Fyfe was convinced that it significantly changed the emphasis of Britain's approach.[8] He meant 'that we would join the Pleven discussions to remould it. We would take a full and honourable part in negotiations which Britain had refused to do over the Schuman Plan, brushing aside the commitment to supranationalism. We all went off to lunch and came back at 5.00 pm when we saw the papers with the headline about Eden's statement in Rome[9] ... The whole thing was unbelievably awful.'[10] Henceforth, 'we were regarded as almost untouchables, and it would be better if we went home.'[11]

On 3 December 1951 the whole Conservative delegation in Strasbourg signed a round-robin letter to Churchill saying their position was intolerable.[12] 'It was a desperate message ... saying we must make our goodwill known otherwise Europe would fall apart and form something without us. It was a really strongly worded letter of protest asking if we had gone back on everything that we said.'[13] In his response which supported Eden's stance, the Prime Minister showed no hint of discomfort.[14] Further personal interventions and individual letters of protest to Churchill[15] and Eden[16] received no reply.[17] 'Nothing happened. Thereafter the European Movement rather sank. Although we went on meeting, the steam went out of it.'[18]

The events of November 1951 proved to be a watershed. Thereafter there emerged three lines of approach in Conservative backbench attitudes to Europe:

(1) Thanks to the twin distractions of German rearmament (and the political form this was taking through the European Defence Community/European Political Community) and imperial preference, only a hard core of MPs within the Strasbourg delegation and in organizations such as the British Committee of ELEC, worked to counter Eden's indifference to the development of 'Little Europe', and sought to promote alternative military and economic arrangements. These MPs were Amery, Smithers and Boothby.

(2) The 'centrist line', favoured by those Conservatives who wanted a British lead within the Council of Europe and a closer association with the European Coal and Steel Community (ECSC),[19] and who were profoundly discouraged by the Foreign Office's indifference. These MPs included

Beamish, Sir Edward Boyle, Lord John Hope, Jack Maclay (after 1954 when he returned to the back benches), Nigel Nicolson, Gilbert Longden, Kerr and Roberts; and Hay, Foster, Reader Harris, Hughes Hallett, Pitman, Cyril Black, Hugh Fraser, and Tilney who were closely connected with Federal Union or its parliamentary group.[20]

(3) the 'Eden thesis': Eden's unwillingness to join moves towards European integration was the obverse of his desire for Britain to continue to play a world role. The Foreign Secretary preferred association with Europe not participation – Bevin's Atlantic approach, which ignored the Council of Europe. The bulk of the Conservative party endorsed this attitude.

CONSERVATIVE EUROPEANISTS AND MILITARY INTEGRATION

'For better or for worse, the ideal of a United Europe [became] identified in the public mind with the plan for the European Defence Community.'[21] Conservatives were agreed that Britain, with its global military, economic and colonial commitments, could not surrender sovereignty[22] over her armed forces to a European political authority – even the European moderates (for example, Hope, Mott-Radclyffe and Longden) who were conscious of the danger of a rearmed Germany allied with Russia.[23] The Commonwealth, the 'most stable force in the world', remained Britain's first priority. At first glance, it seems curious that the Europeanists did not point to French willingness to join such a federation which contrasted so sharply with British animosity. However, it was argued although France might have as many extra-European interests and anxieties, 'Britain was a special case with a completely different approach; the French did not have the equivalent of the White Dominions'.[24] The conviction remained, based partly on long-standing Anglo-French colonial animosity and France's defeat in 1940, that Britain, America and the Soviet Union, were the only true global powers.

Although there was widespread Conservative scepticism about the possibility of European political union and the viability of the EDC,[25] most Tories endorsed Eden's determined support of the EDC process in the absence of a French alternative: 'No one was prepared to contemplate the future without the French'[26] and the French were adamant in their opposition to independent German rearmament within NATO. Only a few Conservative Europeanists argued it *was* possible to put forward a constructive alternative. Boothby vehemently opposed the EDC in favour of German rearmament within NATO, arguing it was indefensible to ask the French and Germans to join something in which Britain was unwilling to participate. He did not believe the French would ratify the EDC, nor that there was any real French support for the idea of a 'Little Europe' federation.[27] Smithers, too, saw growing French concern at the possible repercussions for the French Union in European federation and apprehensions that this would lead to German interference in French colonial policy;[28] by mid-1953 Smithers was convinced that Germany would dominate the Six and that if the EPC failed, 'Germany would emerge from the subsequent chaos as the leader and still obtain American support'. As Germany was not regarded as stable politically, the situation seemed particularly grave.[29] Amery initially urged British association with the EDC, short of full participation. Since a European army was a pre-requisite for West German rearmament and such an army 'will probably not be formed without British participation',[30] a token British force could be placed under European command. In addition, 'if the British contingent were to include a Canadian unit or units it would be a Commonwealth force, and serve as a symbol of the special Europe-Commonwealth relationship, within what is somewhat nonsensically described as the Atlantic Community'. Britain could help prevent a collapse of the European idea by stating plainly she could join a European union run along Commonwealth lines;[31] such a proposal might help assert British leadership in Europe.[32] Amery helped Macmillan[33] draft his submission to Cabinet in January 1952,[34] but Eden's supremacy in Cabinet quashed this initiative.

By late 1953 an unlikely alliance had developed between pro-Europeans and anti-European Tories: both groups were frustrated at Eden's persistence in propping up the French over the EDC and wanted the Government to 'get off the fence'.[35] Amery had come to regard the EDC as 'a mistaken policy'; there was a danger the arrangement would tie France and Germany so closely that this would tip the balance against Britain.[36] He appreciated the difficulty in withdrawing support immediately, but questioned the need 'to make active propaganda' in continued support of the EDC.[37] The anti-Europeans were antagonized by America 'pushing the federal idea';[38] the Government's present 'gutless'[39] policy must change to a decision for or against EDC – if the decision was against, the Conservative government should do its utmost to defeat the EDC.

Eden's approach appeared vindicated when, following the French government's refusal to ratify the EDC treaty in August 1954, his suggestion for German rearmament under the NATO umbrella (extending the Brussels Pact arrangements for West European union) was accepted in October 1954. There was universal Conservative pleasure over WEU, a 'magnificent lead'[40] which 'exemplif[ied] British, rather than Continental techniques, allowed for organic growth'.[41] European enthusiasts hoped the Government would now go beyond its prior 'half-hearted support [to] Strasbourg'.[42] British interests required encouraging a Strasbourg revival now that the federal idea was dead; the moment appeared right to consider advances in economic as well as political integration.[43] The work of the Economic Committee of the Council of Europe should be pushed ahead in cooperation with the new Brussels Treaty organization. Eden was not receptive to these ideas, having no desire to cut across the OEEC's work or to encourage political or economic polarization. Nor did he wish to see a grouping of NATO's European partners which excluded Britain's North Atlantic NATO allies, America and Canada.[44]

CONSERVATIVE EUROPEANISTS AND POLITICAL INTEGRATION

For the Conservative Europeanists, the debate over the most desirable arrangement for German rearmament was part of the wider debate over the question of British leadership of Europe. They appreciated the need for a strong Europe to earn Washington's respect, to forestall American dictation or abandonment. The unspoken question was 'Who is to be America's principal ally in Europe: Germany in the Six, or Britain in the Fifteen?'

After November 1951 continental Europe was 'no longer comforted by assurances of Britain's "close association" or "warm welcome" or by any other euphemisms for no direct participation'.[45] Rudely disabused of the illusion that only Labour's 'selfish' refusal to participate had prevented the Federal Union of Europe, and that a Conservative government could be cajoled into changing policy,[46] henceforth the idea of 'Little Europe' dominated. Eden's acceptance of this, through his support of the French throughout the tortured progress of the EDC treaty towards ratification and his persistent refusal to support the Council of Europe[47] despite appeals from the Europeanists,[48] left the stage free for the Six, and for the Germans to become the Americans' favoured Continental allies through US loans and aid to the EDC. The work of those dedicated Conservative Europeanists who strove to ensure that Britain's voice was heard in the forum of 'Big Europe' was relegated to the side lines.

For the Conservative Europeanists it was 'a black period'.[49] Struggling for Britain to regain the political initiative in Europe, a battle which Eden was content not to fight, they were immensely frustrated at the Foreign Secretary's refusal to exploit an inter-governmental, pragmatic institution which 'was tailor-made for British interests'.[50] They repeatedly urged Eden to demonstrate the value Britain placed upon the Assembly's deliberations in a vain attempt to counter the development of the Six and the corresponding exclusion of Britain. They feared German domination of the emerging entity, particularly once the issue of German reunification resurfaced as the Soviet Union sought to woo West Germany from the Western camp.

The Europeanists scored one ephemeral success. The combined pressure of pro-European junior ministers, backbench delegates to Strasbourg,[51] and civil servants obliged the Foreign Secretary to put forward the 'Eden Plan' in 1952. Drafted by Anthony Nutting, the junior Foreign Office minister leading the Conservative delegation in 1952–4, this plan was designed to harmonize the emerging institutions of the Six with the Council of Europe, by amending the Statute of the Council of Europe to permit its existing organs to become the institutions of the ECSC and the EDC. The enthusiasts publicly welcomed the Eden Plan as an important advance in Britain's attitude to Europe.[52] Britain's relations with the ECSC would be 'scarcely distinguishable from full membership'.[53] The Tory delegates worked hard at their allotted task[54] of showing the Eden Plan was not simply a ruse to allow Britain to control the pace whilst remaining outside the new political organs. Amery was appointed *rapporteur* of the General Affairs Committee of the Consultative Assembly to resolve relations between the inner Six and the outer Nine. By the end of 1952 'Britain's position had greatly improved and much credit was due to Amery';[55] the enthusiasts were boasting 'there seems to be a considerable swing away from "Little Europe" back towards our original ideas'.[56]

But the Conservative Europeanists soon realized that the Eden Plan was merely 'window dressing'.[57] It had created a positive impression among the countries of 'Big Europe' but roused the suspicions of the Six, in particular Monnet and 'the Germans who would prefer that there should be no links between the Six and Britain'.[58] Continental opinion no longer saw Britain as dragging its feet, but instead 'was inclined to suspect that we might be trying through the Eden proposals to mould federal developments our way'.[59] The Eden Plan failed to divert the Continentals from their chosen course,[60] nor did it mark a sea change in Eden's and the Foreign Office's attitudes on the value of the Council of Europe and the desirability of British leadership in Strasbourg. 'The policy of the Government was perfectly clear. They wanted to be in on the act so far as they could be, in order to prevent any excesses which might unify Europe against us.'[61] To the profound disgust of some Tory delegates,[62] the British Government's line remained that every encouragement should be given to the formation of the projected 'Little Europe' and that if federation should fail, Britain must not in any way be to blame.[63] This led to a public split within the Conservative delegation to Strasbourg.[64] Boothby resigned from the European Movement in despair at successive British governments 'who have so often led us up the garden path and left us there'.[65]

These and other protests made through the Whips' Office and to Eden about the damage caused by the Government's negative attitude were to no avail.

It was always made clear in one way or another by the Foreign Office people in charge of the British Conservative delegates that we should not 'rock the boat', 'go native', be too enthusiastic about the pie-in-the-sky ideas of 'integration', and above all not to let the Government down. This... caused even more harm, because 'the British are always so negative and they'll always find some way to argue that any progress towards integration is either impossible, impracticable or dangerous [to British interests]'. [The committed Europeanists] did advocate in speeches and in Committees of the Council of Europe that we were personally in favour of closer links... but these views had to be expressed tactfully so as not to upset our British colleagues nor to exceed the bounds of Government declared policy; there would have been no surer way of being dropped from the Delegation for the following year and therefore robbed of what was at the time the best forum for putting forward our opinions [to say nothing of jeopardizing any possible elevation to office!].[66]

CONSERVATIVE EUROPEANISTS AND ECONOMIC INTEGRATION

The principal division in the Conservative European camp came in the economic sphere: between the 'anti-GATT' MPs and the 'pro-GATT' MPs (such as Hope, Longden, Tilney and Nicolson) who favoured 'Atlantic Union'. To a very great extent, the battle within the Conservative party over Europe in the 1950s has to be seen in tandem with the internal struggle over imperial preference.

Europe and 'Europe overseas'

Boothby, Smithers and Amery continued to argue vehemently that Europe and Empire were complementary, not contradictory, strongly supported by Leo Amery. 'Entry into a European customs union would not by itself create a better balanced economy... Europe and the British Commonwealth as a whole can most usefully supplement each other.'⁶⁷ As the 'only practical means by which that end can be achieved' was imperial preference, this campaign was aimed specifically at America and her campaign for 'nondiscrimination'.

Between 1951 and 1953 there was strong Continental pressure to concentrate on ideas for greater unity of the Six alone (for example, the Pflimlin plan, covering agriculture), particularly for currency union with a European central bank. 'Many of the promoters of [this] did not conceal their intention of waging an economic war against the sterling area and the leadership of the City of London.'⁶⁸ The British section of ELEC felt this would tend to disrupt the European Payments Union (EPU) and might end the greater cooperation in trade and finance between the sterling area and Europe for which it had always worked.

A small number of Conservatives strove hard to counter this movement towards the economic federation of the Six. Boothby's and Hollis' proposals for the possibilities of drawing together the economies of Europe and the sterling area, together with their suggestions that exchange markets should be established in some European centres with upper and lower limits controlled by an equalization fund, were reflected in the recommendations of the Council of Europe's Economic Committee in 1951.⁶⁹ Boothby had already called for a world monetary conference to reconsider the Bretton Woods agreement, on the grounds of constant balance of payments difficulties, inadequate stocks of gold at its present price, and of hard currencies, and the restrictions which nearly all the signatories of the Bretton Woods agreement had been forced to maintain. Amery passionately believed that 'the Commonwealth is the ground plan to which all other things must be attached'. His desire for Britain to take a greater lead in European affairs was a reflection of his reluctance to be dependent upon America.⁷⁰

As these Conservatives saw it, no purely European, nor purely Commonwealth solution was possible. The answer was 'the abandonment of the obsolete doctrine of nondiscrimination', the extension of the preferential system, and the reduction of dollar imports to the level of dollar income.⁷¹ 'It is idle to imagine that a united Europe alone, whether it included Britain or not, could ever provide both the guns and butter or escape from dependence on the United States . . . Only a Europe which has integrated its economy with that of countries... [supplying] raw materials in which it is deficient and for which it is dependent upon America' was a viable economy, and only the sterling area could provide this.[72] Intent on retaining the British initiative of the Eden Plan, Amery suggested to the Conservative Foreign Affairs Committee that 'we should have some new suggestion for debate' at the Strasbourg Assembly in September 1952, which might develop the idea of the Commonwealth and Europe sharing economic resources as a balancing factor in relation to the dollar world.[73]

Thanks to these MPs' efforts – largely on Boothby's initiative as vice-chairman – in 1952 the Economic Committee of the Council of Europe drafted a set of proposals which came to be known as 'the Strasbourg Plan', intended to improve economic relations between the Council of Europe and overseas countries with which these countries had constitutional links. Boothby was building upon the 1951 Commonwealth–Europe conferences in Brussels and London, held under the auspices of ELEC, which had examined the possibility of closer economic cooperation between Commonwealth countries and Western Europe with a view to narrowing the dollar gap. His Strasbourg plan proposed a two-tier preferential system – leaving the existing Commonwealth preferential agreements in place, and developing a second preferential system within the whole group. Its aim was to harness the industrial resources of Western Europe to the raw materials of its associated territories and by providing assured markets for both, to increase trade and production.[74] The plan was overwhelmingly accepted by the Assembly and the Committee of Ministers. Eden sent it round the Commonwealth. It was then pigeon-holed.[75] These proposals received scant attention at the 1953 Commonwealth Conference,[76] and were 'pole-axed' by the British Treasury.[77] While Conservative Europeanists felt that it was 'understandable' that Britain held aloof from the Schuman Plan, 'much less justified was the British failure to exploit... [this] scheme ... [which] would have realized Bevin's ambition and brought Europe and "Europe overseas" together in a vast area of preference and development'.[78]

This small band of MPs persisted in its attempts to foster economic links between the EPU and the Commonwealth. The British section of ELEC devoted its energies to making the British view on European economic integration heard and understood 'against what at one time seemed hopelessly adverse tide'.[79] At the unofficial monetary conference organized by ELEC in Brussels in February 1953, building upon the shared feelings of influential groups in France, Belgium, the Netherlands and West Germany, the British delegation (which included Leo and Julian Amery) managed to deflect the propensity towards smaller areas of cooperation.[80] The final resolution welcomed the Schuman Plan, but stated plainly ELEC's preference for a 'truly European market' which was defined as a common market on the widest possible scale. Julian Amery and Boothby also formed part of the British delegation to the European Movement's second economic conference, held in London in January 1954, whose ultimate aim was 'to favour conditions which will lead to the creation of a free world market with the free movement of goods and currencies between Europe, the Commonwealth and the dollar world'.[81] In order to deal with immediate problems the conference examined the possibility of closer economic and social ties between countries of Western Europe and their associated overseas territories, and the Commonwealth; this was the natural sequence of events from the Council of Europe's recommendations on the Strasbourg Plan. The economic tide seemed to be turning away from 'Little Europe'.

Atlantic Union

> Of course going on at the same time was Atlantic Union. This was quite a considerable movement, although there was not much structural propaganda. NATO was the successful alliance and seen as a thoroughly satisfactory organization. Many people felt this should be kept going and give it more political clout. There was an Atlantic Union Committee, and a lot of people from outside Westminster were interested. It was welcome to the Conservative government for quite a while because the more intrepid people like Amery were so pro-Europe.[82]

These Conservatives opposed increased protection on the grounds that it would limit the field of economic opportunity, and the remedy of Europe plus Empire was inadequate and unrealistic.[83] They looked to the 'oceanwide partnership of the Commonwealth, Western Europe, and the United States', arguing that those who looked to Western Europe, their overseas territories and the sterling area 'would permanently cut Canada away from the Commonwealth'[84] since Canada was not in the sterling area.[85] Canada was the key – 'so close to America economically, yet linked to Britain by friendship and tradition'.[86]

This group firmly believed in the need for closer integration of policy and action between Europe, the Commonwealth and the USA to form a 'more organic organization'. NATO should be expanded beyond a mere military alliance (NATO from the beginning did have a wide remit), as 'such alliances serve only for limited periods of dire and obvious peril'. Nor could effective arrangements in the economic field be secured through *ad hoc* functional bodies which, like the OEEC and the Economic Commission for Europe, often overlapped. An Atlantic Community should not be restricted to the countries of the Atlantic seaboard, but 'embrac[e] the civilizations of the democracies of free Europe'. To further this, a cross-party group, the 'Friends of Atlantic Union',[87] was formed.

In 1954 members of the Committee and Council of Atlantic Union founded a European Atlantic group, to provide a regular forum for members of existing European and Atlantic societies where they could maintain contact and discuss developments of European and Atlantic Communities. Longden and Nicolson were elected Executive members. The aim was to give background information on political and economic cooperation between NATO and various other international associations with the Council of Europe, West European Union, the OEEC and the ECSC. However, 'in the end people became convinced that Atlantic Union did not matter, because they concluded that America would not divorce herself from the NATO alliance. And as long as they were part of the alliance, with NATO defending Europe, why worry about the European movement?'[88]

In marked contrast to their impact when in opposition, during Churchill's peacetime administration the Conservative Europeanists' political influence was negligible. In essence, Conservative backbench support of 'Big Europe' through the Council of Europe foundered on the rock of Conservative front and backbench indifference. Continental opposition dealt the *coup de grace* on the one occasion when backbench pressure succeeded in obliging Eden to offer the palliative of the Eden plan.

There were several causes of this impotence which belied the promise of the Opposition years. The crucial factor was the loss of Churchill's interest and support. 'We all thought at Strasbourg that Winston was fighting a lone and desperate battle against a hostile Cabinet on Europe. Not at all... There was no battle because nobody in Cabinet put in a word for Europe as far as I can make out. Not even Maxwell Fyfe or Macmillan who had been ardent champions of Europe... Winston lost interest.'[89] Churchill's refusal to give the lead, leaving British policy towards Europe to Eden and the Foreign Office who were deeply suspicious of all schemes for European union,[90] seemed incomprehensible to some.[91] Others did not speculate about Churchill's change of stance 'because he had had a thoroughly unreliable political career. We were all aware of his past inconsistencies'.[92] To his personal *coterie*, Churchill's absence of interest was easily explained: 'Churchill's idea of a united Europe was more akin to de Gaulle's *Europe des Patries*. [He] always had at the front of his mind the concept of the close relationship of the English-speaking peoples, and above all of England and the US.'[93] The supranational EDC was not his idea of ideal European cooperation.[94]

In December 1951 Churchill toyed with the idea that the EDC might be transformed into an 'integrated force' which emphasized national units; he was defeated in Cabinet by Eden, supported by the majority of his colleagues, which 'ruled out the danger of Churchill's idea supported by the pro-Europeans'.[95] Churchill's great age militated against a fight with his Foreign Secretary on Europe, as did his 'inherent constitutionalism':[96] he had no wish to saddle his chosen successor with a policy of which Eden disapproved.[97] He was also fighting a war against Eden in the Middle East. 'He was tired and his one big idea was a summit with Russia.'[98] Therefore, 'he did not push the Europe idea as much as he should have,'[99] concentrating 'on the few things that interested him'.[100] Whatever their opinion on the reason for Churchill's silence, 'it was very dispiriting to those of us who saw Europe as the future'.[101] The young Europe enthusiasts were loath to approach the Prime Minister as 'persuading Churchill' (to take a more positive line) was not a promising prospect on any subject, particularly for new backbenchers.[102] Boothby did try and failed.

To the ardent Europeanists, Eden was the villain. 'I am sure that there was a sharp division between [Churchill] and Eden on this subject. The latter thought the whole European "thing" was insubstantial . . . The fact that the first meeting of the Consultative Assembly after the Conservative election victory was ignored by Anthony and that the negative position was stated immediately at it by Maxwell Fyfe, suggests that this had all been definitely settled in opposition.'[103] Eden had indeed already indicated there should be 'no Europe nonsense'.[104] 'When the Government was formed in 1951 Churchill spoke to Eden, saying, "I want you to have a Minister of European Affairs, and I suggest this should be Duncan." Eden was adamant. He said (a) there was no reason for having such a Minister, and (b) he did not want Duncan. He wanted Selwyn and me.'[105]

The pro-European Tories were insufficiently important to counteract Eden's and the Foreign Office's influence.[106] From the outset, Eden was determined 'not to become involved [in European union] and his decision was vital'.[107] Eden's exceptional knowledge of foreign policy conferred an extraordinary supremacy in the Government on such matters.[108] Eden's position was quite clear:

> He intensely disliked the idea of European Union in any form other than the Concert of Europe . . . He did not believe that there was any political substance in the movement on the Continent. His view of Europe was that of a skilled diplomat – a 'concert' – shades of Metternich. If I sat next to him in the smoke room he would say, 'Now, old boy, anything but Europe.' His prestige within the Foreign Office was immense. He was indeed a marvellous negotiator. His hostility to any engagement by Britain in the European process was translated into (i) the Maxwell Fyfe speech (November 1951) and (ii) the appointment of a minor official named Gallagher as British Permanent Representative in Strasbourg. In the Committee of Ministers' Deputies Gallagher systematically obstructed every constructive move: he was the most hated man in Strasbourg.[109]

The Foreign Secretary *was* in favour of greater cooperation within Europe[110] – between nation states. He regarded Britain as 'an active and enlightened European nation with a world role and not as a limb of Europe'. Britain should play a leading part in Europe for three reasons: (i) her history in Europe; (ii) her role in the War; and (iii) the 'three circles'. He and the Europeanists differed in the emphasis they placed on relations with Europe and the clash came because so many of the European enthusiasts' ideas appeared to Eden to underestimate or undermine Britain's role in the world.[111] Eden was 'also very conscious of the general public and he was convinced that Europe could not be sold to the country'.[112] Eden was right: 'The public attitude was a hangover from the War: after the strain of war, most people were so thankful to be at peace. Foreign adventures were not on the agenda, nor did they like the idea of being tied up with the French and the Germans.'[113]

Personalities also came into play. Accusations that he had personally stifled Churchill's pro-European inclinations rankled.[114] Eden was convinced that the Conservative Europeanists 'were not just a policy pressure group, as much as a scheming policy pressure group'.

> The Council of Europe gave them platforms to make speeches with no government backing at all. It was not commonplace then for politicians other than ministers to go abroad to speak in a formal international forum such as the Council of Europe and thereby appear to obtain an international importance for what they said. He had fairly old-fashioned ideas that it was up to the Foreign Secretary to make policy and there should be no free enterprise efforts which made life difficult for him. Even if he had agreed with the content of what they were saying, he would have been tetchy because it was out of his control. People buzzing about on the periphery pretending more influence than they possessed were not welcome. He could not appreciate them, although he could understand them only too well, or at least their motives. Eden was inclined to think it was all much more of a plot than it was, but underlying this was the majority view, which he shared with the Foreign Office, that none of this would come to fruition ... He thought EDC

would fail, and that Britain's proper role was to stand back a bit and to use her diplomatic skill to pick up the pieces, knock heads together, generally get all concerned to see sense and moderation.[115]

His one concession to backbench pressure on Europe, the Eden plan, 'had a good impact on the backbenches. They knew Eden was not a pro-Europe man, but thought it was a very constructive thing to do. Eden took the idea round the capitals of Europe to gain support, which created a very good impression. Nutting [said] later that Eden had not wanted to do so at all, but had been pressured by his civil servants.'[116] But Eden was increasingly less susceptible to such pressure. 'As time passed and Churchill was still in the saddle, Eden was critical of Churchill on an increasing number of matters, and Europe was obviously one of them.' There came a critical moment in the Strasbourg context in 1954 when Lord John Hope, the junior Minister at the Foreign Office in charge of the Europe department, sent a minute to Eden saying it would be a good thing if he came to the next meeting: 'To my amazement, I got a note back, written on my memo, saying, "I am astonished I should be given this advice. Strasbourg is of no importance whatever". Of course he did have a quick temper, and I made allowances, but I was very taken aback.'[117]

Eden's presence at the Foreign Office between 1951 and 1955 probably prevented 'not so much entry into Europe, because Britain had not got to that point, but the advance of real objective thought within the Government and Whitehall as to Britain's place in Europe'.[118] With the exception of Nutting, 'Eden worked entirely with and relied upon his civil servants'[119] who reinforced his natural scepticism. The brilliant and forceful figure,[120] Roger Makins was the most vociferous critic;[121] he and other key Foreign Office advisers were convinced 'the American/British partnership was crucial'[122] and remained deeply suspicious of European union.[123] This sentiment pervaded Whitehall.[124] The Board of Trade, under the leadership of Thorneycroft[125] and Frank Lee, the Permanent Under-secretary, was the notable exception.[126] 'The Treasury and Foreign Office [were] not in favour of us pressing the matter at the time',[127] and as both ministries 'were a very powerful team, with two very experienced ministers at their head, both of whom were in the running for Prime Minister, and certainly not people Churchill wanted to take on',[128] Eden's approach to Europe had very powerful backing.

Then there was the lack of ministerial support. 'With Sandys at Supply, Maxwell Fyfe at the Home Office, and Eccles relegated to the Ministry of Works – to his chagrin – the champions of Europe were isolated.'[129] The heavy burdens of office left little time for outside projects.[130] In addition, 'they were on the fringe. Macmillan did produce a paper, but... he was only Minister of Housing, and did not carry any weight.'[131] Macmillan who had his fingers burnt[132] thereafter confined his energies to his ministerial brief. Of the junior ministers, Hopkinson was rapidly promoted to Secretary for Overseas Trade at the Board of Trade, then was made Minister of State at the Colonial Office in May 1952. Hopkinson led the Conservative delegation to the Council of Europe in 1952, but a severe accident[133] made this a shortlived appointment. Thereafter, his ministerial duties effectively deprived the Europeanists of his support. Lord Glendevon's pro-European inclinations similarly were circumscribed by office.

Eden's 'stay out' view was supported by the majority of the Cabinet; Lord Swinton's opposition was a particularly powerful influence upon older Tories.[134] As Salisbury expressed it, 'We are not a continental nation but an island power with a colonial empire and unique relations with the independent members of the Commonwealth. Though we might maintain a close association with the continental nations of Europe, we could never merge our interests wholly with theirs. We must be with, but not in, any combination of European powers.'[135] This front bench indifference to Europe was mirrored by attitudes on the Conservative backbenches. In the early 1950s generally, 'there was very little in the party's mind, or the House of Commons' mind on the question of Europe'.[136] 'A certain number of people... were very keen on it, but I can't say we would find many people going onto street corners and shouting "Hoorah for Europe". They were open to be led in early stages, but as time went on the thing polarized into people being either for or against it.'[137]

There were the distractions of other, seemingly more important issues. When the Conservative party did turn its mind towards Europe, a 'large element' was opposed to closer links.

There was a general Conservative distaste for the federal vehicle chosen for German rearmament.[138] The majority had no greater love for the idea of 'Big Europe', and their 'healthy scepticism'[139] of the value of Strasbourg was further strengthened by Eden's opposition.[140] Outright opposition came from the 'right wing' but 'was not very dramatic, nor tiresome, in marked contrast to its behaviour in the Suez Crisis'.[141]

Most Conservative backbenchers regarded the Council of Europe as an irrelevance, serving no useful purpose.[142] 'So much talk on Europe centred on Germany. Germany bounded forward with enormous speed and her re-entry into international politics was through France, not through us.' The effect was twofold: 'Germany was not looking to Britain, so the British people were disgruntled [and] as it was obvious Germany was working with France, a decided feeling grew up that this was not a healthy situation. This instinct in the country was shared to a great degree by both parties in the House of Commons. Therefore Europe struck very few chords back home.'[143] There was also a residue of historical animosity towards the French, aggravated by 'French behaviour... which always seemed to be unpredictable. Hostility is too strong a word. The French politicians and Governments always seemed unwilling or unconcerned about the effects of their words and actions on the British, who in turn they distrusted!' Even those Conservatives at Strasbourg who enjoyed good relations with their French colleagues were 'wary of taking them 100 percent at their word!'[144]

Another part of the problem was that the Council of Europe was 'less frequented than formerly by great parliamentarians of weight' and its method of work – meeting for one month – meant that it was not easy to develop at once into a forum for adequate discussion of large issues of foreign policy.[145] The work of the Conservative delegates was also considerably hampered by the poor view party managers and most Tory MPs took of the Strasbourg Assembly, reflected in the lack of debating time made available to the Council of Europe proceedings at Westminster.[146] Going to Strasbourg was regarded by many as nothing more than a 'jolly'[147] or gastronomic jaunt.[148] Trips to the Council of Europe were certainly regarded by Conservative delegates as most enjoyable:[149] 'It was rather like a Christmas game, only this game was called "Foreign Secretaries". You played the role, pontificated on policy, without power and responsibility. [But] it was not a great honour. The Minister and the rest of the party saw it as a joke, and the constituencies did not understand it at all. We were very frustrated by having so little influence and knowing we were regarded with a certain degree of contempt.'[150] 'As to the value placed on the work and recommendations of the Council of Europe, the House of Commons in the 1950s seemed to pay little, if any attention – nor, I suspect, did Whitehall and Ministers. After all, if you sent people to Strasbourg . . . you'd think they were probably just having a good time there and you needn't take their reports, etc, particularly seriously.'[151]

Given the pervading Conservative scepticism towards the Council of Europe and the Government's desire to forestall any freelance promotion of closer links with Europe, the selection of delegates to the Assembly in the 1950s cannot be taken as a guide to enthusiasm for Europe.[152] Indeed, Strasbourg was seen as a distraction from an MP's work at Westminster.[153] Recommendations were made by the Whips' Office on several grounds: support for closer relations with Europe[154] and a facility for European languages. The delegations always included a member of the Ulster Unionists, to counter any accusations of Conservative neglect of the province, and criticism from the Irish Republic over the north; and a Whip.[155] It was a method short of office of rewarding and encouraging promising backbenchers, who might show with Strasbourg experience that they were worthy of junior office. It was also an assessment of the MP's reliability not to get swept away by the heady (and 'unrealistic') rhetoric of the Continentals.[156] Ability and suitability for some area of the Council's work was considered,[157] and there was also an element of 'widening the horizons' of some Conservatives, to cultivate their interest in Europe: as Chief Whip, Heath once asked Ursula Branston, the secretary to the Strasbourg delegation, for suggestions on the composition of the next group.

> I myself was not very enthusiastic about how things were going, and pointed out that the Europeans themselves were disappointed because . . . our delegation was rather *piano* politically, with no sign of it having much clout back home. Heath thought this was rather naïve of me and replied, 'The

more people we can send who are not stars but likely to become interested in Europe in the future, the better.' He persisted in sending [people] with orders to observe and learn; they were to make up their own minds but understand they were to do as directed. Therefore he was a strong force in the Whips' Office for Europe behind the scenes... Those who went to Strasbourg learnt an enormous amount, and the seeds of the future were sown but they did not come up to the extent that Heath hoped. It was very much an uphill struggle. None of the British delegates to Strasbourg were very prominent politicians back home. They had no drawing power. Television was not as powerful as it is now. Rippon, Martin Madden, David Price, etc. were all excellent people but Westminster was the only place they could secure an audience. It was no good their going round the country.[158]

All in all, 'Strasbourg did not make much impact. It did not get much publicity, although [there was] a certain amount in the universities', but it never got a grip on British public or political opinion.[159]

The struggle for Europe in the 1950s must also be seen in tandem with the internal party conflict over imperial preference,[160] as the reverse of Conservative pressure for the maintenance and extension of imperial preference was stout opposition to the General Agreement on Trade and Tariffs (GATT), sponsored by America. Once this cause had been defeated by the President of the Board of Trade, Peter Thorneycroft, at the 1954 party conference, with his successful attack on a critical motion on the GATT, the party was free to look beyond the immediate horizon of the Empire and Commonwealth to closer economic links with Europe.

In the first months of the Conservative Government, Britain's sterling crisis prompted earnest political debate on the optimum way to solve the country's pressing problems. There was a universal Tory desire to escape from the domination of the mighty dollar, but attitudes varied on how best to construct an economic unit 'which can stand on its own feet, in which the countries of the free world outside the dollar area can live and breathe'.[161] For a section of the Conservative party the maintenance and extension imperial preference was the obvious solution.[162] The New Commonwealth (India, Pakistan and Ceylon), and to a great extent the Old White Dominions, were still regarded as an integral part of Britain, and no Conservative politician questioned the thought that the Empire formed an inalienable part of British society, tradition and pattern of trade.

This cause echoed the moves of those who placed greatest emphasis on Britain's links with her Commonwealth and Empire over and above Britain's commitment to NATO and ideas of Atlantic Union.[163] Some 'enthusiasts for the Empire [thought] of Imperial unity and European unity as contradictory causes';[164] others argued, 'There was no cleavage between the two'[165]: Empire and Europe 'were compatible, indeed complementary'.[166]

> It is difficult to realize today [1993] just how powerful [the idea of Empire] was right up to the early Sixties. Many of us thought, including myself, that the concept could be revived and indeed could take on a new and greater dimension in the form of the Commonwealth. This would give Britain a part more in keeping with her post-war capabilities, would free rein to the political aspirations of the Colonial Empire and the Dominions, and would give us a distinctive position in the modern geopolitical scene. It was attractive from every point of view ... No one said and I doubt anybody thought that the Commonwealth was a dead duck from the start.[167]

THE SHIFT TOWARDS EUROPE 1955–1957

European Economic Community vs Free Trade Area

'The great majority of the party did not pay much attention to Messina' (June 1955) as 'we were fully involved on the defence side through Eden's WEU, and through NATO, Germany had come back into "the family"'.[168] However, over the next two years, there was a revival of Conservative backbench interest in Europe. Backbench concern that 'Britain would be left behind again'[169] grew slowly but steadily,[170] building on the feeling of those who had been to Strasbourg that Britain had blundered badly at the start and should 'buck its ideas up'.[171]

The Conservative Europeanists in large part owned this revival to the influx of younger MPs in the May 1955 Parliament. Geoffrey Rippon[172] was 'the main swing' of a small group of new MPs which included Keith Joseph, Peter Kirk, Martin Maddan,[173] Robert Mathew, John Rodgers and – ironically, in view of his anti-Common Market stance in the 1970s and trenchant anti-Maastricht views in the 1990s – Richard Body who 'rather went along with some of the federalist arguments; the constitutional significance had not struck me at that point'.[174] Other incoming Conservatives who were particularly sympathetic were Frederick Corfield (a barrister in the same chambers as Mathew) whose ideas for greater European cooperation stemmed from his lengthy incarceration as a German POW; and David Price, a close personal friend of Kirk.

The British Government had confidently anticipated that, thanks to Eden's success in rearming Germany through WEU in 1954, the British preference for intergovernmental cooperation had triumphed and the French bid for European leadership had been foiled; henceforth there would be no nonsense about supranational structures. The *rélance* following the meeting at Messina in June 1955 thus came as a disagreeable surprise.

Conservative Europeanists not unreasonably hoped British policy towards Europe would take a more positive turn as the Messina meeting followed swiftly on Macmillan's appointment as Foreign Secretary in May 1955[175] – 'but . . . Eden was Prime Minister'.[176] Macmillan was initially keen for Britain to take part,[177] and in his first speech in the Commons referred to the importance of the 'European Idea'. However, thereafter he did nothing to promote it.[178] Macmillan's short tenure at the Foreign Office was not a success; 'I think he found everything much more of a strain than he had expected, and his health seemed to suffer . . . He was a good mixer, clever, amusing and had a lot of backing among young people. But he did not make much of [Europe].'[179] Macmillan's own political courage appeared to be lacking: 'He was never anxious to fall out with those in charge, because he did have ambitions . . . His private commitment was there, but he was not prepared to take an heroic part.'[180]

Eden remained determined to guide British policy. The Prime Minister was convinced any idea of British participation in the Messina process was 'a mad scheme';[181] it was regarded in Whitehall as a 'friendly revolt' against British pressure on France in the OEEC to liberate her trade.[182] The decision to withdraw Russell Bretherton (an official from the Board of Trade) from the Spaak Committee deliberations in Brussels in November 1955 was made by Eden and Butler, the Chancellor of the Exchequor, backed by Foreign Office officials who felt it would be disastrous for Britain to join.[183] Nothing had happened to alter fundamentally British officialdom's perception of European supranationalism as an irrelevance: the *rélance* was 'doomed to failure'[184] because lack of popular support in France for supranational solutions[185] and because of French protectionism.[186]

Despite this complacency at the top, 'there was a ground swell of opinion'[187] between November 1955 and July 1956 in favour of a more positive attitude towards the discussions initiated at Messina. The *rélance* appeared to be the direct 'result of the Government's refusal to assume its responsibility in an intergovernmental organization, the Council of Europe ... and [we] thought it would succeed'.[188] Backbench concern at the EURATOM proposals had already surfaced in party committees,[189] and the Conservative Europeanists were determined that Britain should try to direct this 'impetus'. Boothby raised the topic in the House, pointing out it would be 'very unfortunate if a common market were to be formed in Europe with great reciprocal advantages to the countries concerned and we were totally excluded'.[190] Three weeks later Rippon moved an adjournment debate on 5 July 1956 in which he and Boothby pressed the Government to give reasons for its policy of indifference towards the Messina process. Sir Edward Boyle, the Economic Secretary to the Treasury who was known to be sympathetic to greater cooperation with the Continent, was given the task of replying for the Government. He did this 'unsatisfactorily',[191] although Rippon and his colleagues took some comfort from Boyle's assurance that 'the Government has not got a closed mind on the subject'.[192]

Faced with an impending important OEEC meeting, and concerned that a decision 'cannot be long delayed' while the Government claimed 'that we cannot be sure at this stage that the venture will succeed',[193] Rippon,[194] Mathew, and Rodgers put down an EDM on 10 July 1956,[195] which suggested sending an observer to the Messina talks. They were anxious Britain should play 'a full and effective part in the preliminary stages'.[196] If Britain took a negative attitude, 'we may well have to face the implications of them succeeding without us'. These MPs conceded that given Britain's special position the Government might have to make a number of reservations, especially on agriculture, and that a common market might be acceptable in some form, but not in another. Above all, they did not want Britain to be in a position in which other West European nations signed a draft treaty, and Britain was obliged either to stand aside, or take part on terms that she had no part in settling.[197]

As the enthusiasts admitted, there had been 'remarkably little public interest in the country at large ... focused on the vital question of the establishment of a Common Market'.[198] However, they were determined to demonstrate there was growing backbench 'recognition of the importance of the issues at stake'[199] and support for British moves towards the Six, rather than merely 'letting them get on with it, as we can join them at any time'.[200] 'It seems a comparatively timid move today, but at the time it was a brave thing to do.'[201] The motion expressed agreement 'in principle on the establishment by stages of a common market in Western Europe' and urged the Government to accept the invitation to participate in the negotiations, 'with a view to ensuring that if, or when, any treaty is signed the way will be open for British participation ... on an acceptable basis and in accordance with the interests of the Commonwealth and Empire'.[202]

'There is always an element of Smoking Room jollity in signing EDMs, but they are a good expression of growing opinion.'[203] The signatures revealed age and date of entry into Parliament were closely related to MPs' attitudes to Europe and of the 1955 entry, 'the Europeans outnumbered the Empire men by nearly 2:1'.[204] Rippon and his colleagues hoped to nudge the Government towards accepting the basic principle of British participation, convinced that once this had been achieved, there would be ample room for manoeuvre and compromise, provided there were safeguards and exceptions, notably for agriculture and horticulture. British participation would open cooperation on a far wider basis. They argued 'no fundamental conflict of interest or ideology' existed between those who advocated an expanded Commonwealth and those who urged closer integration of Western Europe.[205] Shuckburgh cynically attributed the sizeable Tory support for joining some sort of European confederal system to baser electoral motives (rather than to newfound attractions of Europe) as the Conservative electoral prospects were 'at present very dim'.[206]

Britain's relations with the Commonwealth and Europe were an increasingly popular political topic in the autumn of 1956 and, apart from the Suez question, represented the main concern at the party conference at Llandudno in early October.[207] The plan for a free trade area – Plan G – which had begun to take shape in early 1956,[208] was paraded before the party at Llandudno,[209] following Macmillan's and Thorneycroft's proposals to Commonwealth Finance ministers gathered in Washington for the IMF meeting in September 1956. This free trade area plan offered 'the way out' between the emerging European Economic Community and the Commonwealth, with the proposal for British 'association' with the Six by means of a free trade area. This preserved ties with the Commonwealth by guaranteeing the continued free entry of goods into Britain.

Most Conservatives favoured a free trade area.[210] By the mid-1950s 'more and more people recognized that the old pattern of trade with the Commonwealth was breaking down, and this involved the exploitation of the European market'. 'The Commonwealth is still our biggest market, [but] it is not the market which is expanding the fastest.'[211] There was a feeling among younger MPs, with the signs of the eventual break-up of Britain's colonial empire, that Britain could no longer have a captive market. But 'we wanted to keep the sterling area: we attached enormous importance to this'.[212]

This backbench support was a welcome prop to the moves initiated by Macmillan and Thorneycroft, ably supported by Frank Lee and other civil servants at the Board of Trade. It was generally felt a free trade area would 'open our export trade to the most rapidly expanding major market in the world', 'prevent the exclusion of the UK from European trade', 'preserve the spirit and substance of imperial preference', be advantageous to the Commonwealth, 'both as a growing market ... and a source of capital'; and British association in the early stages would 'enable us to shape and influence the detailed planning'.[213]

However, there remained an undercurrent of unease on the Conservative backbenches at the implications of a free trade area. There was a residue of opposition from the diehard imperial wing who favoured an extensive preferential system outside as well as within the Commonwealth system.[214] There were also decided and persistent reservations about agricultural and horticultural produce,[215] as Macmillan acknowledged with his assurance to the party conference that it would 'be an absolute condition that agricultural products of all kinds... should be excluded' to preserve the Commonwealth structure and to protect home agriculture.[216] Other Conservatives saw 'great risks... Some industries would be able to seize the greater opportunities abroad, others would feel keener competition at home. There would have to be changes to the industrial pattern... and these would not always be welcome.'[217] Conservative backbench opinion was also divided on the ultimate role of the free trade area: was it a counterweight to the emerging Common Market, or a halfway house?[218] A few saw the whole EFTA exercise as a deliberate wrecking tactic.[219]

Complementing government moves to canvass opinion in industry and the Commonwealth on a free trade area,[220] Rippon and his small band persisted in their efforts to persuade the Government to cooperate the Messina powers, acting as parliamentary sponsors for Federal Union's survey of attitudes of members of Commonwealth Parliaments since the Commonwealth seemed to be the main hindrance.[221] Rippon, Maddan and Rodgers, together with Spens, Stoddart-Scott, and Braine put down a second EDM on 12 December 1956. This was signed by 110 MPs and urged the Government to call a conference with the West European powers to consider further practical steps towards European unity, in the belief that the 'best interests of the United Kingdom and the rest of the Commonwealth lie in the closer association of the United Kingdom with Western Europe in conditions which safeguard existing Commonwealth relationships'.

Although disassociation with America was not in the sponsors' mind,[222] one effect of the Suez crisis was to increase Conservative support for participation in a new West European community.[223] The assumption that 'America would never stand aside if British vital interests were at stake'[224] had been rudely dispelled. 'As a result we must now turn urgently to consolidating our relations with Europe, for example the creation of a free trade area in association with a common market. By moving closer to Europe we stood the best chance of improving our relations with the United States.'[225] Typically, Amery looked beyond this, suggesting a concerted common European policy could be pursued in the Middle East, if possible with America, and without her if necessary.[226] This was not to be: Guy Mollet had ardently hoped that if Britain and France could 'win through' against Egypt and Russia, he would 'make a good European of your Anthony Eden yet!'[227] The failure of the Suez military intervention struck a tremendous blow to the emerging Anglo-French axis as the basis of European progress, instead of a Franco-German axis. Treated like naughty schoolboys by the United States and Russia, thereafter Britain and France went their separate ways.[228]

Rippon's EDMs did not develop into a concerted Conservative backbench campaign: Edward Heath, the Chief Whip told Rippon if he continued with these 'unhelpful' motions he might have to give up being a PPS.[229] There remained deep-seated Conservative backbench animosity towards any attempts to lure Britain into federal schemes which 'incompatible with our free association of sovereign states'.[230] The Conservative Government did not desire a customs union, for the same reasons that had influenced its Labour predecessors, convinced that Messina would weaken the OEEC, the British choice for economic cooperation with Europe.

However, the 'feeling of well-founded backbench support'[231] bolstered government moves towards the Community through a free trade area.[232] The 'greater eminence' of Macmillan and Thorneycroft[233] after January 1957 confirmed the government's commitment to this policy,[234] although in his first months as Prime Minister Macmillan was too busy 'picking up the pieces with America' to concentrate on closer European integration.[235] It was not until after the signature of the Treaty of Rome on 25 March 1957, that the Government took the idea of EFTA seriously.[236] The greatest concern now centred on the decision of the Six to include their overseas territories within the EEC tariff boundaries: this put both the principles of excluding the Commonwealth and agricultural products into question[237] – which immediately raised Tory backbench hackles.[238] Faced with this unwelcome development, the Government determined to try to negotiate an industrial free trade area excluding all overseas territories, rather than to expand the new European grouping to include the whole of the Commonwealth.[239] The Defence White Paper of February 1957 which proposed the withdrawal of 13 500 British troops from West Germany had had 'unfavourable repercussions'. 'It was imperative for Britain to continue to show maximum interest in Europe... and in case the EEC and EURATOM treaties were not ratified, to have a "crash wagon" ready'.[240]

Henceforth, the supreme danger for Britain seemed the creation of an economic bloc in Western Europe without the simultaneous creation of a Free Trade Area.[241] The threat was not solely Britain's economic exclusion: the Third Force ideas inherent in such a customs union 'must lead inevitably to the disintegration of the European policy which we have hitherto pursued, involving the collapse of the North Atlantic Treaty Organisation and the existing system of defence of Western Europe against the Soviet Union.'[242]

This burgeoning British official enthusiasm for the 'lifebelt of EFTA',[243] was matched by the perennial Continental suspicion that British initiatives were intended to undermine their projects.[244] It also ran sharply against the profound and enduring Conservative attachment to the Commonwealth,[245] and raised persistent questions about the possible rise in unemployment because of increased imports, and the erosion of British markets by cheaper European goods, based on lower wage scales.[246] Macmillan went out of his way to reassure his anxious backbenchers that 'the Commonwealth comes first in our hearts and minds' as political observers speculated that 'the issue, opportunity and inclination for another right-wing revolt may be emerging. If the trouble spreads, it could conceivably play a part in Conservative politics similar to... the Bevanite struggle'.[247] Although a Conservative backbench revolt did not materialize over the Macmillan government's attempts to create first EFTA of the Seventeen,[248] and then to establish a rival economic grouping to the EEC, EFTA of the Seven (signed on 21 November 1959[249]), such speculation was a prescient prediction for future Conservative convulsions over closer ties with Europe.

For the Tories in the 1950s, Europe was the dog that did not bark. Contrary to the Europeanists' hopes and Continental expectations, Churchill's peace-time administration adhered to Bevin's foreign policy on Europe and Conservative backbench attempts to foster more positive attitudes to intergovernmental cooperation through the Council of Europe were marginal and very largely ignored. For most Tories, the developments of the Six prior to 1954 were merely a 'temporary emotional aberration';[250] Eden shared this conviction that there was no need for Britain to strive for leadership in Europe to divert attention from federalism.

Although there was no broad policy change when Eden became Prime Minister gradually, the tide turned in favour of the pro-Europeans, thanks in large part to the defeat of imperial preference and the 1955 intake of younger MPs, which provided a welcome prop to Macmillan's and Thorneycroft's moves to associate Britain with the emerging common market in a free trade area. 'Eden's resignation in January 1957 did seem to mark the departure of a generation within the Foreign Office itself, and the arrival of people like Donald Maitland [who went on to help Edward Heath negotiate Britain's entry into the Common Market] who were strong Europeans.'[251]

Thus the EEC provided the catalyst for the shift in the balance within the Conservative party on Europe: from sceptical front bench vs individual committed backbenchers, to committed front bench (with prominent Cabinet sceptics) vs sceptical and hostile backbenchers, vocally supported by *The Express* Newspapers' claim that the Government had no mandate. This pattern has endured to this day.

6 The genesis of the Suez Group and the Anti-Suez Group

The Conservative Europeanists scored their greatest successes in opposition, yet proved surprisingly impotent once their party had been returned to power; the tide only began to turn in their favour after the defeat of imperial preference had 'dragged the party into the 20th century'.[1] The Suez Group fared very differently. This faction's formative experiences were in opposition: the débâcles over Palestine in 1947–48 and Abadan in 1951. Although Conservative critics of the Labour Government's handling of these crises were unable to pressure the Government either into imposing a settlement in Palestine or despatching troops to protect British lives and property at Abadan, both episodes served to identify those Tory MPs who held passionate views about Britain's place in the Middle East[2] and the best means to sustain her pre-eminent position.

As with Europe, so the Middle East: in opposition Churchill and his shadow cabinet could evade difficult choices by giving their backbenchers their head. Although Churchill reined in some of the more extreme utterances of his supporters during the Abadan crisis, there was no need for him to worry too scrupulously about the practical effects of the belligerent approach Conservatives were advocating. In contrast, the resumption of responsibility in October 1951 necessarily demanded a coherent and pragmatic approach; the Government's slim majority (17) also meant the Conservative party could no longer tolerate internal differences to the same degree. The stern instruction to errant backbenchers 'not to rock the boat' had the desired effect in some cases and the first eighteen months of Churchill's government was 'touch and go'[3] which, in itself, instilled party discipline.

But despite the constraints of power, there was a greater tendency to rebellion within the party. As the economy improved and the party's confidence grew, by the 1953–54 session Conservative stirrings were much more noticeable. There were various reasons for this backbench waywardness. Eden's reinstatement as Foreign Secretary, Butler's elevation to the Exchequer, and the despatch of Macmillan to the apparently marginal Ministry of Housing, ensured that Churchill's peacetime government was of a progressive stamp[4] which was not to the taste of the robust element on the Tory backbenches. Even those who accepted the need for Butler's measures craved a policy distinct from the socialists.[5] There was also resentment over the rapid promotion of recent newcomers, such as Hopkinson, and jealousy over Sandys' elevation to the Cabinet.

The non-partisan emphasis of Churchill's administration greatly aggravated party discontent.[6] Backbench dissatisfaction that Churchill had surrounded himself with old cronies, giving little opportunity to postwar entrants at junior ministerial level, necessarily created a ripple effect onto the conduct of foreign policy. It liberated those able, ambitious younger members who might otherwise have been silenced by ministerial office. In addition, lack of contact between senior ministers and their backbench colleagues[7] underlined the importance of the party committees as a vital conduit between the front and backbenches, and meant any lack of information available in committee was all the more keenly felt.[8] It became increasingly difficult for the Whips to maintain the high degree of public unity that had characterized the Conservative party since 1945. The Government faced internal revolts on a wide range of issues: fiscal policy, transport policy, commercial television, MPs' salaries, imperial preference/opposition to the GATT treaty, and foreign policy.[9]

THE SUEZ GROUP

The strength of Conservative backbench feeling on Europe between 1951 and 1957 was insufficient to stimulate even a pale imitation of a backbench revolt. In contrast, of all the backbench rebellions facing the Conservative Government in these years the Suez Group was the most serious. Butler as Chancellor encountered considerably less difficulty from the backbenches than Eden – undoubtedly because the Suez Group enjoyed the tacit support of Churchill. The economic ginger group led by Assheton and Waterhouse enjoyed no such favour from their party leader, although they might have expected more support from a former Chancellor; Churchill's experiences in the 1920s had undoubtedly made him extremely wary of economics.

Unlike the Europeanists, whose cause enjoyed active cross-party support, the Suez Group was a Conservative creation.[10] It comprised approximately 40 MPs, with a core of approximately 28. It enjoyed the private support of a far wider circle, but these 'crypto-Suez Group' MPs were not prepared to sign critical EDMs, let alone carry their opposition to Eden's Middle East policy into the division lobby.[11] The two prime movers in the creation of the Suez Group were Captain Charles Waterhouse and the son of his former ministerial colleague Leo Amery, Julian Amery.

The patrician Waterhouse, who first entered Parliament in 1924, was a member of the Tory old-guard who preferred private meetings with the minister concerned as the means to iron out differences over policy. A former junior minister under Baldwin and Churchill and a Privy Councillor, he was unfailingly courteous to friends[12] but somewhat distant to the new boys of 1950 and 1951[13] – unless they were the sons of friends, or shared his robust views on the requirements of the continuation of Britain's imperial role. Some of the newer entrants tolerantly described him as 'an old war horse'[14] and dismissed his interventions. Others regarded him as a 'most unattractive character',[15] commenting that his retention of the rank 'Captain' in peace-time was revealing,[16] and interpreted his role in the Suez Group 'as a sort of redemption' for his support for Munich.[17] However, among Waterhouse's older pre-war colleagues there was greater sympathy and understanding for his outlook,[18] even if these MPs did not share his views. It was recognized that Waterhouse's stance had a resonance in the constituency associations, even if it appeared increasingly outdated in the cold light of Britain's parlous economic position in the early 1950s; and he exercised considerable influence behind the scenes, particularly in the Foreign Affairs Committee. He was less influential in the 1922 Committee and in the House because of his 'right-wing' views.[19]

Through his service in the Life Guards and his younger brother, Major General Guy Waterhouse,[20] Waterhouse enjoyed widespread contacts with the military; these contacts were reflected and enhanced by his election to the Chairmanship of the backbench Defence Committee in November 1951. Waterhouse also took a leading position in the backbench ginger group which was fiercely critical of Butler's economic policy. Known as 'Slasher Waterhouse'[21] because of his ardent campaign for large cuts in spending – which could only mean slashing social services – in July 1953 he was chosen as the Chairman of the Select Committee on Estimates. Waterhouse had also served as Chairman of the Conservative party conference in Scarborough 1952 and had given 'tacit approval to extremists' demands for a 2/- (i.e. 10 per cent) cut in income tax.[22] His detractors held that his widespread business interests in the colonies[23] had a direct bearing upon the areas of his political activity. Certainly, Waterhouse did have close business links with the British colonies in Southern Africa (his son also lived in Southern Rhodesia), and he was one of those who later formed the pro-Rhodesia group in the 1960s.

Through his personality and ability, Julian Amery rapidly came to outshine most of the Suez Group rebels, including Waterhouse, the Group's official leader.[24] Amery was one of the leading Conservative critics of Labour's mishandling of the Abadan crisis, but it was the Conservative Government's seemingly imminent grant of self-government to the Sudanese in early 1953 which spurred him and like-minded colleagues to take coordinated action. He and Waterhouse had been on civil, if rather distant terms since Amery's arrival in Parliament in 1950. A chance meeting in a lift in Cape Town in January 1953 proved decisive: Waterhouse had just visited the Sudan and was deeply disturbed that Eden seemed poised to 'give it away'. Amery regarded the rumour that, under American pressure, Eden was considering pulling out of the Suez Canal base as far more serious, as this would mean that Britain could not hold the Sudan anyway. On their return to London, both men began talking to friends.[25]

Amery was a paradox, a true latter-day Social Imperialist: his pronounced liberal views in social and economic policy accorded ill with the Suez Group's older members' more traditional views of the efficacy of capital punishment and the pernicious effect of the welfare state. His passionate advocacy of the compatibility of an expanded Commonwealth and closer links with Europe was diametrically opposed to the opinions of many of his chosen colleagues in the Suez Group (such as Legge-Bourke and Sir Herbert Williams).

Highly intelligent, articulate, able, from an impeccably imperialist stable and married to Macmillan's daughter, as a new backbencher Amery enjoyed a multitude of advantages. He was one who had 'enjoyed the habit of power' from an early age, and he unquestionably benefited greatly from the considerable respect and affection for his father whose connections he exploited with great effect. However, his energy and drive raised some eyebrows among the more sedate and orthodox members of the party. Amery was respected and his ability was unquestioned, but the man and his political methods were not widely liked nor approved.[26] Amery was a natural 'plotter' – an arch plotter in some people's book – with an innate passion for intrigue. Through no fault of his own, he suffered from 'too much political baggage'. His and his father's determination to overcome the tragedy of his brother commanded widespread sympathy and admiration, but there remained a residue of the memory of this family connection; and although in the eyes of many he had had a 'good War', with his exploits among the Albanian partisans being legendary, not all middle-ranking Conservatives approved of the circumstances surrounding his involvement in Balkan resistance to Nazi Germany and regarded him as a youthful adventurer who had manipulated his father's position in Churchill's Cabinet to his own personal glory.[27] Nor did his friendship with Randolph Churchill commend him to everyone, some of whom questioned his judgment of men. In all, he made an exhilarating, if rather exhausting political stable mate.

'Treading on Amery's heels'[28] on the topic of the future of Suez Canal base, Lord Hinchingbrooke was never shy of expressing his views on any subject. His house in Great College Street had been an important venue for backbench ginger groups since the days of the Tory Reform Committee.[29] A traditional High Tory – or rather 'an old-fashioned Whig'[30] – of patrician appearance and always immaculately dressed, 'Hinch' was regarded with tolerant affection by his colleagues, even though his opinions became more and more 'manifestly mad' with the passing years.[31]

At first glance there appear glaring contradictions in

Hinchingbrooke's thought: his statement 'at home and overseas our commitments exceed our power'[32] seems at odds with his support for retaining a British presence at the Suez Canal. However, this was a question of political perspective. A supporter of a more liberal economy, Hinchingbrooke advocated a fundamental shift in the Government's approach to domestic and foreign policy, based on reducing the burden of taxation and state controls, expanding the frontiers of free trade, reducing tariffs and quotas, while maintaining imperial preference, and seeking peace by negotiation not by threat of force.[33] He was vehemently opposed to rearmament, German or British, on economic grounds, arguing vociferously that the burden this would impose would prove disastrously counter-productive; there was no evidence that Communist countries wanted to capture countries by military means; rather they wanted to capture them by policies and processes of the mind. That could be realized if Britain reduced her standard of life by too much rearmament and by denuding the country of goods and services.[34]

The heir to the Earl of Sandwich whose family had been in politics for three centuries, Hinchingbrooke benefited from his aristocratic political connections. However, he had always avoided the comfortable route in politics. Before entering the political arena he had spent two years working as a Woolwich factory hand, where he had joined a union. In 1938 he had supported the anti-Chamberlain lobby, and had been one of the prime movers in the establishment of the Tory Reform Group, constituted to implement the Beveridge Report, and acted as the Group's first chairman. Ironically, Hinchingbrooke later became a member of the Progress Trust.[35]

Hinchingbrooke held a decidedly independent, Burkean view of the responsibilities and duties of an MP[36] and put loyalty to conscience above loyalty to party – which sorely tried the patience of his local constituency association. When Hinchingbrooke's campaigns of criticism against Britain's rearmament programme and the Government's transport policy coincided with his part in Conservative backbench moves to oust Churchill,[37] in the autumn of 1952 the South Dorset constituency association tried to deselect him on the grounds that Hinchingbrooke's 'repeatedly publicly expressed opinions ... on foreign affairs [notably the Middle East and German rearmament] and repeated attacks on party leaders, . . . [had] gradually built up the possibility, in the opinion of the Executive, that would make a present of the seat to a Socialist if our member were again a candidate.'[38] Happily for Hinchingbrooke, this deselection attempt failed.

Major Harry Legge-Bourke was another prominent member of the Suez Group; regarded as 'the most popular man in the House of Commons',[39] his charm and sincerity enhanced the influence of his contributions to political debate.[40] A former regular soldier in the Royal Horse Artillery, who had been ADC to Lord Killearn (the British Ambassador in Cairo during the War) he was a man of great integrity and simplicity, to whom honour was paramount. In the general elections of 1950 and 1951 Legge-Bourke publicly declared on the hustings that he reserved the right to disagree with his party 'on matters such as foreign affairs which ought to transcend party considerations',[41] and had already disobeyed the party whip on Palestine and the Schuman Plan.

Legge-Bourke's first meeting with Amery on the Egyptian question took place in July 1952, just after the group of radical nationalist officers had seized power in Cairo. 'It was in the following winter recess that Julian rang me up and asked whether I would come to a meeting in his father's house [in Eaton Square] if I was not satisfied with what was happening in Egypt.'[42] As a long serving officer accustomed 'when the firing is going on [to] concentrate on firing back', Legge-Bourke's membership of a rebellious faction was unusual.[43] Although he was the only Suez Group member to go to the extreme of resigning the party Whip in July 1954 following the conclusion of Heads of Agreement on the Suez Canal Zone base, throughout the 1956 crisis he maintained a deafening silence in public and was very measured in private: 'It was "I told you so". Things were going exactly as he had warned, but he had done all he could [in 1954].'[44]

Other vocal members of the Suez Group were Patrick Maitland, the heir to the Earl of Lauderdale, who had 'a distinguished record as a correspondent for *The Times*' and as an ex-diplomat had had long-standing interest in foreign affairs; and Angus Maude, a fellow journalist, a leading member of One Nation and a member of the party's backbench Education Committee. Intelligent, articulate and caustic, Maude lent forceful intellectual persuasion to the Suez Group's cause. So did Enoch Powell, intellectually the most formidable of these younger MPs; an original member of the One Nation group, Powell's powerful arguments in the Chamber savaging Labour's policies were the talk of the smoking rooms. Powell was not invited to the original meeting of the Suez Group, but joined the group later.[45] Paul Williams (whose election for Sunderland in May 1953 provided a great tonic to the Tory party) was a rapid active recruit for the Suez Group's crusade, as were Neil ('Billy') McLean[46] and John Biggs-Davison following their election to Parliament in December 1954 and May 1955 respectively. A long-standing friend of Amery and Neil McLean, Biggs-Davison was well versed in the Suez Group's arguments through his role as secretary to the Foreign Affairs Committee while working the Conservative Research Department, and through his regular attendance of the Suez Group's meetings.

Other important members included Fitzroy Maclean,[47] Sir Guy Lloyd (very much a Tory grandee, and one of Eden's few close friends), and the erudite and immensely likeable Hamilton Kerr, Macmillan's PPS when the latter was Minister of Defence. Another larger-than-life character, Fitzroy Maclean had had a 'good War' as Churchill's special envoy to Tito's partisans, was a former diplomat, an author and a man of great personal courage and integrity. However, Maclean was not a 'natural politician'.[48] Macmillan, when Prime Minister, was to drop him from his government with regret, commenting that sadly Maclean's literary fluency was not matched by any parliamentary oratory.

In the party behind the scenes no less important were Ralph Assheton and Christopher Holland-Martin. A former Financial Secretary and Chairman of the Party, to his bitter disappointment Assheton was one of several former Tory ministers omitted from Churchill's government[49] – by his own choice as he had not been offered a post 'in charge of a department' responsible for economic and financial policy. Assheton served as Chairman on the Select Committee on Nationalized Industries between 1951–3 and, together with Waterhouse, he led the backbench group which was fiercely critical of Butler's fiscal policy. Assheton and Fitzroy Maclean were both Lancashire MPs whose constituency industries were dependent upon Sudanese and Egyptian cotton. Holland-Martin's name

The genesis of the Suez Group and the Anti-Suez Group

was 'rarely in the news';[50] a banker who had only entered Parliament in 1951, he was also Macmillan's brother-in-law, which gave him an additional connection to Julian Amery. His lack of public eloquence was more than compensated in private where, as the holder of eight directorships, he was a powerful advocate for the City. Tall, bespectacled and retiring, *Crossbencher* described him as a 'chief strategist for the Suez Group'[51] canvassing MPs, organizing two secret memos for Churchill and helping to draft the dissident EDM of December 1953.

The spur to the formation of the Suez Group was not only Eden's proposed treaties with Egypt over the Sudan and the future of the Suez Canal base. These MPs were fundamentally dissatisfied with the impact of their opinions through the official channels of the party, notably the Foreign Affairs Committee. While the formation of their ginger group was in fact an admission that their influence had failed thus far, these MPs felt that more could be achieved by public dissent.

The first meeting of 'the Suez Canal Committee' was held at Leo Amery's house, No 112 Eaton Square, on 5 October 1953.[52] Thereafter there was an inner group[53] which met regularly, invited by Julian Amery on Waterhouse's instructions,[54] and an outer group 'that was more amateur'.[55] Waterhouse also usually invited a Whip to the meetings,[56] 'so that he could see for himself what views were held and by whom'.[57] Afterwards Waterhouse would write to Churchill, Eden or Buchan-Hepburn (the Chief Whip) reporting the group's views.[58] Maitland, a journalist with wide-spread connections, was in charge of briefing the press, both formally at press briefings, and by the more devious route of private briefings for a friendly agency stringer, as the Suez Group could then use the foreign date-line report as the basis for embarrassing questions in the House.[59] Amery also used his contacts in the press to great effect. Derek Marks at *The Daily Express* was an ally (although at times an unreliable one[60]), as were Colin Coote, Ivor Thomas and Peregrine Worsthorne at *The Daily Telegraph*, Malcolm Muggeridge, the editor of *Punch*,[61] and John Junor.[62] Inevitably, the Suez Group targeted the Northcliffe and Beaverbrook press which were inherently well-disposed to their cause.[63] Biggs-Davison acted on Amery's specific instructions[64] to ensure that *The Daily Telegraph*'s and *The Times*' editors were kept up-to-date of the group's meetings and deliberations, drawing their attention to specific points 'to make sure they understand the significance'.[65] The composite column, *Crossbencher* – 'quite an important and influential column; its touch of scandal certainly made it more interesting to read!'[66] – was particularly useful. To begin with, only British newspaper correspondents were invited to the press briefings which following the Suez Group's meetings. 'However, the Group realized then that it was very important to influence opinion overseas, and especially American opinion, and therefore began to see foreign correspondents privately.'[67]

As far as running the Suez Group was concerned, Amery and Powell acted as secretaries.[68] Amery organized hiring committee rooms for Suez Group meetings,[69] and together with Powell arranged for information to be distributed.[70] Amery also had the political connections; his father was very active in opposing Eden's policy on Egypt until his death in 1955 and Amery benefited enormously from contacts made through his father, at school (Eton), university (Balliol) and during the War (intelligence service).[71] In comparison, Waterhouse had the 'political form'.

In July 1954 the Suez Group lost Fitzroy Maclean (who later joined the Government as Under-secretary of State for War), Bell and Bromley-Davenport. In addition, Powell came to the conclusion over the summer that the British 'empire of positions' which had replaced 'the empire of government of peoples' after Indian independence, was an inconceivable theory if Britain could not hold Suez.[72] The Group lost further supporters in the May 1955 election through boundary changes (Assheton) and decisions not to stand again (Donner, Mellor, Rayner and Savory).

But 'most of us... remained convinced that we had been right in our assessment of the consequences of abandoning the base and believed it would still be possible to retrieve the ground that had been lost.'[73] There were more active recruits in 1955 as anxiety over Britain's future in Cyprus provided the momentum for the Suez Group's continued existence. The Group's dissatisfaction with the Foreign Affairs Committee persisted, fundamentally unimpressed by the argument that the Foreign Affairs Committee 'enabl[ed] backbench MPs not only to receive information from the Government but to clear their minds in general discussion',[74] and with the information available from the Government on, for example, the details of the offer to Archbishop Makarios.[75] Indeed this Committee appeared one of the 'organs of party control, registering favourable or unfavourable reactions',[76] rather than as a means to promote an alternative approach; it 'met more often to learn of decisions already taken instead of helping to make them'.[77] Pressure from these rebels led to the formation of the Middle East Subcommittee in April 1956, to meet fortnightly: as Hinchingbrooke was elected chairman, Neil McLean served as secretary and the subsequent lists of those attended included Maitland, Legge-Bourke, Paul Williams, Hugh Fraser and Biggs-Davison, this represented the official coming-of-age of the Suez Group.

Although the Suez Group was later described as the 'whiff of grape-shot school,'[78] they cannot all be dismissed as 'crusty right-wingers',[79] or 'embittered ex-ministers and ambitious young men'.[80] A considerable number of these MPs held important positions behind the scenes in the official and unofficial backbench committees of the party, which contradicts the received wisdom that the Suez Group could be summarily dismissed as diehard reactionaries on the periphery of the party. Assheton was one of the most senior Conservative backbenchers, whose considerable influence[81] was not widely recognized outside Westminster.[82] Waterhouse was Chairman of the party's backbench Defence Committee, Hinchingbrooke was chairman of the Transport Committee and Holland-Martin served as joint Treasurer of the Party. Six of those who signed the Suez Group's critical EDM in December 1953 were executive members of the 1922 Committee;[83] John Morrison who had been elected vice-chairman of the 1922 Committee in 1951, went on to become an extremely influential Chairman[84] in 1955. By 1956 Amery, Maude and Hinchingbrooke were members of the 1922 executive; Hinchingbrooke was also vice-chairman of the Foreign Affairs Committee, and Chairman of the Middle East Subcommittee.

The fact that at least five Suez Group rebels in 1953–4 and 1956 were also members of the Progress Trust[85] demonstrates that in the eyes of their peers they were not negligible politicians, and places their opinions more squarely in the centre of the party than other political writers have appreciated. Conversely, membership of the Progress Trust gave the Suez Group an exceptionally powerful forum in which it could air and appeal for support for its views, and offered the opportunity to exploit the political links offered by the Trust as the organization was a source of powerful political patronage and formed a bond between its former members in the Cabinet and on the backbenchers. Thus Conservative party managers could not easily dismiss their views.

The Suez Group MPs did not all conform to a stereotype of older, imperially-minded 'backwoodsmen' with decidedly reactionary views on economic policy and capital punishment. Admittedly, a considerable number enjoyed close links with Britain's colonies, both through family connections and through business interests; and Sir Herbert Williams, Legge-Bourke and Biggs-Davison held important positions on the Council of Empire Economic Union, founded by Leo Amery in 1929.[86] However, eight were 'political youngsters of 40 or less and nearly half [were] under 50'.[87] It contained several ardent Europeans, and keen partisans of World Government,[88] and certainly included young men in a hurry, anxious to make their political mark. Amery, Biggs-Davison, Hinchingbrooke, Maude and Powell held progressive views on domestic reform[89] and, together with Hyde and Reader Harris, had voted for the abolition of capital punishment. In fact, of the Suez Group in 1956, approximately half had voted against hanging.[90] In other spheres they made a considerable contribution to political debate: Enoch Powell, in particular, was at the forefront of the new progressive Conservatism spearheaded by Butler at the Conservative Research Department. The Suez Group also benefited from individual members' war experience and contacts – many had served in the Middle East, whilst others profited enormously from their war-time association with the diplomatic and intelligence services.[91] The inner core of the group was particularly well-informed.[92]

Unfortunately for their cause, the Suez Group was not a sum of its parts; the Group did suffer from the image of being composed of 'political lightweights'[93] – backwoodsmen who had an out-dated view of British resources and power. It was true that, although the Group included influential and respected politicians, many of its members remained marginal politicians. Some cut amusing figures: Bromley-Davenport, whose booming interventions invariably attracted opposition cheers; Brigadier Ralph Rayner, who was greeted frequently with cries of 'Tally ho!' from the Labour benches (a reference to his passion for hunting) when he rose to speak; William Rees Davies whose raffish air, (heightened by his habit of wearing a cloak) together with the accident during a tank exercise in the Second World War which had cost him an arm, earned him the nickname 'the One-armed Bandit'. And not all MPs lent a particular *cachet* to the Suez Group: Montgomery Hyde (once described as the 'kiss of death' to any pressure group to whom he belonged)[94] was an inveterate member of rebellious factions. Hyde, an Ulster Unionist, was not widely liked, and his occasional salacious interest in more prurient topics was viewed with distaste. Gerald Nabarro was another outsider: loud, brash and widely unpopular, his dogged persistence – over the Clean Air Act, for example – was admired, but frequently viewed as misguided.[95] Captain Kerby, a quiet, somewhat secretive man, sought to create the aura of diligence with his constituents through his assiduous use of written parliamentary questions and letters to his local press; dining-room gossip that he was a Russian spy[96] did not lend weight to his contributions to political debate.

Superficially the Suez Group appeared a polyglot 'colourful' group[97] whose common denomination was eccentricity. Certainly, given the disparate nature of the Group which included several ardent Europeans with the 'empire stalwarts', no overall hard and fast philosophy pervaded. However, the Suez Group's members did share a coherent view about the position of the British Empire and Britain's role in world affairs. They were determined to maintain the Commonwealth as a political and military entity[98] and hotly denied accusations that they were chauvinists with an illusory view of Britain's potential influence.[99] As Amery expressed it, 'our position – power-political as well as geographical – is one of being between Russia and America, or if you prefer to think ideologically, between Totalitarian Socialism and Liberal Capitalism... Our survival must depend on our ability to provide a solution for the problems first, of our own people, then of the different grades of the nations drawn naturally into our orbit under the present political constellation, i.e., the colonies, Mandates, Dominions, Middle East, the sterling bloc and Western Europe.'[100]

This view of Britain's natural position being between Russia and America was key to their beliefs. Britain remained one of the Big Three: she should continue to be and act as America's equal, on the basis of diplomatic tradition and experience and her position as head of the Empire and Commonwealth. Any retreat from Britain's global commitments was viewed as fatal to her prestige: it would destroy the illusion of 'the empire of positions'[101] and admit decline into second class power status. The answer to the erosion of British influence and prestige was seen to lie in the extension and consolidation of imperial preference. Welding the Commonwealth together into a united bloc would ensure continued British influence in world affairs, for as leader of a large unit her wishes and opinions could not be ignored.[102] After the defeat of the imperial preference issue at the party conference in 1954, a considerable number of Suez rebels sought to give cohesion to the Commonwealth through the Expanding the Commonwealth Group: Maitland was chairman; other Suez Group members and sympathizers who were involved included Amery, Tilney, Hinchingbrooke, Biggs-Davison, Paul Williams, Beresford Craddock, Ronald Russell and Angus Maude.

As the principal enemy of imperial preference, America seemed the relentless foe of British interests. There was a common desire for Britain to assert her independence of the United States[103] politically and economically. The Suez Group's gut feeling was that Britain had been 'dead wrong'[104] to take the American loan in 1945; the British economy should be consciously directed to the Empire and – for the Europeanists within the Suez Group – Western Europe. Marshall Aid was seen as American economic imperialism. The US was 'a young and ebullient nation', so it was essential that Washington should look to London for diplomatic leadership. Britain was fatally cast in that role by her economic and geographic situation.[105] The sinister hand of American influence was seen in every British overseas loss, especially in the Middle East where America appeared a dangerous, untutored rival. Everywhere was seen 'the State Department's desire to break the British Commonwealth and establish Britain and Europe as satellites of the US defence network'.[106] Their passionate conviction that Britain was America's equal was a recurrent theme – as was their belief that successive British governments had been lamentably subservient to Washington with dire results, and that Britain was being reduced to being America's 'lackey'.[107]

In the eyes of the Suez Group, there was insufficient concentration on the aims and purposes of British foreign policy generally: for example, with regard to America, did Britain want an unqualified, unreserved alliance or some kind of balance of power? Maitland felt that the Foreign Affairs Committee should discuss 'regularly, seriously, and methodically our objectives around the world'.[108] Just as anti-American feeling was engrained in the Suez Group,[109] so too was a pronounced distrust of the United Nations. Not only had the Labour Government lamentably failed to use the new organization as an effective tool in international diplomacy, 'we seem to be the hacks and serving men of the UN, waiting for other nations to act and not exerting our own rights and insisting on united action'.[110] Extensive use of the Russian veto had crippled the organization, therefore Britain should return to traditional methods of great-power diplomacy.

The Middle East was 'the new Empire'[111] for the Suez Group and their sympathizers: Britain's position there was pre-eminent and should remain so. Even the less emotional Tories regarded the area as vital to the Commonwealth.[112] Departure 'would be the beginning of the end of the greatness of ourselves as a Great Power and be the beginning of further troubles for that area'.[113] Conservatives persisted in their pre-war view of the strategic importance of the whole region, despite the independence of India, Pakistan, Ceylon and Burma in 1947. The emotional tie to India had not been severed with the lowering of the British flag on the Indian subcontinent,[114] and this belief in the need to protect the route to India was extremely influential upon Conservative opinion. Hopes persisted that the two great Indian dominions would go on cooperating with London, as would the old White Dominions.[115]

There was an overwhelming necessity to keep key positions; first and foremost was, of course, the Suez Canal base. Britain's position in the region appeared to be under threat from two fronts: America – whom the Suez Group firmly regarded as Britain's junior partner in the region on the basis of tradition and Britain's 'superior knowledge',[116] rather than raw military power – and Russia. Ironically they shared their conviction of the need to maintain British prestige in the Middle

East with Eden; Eden, however, pinned his hopes upon regional treaties and (hopefully) accumulated goodwill to bolster British prestige and influence in the region.

The age and political experience of these MPs was very relevant to their views on Britain's natural position in the world. Just as the Suez Group's older members were of a generation which had never doubted that Britain was great, the younger MPs were the children of the appeasers, to whom Munich had been a sign that, to put it politely, their elders had lost their nerve. This idea of the critical importance of 'holding one's nerve' recurs again and again in the Suez Group's arguments. Throughout Britain's dealings in the Middle East in the decade after the War, the Suez Group was to call constantly for Britain to stand firm – convinced that the other side would eventually come round to the British position, and a satisfactory conclusion could be reached. The Suez Group were not impressed by arguments of the debilitating effect on Britain's influence of British material weakness, echoing Marshal Foch's opinion that morale is to *matériel* 20:1. It was not vast numbers of British troops that were required, 'but an awareness of minds ... that Her Majesty's Government is determined to protect the King's subjects and the nation's treasure, wherever and whenever endangered'.[117]

Throughout this period the Suez Group was united in its opinion that successive British governments were following a 'policy of drift' in the Middle East. Its consistent view was that Britain 'still has a major role to play in world affairs'.[118] Its anger was directed at British dependence upon America, frustrated that support for America elsewhere, especially in Korea, had not led to any corresponding support for Britain in the Middle East. Many members harboured a long-standing dislike of the Tripartite Declaration (of 1950 which guaranteed the armistice frontiers of 1948), which they felt 'could land Britain in an appalling situation'.[119]

Throughout the internal party debate on the future of the Suez Canal Zone base, the Whips were hard at work to minimize the effect of rebel views on the bulk of the party. 'Patrick Buchan-Hepburn[120] was frightened of the Suez Group; he took a lot of private soundings about them, as he really thought the Suez Group could derail the show. He campaigned very hard.'[121] Assiduous attention was paid to their behaviour, and great efforts made to develop and maintain good contacts with the dissidents.[122] 'The Suez Group was not just a "one-off" thing. It was a last glow of Britain's imperial era . . . a string of people who were inclined to believe that the Government had made a fatal switch of emphasis with the liquidation of the Empire after the War and in throwing our lot in with America. It was too high a price to pay for American support. Therefore the Whips' Office paid quite a lot of attention to them. We had endless meetings and debates about it all . . . The Suez Group had a resonance within the party and the constituency associations. They were much more than a safety valve.'[123]

Throughout the spasmodic negotiations with Egypt the Whips were pressed hard to keep the party on the rails, as there developed 'an enjoyable cat-and-mouse game . . . behind the Westminster scene between the Whips and rebels'.[124] The Whips were prepared deliberately to limit public debate in Parliament on the issue if the need, and the opportunity, arose. In December 1953 Government whips quickly realized Churchill's and Eden's interventions might not be enough to head off a public expression of unease from the Suez Group and 'glumly resigned themselves to a two-day debate which would allow plenty of time for the Tory malcontents. The Whips were therefore wreathed in smiles when the Socialists decided on their vote of censure on the African muddle[125] [since] it gave them the perfect excuse to cut the debate down to a single day.'[126] In July 1954, Buchan-Hepburn left 'nothing to chance',[127] sending three-line whips by telegram to all Conservative MPs to ensure their presence at the division on the Heads of Agreement of the Suez Canal base.

Similarly, throughout the protracted Suez crisis, the Whips paid close attention to the Suez Group's activities[128] and cultivated their contacts with the dissidents. A young backbencher curious about the brouhaha, joined a Suez Group meeting at the Carlton Club. His innocent inquiry of 'Why was it all so secret since surely the Whips had a good notion of the goings on?' was quelled by a terse 'Shut up!' from one of the Group's leaders. 'But I was right, for when we came out of the room, there in an armchair at the end of the corridor sat one of the senior Whips, ostentatiously holding a copy of *The Times* in front of his face. He had, however, cut a large hole in the middle of the paper, and was busy writing down names as we came out.'[129]

THE ANTI-SUEZ GROUP

This small group of Conservative MPs only emerged in the Suez Crisis of 1956; it did not play any part in the fight Eden encountered within his party in his determination to negotiate the Anglo-Egyptian agreement on the Sudan, nor the Suez Base Agreement in 1954.[130] This faction contained varying degrees of antagonism to Eden's Suez policy, ranging from unease to active opposition. In addition to the six MPs who publicly abstained on 8 November 1956,[131] the views of Sir Lionel Heald, Walter Elliot and Alexander Spearman were well known in Westminster. Beyond these were approximately 20–30 Conservatives whose profound concern caused them to contemplate seriously rebellion against the Government.[132] Dumbfounded by the news of the initial assault, 'they felt they deserved time to reflect before committing what they assumed would be personal as well as party political suicide and the noisiness of the Opposition benches did not make things any easier since it suggested that any surrender would be surrender to disorder'.[133] As *The Economist* predicted, in the end most stayed quiet and eventually rallied round Eden.

In contrast to the well-organized Suez Group, the Anti-Suez Group had no recognized leader, nor did its members fit easily into any particular category. All of those who publicly abstained in November 1956 had already antagonized their local constituency associations through their opposition to capital punishment. Paradoxically, the group contained two Jewish MPs, Joseph and D'Avigdor Goldsmid, as well as the inveterate Zionists, Elliot (who had supported Zionism since the 1930s influenced by his relationship with the ardent and active Gentile Zionist, Baffy Dugdale) and Robert Boothby.[134] Overall they represented a motley collection of independent minded, 'liberal intellectual'[135] Conservatives: Spearman was on 'the left' on foreign policy issues but on 'the right' on economic matters;[136] Frank Medlicott, a National Liberal, was one of the 1945 'Brigadier Group'; John Jacob ('Jakie') Astor[137] was a former

PPS to Selwyn Lloyd, who had already informed his constituency association that he would not be standing again; the political buccaneer, Boothby was, of course, an ardent European;[138] and Nigel Nicolson's instincts were not those of a politician at all. 'His adoption of a high moral line – a very difficult thing to do in politics – was that of a member of the intelligentsia.'[139] It was ironic that his political neighbour in Bournemouth West was John Eden, whose warlike utterances caused his uncle considerable embarrassment.[140]

The Anti-Suez Group was formed as an instinctive reaction to the Government's military intervention in November 1956. Conservative backbench opposition to the use of force to settle the dispute over the Suez Canal had been growing in a haphazard manner prior to Eden's decision to launch a military operation against Egypt. Heald's speech in the House of Commons in September 1956, calling for a referral of the dispute to the UNO provided a rallying point for these dissidents, but hopes that Heald would thereafter lead the little group were dashed[141] when Heald refused to carry his criticism of the Government any further.

'It was a gradually coalescing movement. One would sound out others quite openly in the smoking rooms, who might point out a fellow dissenter, along the lines, "I know old George over there feels as you do".' Spearman came to act as their co-ordinator and quasi-leader in that 'he was the man in whose flat we met'.[142] Spearman was not very senior, but from his seat below the gangway, he had earned the reputation of an independent thinker, and 'respect as one who understood finance'.[143] There was an element of older MPs, such as Walter Elliot, whose unhappy feelings about Eden's policy encouraged their younger colleagues into open defiance; however, once the younger men had 'gone over the top', their elders declined to commit what appeared to be political suicide – there was a tendency to shake their heads in sorrow, along the lines of 'Poor fellow, I knew his father'.[144]

Although these MPs did not hold a coherent philosophy on Britain's place in the Middle East, they were on the party's progressive wing; they were traditional Tories who were anti-Socialist. With their mixture of ages, political experiences and political generations, they held markedly disparate views on ideal links with the Middle East. In marked contrast to Elliot and Boothby, William Yates was an ardent Arabist, who once appeared at the count in his constituency (The Wrekin) wearing an Arab headdress[145]; and Cyril Banks had taken a long-standing interest in the problems of Palestinian Arab refugees, and whose objections to Eden's Suez policy were no secret in Westminster. Banks' keen interest in Egypt had been demonstrated by two visits to that country over the previous two years; in December 1955 he had made an unofficial attempt to start talks between Egypt and Israel. Nor was there a common theme of 'anti-appeasement': Boothby and Nigel Nicolson, as the son of Harold Nicolson, were in the Churchill camp, and Medlicott had voted against Chamberlain in May 1940. On the other hand, Walter Elliot who was known to have been deeply unhappy about Munich, had not resigned over the issue – much to his later regret.

Despite their individualist approach to politics, these MPs shared a respect for the rule of law and diplomacy, together with a respect for observance of the Charter of the UNO. There was an acceptance of the necessity of the American alliance and many of these MPs had personal and/or business links with America.[146] Like the Suez Group, the Anti-Suez MPs jealously defended the right of an MP to exercise his individual judgement on behalf of his constituents. But unlike the Suez Group, all save one (Banks) kept their opposition within the scope of the party. In the violently partisan crisis, these dissidents took an extremely courageous stance, politically and personally, faced with trenchant opposition from many of their Conservative colleagues[147] and outright hostility from their constituency associations. Unlike the more reactionary rebels, the Anti-Suez group MPs did not escape censure by their local parties in the Suez crisis; only Boothby and Boyle survived politically unscathed.[148]

The respective fortunes of the Suez Group and Anti-Suez Group were paradoxical. Individual members of the Suez Group held a more important place within the party than has been appreciated hitherto, but despite excellent contacts and sizeable support in the House of Lords and in the country, its skilled organization and lobbying, the Suez Group suffered from the image of being composed of 'yesterday's men', which detracted from the force of its message. The faction exercised a powerful, but ephemeral influence. Ironically, the Anti-Suez

Group, despite its apparent small size, lack of organization and *ad hoc* nature, exercised a significant brake on the Cabinet in September and November 1956.

Some political commentators felt that the confrontation between the two factions was a battle within the aristocracy. The comment, 'Suez was lost on the playing fields of Eton'[149] holds a superficial truth in that some of the protagonists were old Etonians: Amery, John Eden, Hinchingbrooke, Pitman and Sir Charles Williams vs Astor, Boothby, Boyle, Nicolson, Nutting and Price. The bulk of the party was irate at the lengths to which these rebel MPs were prepared to carry their opposition to the Government. 'They feel lately that the divisions of the party have mostly been the work of the "aristos". "Our betters", laments Dr Johnson, "indulge in fratricidal strife while we the party proles look on helplessly at the ruin of our fortunes".'[150]

7 The Conservative Party and the Middle East: 1948–51

The Palestine crisis, Britain's relations with Egypt and the Abadan crisis provided the formative experiences for the Suez Group. While the Conservative party was in opposition, this was an inchoate group – indeed between 1948 and 1950, many of those who later became stalwart members of the Suez Group were not MPs – but their views coalesced with each successive crisis in the Middle East, and their determination to influence their party and the government increased accordingly.

Britain's paramountcy in the Middle East had evolved from the collapse of the Ottoman Empire after the First World War, through treaty rights, business interests, the Mandate in Palestine, and part-ownership of the Suez Canal Company. Britain's dominant position was reinforced after the Second World War by a network of treaties, her position as one of the victors in the recent struggle, the huge military base at the Suez Canal, a naval base at Aden, air squadrons stationed in Iraq, and rear bases in Cyprus and Malta. In addition, the commander of the Arab Legion in Jordan, General Sir John Glubb, was provided and paid for by the British Government; Britain had protectorates over the Persian Gulf Sheikdoms and conducted their foreign affairs through a Political Resident based in Bahrain. Britain also had enormous oil investments in Persia through the Anglo-Iranian Oil Company and a growing interest in the oil reserves of the Persian Gulf.[1]

PALESTINE

Palestine was the bastion in the informal empire in the Middle East. Britain had acquired the Mandate for Palestine in 1922; thereafter the territory was supposed to be the shield of the Suez Canal, the 'Clapham Junction of the British Commonwealth'.[2] Palestine offered the overland route between Iraq (where there were key British air bases) and Egypt (the Suez Canal Zone base), and the air route to India and the Far East passed through the Mandate territory. In addition, Haifa was at the Mediterranean end of the vital oil pipeline from Iraq and Iran (crucial to Britain's oil supply), and was potentially significant as an alternative to the Suez Canal base. This was to assume greater importance for Conservatives when Egypt demanded revision of the 1936 Anglo-Egyptian Treaty.

Conservative opinion varied on the best way to maintain Britain's prestige and influence in the region. Balancing the view of Palestine's strategic importance, which required a continued British presence or controlling influence, was the party's position as the heir to the 1917 Balfour Declaration which had promised a homeland to the Jews. In the Palestine conflict the Tory party was torn, privately and publicly, between moral duty and views of military necessity.

Whatever their views on the relative merits of Zionism, Conservatives concurred on the vital necessity of maintaining Britain's standing in the Levant. Just as before the Second World War, the major considerations were military: the need to protect Britain's position in the Middle East when the international horizon seemed likely to continue to be stormy. All saw the Palestine problem as 'linked to all the other questions in the Middle East',[3] especially Britain's future position in Egypt.

The Conservative party was also united in its desire to separate the twin problems of what to do with the European Jews and the Mandate. On the issue of Jewish immigration, Conservatives had tended to side with Arabs, fearing that to do otherwise would forfeit the confidence of the Moslem world[4] and the 90 million Moslems on the Indian subcontinent. Tories stoutly refused to concede that the Jews' suffering during the War gave them a unique claim upon the world's conscience and entitled them to unlimited immigration into Palestine.[5] For the most part Conservatives confined themselves to recommending the amount of immigration permitted should be to 'the limits of economic capacity'; it was repeatedly stressed that Britain should prevent 'putting an over-supply of Zionists into Palestine'.[6] Even Churchill, who had taken a highly unpopular line within his party by publicly supporting the Zionists, persistently encouraged the Labour Government to investigate other avenues in resettling the Jewish Diaspora from Europe.[7]

There was universal Tory criticism of extravagant promises made by Labour MPs during the 1945 election campaign in support of the Zionists,[8] which had raised hopes yet offered no decided policy.[9] There was general agreement that Conservatives must demand from the Government a much more firm and positive policy than hitherto[10], and widespread Tory concern at the apparent power vacuum in this key strategic region and its vulnerability to Russian infiltration.[11]

On the question of the political future of Palestine, the Conservative party was openly fractured[12] between the pro-Zionists who favoured a Jewish national state; the supporters of partition as an interim measure, leading to the eventual creation of a binational state;[13] and those who regarded the indigenous Arab population as the more important. Varying attitudes to America further complicated the picture.

The post-war Conservative party was at best ambivalent towards the Jews. The party had few Jewish voters and hardly any Jewish MPs. Many Tory MPs were fervently pro-Arab, influenced in part by a romantic idea of the Arab fostered by T.E. Lawrence[14] which had survived war-service in the Middle East. However, several senior Tories were Zionist supporters of long standing who felt, as heirs to the Balfour Declaration, it was their moral duty to support the Jews. It also seemed practical politics.

Churchill's position on the Palestine issue was crucial, given his extraordinary position on the Opposition benches as a foreign policy expert, world statesman, ex-prime minister, and prime minister-in-waiting. Churchill was an inveterate advocate of a Jewish homeland.[15] His support for Zionism had led him to oppose the 1939 White Paper which limited immigration into Palestine, and he had persisted in his proposal for partition against the advice of his Cabinet in 1945. Despite this opposition from his colleagues, notably from Eden, Churchill remained committed to the idea of partition.[16] Some Tories remained very suspicious of Churchill's Zionist/Liberal credentials and his stand was not popular with his party,[17] although Churchill was always careful to state that his stance was a personal view, and was measured in his support for Zionism in Parliament and his recommendations to Bevin. James Henderson Stewart was similarly restrained. Macmillan and Elliot, despite their pre-war support for the Jews, did not express an opinion in

Parliament at all. Boothby was the only other prominent Conservative publicly to back the Zionists which earned him opprobrium from his party[18] as the Jewish terrorist attacks against British troops escalated.

The bulk of the party accepted 'local home rule'[19] and were anti-partition. These MPs could use irrefutable geopolitical arguments to back their case. The Arab revolt in Palestine in the 1930s had demonstrated the indigenous population's opposition to unlimited Jewish immigration and partition, and turmoil in the area had offered outside hostile powers the opportunity to meddle. Britain's policy had increased Arab nationalism to Britain's later cost.[20] The Balfour Declaration was seen as 'a mistake';[21] the Conservative party's real moral duty lay in protecting the interests and desires of the indigenous Arab population who should be consulted first before any decisions were taken about their country's fate.

From the start many Conservatives were deeply concerned that by failing to put down the Jewish revolt, and by bowing to American pressure on immigration, Britain was by implication pursuing too Zionist a policy which would have a catastrophic impact on Arab opinion. The Zionists in Palestine, backed by America, were challenging the *status quo* with potentially disastrous strategic implications for Britain, at a time when Egypt was demanding a revision of the 1936 treaty, Britain's treaty relations with Iraq were under question, and Russia appeared to have revived to her traditional imperial quest for a warm water port.

There was a decided strain of anti-Semitism within the Tory party.[22] 'In spite of the Nazi atrocities against the Jews in the war, British public opinion and Conservative opinion remained ambivalent.' But when the fight against the British Mandate began in earnest and British troops were being killed 'an ugly Jewish backlash resulted... Episodes such as the hanging of the two British sergeants and the explosion at the King David Hotel inflamed anti-Jewish feeling in Britain and particularly in the Conservative party.'[23] Jewish outrages destroyed any inclination to make further efforts on behalf of Zionists. Conservative MPs recognized the paradox of the British Government using armed force to compel the Arabs in Palestine to take more Jews than they wanted and were furious at the 'disgraceful' government policy which had placed British troops in such an impossible position.[24] There should be no partition, because it would be 'utterly impossible to enforce partition on an unwilling Arab population without an international police force'.[25] There should be no Jewish state, and Britain should stand firm until the Zionists' attitude changed completely.[26]

The greatest source of Conservative anxiety derived from the Labour Government's failure to secure American cooperation over the Palestine question, despite an apparent affinity of interest in the region. There was a decided Tory ambivalence over America's proper place in the Middle East: Conservatives recognized that American support was vital to underpin any settlement,[27] but Britain was the rightful pre-eminent power in the region and should unashamedly assert her great power status.[28] Convinced that Bevin, if he was sufficiently firm, could persuade America to accept the responsibility for urging partition upon Britain,[29] Tories were exasperated by Washington's calls for unlimited Jewish immigration and contemptuous of Truman's susceptibility to domestic Zionist pressure: America seemed unfairly to be forcing Britain to bear the whole weight of Washington's policy, while the Moslems who were so important to the Empire were alarmed and estranged, with America sitting on the sidelines criticizing 'Britain's shortcomings with all the freedom of perfect detachment and irresponsibility'.[30] This frustration with American policy hardened into antagonism among the MPs who later came to form the Suez Group.

Similarly Conservative contempt for the role of the UNO grew as the crisis dragged on and permeated the entire party.[31] The majority of Conservatives had been initially shocked[32] by Churchill's call for the Mandate to be referred to the UNO in August 1946.[33] Gradually Tory opinion shifted, albeit reluctantly:[34] some backbenchers had reservations, on the grounds that UNO had already failed because of the attitude of Russia,[35] but the official Tory line was that whilst there was no complaint against this referral, the Labour Government's method and timing of the appeal was lamentable.[36] America and the United Nations should look to Britain for the lead;[37] it ill-accorded Britain's great power status to refer the issue to the Security Council with no recommendation on the desired settlement.

Had there been a united Tory cavalry charge upon the Treasury bench, a Conservative thesis might have stood a greater chance of influencing the Government, for although Labour's parliamentary majority was 146, the Labour party, too, was riven on the issue.[38] Despite the overwhelming and manifest Conservative sense of frustration that the Government was drifting at the mercy of outside events, having missed key opportunities,[39] the Conservative front bench throughout the crisis was careful to support Bevin in his attempts to involve America, and taking the matter to the UNO; criticism was reserved for method and timing. Eden recognized the problems Bevin faced as he struggled to deal with a difficult and emotive issue. More hard-headed on the problem of Palestine than his emotional leader, in a Cabinet paper before the War Eden had argued for limiting Jewish population in Palestine, on the grounds that the Middle East was an organic whole; Palestine in Arab eyes was an Arab country, the most fertile area of which was being handed over to an alien and particularly dangerous invader.[40]

Eden's support, as an ex-Foreign Secretary and acknowledged foreign policy expert, was of great value to the beleaguered Foreign Secretary throughout the crisis.[41] Bevin had to contend with an outspoken section of his supporters which was ardently pro-Zionist, as well as with an American Administration which was heavily influenced by the vociferous American pro-Jewish lobby, but which stubbornly refused to enforce the policy it advocated so publicly. Bevin's vain attempts to placate the Arab nations whilst reining in the more extreme Zionist demands merely served to alienate both camps in Palestine, and incurred the distrust of Washington.

Despite the Foreign Secretary's best efforts, Britain was obliged to relinquish the Palestine mandate without securing a satisfactory settlement between Arab and Jew. Conservatives no matter what their opinions on the ideal solution in Palestine regarded the decision to withdraw on 15 May 1948 as a total abnegation of Britain's responsibility to ensure a just settlement.[42] The party was 'unhappy and divided'[43] by the outcome of the Arab-Israeli war – which had proved contrary to popular Tory expectations that the Jews would to be annihilated[44] – and found it difficult to come to terms with the new State of Israel which, it was feared, would prove a disruptive force in the region. It had been established by 'completely casting aside the rule of law and the principles of the UN

Charter and of the Atlantic Charter'.[45] Unchecked immigration into Israel might prompt Israel to seek new borders for her burgeoning population. King Abdullah of Jordan was also suspected of territorial designs which might one day be detrimental to Britain's position and interests in the Levant.[46] Boothby was one of the few who drew the obvious conclusion that as the Israeli army was one to be reckoned with, there should be a realignment of Britain's treaties in the Middle East: King Abdullah, ruling the most progressive of the Arab states, should be encouraged to make a separate peace with Israel,[47] whatever the objections from Egypt. The two 'strong' states in the Middle East – Israel and Turkey – were being ignored: both were 'modern', 'significantly non-Arab' and firm in their opposition to Russia – all of which should make these two countries the natural pivot of British policy in the region.

Churchill and Eden urged Conservative dissenters and the Labour Government alike to 'face the facts': the Jews had established a government that functioned effectively and which had been recognized by the United States and Russia. Britain, with her 'many interests, duties and memories in Palestine and the Middle East... would surely be foolish in the last degree to be maintaining a sort of sulky boycott'.[48] A powerful additional reason was Britain's treaty obligations to Jordan. Notwithstanding this Conservative front bench endorsement for immediate recognition of the new State of Israel, Conservative criticism of Labour's handling of the Palestine question culminated in the decision to divide the House[49] in protest at the Government's policy of 'folly, futility and fatuity'. It was the first occasion in the 1945 Parliament in which the Conservatives had voted against the Government on a major issue of foreign policy. Even though the Government's majority dropped to 90, Labour's authority was not gravely damaged, merely shaken,[50] and Churchill was careful to explain that his party was not withdrawing its support for Bevin's foreign policy in general.

For the imperial wing of the party, many of whom later became stalwart members of the Suez Group, the Palestine débâcle was the first in a series of major disasters for British policy in the Middle East; it appeared an integral part of Labour's disastrous policy of retreat from Empire as Britain's abandonment of India, the jewel in the imperial crown, had immeasurably weakened her position in the Middle East.[51] Britain had let down the Arabs in Palestine; she had not ensured a just settlement[52] and had made enemies without rewarding or strengthening her friends. Britain's position, power and prestige had been damaged, as the British Government had not been able to impose its will on the region, was unable to hold sway against America, and had inflamed Arab nationalism, to the detriment of Britain's position in other Arab countries. This emerging faction of the party was anti-Israel for the most part, suspicious of American policy and designs in the Middle East and contemptuous of the UNO. The departure of Britain from Palestine without any residual influence strengthened these MPs' conviction that Britain must have a physical presence in the Middle East – and Labour had committed the cardinal sin of opening the question of Britain's withdrawal from the Suez Canal. The Palestine conflict did nothing to alter strategic perceptions that had endured since the 1930s.[53] The festering conflict between Arab and Jew which offered opportunities for Communist subversion further underlined the need for a secure British presence on the Suez Canal.

BRITAIN'S RELATIONS WITH EGYPT 1948–51

In considering Conservative reaction to later events in Persia in 1951, the history of Britain's relations with Egypt following the Arab/Israeli war of 1948 was of crucial importance. The Conservative party as a whole believed Labour's decision to open the question of the Suez Canal base immediately after the War had placed Britain in an unnecessarily vulnerable position in the Middle East.[54] Nor had the Tories believed it was justified: Britain would need to import military supplies through Egypt[55] to protect her position in Palestine. The idea that Egypt 'could ensure by her own resources the liberty and entire security of the Canal' (Article VIII of the 1936 Anglo-Egyptian treaty) was frankly laughable. While there was private awareness that the defence of the Canal might be affected by the atom bomb,[56] more immediate concerns focused upon the possible effect on the Sudan, an Anglo-Egyptian condominium.[57]

Conservative opinion concentrated upon the strategic importance of maintaining a British military presence in the Middle

East: control of this bridge between continents was seen to be of the 'first importance to any aggressive power in the Eastern Mediterranean and Levant'; therefore it was imperative that Britain, through her base at the Suez Canal, continue to hold this keystone in the arch of Western and Commonwealth defence, enabling Britain to act as a deterrent to possible Russian military aggression, and to react quickly should a crisis develop.[58]

By the late 1940s the problem of the future of Britain's substantial base in the Suez Canal Zone was compounded by the Labour Government's inability to settle the problem of Arab/Israeli animosity. Egypt refused to permit the passage of Israeli-bound cargo through the Canal, in direct contravention of the 1888 Convention governing international use of the Canal. Cairo's intransigence and the closure of the oil pipeline to Haifa from Iraq following the 1948–9 war meant the Haifa refinery was lying idle at a cost of $4 million a month to the British economy.[59] Some Conservatives feared that as the British economy became increasingly dependent upon Middle Eastern oil (rising to an estimated 82% in 1951), the success or failure of the European Recovery Programme would be tied more closely to the continued security of the Middle East.[60] The closure of the Haifa refinery was of particular importance during the Abadan crisis.[61]

For the Tories, the problem of securing passage through the Canal was twofold: the need to gain passage for vital oil supplies;[62] and the danger of British power and prestige being eroded by an inferior nation's ability to flout Westminster's will (and incidentally the rule of law) with impunity.[63] It was obvious Egypt's success in barring Israeli-bound traffic from the Canal spurred the nationalist clamour for Egyptian sovereignty over the Canal Zone base. Conservatives felt that the Egyptian people should be far more cooperative with the United Kingdom, in gratitude for Britain's sacrifice during the Second World War, both in terms of loss of life and the considerable cost of defending Egyptian territory from her Nazi/Fascist aggressors.[64] There was a large element of racism, albeit cloaked in a paternalistic guise, in Conservative attitudes to the Middle East, and in particular, towards Egypt. Many Conservatives were former soldiers who had served with the 8th Army in the Middle East, an experience which had done nothing to improve their poor opinion of Egyptians, either as soldiers or as administrators.[65]

General Conservative impatience with Labour's inability to settle these outstanding issues was mirrored by the feeling that Egypt should be concentrating on the wider issue of uniting against the threat of Communism, rather than taking a narrow nationalist view about the Anglo-Egyptian treaty. The outbreak of the Korean war in June 1950 inevitably reinforced Conservative anxiety of Russian encroachment in other areas of the world which were vulnerable to Communist infiltration. Now more than ever the Middle East appeared to be a power vacuum which posed an irresistible target for Russian aggression,[66] making a substantial British military presence in the region seem all the more imperative. The notion that Egypt could become neutral in any future conflict was simply not practicable.[67]

Conservatives were united on the need for international solidarity and preferably for active allies in the Middle East to bolster Britain's position.[68] Labour's crowning error was seen to be its persistent failure to persuade America that its vital interests were equally at stake and to secure joint cooperative action.[69] The Tripartite Declaration, signed by Britain, America and France in May 1950 which guaranteed the armistice frontiers of 1949, appeared a poor substitute for active cooperation, or even better, an Eastern Mediterranean or Middle Eastern pact – witness the efforts made by Churchill's government to secure a Middle East defence organization in 1951–52. A very small group of Tory MPs, notably Boothby and (after 1950) Julian Amery and Somerset de Chair, felt Israel was the obvious ally capable of providing effective resistance to Russian aggression. These MPs were increasingly critical of what they perceived to be the failure by successive British governments to harness Israel as a progressive and stabilizing force in the region.[70] Israel was denied arms necessary for its survival, while Britain continued to supply arms to Egypt, a nation that openly flouted British will by refusing free passage through the Suez Canal.

The nascent Suez Group carried the general Tory low opinion of Egyptians to extremes. Egyptian independence was regarded as an unhappy experience: 'Egyptianization' had been pushed through too rapidly, to the detriment of Egypt's real industrial interests, and misgovernment with the accompanying search for scapegoats – in particular foreign powers, with Britain as the ex-imperial presence leading the pack – had led to a decline in the rule of law and an increasing disrespect for international conventions. They endorsed the strategic arguments for a British military presence in the region and the need for the ability to react to a sudden and unexpected threat.[71] Convinced that there was no military justification for a revision of the Anglo-Egyptian treaty, they firmly contended that the treaty contained a provision for its indefinite continuation (Article X), as Britain had the option to take to arbitration the question of whether Egypt was capable of maintaining full security at the Canal – which most, if not all, Tories felt she was not. After the outbreak of the Korean war, these MPs regarded it as inconceivable that Britain could abandon the base and move it somewhere else in the Middle East, like 'some sort of suitcase'.[72] The Suez Canal and the Panama Canal were comparable in importance to Britain and America respectively.[73] Quite simply, Britain had to maintain a position of strength in the area to make an effective contribution to world security.

To these MPs, the Suez Canal base was vital to the maintenance of British leadership of a strong Empire; if Britain was pushed out of Suez the country would be dependent upon America and the Panama Canal for her air and sea communications with Australia and New Zealand.[74] They had no desire for Britain to be as dependent upon the United States for her defence in the Middle East as Britain was in Europe. Although they agreed with the official Conservative line on the need for Anglo-American cooperation in the region since Britain could not act alone,[75] they felt Britain's pre-eminent position in the region should be maintained and respected.[76] America should play a supporting, junior role,[77] while the gap in manpower created by the loss of the Indian Army should be filled by colonial troops recruited from East and West Africa.[78]

The emerging Suez Group disliked the Tripartite Declaration which was clearly aimed at eliminating traditional spheres of influence. If Britain was to continue to play its part effectively against Communist aggression in the Middle East, she must retain her sphere of influence[79] – a clear warning that the Government should impress upon the American administration that it interfered with British interests in the region at its own peril. The signature of the ANZUS pact in September

1951 governing the defence of the Pacific, which specifically excluded Britain from a region previously regarded as one of rightful influence, was to reinforce their determination that British influence in the Middle East was not to be eroded in a similar fashion. There was a decided feeling that the US attitude to 'colonialism' should not go unchallenged, and the general effect of regional pacts concluded piecemeal would be to dismember the British Empire.[80]

Despite initial Tory hopes[81] that the return of Nahas Pasha would signal an era of better understanding, negotiations on a revision of the 1936 Treaty continued in a desultory fashion throughout 1950 against a background of increasing Egyptian restrictions on British ships. Tories fumed at Labour's persistence in trying to negotiate with a blatantly unreliable nation[82] and at Cairo's ingratitude and unreasonableness,[83] accompanied by strident anti-British propaganda in the Egyptian press. 'If only the Government had pushed a stronger line of action our tankers would now be passing through the Suez Canal',[84] and the Haifa refinery would be going again. Such comments implied it was outrageous that an inferior nation should try to hold the British Empire to ransom. They urged the use of economic sanctions to force Arab cooperation over Haifa.[85] The incipient Suez Group's calls for the use of military equipment sales to Egypt to extract her compliance with Article IV of the 1888 Convention[86] enjoyed wider Conservative backbench support.[87] Churchill was in favour of using such pressure[88] whereas Eden was more cautious[89] – reflecting the Conservative party leader's affinity with this belligerent group and Eden's opposition, running contrary to the alignment one might have assumed of a particular group striving to capture the leadership's attention.

Britain's relations with the Wafd government came to a head with Cairo's call for an unconditional withdrawal of British troops from the Canal Zone and the unity of the Sudan and Egypt under the Egyptian crown on 15 November 1950. This coincided with the Attlee Government's decision to resume despatch of jet fighters and tanks to Egypt (suspended in September 1950 because of the demands of Britain's rearmament programme). Thereafter there was a marked Conservative backbench swing to support the use of the obvious levers of sales of military equipment.[90] Tories were incensed that the

Government appeared to be selling much needed equipment abroad – and to a suspect nation – ignoring the prior claims of the Commonwealth. Conservatives were also acutely aware of the interaction of events in the Middle East:[91] difficulties with Cairo coincided with problems with Tehran, where the Persian Parliament was steadfastly refusing to ratify the Anglo-Iranian Oil Company's Supplementary Agreement of 1949. Thereafter, the Conservative front bench adopted the tactics advocated by their robust backbench colleagues,[92] with Eden notably in the vanguard of the attack. Political circumstances favoured the Conservatives in the short term. Faced with a knife-edge majority and widespread Labour backbench unease about the wisdom of sending military equipment to a truculent government,[93] the Government was forced to concede a temporary suspension of arms shipments.

Gaitskell's announcement of the conclusion of the Anglo-Egyptian financial negotiations on 16 March 1950 similarly prompted the Conservative front bench to take up backbench suggestions of using Egyptian sterling balances in London[94] as a *quid pro quo* for free passage of British tankers through the Canal. Responding to Conservative disgust at Labour's failure to use a readily available lever, Eden moved an adjournment debate on 20 March 1951. The wider political implications could not be ignored: this lily-livered approach would have serious repercussions on Anglo-Persian relations, currently at a very critical stage with the proposal before the Persian parliament for the nationalization of the Anglo-Iranian Oil Company's interests. The more the Chancellor gave way to Egypt the more difficult it would be to stand up to Persia.[95] Despite this Conservative outrage and profound Labour backbench misgivings,[96] on this occasion there was no repeat of the Government's retreat of the previous autumn.

Throughout the Abadan crisis of 1951 Conservatives saw a continued interaction of events between Britain's positions in Egypt and Persia.[97] Britain's humiliation in Persia led to a stiffening of the official Tory line on Haifa and the Suez Canal. With the two largest British owned oil refineries in the world out of action, the time had come to take steps – if necessary a tanker escort through the Canal – to ensure that British tankers could go through to Haifa and other countries could have refined oil products to which they were entitled under international law.[98] And as negotiations on the Anglo-Egyptian Treaty stalled, Conservatives repeatedly raised questions on the continued sale of military equipment to the Cairo government, prompted by a fear that the British Government had not taken into consideration the demands of the country's own rearmament programme, in addition to a violent dislike of supplying a country which had 'behaved in such a shabby manner' towards Britain.[99] Tories were agreed no further supplies should be forwarded until treaty rights were observed. Their efforts were to no avail; Labour ministers insisted that substantial items of equipment were not being supplied and the complete cessation of all arms supplies might prejudice future talks.

THE ABADAN CRISIS: 1951

The Mossadeq government's decision to nationalize the Anglo-Iranian Oil Company, together with its subsequent refusal to submit to arbitration or to permit the export of oil under the old terms,[100] appeared the last straw to Conservatives, whose sensibilities were already flayed by Egyptian truculence over Haifa and the Canal Zone base. There was universal concern at the lack of effective protest and determined approach.[101] All sections of the party concurred it was the culmination of the absence of any effective policy in the Middle East.[102]

The Abadan crisis was more straightforward for the Conservatives than the Palestine débâcle. There were no complicating factors of prior commitments to an unpopular minority, nor arguments over Britain's moral obligations. Nor was there a problem over the appeal of differing Arab countries. However, again, there were differing currents of opinion on how best to respond to the challenge to Britain's position. Since the end of the Arab/Israeli war the existence of a group of MPs who were 'critical of the policy pursued generally by the Government in the Middle East'[103] had been increasingly apparent in the frequency with which certain names recurred on the Order Sheet, and interventions and speeches in debate. Their number was strengthened considerably after the General Election of February 1950 with the return of independent-minded pre-war MPs[104] and the election of younger MPs, whose war-time experiences and interests had given them a wide knowledge.[105] Although in the Abadan crisis this remained an informal group,[106] in essence the events of 1951 were the skirmish which determined the battle lines within the Conservative party over the Sudan and the future of the Suez Canal base once the Conservatives were returned to office.

The presence of two acknowledged experts on foreign affairs on the Tory front bench was increasingly an explosive cocktail as the informal hawkish faction knew they enjoyed Churchill's sympathy, if not his explicit support.[107] Throughout the Abadan crisis Churchill was more inclined towards the robust view than his deputy. Although Churchill enjoyed 'proper backbench pressure',[108] 'he always spoke with two voices on this'. As leader of Her Majesty's Opposition it was perfectly proper to attack the incompetent policy of a disastrous Foreign Secretary, and the opportunity was there to shy away from the unpleasantness of knowledge and the inevitable accompaniment of responsibility. On the other hand, as the possible future Prime Minister in an election year, circumstances demanded temperance and statesmanship. Therefore, for Churchill, the Abadan crisis was something of an uneasy balancing act for he 'loathed to be drawn into a position where he could be seen as in cahoots with the Government'.[109] Although emotionally drawn to the nascent Suez Group's remedy, Churchill counselled restraint in private meetings and in the party committees, and was noticeably subdued in public. His message was clear: he opposed evacuation, but only if British personnel were physically threatened should the Government send in troops.

Throughout the Abadan crisis Eden was the most prominent Opposition spokesman on Persia. Initially Eden had favoured doing 'nothing ... in a hurry',[110] but by mid-June he was leading vigorous Conservative calls for firm, effective action: namely a declaration that there would be no evacuation of British personnel from Abadan.[111] 'Privately, Eden agreed with Labour that the wisest course was to handle the matter calmly and not to get into precipitate action in the volatile Middle East.'[112] His robust line in public was undoubtedly fuelled by his poor opinion of Herbert Morrison's performance as Foreign Secretary and Conservative backbench pressure.

Eden and his moderate colleagues stopped short of calling for the Government to protect lives *and* property. Nor did they ask for troops to be sent in immediately. Military intervention should 'only [be] in the final resort'; it was hoped that the matter would not be allowed to drift to a point where the only choice facing Britain would be complete withdrawal from Persia and sending in troops.[113] Moderate Tories were acutely aware that if British troops moved into the oil fields, it would be very difficult to represent it as protective action, whilst accusing others of aggressive behaviour (i.e. Korea).[114] British intervention might lead to revolt in Tehran,[115] raising the spectre of Russian inspired intervention. 'Eden also knew the Truman Administration considered Mossadeq as a barrier against Communism who should be supported.'[116]

Eden moved to restrain the atavistic jingoism of some Tory backbenchers, ensuring that it was the Shadow Cabinet which led pressure upon the Government for debates on the crisis, and in trying to channel backbench agitation. On 7 June 1951 Fitzroy Maclean, Viscount Cranborne, David Ormsby-Gore, Amery, Anthony Head and Oliver Stanley tabled an EDM which accused the Government of failing to provide 'firm or coherent policy in the Middle East' which had gravely endangered British interests in the area, especially Persia, and deplored the weakness shown by the Government in its dealings with Egypt over the Suez Canal. The EDM urged the Government to take immediate steps to 'establish, after consultation with the Commonwealth, the United States of America and France, and in cooperation with the Governments of Greece and Turkey, an effective Middle East defence system designed to ensure the maintenance of peace in the area'. It was signed by 157 Conservative MPs, an extraordinary demonstration of the strength of party feeling on the Abadan issue, and the list included many senior backbench committee officials. There had clearly been a concerted effort by Tory whips[117] to turn this EDM into the Conservatives' manifesto on the Abadan crisis, and Middle Eastern affairs generally.

As the dispute with Persia appeared to reach a climax in mid-1951, it became increasingly difficult for Conservative party managers to ensure that the party spoke with one voice. At the outset of the crisis, unlike the later party disagreements over the Sudan and the Suez Canal base, the nascent Suez Group did appreciate and applaud Eden's position on Abadan;[118] similarly, the Conservative front bench reluctance 'to make the running' in challenging Morrison 'for fear of acquiring the label of "Warmonger" was understood.'[119] All Conservatives were aware of the party's conflicting roles: as the party of opposition, 'we were all free to say what we thought, and let fire over Abadan';[120] yet in its role of responsible government-in-waiting in a year when a general election seemed imminent, it behoved the party to be cautious, moderate and restrained.

Initially the informal Suez Group 'emulated the reserve of the Conservative front bench',[121] but rapidly came to describe publicly Morrison's policy as one 'of despair'.[122] These MPs did not regard the Persian crisis as an isolated phenomenon: the 'scuttle' from Palestine and sour relations with Egypt and Iraq had created a background of weakness and withdrawal which went a long way to explain recent events in Persia.[123] 'The nationalization of the Anglo-Iranian Oil Company's holdings by Mossadeq immediately raised the whole question of British influence in the Middle East. If he was allowed to get away with it, it followed almost automatically that someone [like Nasser] would want to nationalize the Suez Canal Company.'[124] They fumed at Herbert Morrison's inadequacies.[125] Nothing less than the survival of the British Commonwealth and Empire as an independent force in the world was at stake.[126] Legge-Bourke was goaded into throwing a penny contemptuously across the floor of the House at the Foreign Secretary, with the instruction that Morrison 'should put on another record'[127] – a gesture which was regarded as particularly shocking and received extensive press coverage.

Britain's commercial[128] and strategic interests in the Persian Gulf appeared to be under attack from two, equally undesirable quarters: Russia and America. Just as Persia was a traditional target of Russian expansion,[129] now there was a desire to deny Russia control of the oil fields of the Gulf as this would immediately treble Russian oil reserves.[130] Persistent rumours that Persia was in negotiation with US oil companies to take over the AIOC concession[131] fuelled Conservative suspicions of American oil interests over-influencing Truman's policy in the region; although there was little evidence of any such negotiations, it was undoubtedly in the back of the Persian government's mind that if agreement with Britain was not reached on Persia's terms, then US technicians could fill the breach.[132]

In addition to these MPs' fear that the Tudeh party would

triumph and that Persia would become a Russian satellite,[133] there was also the wider concern for Middle Eastern defence: if Russia swept through Iraq, Persia and the Levant, it would be of no avail that Greece and Turkey were members of NATO.[134] Since a purely British organized defence system in the Middle East was not feasible, reluctantly, they accepted the need for Anglo-American cooperation, but with the US playing a subsidiary role.[135] America should realize that 'the defence of the Middle East must primarily be a British responsibility' as 'the Middle East is the backbone of the Commonwealth and Empire'; these MPs had no desire whatsoever to see the sea and air routes to Australia and India lying through America and the Panama Canal.[136]

Implicit in this was the belief that Britain should not be constrained in the Middle East by Washington's attitude; it was, of course, desirable to act in concord, but this was by no means obligatory – a view surfaced repeatedly in the Conservative party in the 1950s, only to be refuted brutally in the Suez crisis. Their ideal was for a joint Middle Eastern defence force,[137] but its composition varied. Amery preferred an arrangement whereby the British and Turkish armies should have primary command, with contributions from Israel and the Arabs nations, together with American and French contingents.[138] Other future members of the Suez Group were decidedly unenthusiastic about the inclusion of Israel; Fitzroy Maclean's stated preference was for a strong Western force, together with troops from the Commonwealth, America and France.[139]

As their frustration with Labour's policy, or lack thereof, mounted, so the demands of the incipient Suez Group grew more vociferous. While these MPs agreed with their senior colleagues that there should be no evacuation of AIOC personnel, they wanted a stout declaration that force would be used if necessary to protect British lives and commercial and strategic interests, on the grounds that if the Government were to declare its determination to send in troops this would make war less, not more, likely.[140] These MPs was aware of a Cabinet split on the issue: 'At first Morrison was very friendly and sympathetic ... in his replies. Then I noticed he got increasingly irritated and uncomfortable about the whole matter. I was stopped in the lobby by Hector McNeil [Minister of State at the Foreign Office] who said "You're going for the wrong man. He wants to put troops in. The Cabinet are stopping him on the grounds it would upset the UNO [in Korea] – the Americans would not wear it".'[141] Conservatives were singularly unimpressed by such arguments. In the first place, as Eden had pointed out, they felt entitled to unstinting American support in Persia in return for Britain's loyalty to the US in Korea. Washington should be made to acknowledge that it was in her interests, economically, politically and strategically, to have continued British pre-eminence in the Persian Gulf. Secondly, in this faction's view, Britain did not have to defer to American wishes. Once aware of the schism within Cabinet, these MPs were relentless in trying to drive a wedge publicly between Morrison and Attlee, pressing the Foreign Secretary to admit that by his earlier statements to the House he had given the impression that he was prepared to use force, and urging troops to be sent in immediately[142] – the principal effect would be psychological.[143]

Infuriated by Morrison's refusal to be drawn on a specific line of action,[144] this faction was also determinedly pressing its line on the Conservative front bench, through an EDM[145] and in the party committees. Their efforts, which enjoyed wider support from senior Tories such as Lord Salisbury,[146] Lord Dunglass,[147] Sandys[148] and Head,[149] prompted swift moves by Conservative party managers to avert a public and potentially damaging split by public disclaimers of internal strife,[150] and attempts to coordinated party line through the 1922 Committee.[151] Dissatisfied with the Labour Government's response to their critical backbench motion, and what they regarded as Labour's continued pusillanimous behaviour, immediately after the Persian oil debate on 21 June 1951 Fitzroy Maclean and 28 Conservatives tabled a further EDM[152] deploring the Foreign Secretary's refusal to give an assurance that the Government would take the 'necessary measures to protect British lives and installations'. Unlike the earlier more moderate EDM this motion was phrased in stronger terms, calling on the Government to use force to defend property as well as lives. This went further than the Conservative leadership and the more moderate wing of the party were prepared to go, since in the debate Eden specifically had excluded the protection of installations.

Hugh Berrington describes these MPs as being predominantly younger, elected since the War who had had 'no share in the pre-war policies of appeasement but would have absorbed its lessons. To such men Labour's policy of imperial retreat and its compliance with the demands of local nationalist leaders may have been reminiscent of what, by then, was regarded as the disastrous course of the Baldwin and Chamberlain governments.'[153] There were, however, notable exceptions: although the average age of these MPs was 42, Sir Herbert Williams, Captain Waterhouse and Viscountess Davidson were noticeably of a different political vintage and certainly had participated in the 'pre-war policies of appeasement' through their support for Chamberlain in 1938 and 1940.

Although this group 'was still spontaneous'[154] it was increasingly obvious that there was a discrete Conservative backbench faction which was prepared to take a vociferous interest in Britain's position in the Middle East. Of the above signatures, six went on to be active members of the Suez Group in the 1950s.[155] Soames' signature is a conundrum: was he acting as his father-in-law's spokesman on the backbenches, or on his own initiative? Soames had not impressed his contemporaries with his political acumen at this point, which, to every one's great surprise, he was later to display as Churchill's PPS.[156] 'I would guess he would have had Churchill's tacit support. To sponsor an EDM is such a natural action for a backbencher, that I am doubtful whether Soames felt the need to *consult* his father-in-law. But he could count on his natural feeling of support... I think it was a question of Churchill letting the backbenchers "fly the flag", while he looked round in a supportive way – though not actually "tipping them the wink".'[157]

As the AIOC staff were increasingly beleaguered, this emerging faction pressed their front bench in the party committees that a firm line should be taken with both Persia and Egypt.[158] Despite their leaders counselling caution, the weight of opinion shifted in these critics' favour as they tapped the profound concern over the possible effects on British prestige throughout the Middle East[159] and the deep sense of humiliation within the party; Britain seemed to being seen off by a 'Persian jack-in-office'.[160] The critics seized the opportunity of the debate on the Middle East at the end of the summer session to issue a firm statement of their views. Undaunted by the clear instruction from their front bench that Conservatives should not demand that the installations be protected,[161] Amery and Maclean pressed the Prime Minister to give a declaration that the Government would use all means at its disposal to protect British lives and interests. If British objectives were achieved by negotiation so much the better, but the Government was urged not to negotiate while AIOC personnel were being harassed.

Although the emerging Suez Group failed in its efforts to persuade Churchill and Eden to press for military intervention – the more moderate recognized that this demand for action would have taken the Government a good deal further than it had so far been willing to go, or indeed that the Opposition leaders in the Commons had urged they should go[162] – under pressure from the Tory backbenches Eden and his more moderate front bench colleagues demanded that AIOC personnel would not be evacuated from Abadan, and that the Conservative party would support any Labour Government measures to defend them at the refineries. Eden's robust (but still qualified) stance also undoubtedly raised expectations that he would be similarly hawkish in defence of British interests elsewhere in the Middle East.

The Tory militants did have another, less positive influence upon the public bearing of their party in the crisis. The Conservative front bench needed to promote a responsible, coherent line in an election year, yet was faced with wayward and extremely vocal backbenchers. This, combined with the political luxury of opposition, meant that the party never confronted the question of how a Conservative government would have risen to Mossadeq's challenge. As *The Times* commented,[163] it was never possible to say how the Tories would have handled the dispute.

The Conservatives felt they had succeeded in finally wringing an admission from the Labour Government that Britain was prepared to stay in Abadan.[164] Such satisfaction proved short-lived. Tory relief at Attlee's decision to call a general election in October was balanced by the fear that events in Persia were moving inexorably towards disaster, while the Labour Government wrung its hands.[165] The worst Tory fears were realized. Denied American support and outmanoeuvred by Mossadeq in referring the matter to the UNO, the Attlee Government had no choice but to sanction the withdrawal of the remaining AIOC personnel. The Conservative assault on Labour's policy during the election campaign was 'to a large extent neutralized, since the Government was able to create the impression that the Opposition would have handled the matter even more disastrously'.[166]

Conservative urgings to use force did not affect the debate within the Cabinet, although these may have goaded Morrison on since the Foreign Secretary was enthusiastic for intervention, as was Shinwell, the Minister of Defence. The crux of the matter as far as the Cabinet was concerned never surfaced in public debate: namely, the impossibility of using force in the dispute in opposition to America, given Britain's support for America in the UNO over North Korea's invasion of South Korea. The outcome of the Abadan crisis revealed Britain could not take military action in the Middle East with impunity. However, a sizeable section of the Conservative party refused to accept the logic of the need to observe the UN Charter and to act only with American support. Britain's humiliation was attributed to the Foreign Secretary's 'ignorant laziness and lack of understanding of foreigners',[167] his 'flabby diplomacy',[168] not deference to Britain's mainstay in Europe.

To a great extent Eden was also guilty of this, with disastrous results in the Suez Crisis. He and Churchill were briefed by Attlee following the Cabinet's decision on 27 September 1951 not to use force without American support, on the grounds that Britain did not have the strength to act alone in defiance of America. In 1956 discussions with Washington never precisely considered the use of force[169] and Eden never asked himself the difficult question of whether America would oppose British military intervention.

As far as the Suez Group was concerned, Abadan was the 'preparatory exercise' in the Conservative party's future relations with Egypt. It helped identify people who cared about the Middle East, and who worried about the appeasement of Middle Eastern radicalism.[170] The crisis helped coalesce ideas about Britain's ideal place in the region, and the optimum defence arrangement. Specifically the events of 1951 helped concentrate Conservative attention on Britain's future in the Suez Canal Zone, causing an early declaration of what was to become the Suez Group's thesis: a request for the reaffirmation of Britain's treaty right under the Anglo-Egyptian treaty to maintain a garrison in the Canal Zone, that all measures be taken to restore free passage through the Canal, and a clear expression of determination from Westminster not to leave the Sudan 'until such time as the Sudanese people can freely determine their own destiny'.[171] In the critics' view, Britain had taught that terrorism paid: King Abdullah of Jordan[172] had been 'killed because he was a friend of Britain and the Middle East no longer believed that Britain could or would protect her friends . . . For six years the Government have sought to conciliate the Egyptian regime . . . It is high time that we turned our backs on any attempt to appease the Egyptian government.'[173] The incoming Conservative Government had been warned.

8 The Conservatives in power: Egypt and the Sudan 1951–53

The relatively short, but very heated party battle over the Anglo-Egyptian agreement on the Sudan proved a watershed in backbench opinion. It provided the catalyst for the 'Sudan Group',[1] from which grew the active and extremely vocal faction, the Suez Group. The furore over the proposed agreement was the most serious revolt Churchill's government had yet faced, coming on top of internal wrangling over transport policy, commercial television and government expenditure. The party was already excited by Egyptian truculence over Britain's future in the Suez Canal base, the strategic importance of which was believed to have increased with the tension of the Cold War, and it was well known on the backbenches that Churchill was at loggerheads with his Foreign Secretary in Cabinet on Eden's Egyptian policy.

Backbench unrest over the issue of Sudanese self-determination equalled later Conservative discontent over the Suez Base Agreement; indeed, 'some said Eden had even more of a fight [over the Sudan]'.[2] Certainly, Eden was on the point of resignation,[3] a possibility of which he never hinted in his autobiography when writing about his battle over the future of British troops in the Canal Zone. It was to prove a considerable test of the Foreign Secretary's powers of persuasion, and cost him dear in terms of his support from those who had been persuaded by his vigorous statements in the Abadan crisis that he was 'sound'. Eden did not command uniform respect in the Parliamentary party, although he was firmly entrenched as a leading member of the pantheon of Conservative gods as far as the party in the country was concerned. Admittedly in 1951 his parliamentary supporters far outnumbered his critics. However, those Conservatives (such as Waterhouse and Sir Herbert Williams) who did not trust his espousal of more progressive domestic policy, came to form an unlikely alliance with those

Tories who were at odds with Eden's indifference to Britain's involvement in European integration (Amery, and later Biggs-Davison). This coalesced into the third strand of opposition to Eden: criticism of his Middle East policy.

As questions persisted about Churchill's continuing leadership, the rumbles of discontent grew. The party rank and file felt increasingly ignored by their aging leader,[4] just as the friction between Eden and Churchill, which belied the public image of the Prime Minister and Foreign Secretary working in perfect harmony, opened the door for the critics of the Government's Middle East policy. As well as being the 'arch-appeaser' in the Middle East, Eden was also Churchill's heir apparent.[5] His assumption of the party leadership could not fail to affect the balance of power within the party. This internal political discontent obliged Eden to pay assiduous attention to the presentation of his policy on the Sudan and Egypt to minimize backbench objections, and magnified his conflict with Churchill, since the Foreign Secretary could not count on the good temper of the party in the Commons in his battle with the Prime Minister. Although Eden's policy enjoyed the support of the majority of his Cabinet colleagues,[6] the existence of a sizeable faction of discontented backbenchers enabled Churchill to conduct his own war of attrition.

Although the legacy from the Labour Government in the Middle East did not seem a happy one, there was considerable optimism that Britain's position in the region could be restored after the rout from Abadan, or at least the line held: Churchill the titan who had fulminated against the 'scuttle' of Palestine, was in charge once more; and Eden was back at the Foreign Office, the man who had originally negotiated with Nahas Pasha the 1936 Treaty, a man of proven diplomatic ability and undisputed knowledge of world affairs, and who had encouraged the Conservative diehards by his strong stand in the Abadan affair. Thus Conservatives hoped that the Persian fiasco would prove merely a setback, and with assiduous attention, Britain's former position and prestige could be recovered; the damage, although acknowledged to be serious, was not seen as irreparable.

Eden believed there were only two great problems facing Britain on the international scene: Persia and Egypt.[7] The former ceased to be a bone of contention within the Tory party. With Eden's policy of 'cautious restraint'[8] towards the Mossadeq government over London's outstanding claims for compensation,[9] the issue dropped below the political horizon as far as the mainstream of the party was concerned. Occasional questions were raised in the House and in the Foreign Affairs Committee over the likelihood of a settlement, but on the whole the matter was left to the Foreign Secretary's discretion. For this Eden had to thank private knowledge among MPs[10] of the contacts between the CIA and MI6 in Persia. The calming effect of their inside information (confirmed by Eden's hint in the Foreign Affairs Committee that 'America will never let anyone alone'[11]) was not apparent at the time.[12] A final settlement of Britain's outstanding claims had to wait until after the fall of Mossadeq in July 1953, following a *coup* inspired by the CIA using the contacts established by MI6.[13]

Despite initial Conservative hopes, the nationalization of the AIOC proved the harbinger of increased threats to Britain's commercial and military interests from Arab nationalism. Relations with Egypt over the Anglo-Egyptian condominium of the Sudan and the continued presence of British troops in the Suez Canal Zone proved the main points of contention in foreign policy for the Conservative party between 1951 and 1954. The swell of feeling had been mounting throughout 1951: the negotiation of the Egyptian Sterling Balances Agreement in March had drawn sharp Tory criticism and Conservative feeling throughout the Abadan crisis had been exacerbated by difficulties with Egypt over the 1936 Treaty. The humiliating evacuation from Abadan in October 1951 compounded London's difficulties: encouraged by the spectacle of Tehran's successful defiance of John Bull, Egypt was spurred on to commit further outrages in her war of attrition to force Britain's withdrawal from the Canal Zone base, and to press more fiercely King Farouk's claim to sovereignty over the Sudan and the Nile waters.

The Conservative backbenches were united on three points: they supported their government as it held to the outgoing Labour Government's refusal to accept Egypt's unilateral abrogation of the 1936 treaty (announced on 8 October 1951); they concurred with Eden's desire to protect Britain's power and prestige in the Middle East; and it was their universal view that the base remained the best point from which the defence of the Middle East could be conducted. Whatever Tory appreciation of the validity and strength of nationalism in Egypt, the Conservatives, leaders and supporters alike, all felt Egypt was making a tragic mistake if she thought she could remain neutral in an East–West war as long as there remained a threat of Soviet aggression. Convinced that Cairo must be brought to face wider realities posed by the Russian threat to the Northern Tier, to which all requirements of satisfying national feeling should be subordinated,[14] these politicians regarded the Wafdist government's arguments of the threat posed by the continued presence of British troops merely as proof that the Egyptian leaders were victims of communist propaganda and misinformation.

Thereafter, the strands of party opinion divided. The Conservative mainstream accepted Eden's assessment of the requirements of Britain's post-war role balanced against her straitened resources. In Eden's opinion, it was vital for London to reduce Britain's global military commitment, whilst maintaining British prestige. He recognized the danger involved in this retreat and was profoundly concerned that too rapid a reduction of Britain's presence might destroy Britain's credibility abroad. In any case, his party's internecine conflict denied the Foreign Secretary this option since the Government could not carry its supporters, let alone public opinion,[15] on a policy of running down boldly Britain's onerous overseas commitments.

But Eden was convinced a contraction of the British presence in the region was imperative, gambling that once the irritant of British troops was removed from the Canal Zone base, Anglo-Egyptian relations would improve sufficiently to allow a regional defence organization to offset this shedding of Britain's responsibilities and encourage America to take the lead.[16] There was general Conservative support for a Middle East Defence Organization,[17] but the Conservative Government's attempts to involve Egypt with Britain, Turkey, France and America in a Middle East defence organization between 1951 and 1952 foundered on Egyptian determination to remove all foreign troops from her soil, and Washington's refusal to join except at Egypt's express invitation.

Eden's view of the vital necessity of removing British troops was not shared by a vocal section of Tory backbenchers, whose opinions enjoyed wider support within the party. From the start of Churchill's peace time administration, these MPs urged the Foreign Secretary to take a 'firmer line' with Egypt.[18] Whilst this incipient group recognized that the number of British troops currently in the Suez Canal Zone considerably exceeded the allocation under the arrangements of the 1936 treaty, these MPs saw no reason to renegotiate the terms; these, they argued, entitled Britain to remain in the Canal Zone beyond 1956, and they entertained an increasingly sceptical view of the benefits to be derived from negotiating with such an unreliable and improvident people. This faction was infuriated by Eden's determination to try to negotiate a replacement treaty with Egypt against a background of continuing guerilla warfare in the Canal Zone, and attacks on British lives and property which culminated in the Cairo riots of January 1952. Increasingly alarmed at possible concessions to Egyptian nationalism, they feared that Britain was incurring the odium of using strength without any of the stability which a policy of strength, if wisely applied, should have secured.

This section of the party regarded as specious in the extreme the argument that Britain's continued presence could only bring about the war which it was supposed to avert. Egyptian nationalism appeared narrow-minded and misplaced; the nationalist movement was dismissed as a motley bunch of pilferers, religious extremists, and communist agitators bolstered by the Cairo poor and the press, in the face of which the Wafdist government was proving lamentably feeble. Yet, there remained a hangover of Britain's nineteenth century 'civilizing mission', and the assumption that Britain was only acting for the good of the (unworthy and ungrateful) Egyptian populace was deeply engrained in their psyche.

While their opponents criticized them for being 'less solicitous about money and resources',[19] these MPs were far from blind to the parlous state of the British economy. But they refused to accept the logic of wholesale withdrawal overseas, and bitterly resented the passing of Britain's imperial greatness. They were aware through their contacts with the Army that military opinion was 'almost unanimous that the best base for defending the area will always be the Suez Canal because of communications and existing installations'.[20] Therefore for the emerging Suez Group, its sympathizers and the Conservative press (especially the Northcliffe and Beaverbrook groups) the region remained a vital sphere of influence and nothing should be done which might undermine the country's reputation and resolve. Britain's pre-eminence there was part of the natural order.

Eden very quickly encountered difficulties with backbench colleagues and the Cairo authorities in his determined pursuit of a negotiated settlement with Egypt – seen in the extraordinary letter written by the Chairman of the 1922 Committee, Derek Walker-Smith, to Eden in February 1952, giving the Committee's support to the Foreign Secretary on Egypt and the Sudan.[21] By the spring of 1952 Eden had also aroused the wrath of his leader. Concerned about the 'strong forces within the Tory party which were deeply stirred by the prospect of moral surrender and physical flight',[22] of which he was well aware from reports from the Chief Whip, Churchill himself was congenitally opposed to any imperial retreat and was furious with the conciliatory line his Foreign Secretary was taking with the Cairo government.[23] Churchill was in no hurry to renegotiate the pre-war treaty; he was firmly of the view that Britain was in a position of strength and there was no urgency to conclude an agreement 'which sacrificed all Britain had striven for for so many years'.

After the overthrow of King Farouk in July 1952, the majority of the Cabinet concurred with Eden on the need to conciliate the new Neguib regime, in marked contrast to Churchill who felt that Neguib's increasingly critical and hostile statements about Britain as the autumn went on should be met with clear signs that Britain would not appease the new government. Churchill was extremely reluctant to concede that Britain had to withdraw from the Canal Zone base. He wanted Britain to hand over her responsibilities in Egypt to an international organization and he fervently hoped that America would take some share in the responsibility of protecting the waterway.[24]

Division at the top gave backbench critics greater opportunity to press their case, just as the emergence of a vocal backbench faction gave the Prime Minister powerful ammunition in Cabinet. The demand by the young Egyptian army officers for serious negotiations for British withdrawal prompted Amery and Waterhouse to take further soundings within the party to form a cohesive group to fight any such proposal; and fortified by backbench support, Churchill conducted a determined rear guard action, both within the Cabinet, and by nods, winks and asides in the corridors of Westminster in support of the rebels on his own benches.

CONSERVATIVES AND THE SUDAN

The Conservative Government's reaffirmation of Britain's commitment to Sudanese self-determination[25] had further complicated Anglo-Egyptian relations, already strained by the Cairo government's unilateral abrogation of the 1936 treaty, as King Farouk's ministers were determined to assert sovereignty over the whole of the Upper Nile. Conservatives had been concerned about the future of the Sudan since Attlee's statement in 1946 on the withdrawal of British forces from Egypt.[26] Eden's expressed determination to honour Bevin's pledge of 27 March 1946 to Sudanese self-government, together with his view that the burden of defence could, and should be reduced, ran directly contrary to the beliefs of a sizeable faction of Tory backbenchers, who stoutly advocated that the Sudanese should not be sacrificed to conciliate the Egyptians.[27] These critics assiduously cultivated their links with Sudanese politicians to glean information which could be used as ammunition to prevent a 'sell-out'.[28]

The feeling that the Sudan was being thrown away to appease Egypt went far beyond the emerging Suez Group's apparent numbers in the Commons, and was supported by elements in the Conservative press. Throughout 1952 there was great anxiety lest the Government would make extensive concessions to the Egyptians on the Sudan, under pressure from the Americans who were strongly suspected of a pro-Egyptian bias.[29] These fears, already buoyed by the behaviour of Caffrey, the American Ambassador in Cairo, were aggravated by press reports covering the arrival of H.M. Hoskins as Head of the Middle East Department at the State Department, who was 'understood to have tried to persuade the Sudanese leaders to support the Egyptian demand for Egyptian sovereignty.'[30]

Negotiations with Egypt prior to July 1952 foundered on

Egypt's refusal to separate the issues of the Sudan and the British presence in the Canal Zone. Although the Neguib government proved no more susceptible to the idea of Egypt joining a Middle East defence organization, the July revolution did open the way to a negotiated settlement of Anglo-Egyptian differences, since it finally separated the two contentious issues. The fall of King Farouk removed all legitimate claim by the Egyptian government to sovereignty over the Anglo-Egyptian condominium. However, this did not diminish Cairo's hopes of ultimately controlling the whole of the Upper Nile. Neguib, himself half-Sudanese and educated at Gordon College in Khartoum, hoped to use his origins and the Egyptians' newfound role as comrades-in-arms with the Sudanese to tie an independent Sudan firmly to Egypt. In the meantime, Egypt could pose as the champion of Sudanese independence. Britain could not now renege on her public commitment to Sudanese self-determination.[31]

Conservative anxiety hardened into outrage when the details of the proposed Anglo-Egyptian agreement over the condominium became known in January 1953. This concern extended far beyond the diehard wing of the party, who opposed self-government on imperial grounds. Other Conservatives sympathetic to Sudanese self-determination, such as Douglas Dodds-Parker who had served in the Sudan Civil Service, and Edward Wakefield, a former member of the Indian Civil service (both of whom had friends and excellent contacts in the Sudan) were profoundly disturbed. These MPs agreed that the Foreign Office line on the Sudan was correct on the importance of taking the problem of the Sudan out of Anglo-Egyptian relations,[32] but they were fearful of future independence of the Sudan after self-government. Tories were convinced that the interests of the Sudanese had been jeopardized by the proposed agreement;[33] Britain's administration of the condominium through the Sudan Civil Service was seen as an outstanding feat of government by all sections of the party,[34] and the proposed replacement appeared fraught with difficulties.

This party discussion on the Sudan was part of the 'gradual decolonization debate ... It struck very deep emotional chords in the Tory party; there was an emotional depth to duty. They hated the fashionable view which mocked Britain's contribution to development.'[35] In these MPs' eyes, Britain was rushing

Sudanese self-government for misguided reasons. Critics questioned Eden's arguments that the deteriorating relations between London and Khartoum justified a speedy resolution to the matter and early elections; Patrick Maitland and Fitzroy Maclean argued that reports of Anglo-Sudanese tension were completely at variance with previous appraisals, and suggested that the Government's sources were unreliable. In addition, there was a widespread conviction that Britain was reneging on her responsibility towards the Southern Tribes of the Sudan who were culturally and racially very different from their Arab, Moslem northern neighbours. There was an underlying concern that a mere political settlement could not protect the Southern tribes from incursions from the North.[36] They argued that less than one per cent of the Southern Sudanese were literate, or had any sort of political knowledge or experience: to talk of self-government for such a people was 'only a mockery, and an abandonment of our trust'.[37] If the Noble Savage tried to protect himself, the result would be civil war. The memory of the bloodbath that had accompanied Indian independence was fresh in people's minds.[38]

Deeply worried that Egyptian money would corrupt Sudanese politicians and the electorate, many backbench MPs were unhappy with Government assurances that the Sudan would be free to seek Commonwealth association with Britain after independence.[39] Eden's assurances that the Sudanese could choose between complete independence, a link with Egypt or a link in some form with Britain were seen as empty promises. As far as his critics were concerned, Eden could promise until he was blue in the face that 'complete independence did not exclude the right of any country to apply, if it so wishes, for association with or membership of the British Commonwealth';[40] he had not made this sufficiently clear to the Egyptians[41] – Neguib's swift contradiction of the Sudanese right to associate with Britain once the country was independent seemed to demonstrate that it was 'quite impossible to accept the word or the signature of the Egyptians'.[42]

There had been private Conservative suggestions for Britain 'to make arrangements with the Sudanese even in defiance of the Egyptians if necessary'.[43] These plainly extended beyond Commonwealth status, to include a separate arrangement for the Southern Sudan, whose tribes were known to be profoundly disturbed by the proposed settlement. Eden refused to countenance such suggestions, stressing in his statement on the progress of negotiations concerning the Sudan's future on 20 January 1953, that the Government did not propose to add to the safeguards in the draft self-governing statute which gave the Governor General special powers to protect the interests of the Southern provinces. This and his comment regretting the suspicion Britain had wanted to detach the Southern provinces, were clear indications that the Foreign Office had been under pressure to implement this option. His backbench critics regarded his refusal to make active provision for either Commonwealth status or certainly a special treaty relationship[44] as 'a great mistake: it was a passive, not an active foreign policy'.[45]

In the view of Conservative backbench critics, any settlement should be based on the long-term welfare of the Sudanese. This was interpreted as an unhurried progression to self-government, involving the continued, long-term presence of the British in the country. What was needed was a barrier in the region, not a bridge between Africa and the Middle East, to prevent Middle Eastern disorders spreading south into the East African colonies. The Mau Mau emergency in Kenya merely underlined the argument for the need to protect Britain's air communications with East Africa;[46] and the unrest in the colony undermined the notion that Britain could establish an alternative military base there.[47]

Other backbench critics were convinced that self-government would be detrimental to the security in the area: an independent Sudan alongside Egypt with the British administration withdrawn was very likely to be a source of constant friction in the region. They entertained fears of Sudanese claims that Britain had allowed Egypt too much Nile water, with the ever-present threat that the Sudan might interfere to alter the allotment in her favour. Given that the Sudan was sparsely populated while Egypt was manifestly overcrowded on the available cultivated land, Egypt would be subject to immense economic pressure to widen her boundaries; if matters did lead to armed conflict the Sudan was unlikely to be able to defend herself, faced with her northern neighbour's industrial and financial potential.

For the 'Sudan Group', this untimely withdrawal from the Sudan also had to be seen in the context of Britain's future in the Canal Zone base. By the time of the young Egyptian army officers' *coup d'état*, there had been a widespread suspicion in Conservative circles that the question of the evacuation of British troops from the Suez Canal (along with the problem of the defence of the Canal) had been settled in the confidential talks. Reports had appeared in the press at the beginning of May 1952 that it seemed that Britain's acceptance of evacuation from the Canal Zone would be met on the Egyptian side by a willingness to negotiate an engagement of foreign technicians to help the Egyptian Army to make the Canal base safe and to discuss in detail Egypt's part in Middle East Defence. Foreign Office disclaimers of the alternative of Cyprus[48] seemed highly suspicious. Britain's departure from the Canal base would remove any sanction London possessed over Egypt's continued observance of the Anglo-Egyptian agreement on the Sudan.

These critics also questioned the benefit such an agreement would confer on Anglo-Egyptian relations, arguing that Eden was grossly misinformed if he thought that settlement of Anglo-Egyptian differences over the Sudan would improve Anglo-Egyptian relations. Selwyn Lloyd, the Minister at the Foreign Office, was forced to concede that Egypt might negotiate just as hard over the Canal question.[49] The Conservative stalwarts feared that the termination of the Anglo-Egyptian condominium would only serve to strengthen immeasurably Cairo's hand in its attempts to secure the evacuation of the Canal base: the presence of British administrators was a necessary counterweight to the continued presence of British troops in the Canal Zone.

Therefore, not only was Britain failing in her responsibilities, but the proposed arrangement appeared to offer boundless opportunities for increased Egyptian influence over a newly independent southern neighbour. Conservative opponents of imminent Sudanese independence feared that the Foreign Office was being seduced into an agreement which, once concluded, would free Neguib and his colleagues to pressure the Sudan by bribery and other means to seek unity with Egypt. They had little hope that Egypt would respect an agreement, and it would be highly dangerous to assume that Cairo would do so.[50]

Eden was well aware that he had a fight on his hands with his backbenchers.[51] He had appeared before the Foreign Affairs Committee in December 1952[52] to inform his backbench colleagues on the progress of the 'tough negotiations on the Sudan', and was obliged to address the committee again at the end of January to ward off growing criticism, assuring his colleagues that two particular points required attention: the power of the Governor General to act in an emergency, and safeguards for the Southern Sudanese. The Foreign Secretary insisted that the Governor General should press ahead with elections, and that if no agreement was reached 'it must not appear to be our fault'.[53]

However, Eden had not anticipated the mammoth battle he faced in the combination of a defiant Churchill in Cabinet and outrage on Tory backbenches. Although he and Churchill had clashed over their preferred approach to Egypt during the autumn, Eden's view had apparently prevailed; and Churchill had 'allowed Eden a pretty free hand'[54] over the Sudan. Although the Prime Minister favoured a more hard-line approach to Egypt, he had no coherent alternative policy to offer his Cabinet colleagues,[55] who accordingly supported Eden's line of attack. With the publication of the proposed agreement in mid-January 1953 against a background of more press reports of Southern fears of Northern domination, Eden was suddenly confronted with a major crisis. The Sudan Group and the Beaverbrook press were 'in full cry'[56] and most important, given this ground swell of feeling, he had incurred the animosity of Churchill.[57] To some political commentators it was comparable to the Bevanite split within the Labour party.[58] Eden was also in the doldrums politically,[59] compared to the meteoric rise in the fortunes of his rival Butler.

'He did have a great battle over it.'[60] Churchill had just returned from his holiday in Jamaica, and was 'passionately interested in the Egypt situation'.[61] The Prime Minister ardently hoped Neguib would 'kick us and show him we did not run ... (for) unless you can show that we have imposed our will upon Neguib you will find it very difficult to convince the Conservative party that the evacuation of the Suez Canal Zone conforms with British interest or prestige.'[62] 'Churchill was always trying to avoid having to make a decision to "scuttle", as he called it. He did not like the Sudan agreement because it was hauling down the flag, although the Sudan was not part of the Empire. Churchill had a romantic concept; the feeling [probably because of his participation in Sudanese history] that we must always hold firm, and that British rule was beneficial [to the Sudanese people].'[63]

Churchill was well aware of the depth of backbench feeling on the issue. The Sudan Group had conveyed the intensity of their wrath up the party ladder,[64] the Progress Trust MPs were united in their concern,[65] and with the party in uproar, the Government was obliged to reveal details of the agreement to its supporters before it was put before the House. Tory opposition now came out in to the open: Legge-Bourke 'fired the first shot'[66] with his intervention in the Chamber on 10 February 1953. That afternoon Selwyn Lloyd attended a tumultuous meeting of the Foreign Affairs Committee and was bombarded with questions. Conservatives across the political spectrum rose to voice their concern at the inadequacy of the agreement. The press reported that Selwyn Lloyd who 'undertook to convey the feeling of the meeting to the Foreign Secretary',[67] was 'so roughly handled that Eden felt obliged to come and defend [the Sudan agreement] himself at a separate meeting'.[68]

The truth was somewhat different. Churchill was openly on the side of the protesters and the fact that the Prime Minister saw fit to summon Waterhouse and Assheton 'to a personal interview indicates the importance the Government attaches to the revolt. It should never be forgotten how slender the Conservative majority is.'[69] The following day (11 February 1953) the Cabinet considered a draft of the Sudanese agreement with Egypt. Churchill brusquely informed his Cabinet that he doubted whether Eden's proposals on the Sudan as an independent state would have sufficient support from the Conservative backbenches; he charged that it would be seen as 'an ignominious surrender of our responsibilities in the Sudan and a serious blow to Britain's prestige throughout the Middle East'. He believed it would be sharply criticised by the Press. It seemed likely to involve the Government in serious political difficulties which would doubtless be exploited to the full by the Opposition. He would therefore prefer that no decision should be taken until early the following week, by which time it would be easier to forecast the probable reaction of public opinion.[70]

In the Cabinet discussion which followed it was clear that Churchill was in the minority. He was informed that the Sudanese expected self-government and that nothing could be gained by delay. But although Eden secured the support of the majority of his Cabinet colleagues, the Prime Minister was adamant in his opposition to the proposed agreement. 'There was a big row between them. Finally Churchill said he would give his consent if Eden could get the party to accept. Eden asked, "What do you mean?" Churchill replied, "There is a meeting of the 1922 this afternoon. If you can convince them, I will agree to the Agreement." Eden was furious; he said it was totally unconstitutional and how could anyone expect him to operate under such circumstances.'[71] However, he was determined to persevere and thought he could win. In a fury, he went upstairs to the 1922 meeting and stated his case, 'using all of his great charm and persistence'.[72] The meeting was 'well attended' and he had a stormy reception. Eden knew he was arguing for his political life,[73] and told his critics that if they did not support the agreement, the remedy was in their own hands.[74] His impassioned advocacy 'made a profound impression at this meeting ... after all his personal experience of foreign affairs exceeded the collective knowledge of every one else in the room. Even the incalculable Boothby ran ... to his defence.'[75]

This was still not quite enough, and Eden was saved – literally – by the bell. 'Just as he finished his speech the division bell rang. I think he would have won the vote anyway, but by the time the division was over, the opposition had melted away. Only his supporters came back, and voted for him.'[76] The Sudan Group, although they sensed they had Churchill's backing, realized when the division bell rang that Eden had triumphed.[77] Eden's successful advocacy enabled him to report to the full Cabinet later that evening that his explanation 'had removed many of the misunderstandings which had been current in the Party and had gone a long way towards allaying the anxieties mentioned in the Cabinet discussions earlier in the day.' Although many Conservatives remained anxious about the situation, 'they now recognized that the course which the Government was proposing to follow was the most satisfactory of the alternatives open to them'.[78]

Thus the Sudan issue was settled with Churchill and the Sudan Group beating a grudging, temporary retreat in the face of Eden's argument, supported in Cabinet and the rest of the party, that the agreement offered Britain the best opportunity to secure the foundations of a stable peace in the area. The signature of the Anglo-Egyptian agreement was announced by Eden in the House on 12 February. Although it was 'widely welcomed for the hope it offered in improving Anglo-Egyptian relations', 'a cold douche of misgiving about the effective self-government of the Sudan was given by Assheton and Legge-Bourke'.[79] The Suez Group MPs had agreed to hold their fire over the Sudan agreement, but these critics were determined that the Foreign Secretary's triumph should prove ephemeral. Waterhouse rapidly served notice that he and like-minded colleagues were bloodied, but unbowed.[80]

The cost of the Sudan agreement for Eden in terms of political support within the party was severe. The Foreign Secretary had succeeded 'in soothing over his backbench critics [on the Sudan] but only at the cost of awakening the party'.[81] Eden was keenly aware that the spirit in which the Anglo-Egyptian agreement on the Sudan was received in Egypt and the degree of good faith with which it was implemented was of the utmost importance. 'After the Sudan, Suez [was] the issue of the hour throughout the Tory Party.'[82] Eden had done nothing to dispel Conservative criticism of proposals to evacuate the Canal Zone base. The dissenters were encouraged by the breadth and depth of feeling inspired within the party by the Sudan affair, and a certain vulnerability of the Government: those outside the future Suez Group recognized that, given the slender government majority, there was 'a real danger of a minority group in the House of Commons holding the balance of power and forcing the Government to dance to its tune'.[83]

9 Negotiating the withdrawal from the Suez Canal Zone base 1953-54

The Anglo-Egyptian agreement on the Sudan sealed the Suez Group's determination to oppose Eden's 'appeasement' of the Cairo regime. In the succeeding seventeen months, these MPs conducted a highly public campaign to obstruct Eden's answer to the problem posed by Britain's straitened finances on her position in the Middle East.

Eden's argument throughout remained that the presence of troops in the Suez Canal Zone was a heavy political and military liability, and served no useful purpose.[1] Britain needed access to base and transit facilities in peacetime and the right of re-entry in wartime, and this could only be done with Egypt's agreement. Redeployment without agreement would be far more damaging to Britain's prestige.[2] While no Conservative liked the idea of evacuation, by 1954 more moderate, younger Tories accepted the logic of seeking an agreement with Egypt, albeit some more reluctantly than others. They appreciated that the present treaty had only two more years to run and that the base, even if it were drastically reduced in size, could only function efficiently with a large, cooperative Egyptian workforce. In the present circumstances, Britain was being obliged to keep far more soldiers in the Zone than the country could afford, given her other global commitments, and far more than Britain's entitlement under the existing treaty. Yet, even with the enormous garrison there, Britain was being hard pressed to maintain order and the efficient running of the base for lack of Egyptian labour,[3] and the installations were deteriorating despite an annual expenditure of £50 million.[4]

Some Conservatives recognized that Egyptian nationalism should be acknowledged. The current spectacle of 80 000 British soldiers defending a vast ammunition dump, whilst unable to prevent Egypt denying use of the Canal to Israel-bound cargo, did not impress other Arab nations.[5] The pragmatists felt the Suez Group's thesis of contracting the Canal Zone base to

10 000 troops had not been very well thought out.[6] The crucial question was, if no agreement was reached with Egypt, was the retention of the base in peacetime worth its present cost in money and manpower? Agreement was essential; the alternatives were abandonment or the reoccupation of Egypt.[7]

Moderate Tories argued that the enormous Suez Canal base made little sense in the shifting dimensions of the post-war world. If Russia advanced through the Caucasus, the base would be 300 miles away from the line Britain wished to secure.[8] Egyptian ill-will meant the Canal Zone base was a rapidly depreciating asset[9] and they shared Eden's hope that once the irritant had been removed, Anglo-Egyptian relations would be restored to their 'natural alliance'. To most politicians, Britain's right of re-entry was a bargaining point: it was patently a political move – once the treaty was signed, they agreed with the Suez Group that it made no sense as a strategy. But even those who accepted the logic of evacuation firmly believed that the base could not be run without the assistance of British technicians;[10] there remained considerable concern that these technicians would be excessively vulnerable to Egyptian attack,[11] and that Egypt might seize on the evacuation of British troops as her golden opportunity to attack Israel.

There was irritation that the Suez Group's organization and methods were 'bypassing the party committee dealing with the subject and the 1922',[12] and were trying 'to hold a pistol to the Government and their colleagues in the House [which] could not be tolerated'.[13] Some backbenchers took a sour view of the dissidents' motivation and felt, as former Whips, Waterhouse's (and Grimston's) behaviour was particularly unbecoming,[14] but Lord Lambton's explicit suggestion that several rebels were spurred solely by political pique[15] greatly angered many of his colleagues,[16] who sympathized with the Suez Group's views.

Many of the arguments rehearsed in the previous skirmishes over Palestine, Abadan and the Sudan were redeployed by the Suez Group. Irrevocably opposed to the total withdrawal of British troops from the Suez base on psychological, political and military grounds,[17] the Suez Group believed that under Article X of the 1936 Treaty, Britain had the legitimate right to remain in the Canal Zone beyond 1956, even if London failed to negotiate a new treaty with Cairo.[18] The Suez Group was not opposed to a negotiated settlement *per se*. It accepted that the number of British troops currently in the Canal Zone grossly exceeded Britain's needs,[19] 'eventual redeployment would release much needed forces' and it appreciated the 'deplorable conditions under which many units were serving'.[20] However, the rebels contended that reducing Britain's commitments would not produce a strategic reserve if this led to new pressures on Britain's position in the region.[21]

The Suez Group felt Eden and his supporters were deluding themselves in imagining there would be a dramatic improvement in Anglo-Egyptian relations once the issue was settled. Nor had Britain any basis whatsoever for confidence in Egypt's willingness to abide by a diplomatic settlement.[22] Egypt repeatedly demonstrated her bad faith by attempting to undermine the agreement over the Sudan. Britain as the former imperial power had a continuing responsibility to protect the Sudan from possible Egyptian encroachment,[23] and the future presence of British troops in the Canal Zone was rendered imperative by the unstable situation in the Sudan.[24]

The Suez Group argued the Cold War had conferred on the Canal Zone base a significance far beyond its original function as the guardpost for an international waterway. It disputed that the NATO alliance obviated the need for the base: protecting NATO's supply of vital Middle Eastern oil and Turkey, the exposed flank of the alliance, demanded a base in the Canal Zone, with perhaps smaller advanced bases near the battle front. Should Turkey fall, at present there was nothing beyond it to stop Russia from sweeping into Palestine, Egypt or the Persian Gulf. Despite Stalin's death in March 1953 and the hope inspired by Churchill's summit offer in May 1953, these MPs felt the international climate remained uncertain: the Middle East appeared one of the most vulnerable sectors in the worldwide front against Communism, vulnerable to political infiltration and to overt aggression. There was also the festering sore of Arab/Israeli animosity; recent frontier clashes and guerilla incursions had only served to underline the dangers of another conflict – anarchy in the Middle East and possibly erupting into a wider conflict with irretrievable consequences. The withdrawal of British troops might encourage an Egyptian attack on Israel, quite apart from the advantage conferred by the *matériel* at the base.[25]

The dissidents also felt there was a lamentable tendency to

lose sight of Britain's major commitment to protect communications with the Empire.[26] Despite the increase in air traffic, the Suez Canal remained the main thoroughfare for the Commonwealth.[27] There was also the issue of Britain's responsibility for ensuring free navigation of the Suez Canal. There were two crucial considerations: Egypt was not yet in a position 'by its own unaided resources to ensure the liberty and entire security of the Canal', and Britain was in the Canal Zone not only to protect British interests, but to discharge her responsibilities under the 1888 Suez Canal Convention. The critics warned that if Britain evacuated her garrison, Egypt would grab the Canal;[28] and Egypt had already 'repeatedly flouted her duties'[29] by preventing passage of Israeli-bound traffic. Britain could not unilaterally divest herself of these responsibilities 'without the fullest prior consultation of the other signatories of the Convention and other interested parties', nor before 'adequate alternative provision' had been made for the discharge of those inherited responsibilities.[30]

The Suez Group argued that there was Commonwealth disagreement on the correct line to take on the future of the Suez Canal base.[31] Through its contacts in the military, the Suez Group was aware of divisions within the British Army on the base.[32] Tory pragmatists might argue that soldiers in the base uniformly wanted to withdraw,[33] but the Suez Group found a powerful ally in General Sir Cameron Nicolson, Commander-in-Chief, Middle East Land forces, who publicly rejected suggestions that smaller bases in Cyprus, Iraq, Jordan, and North Africa were viable alternatives.[34] As secretary of the Suez Group, Amery also got in touch with the Indian general staff who informed him that although the Indian government felt differently, in its opinion if British troops were pulled out of the Suez Canal base, the Indian Army would have no more use for Britain.[35] Therefore, a British presence in the Canal Zone base appeared vital to maintain the London/Delhi axis in the Commonwealth system.

Then there was the question of prestige. 'After Britain's withdrawal from India, Palestine and Malta, it was only the Suez Canal Zone base which enabled Britain to exert influence westward in the Mediterranean, including North Africa, and eastward into the Indian Ocean and southward into Africa.'[36] The Government had to hold the line at the Canal if Britain was to have any hope of retaining great power status, leadership of the Commonwealth[37] and Empire.[38] These MPs were convinced that their government's persistence in seeking terms and in permitting commercial and financial deals (for example, the sale of aircraft, and the release of sterling balances) in the face of Egyptian intransigence demonstrated a fundamentally misguided, pusillanimous policy.[39] The issue was an acute political one.[40] Irrespective of the massive blow that withdrawal from the Suez Canal base would deal to Britain's position in Africa and the Middle East, Britain's standing would be fatally undermined by acceptance of terms negotiated and granted under duress,[41] with 'disastrous results' abroad and at home.[42]

The Government's policy should be to withdraw the terms offered to Egypt. With 'firmness and patience', Britain would exert sufficient pressure, persuasion or force to bring to power an Egyptian government who would accept its minimum terms.[43] Britain could not agree to reduce her forces to a mere handful of care and maintenance technicians, merely for the sake of reaching a settlement on paper. The Suez Group conjured the nightmare of British technicians in mufti without sidearms being overrun by fanatics[44] equipped with British weapons. It remained overwhelmingly sceptical that Egypt could fulfil her promise that the existing base should be efficiently maintained, while talk of Britain's right to reactivate the base was seen as pure fantasy.[45] Against the 'many dangers of the situation', (a British garrison) was the only guarantee which held the slightest value.[46]

Arguments of the diminishing value of the Canal Zone base, surrounded (as it was) by a hostile population on whom the efficient functioning of the base depended for its pool of labour, were dismissed; the answer was foreign labour.[47] (This would not solve the crucial problem of fresh water, obtained via the Sweet Water Canal from Egypt – an issue the rebels never addressed.) They conceded the argument that Britain could not afford to exercise her responsibilities had some merit, but responded that the anti-British propaganda and agitation in Egypt did not reflect the true will of the Egyptian people.[48] Similarly, suggestions that the base was not the only station for operations in the Middle East were brushed aside. The rebels also dismissed the menace of the atomic bomb – 'Mr Sandys has told us it can be met by a strong air force on the spot backed by all the most modern anti-aircraft devices' – pointing out that if the Government truly wished to see a continued military base in the Canal Zone, it would not be contemplating handing over responsibility to Egypt since 'in neither respect has Egypt the resources which would enable it to exercise that response'.[49] A base located anywhere else in the region would be just as vulnerable to possible atomic attack: selecting Cyprus as the replacement headquarters for Middle East command made no sense whatever.

The Suez Group was also determined that Britain should not be further dependent on America. 'Post-war governments have paid too much attention to the well-meant, but often unsound, advice of the USA, who have no responsibility and much less experience of these oriental peoples than we have ourselves.'[50] The critics bitterly resented what was seen as undue American pressure on Britain to come to terms with Egypt.[51] Washington's unreasonably sympathetic policy to Cairo seemed part of America's systematic attack on Britain's position in the Middle East and Empire[52] using political, commercial and military levers,[53] increasingly influenced by US interests in Middle Eastern oil.[54] Through their contacts, the Suez Group was well aware that 'when the Egyptians had got the British . . . out of the Suez Canal Zone, the Americans would step in and give all sorts of help to Egypt'.[55] The prospect of Britain being 'jockeyed out to enable God's Own Country to take our place'[56] was deeply galling.

It was Eden's firm hope that once Britain's withdrawal from the base had been conceded, Egypt would be ready to enter into discussions for the maintenance of the base for a Middle East defence organization in which America would play a leading part. All Conservatives remained dedicated to a more coherent organization to provide Middle Eastern defence, but in the rebels' opinion, even if Britain did secure Cairo's adherence to a regional defence organization, Egypt would inevitably be the weak link. Their scant respect for the Egyptian soldier as an opponent had been reinforced by the recent spectacle of the Egyptian army being trounced by the woefully outnumbered Israelis. The Suez Group argued 'the only body which we would be justified in inviting to share our responsibility [to protect the Canal] would be one representing the whole free world including Egypt, but in which we should retain the leading position to which our historical connection to the Middle East and the security of the whole Commonwealth entitles us'.[57] America's contribution was conceded, but this should be a decidedly junior role.

In the meantime, in the absence of a coherent Middle East defence system, there was only one possible and morally justifiable policy: 'to remain in the Canal Zone in sufficient strength so that it can be reinforced at short notice to meet whatever storms may break upon us.'[58] The Suez Canal Zone base was the only base which offered equally the opportunity to send reinforcements to the eastern Mediterranean or to the Indian Ocean. Its importance therefore, in peace or in war, lay in its crucial position in the 'strategy of the free nations and the keystone in the structure of imperial defence'.[59] Eden's proposed formula would create a vacuum, with disastrous consequences for international peace and stability: it constituted nothing less than a dereliction of duty.[60]

The professed aims of the 'Suez Canal Committee'[61] were:

(i) to remind public opinion of the true nature of Britain's obligations and interests in the Suez Canal Zone; (ii) to strengthen the hands of all those in government, Parliament and outside who are anxious to resist the unreasonable demands of the present Egyptian government; (iii) to work for an agreement with Egypt under which Britain shall retain in the Canal Zone bases, airfields, port facilities and sufficient British personnel to maintain and operate these; and British fighting units, strong enough to make effective Britain's right to reinforce the base in the event of necessity of which Britain must be the sole judge.[62]

10 000 British troops should remain in the Canal Zone base.[63]

The Suez Group enjoyed an unofficial alliance with a small but extremely influential group of peers – the Lords Vansittart, Rennell, Killearn, and Hankey[64] – who were former public servants with 130 years service between them. A number of other influential peers also lent support to the Suez Group's campaign[65] and Leo Amery, who instigated 'the Suez Canal Committee', remained an active conspirator until his death in 1955; these men shared strong links through membership of other political organizations and wartime connections.

There was a marked absence of the same 'so-called right-wing group in domestic policy'[66] and on other aspects of foreign policy. 'Suez was the glue'[67] for these rebels who operated as individuals as well as members of an organized, well-briefed committee. 'There were conversations both private and by telephone between members of the group. There were social occasions such as lunches at my father's house ... individual members [also] took it upon themselves to ask questions, make speeches in defence or foreign affairs debates and express their views in the ordinary party committees.'[68] Each MP possessed a different threshold to which he was prepared to carry his opposition:[69] 'protest in the party committee; open opposition on the floor of the House; abstention; voting against the Government; and lastly, resigning the Whip. It was obvious to me that an awful lot would fall out along the way.'[70]

The question arose of whether or not to carry the fight beyond the field of foreign affairs as the Government's small majority (17) offered the rebels the opportunity of coordinating their campaign with Labour. Government difficulties in the committee stages of the Finance Bill in May 1953, in which the Government's nominal majority fell to three, drew some dissidents' thoughts towards the use of votes and abstentions on major pieces of domestic legislation,[71] but this tactic was not considered 'cricket' by their Suez Group colleagues. Instead, the Group relied upon the implicit threat that its opposition could bring the Government down, which enabled the rebels to proclaim their supreme loyalty to the Conservative tradition (if not the party); they were also well aware that a Labour government would pull out of Suez. The Group was publicly disdainful of Labour's 'blatant political manoeuvres'[72] to lure the Suez Group into inflicting a humiliating defeat on its own side.[73] Amery privately argued even the risk of letting in a Socialist government would only be a short-term disaster, 'less than the permanent disaster of a Conservative government staying on after our surrender'.[74] For the overwhelming majority of the Suez Group, had Labour decided to try to vote the Government down, abstaining in the division lobby was the limit of acceptable opposition.[75]

The principal sceptic of reconciliation with Egypt was Churchill himself.[76] His was an emotional resistance to the process of 'scuttle' which had begun in India, continued at Abadan and which he feared would end in British retreat from Africa.[77] His reluctant acquiescence to the Anglo-Egyptian agreement on the Sudan was an open secret in Westminster, as was his resistance to evacuation from Egypt.[78] The Suez Group's morale was bolstered by its knowledge of this schism between Eden and Churchill[79] and by Churchill's private encouragement to keep up the 'good work'.[80]

The Suez Group hoped it would be able to exploit Churchill's distaste for the whole business to its own advantage;[81] in the opinion of Jane Portal, his secretary, Churchill was open to constant influence – in particular Soames (now his PPS) egged him on over the Sudan and Egypt[82] – and Labour certainly attributed the strength of the rebels' obstructive influence to Churchill's support.[83] As matters transpired, it was the presence of a sizeable group of disgruntled backbenchers which enjoyed the sympathy of approximately 100 other less committed Conservatives,[84] that strengthened Churchill's own hand as he sought to counter his Foreign Secretary's Egypt policy. In contrast to the Suez Group, Churchill recognized the economic and military logic behind Britain's proposed withdrawal.[85] Contemptuous of the Egyptians, he felt that Eden's approach smacked of 'appeasement'[86] and was determined to drive a much harder bargain with Neguib. Perhaps there was also an element of mischief in Churchill's encouragement of the Suez Group – regarding all 'as rather fun, seeing what would come out of it'.[87]

Neither the Suez Group nor Churchill made much progress while Eden remained at his desk, supported by the majority of his Cabinet colleagues. Eden's illness and absence from the political scene from April to October 1953 offered the Prime Minister a golden opportunity[88] and Churchill was determined to preside over 'the Egyptian business' himself.[89] The Suez Group quickly seized the opportunity of a change at the helm to reiterate[90] its position to Churchill,[91] pointing out that although Eden had assured the Foreign Affairs Committee[92] that the Government had minimum terms on which it would insist, since this meeting there had been disquieting press reports; the Chief Whip was also alerted to its concern about the course the negotiations might take.[93]

Buchan-Hepburn realized from his own soundings that the Suez Group's views reflected 'a real anxiety in the Party'.[94] This agitation was attributed 'to fundamental strategic facts not being fully understood', but Buchan-Hepburn appreciated that there was a general sense that the Government was out of touch with the backbenches on the matter.[95] At his urging, Churchill addressed the Foreign Affairs Committee on 29 April 1953, and his tougher stance with Egypt,[96] confirmed in the Commons,[97] was welcomed by the critics.[98] Robin Hankey's appointment as *chargé d'affaires* in Cairo seemed to hint that Lord Hankey's (and the Suez Group's) views would now have more weight.

This satisfaction was short-lived. Press reports continued[99] to suggest a basis of agreement with Egypt that cut across Churchill's assurance of minimum demands that would not be conceded. Selwyn Lloyd's remarks to the Foreign Affairs Committee on 12 July 1953 appeared to confirm reports that Britain had agreed to the withdrawal of all combat troops.[100] Accordingly, the Suez Group used *The Daily Express*[101] to leak Lord Hankey's 'confidential report' sent to Eden in February 1953 which warned that 'if British troops were withdrawn from the Suez Canal Zone, the Canal would be impassable to all shipping in little more than a year'.[102] For the Government 'the disclosure could not have come at a worse time'[103] – as Amery undoubtedly knew – since it coincided with secret talks in Washington with the Americans and the French about the freedom of the Canal.

Although this leak caused considerable consternation in Whitehall,[104] the hardliners' initiative was lost with Churchill's continuing indisposition following his stroke in late June. Salisbury, Lord President of the Council, assumed control of the Egyptian discussions and gave an early indication of his determination to pursue negotiations,[105] rather than imitate Churchill's procrastination. 'The Government had no real worry of getting parliamentary approval; it was assumed that Labour would not vote against a treaty and ... [it] seemed unlikely that the disturbed Tories would go as far as to force a vote against the Government; even if they did Socialist non-intervention would ensure a ... Government majority.'[106] On this line of reasoning negotiations with Egypt progressed rapidly. The outstanding issues were reduced to four main points: reactivation; duration of the agreement; uniforms; and a time limit for withdrawal.[107]

As the talks appeared to be drawing inexorably towards a

highly unsatisfactory conclusion,[108] the dissidents went on the offensive in mid-September 1953. With Parliament in recess, letters to the national press were the most obvious tactic[109] and there ensued a very lively correspondence in *The Times* on the future of the Suez Canal Zone base, which discussed the issues at length. Newspaper coverage of the Margate party conference[110] also paid great attention to Julian Amery's contribution to the debate on defence and foreign policy, which was received with rapturous applause. Salisbury, who found the Suez Group's views 'extremely irritating',[111] replied for the Government and directed much of his argument towards rebutting the critics' accusations and seeking to play down expectations of the sort of agreement the Government could reasonably achieve.

By the autumn of 1953 the Government 'was in serious trouble'[112] over its policy towards Egypt. The Suez Group, through letters, private meetings and public speeches, had succeeded in stirring the party. Despite Salisbury's exhortation that the party conference trust its leaders, Conservative MPs became 'highly alarmed'[113] by the persistent rumours of a total withdrawal from the Canal Zone base which 'went undenied'.[114] Ministers began to realize that Labour might 'cash in' on defections of a group of Tories, to whom Eden's announcement of a resumption of negotiations in mid-October proved most unpalatable.[115] 'If 25 [Tories] went as far as to abstain the Government could be defeated, assuming the Liberals and Labour opposed the Government.'[116] Churchill had altered political calculations of an imminent general election by his declaration at the party conference that there would not be an election until 1955. Labour leaders had no desire to go to the polls whilst their party was racked by disagreements over rearmament, but did not want to wait another two years. Defeat on Suez might 'catch the Tories at a disadvantage'.[117]

Churchill's continued opposition to Eden's policy[118] was bolstered by his awareness of this 'stentorian belly rumble'[119] of dissent on the backbenches. Although he reluctantly supported Eden and Salisbury on 15 October 1953 over new proposals to Egypt,[120] Churchill was determined these should be 'presented to the Egyptians as our last word'. He was equally 'anxious that no final agreement should be reached . . . until Parliament had reassembled'. It was of great importance that 'ministers should have that opportunity of preparing the way for the agreement, if it was to be concluded, and doing their utmost to reduce the risk of it being subjected to damaging criticism by their own supporters'.[121]

When Parliament reassembled, the Suez Group began to coalesce as Waterhouse and Amery made discreet approaches to certain members.[122] These moves were matched by 'strenuous efforts'[123] by senior Tories to manage the 'very substantial swell of opinion' on the issue.[124] Only Churchill's personal intervention in the 1922 Committee in October prevented an open revolt.[125] Eden wrote to Waterhouse assuring him that the Government was very conscious of the importance of a workable agreement over the Canal base: 'We should not sacrifice our minimum conditions for the sake of Egyptian goodwill, essential though we believe this to be.'[126] The presence of five members of the Government (Churchill, Eden, Lloyd, Salisbury and Nutting) at the Foreign Affairs Committee on 21 October 1953 was eloquent testimony of the Government's concern.[127] Despite Buchan-Hepburn's initial hope that thereafter 'things would be much better',[128] 'this sledgehammer did not crack the nut'.[129] Appalled by the confirmation of the Government's intention to withdraw all fighting troops, the Suez Group immediately began to increase its pressure.[130] Powell and Amery were spurred into public criticism.[131] Hinchingbrooke, widely tipped for the position of Parliamentary Secretary to the Minister of Transport,[132] let it be known that he declined the offer because of 'differences with the Government on the evacuation of the Suez Canal'.[133]

The Whips realized that the Suez Group had struck a chord of profound unease within the party.[134] In the party committees MPs questioned the logic of complete withdrawal[135] and relocation to Cyprus; for others the right of re-entry was the crux.[136] Eden was only too well aware of the tightrope he was walking: given the volatile temper of the party, logic might fall prey to national pride and fears of a Middle East conflict. Buchan-Hepburn was warning Churchill there were 'quite enough' members of the Suez Group 'for it to be difficult',[137] and urged if an agreement was reached 'you or Anthony will have to talk to people alone'.[138]

The political temperature rose dramatically in late 1953 with the news of Egyptian interference in the Sudanese elections.

This appeared to confirm the Suez Group's worst fears that Britain had failed in her duty to ensure Sudanese self-determination. From Eden's point of view, this evidence of Egypt's unreliability came at a highly embarrassing time and he was at pains to address backbench alarm.[139] Eden had braved the wrath of his leader and a sizeable portion of his party to force through the treaty for the Sudan; he remained determined to secure a negotiated agreement with Egypt involving British evacuation from the Canal Zone base. Yet here was undeniable grist for the Suez Group's argument that no satisfactory agreement could be reached with Egypt.[140] Fearful that, under American pressure,[141] the Government would try to sneak through a 'disastrous' agreement with Cairo during the Christmas recess,[142] the Suez Group was determined 'to tie [Britain's] hands'.[143] Talks were currently at a standstill, which gave the critics 'an opportunity to make their views heard in time'.[144] The terms offered to Egypt should be withdrawn, so that 'if the circumstances justified a new approach Britain could enter negotiations with her hands free'.[145] Private conversations with the Whips, objections in the party committees,[146] letters to Churchill and the explicit threat[147] of a critical EDM, designed to press the Government to commit to prior discussion in Parliament before it entered into 'any commitment to modify their rights under the Treaty of 1936'[148] (which was 'precisely what [Eden was] not prepared to do'[149]) – none of these apparently had the desired effect.

The idea of a critical EDM was, however, causing considerable consternation within the Cabinet which was aware that as a result of the Sudanese elections,[150] there was extensive sympathy for the Suez Group's arguments;[151] the motion seemed likely to attract at least 35 signatures.[152] The Cabinet was in 'no doubt that [the Suez Group] held very strong views and could not be relied upon to refrain from causing acute embarrassment to the Government'.[153] However, government attempts to head off a backbench rebellion[154] with an exploratory meeting between Butler, Crookshank and Nutting and those Privy Councillors who were not in the Government[155] were unsuccessful. At Nutting's urging, Assheton and Waterhouse agreed not to put down an EDM while Churchill and Eden were in Bermuda;[156] but Nutting's refusal to give any undertaking or any new interpretation of government policy goaded the dissidents into briefing the press of their intention 'to carry on their campaign in public by party motions, on the order paper, and public speeches'.[157]

On their return from the Bermuda conference on 11 December Churchill and Eden found themselves confronted with a 'serious demonstration'.[158] The Suez Group's threat was not an idle one: a revolt of 37 'would be sufficient to bring great pressure on a government with a majority of only 16'.[159] The Whips were warning that 'the strength of the rebellion is growing'.[160] 'The big danger for the Government is that the Socialists may vote against any evacuation plan which does not safeguard the position of Israel.'[161] Convinced that, however disagreeable, a negotiated withdrawal from Suez remained the only viable option,[162] Eden immediately set about the business of pacifying restive MPs. On 11 December he held a private meeting with Waterhouse and his fellow critics,[163] aware that if he was not successful they would use the forthcoming foreign affairs debate to air their grievances.[164] There was considerable Cabinet discussion over the best way to defuse the incipient rebellion.[165] On Buchan-Hepburn's recommendation, it was agreed[166] that Alexander should address the Foreign Affairs Committee, rather than the smaller Defence Committee,[167] on military strategy and economic facts of the case to detach a large number of restive backbenchers, and isolate the hard core.[168] Thus 'at least an attempt could be made to avoid a large number of Conservative [signatures to the EDM], which might well turn out to be considerably more than the 40–50 quoted in the press.'[169] The forthcoming debate on foreign affairs due on 17 December 1953 was deliberately curtailed.[170]

When its threat failed to elicit a satisfactory change of tack, the Suez Group publicly placed its objections on the record on 15 December 1953, the evening before Churchill's annual luncheon with the 1922 Committee and just before Alexander's appearance before the Foreign Affairs Committee.[171] Described as 'a virtual vote of no confidence',[172] and 'the most serious revolt the Government had met on a major policy issue',[173] this rebellion was 'a more serious matter than an ordinary flurry of backbenchers'[174] since the list included 'three Privy Councillors, a Joint Treasurer of the Party and many MPs who have expert and specialized knowledge of the Middle East and whose views cannot be lightly disregarded ... [The] body of opposition which Eden faces is a really formidable one and it is evident that the Cabinet is taking the challenge as seriously as it deserves.'[175] 'Minority movements within parties are usually drawn from a fairly narrow field, but among the 39 are to be found representatives of practically every distinctive Conservative group: the 'Old Guard'; One Nation; ex-army types; rural MPs; industrialists; veterans; new boys.' It was 'probably as complete a cross-section as could be got'.[176]

Churchill was more inclined than his Cabinet colleagues to take a robust view that the EDM would be 'a timely reminder to [Egypt] that Britain had to consider public opinion'.[177] He also hoped to use this lever of a 'disturbed and increasingly angered section which could at any time cancel [the Government's] modest majority' to dissuade Eisenhower from granting economic aid to Egypt before agreement was reached.[178] Churchill's own inclination was to send troops to Khartoum to offset the 'disgrace' of retiring from the Canal Zone, to stop negotiations with Egypt and announce that Britain would leave in its own time, destroying or removing the base before departure (the latter was hardly a feasible proposition given the enormous quantity of stores there).[179] However, he assured Eden, currently in Paris, that he would tell the 1922 Committee its members must have faith that the Government was 'not animated by fear or weakness'.[180]

The Suez Group succeeded in wringing two apparent concessions from the Government. Churchill's appeal at the 1922 Committee annual luncheon 'for the Suez rebels not to threaten the small Tory majority... and to argue in the privacy of the 1922 Committee, rather than in public' included the specific 'promise that an agreement with Egypt would not be rushed through in the recess'.[181] The previous day the Suez Group had won an admission from the Government that any proposed agreement would be debated by Parliament before ratification.[182] There the concessions ended. In the foreign affairs debate Eden 'firmly and flatly' refused to 'break off negotiations with Egypt in the existing circumstances', or to refuse to promise that if the British Ambassador reached heads of agreement that the Government would not go on to try to prepare a treaty to replace that of 1936.[183] Similarly Churchill stated that the Government's actions would not be dictated by the violence of our foreign enemies or 'by the pressure of some of our best friends' (a reference either to America, or the Conservative backbenches).

Churchill's personal appeal to the 1922 Committee had succeeded in quelling some dissent on Egypt but the Suez Group remained defiant in debate.[184] It regarded Eden's speech as 'a slap in the face',[185] and warned the Whips of its intention 'to appeal to the party in the country with speeches and letters to the press', bolstered by the belief that although military opinion led by Alexander supported Eden, 'an important military element' and some Cabinet members shared its view.[186] The press was rapidly appraised of its determination to continue the fight;[187] and it was strongly hinted the EDM would not be withdrawn.[188]

The Suez Group continued their campaign to persuade the Government to break off negotiations[189] and to withdraw the present offer[190] in the party committees, in Parliamentary debates,[191] in articles in journals[192] and through briefings to the press. It warned of continued Conservative suspicions of 'too tender an attitude towards Egypt were still very much alive within the party'[193] and many more Conservatives would now be prepared to back the December EDM. (Darling and Kerby were the only ones who did so.) With the recrudescence of attacks on British troops in the Canal Zone, the dissidents pressed the Government to halt all discussions until these disturbances had been firmly crushed.[194] Egypt's failure to put down the violence demonstrated official encouragement for sabotage, while the 'Neguib-out, Nasser-in, Neguib-in again fiasco' in February 1954 demonstrated a dangerous instability in the Cairo government[195] which vindicated the stand they had taken.[196] Their gathering frustration led them to accuse Eden of a policy of 'appeasement'[197] – the ultimate political insult – and to decide to vote against a Heads of Agreement.[198] While Amery and Waterhouse realized that it was unrealistic to expect to get 40 MPs to vote against the government, 'no government can lightly disregard a warning of this kind'.[199]

Despite their public united front, tensions persisted between Churchill and Eden in private. Much to the alarm of the Foreign Office, the pressure of backbench dissent and his own Prime Minister's opposition was beginning to tell on Eden's resolve.[200] Armed with the backing of the Suez Group, Churchill at the end of December told the Cabinet that negotiations should be abandoned if an agreement was not reached in the near future.²⁰¹ Eden was acutely aware that if he succeeded in getting Egyptian agreement on the present proposals, he would carry the party, but with 20 or 30 voting against this might 'gravely compromise his position'.²⁰² Racked by indecision, Eden was torn between the Prime Minister's 'so-called alternative to agreement with Egypt – i.e. breaking off negotiations, and announcing that Britain would redeploy her troops in her own time' – and his own wish not to 'throw over the Arabs altogether and rely on Israel and Turkey' – the Prime Minister's strong choice.²⁰³

Meanwhile Eden's deputy, Selwyn Lloyd, seemed even more influenced by the Tory rebels, suggesting that 'redeployment' should mean that British troops would stay in Egypt in some force until 1956 and even thereafter.²⁰⁴ To Eden's consternation, in February while the Foreign Secretary was in Berlin for the Four-Power conference on Germany, Selwyn Lloyd gave a lunch in London for the Persian Ambassador to which he invited Assheton, one of the leading rebels. This raised fears in the mind of the highly strung Foreign Secretary that Selwyn Lloyd was plotting against him. Churchill had again seized the chance of overall control of Egypt negotiations with Eden's absence and was giving Eden 'a rough ride'.²⁰⁵ 'Quivering with sensitivity to opinion in the House, the party, the newspapers', Eden was 'beginning to find the unpopularity of his Egypt policy with the party too heavy a burden and [was] seeking ways to abandon it'.²⁰⁶ The Cabinet, led by Salisbury, was in favour of a new plan of refusing to renew talks until Egypt had done certain things to restore confidence (stop anti-British propaganda, undertake not to upset the Governor General's commission in the Sudan, etc), in opposition to Churchill, supported by war cries from the backbenches, and 'egged on' by Soames,²⁰⁷ who still wanted to send troops to Khartoum, keep 10 000 men on the canal, and break off all discussions.

To the relief of the Suez Group²⁰⁸ Eden announced on 22 March that negotiations had been broken off.²⁰⁹ However, initial hopes that the severance of negotiations would be followed by 'a material change of approach'²¹⁰ were not fulfilled. Eden persisted with his policy, convinced there was no viable alternative.²¹¹ Caught between American pressure to concede terms to Egypt and Churchill's pressure to stand firm, backed by the

Suez Group, for the beleaguered Foreign Secretary the solution to maintaining Britain's Middle Eastern position after withdrawal from Suez, lay in 'close relations with Jordan and Iraq'[212] building upon the Turkish-Pakistani pact.

By early summer faced with the spectre of an imminent Anglo-Egyptian settlement, the Suez Group MPs and their aristocratic allies were spurred into frenetic activity, despatching articles[213] and letters[214] to the press, to Selwyn Lloyd[215] and to Eden,[216] 'warning that the group ... was now even more strongly of the view that British forces must be maintained in the Canal'[217] because of the situation in the Sudan rendered this imperative. Through informal chats with Eden, deputations to Churchill[218] and private meetings[219] it sought to defend Britain's honour as well as her interests.[220] As the process of proposal and counter-proposal was followed avidly in the press, the Suez Group's efforts to broadcast its dissatisfaction were extremely successful, as were its efforts to stimulate wider party unrest.[221] As the press picked up this backbench dissatisfaction – 'another Tory civil war warms up'[222] – there was sharp Conservative protest at the reopening of negotiations in mid-July.[223] Diehard opinion within the party was also enraged by Eden's 'supine attitude'[224] to China at the Geneva conference convened to discuss Indo-China: there were private fears that America's agreement for Eden's brokered deal in Indo-China was at the expense of British concessions over the Suez Canal base.[225] Yet, again, there was no uniform Suez Group view on Far Eastern matters.[226]

The Government was considerably alarmed at the prospect of a general backbench revolt over the resumption of negotiations. Eden wrote at length to the Suez Group's leader insisting 'any alternative policy will not give us what we want';[227] and the very considerable weight of senior Tories had to be brought to bear upon the critics to bring them to order.[228] First Selwyn Lloyd, Nutting and Dodds-Parker faced the Foreign Affairs Committee on 12 July 1954, and Churchill met a deputation from the Suez Group.[229] The following day Churchill, Butler and Head addressed the Army Subcommittee convened specifically to discuss the Suez question further before the forthcoming Commons debate.

It was Churchill's emotional arguments, rather than strict military logic, that won the day for Eden. Churchill had only conceded defeat very reluctantly.[230] His favoured solution of an international base, with a few thousand British troops and American support[231] foundered when America refused to co-operate at the Bermuda conference in December 1953.[232] By March, as the result of grim discussion of Britain's financial position,[233] the Prime Minister was no longer talking of sending troops to Khartoum. And the American reports of the Eniwetok nuclear test had a decisive effect on Churchill;[234] he was powerfully affected by the scientists' conclusion that this nuclear test had come very close to cracking the earth's crust.

By this point Churchill's ability to stimulate trouble for Eden using the Suez Group was greatly curtailed by the uncertainty of his own future.[235] In addition, Churchill still hankered after a summit with Russia, a notion which his Foreign Secretary heartily opposed. The Cabinet furore in July 1954 over Churchill's private attempts to secure a summit meeting – during which it was noticeable that whereas Salisbury was prepared to resign on the issue of collective cabinet government, Eden was not[236] – demonstrated to Churchill the limits of his authority. A general election seemed highly probable within the next year; Churchill would be 80 in November 1954, and no one expected him to lead the party into the next election. In contrast, Eden's star shone brightly: that year he was acclaimed as Churchill heir apparent and the chances of the Suez Group were necessarily diminished. With Eden's successes (real or apparent) in Indo-China, Trieste, and Persia, never had his standing within the party in the country been higher.

Despite his sympathy with the Suez Group's stance, outnumbered in Cabinet and awed by the vulnerability of the Suez Canal base to nuclear attack, Churchill bowed to reality. His public support for Eden in the party's committees in mid-July was crucial: 'Conservatives attach great importance to [his] intervention at this stage. Though he produced no new arguments, it is felt he was at pains to align himself personally and unmistakably with a negotiated settlement with Egypt.'[237] However, the Prime Minister still disliked the agreement intensely, and made Eden present it to the Commons.

With Churchill's change of heart, the Suez Group's campaign was stalemated.[238] However, the dissidents were still determined to draw as much public attention as possible to their dissatisfaction with Eden's policy, convinced that the proposals currently under discussion with Egypt were an 'unconditional surrender',[239] and profoundly unimpressed by the Prime Minister's arguments.[240] How could Britain hold the Empire together if Churchill's statements about the bomb and the impossibility of holding a base surrounded by a hostile local population were taken seriously?[241] And 'to argue that Britain could re-entry the base because of her position in Cyprus, Jordan and Kenya, was self-delusion.'[242] At midnight after this meeting the Suez Group formally declared its decision to vote against 'any treaty, which involved the removal of all fighting troops from the Suez Canal area'.[243]

It is plain that the full weight of the Whips' Office was brought to bear on the rebels. While Waterhouse's public statements sought to put a gloss of principle on his resignation from the Chairmanship of the Defence Committee, the Suez Group's leader was patently forced out by government supporters.[244] Legge-Bourke's decision to resign the party Whip on 14 July 1954[245] was a courageous gesture in the face of considerable pressure from the Whips, and one which made the Prime Minister very angry indeed.[246] No other member of the Suez Group was prepared to resign the Whip.[247] The resignations of Legge-Bourke and Waterhouse made little impact, though they attracted considerable press comment and there was evidently considerable Tory sympathy[248] for their stance. Sir Thomas Dugdale's resignation as Minister of Agriculture over the Crichel Down affair was a political event of far greater importance, and cast their resignations completely into the shade.

The many doubters were swayed by Churchill's personal intervention, if not by his sombre analysis of the vulnerability of the Canal Zone to nuclear attack. Certainly, 'to vote against Churchill was to lose sleep'.[249] The Whips' moves to contain the rebellion proved effective as hints emerged that not all the Suez Group were prepared publicly to defy their front bench and risk a Government defeat.[250] In the event Labour supported the Government, which enabled the Suez Group to register its displeasure in the division lobby, rather than having to take the less obvious route of abstaining to avoid the odium of voting with Labour. Contrary to earlier press predictions of a larger revolt,[251] only 26 rebels voted against the Government. Of the remainder of the December 1953 rebels, 7 abstained (including Morrison, Hall, Hicks Beach, Rayner and

Fell); Burden, Reader Harris, Frederick Harris and Clarke were paired; and Savory and Baker were in hospital. Herbert Williams had died three days before the debate. 'I think two or three others abstained who were not in our group, but sympathetic to us, among them Jocelyn Lucas. We would have done better if Churchill had not been against us.'[252]

'Fitzroy, Bell and Bromley-Davenport were the only three defections.'[253] In the debate Maclean declared that he had been sufficiently convinced by the strategic arguments and was now prepared – reluctantly – to accept the Government's argument. His former fellow conspirators were livid at this betrayal of their cause. Their reason was simple:

> At the meeting before the vote in one of the Committee rooms upstairs ... Waterhouse went round the table, asking us all whether we would oppose the Government. He said anyone who wanted to quit could do so; there would be no dishonour. I remember Fitzroy declaring, 'I'm certainly not going to support the Government. I'm probably going to abstain.' Waterhouse then submitted the names of those who would like to be called in the debate. Fitzroy was called ... and supported the Government. After our meeting closed he must have trotted down the corridor to the Chief Whip. When Fitzroy was made Under Secretary for War soon afterwards, Julian sent him a note saying, 'As you are incapable of shame, accept my congratulations'.[254]

The Suez Group had in essence 'shot their bolt' as a crusade against the withdrawal of British troops from the Suez Canal Zone base.[255] Despite warnings of its continued opposition to evacuation,[256] the issue of the Anglo-Egyptian agreement was totally eclipsed at the Blackpool party conference by the party's preoccupation with German rearmament. Legge-Bourke's application to have the Whip restored to him on 19 October 1954, together with the 'quietness' of the Suez Group at the party conference, seemed indicative that 'politically the issue of Suez withdrawal was dead'.[257] However, most of the rebels wanted to continue as a cohesive group.[258] Their opposition to withdrawal from the Suez Canal base had been symptomatic of a far deeper disagreement with their government: Eden's foreign policy involved 'the surrender of our rights to decide our own actions and reluctance to give a lead to the rest of the Commonwealth in economic and commercial matters'.[259] Therefore it was hardly surprising that 'from the débris of the Suez Group now springs a new backbench Empire group'.[260] The rebels took steps in the recess to maintain the solidarity of the group, through letters and private meetings, and to sort out an 'after Suez' policy.[261] 'The only possible way the Suez Agreement can be lived down is if we could make a reality of all the talk about Middle East redeployment.'[262] Henceforth Cyprus was to be 'the glue'.

Although the Suez Group was recognized as the most serious backbench challenge to the Government's foreign policy since 1951, its primary influence was as the Prime Minister's tool, rather than as an outside agency exerting pressure on the Foreign Secretary. Churchill came to appreciate very clearly the strategic absurdity of a huge base at the mercy of one nuclear bomb, and was haunted by his experience in the 1920s as Chancellor of the Exchequer, when it became apparent that the rearmament programme initiated by the Attlee government in 1950 was making Britain bankrupt. With his defection, the Suez Group's fight became a rearguard action. When the terms of the final agreement were announced on 20 October 1954, there was 'no longer much fight left in these dissidents'.[263] However, as observers commented,[264] all depended on the spirit in which the agreement worked, as there remained many possible sources of conflict. Eden was hostage, in the eyes of the Suez Group, to Nasser's continued observance of the treaty.

10 The Conservative Party and the Middle East: 1955–57

The Suez crisis was the most divisive event to confront the Conservatives since 1940, and very nearly broke the back of the party in the aftermath of military intervention. There were several decisive domestic and foreign developments prior to July 1956 which helped the frustrated, angry, yet containable group of July 1954 evolve into the faction that seized the ear of the party and the Prime Minister in 1956, setting the parameters of party debate on the best way to deal with Nasser's challenge to Britain's position in the Middle East. These developments were Churchill's resignation from the premiership in April 1955, Conservative opinion of Eden as Prime Minister, and events in Cyprus, Egypt and Jordan.

The importance of Churchill's retirement was twofold: firstly, the departure of the titan was akin to the lifting of a great repressive force. All kinds of tensions could and did well up.[1] Eden did not command the same loyalty and respect, and the Suez Group's reluctant support became dependent upon Egypt's continued 'good behaviour'. These MPs wanted a more 'Conservative' foreign policy generally and felt their government's increased majority after the general election in May 1955 (60) gave the backbenches greater room for manoeuvre.[2]

Secondly there were the questions of Eden's own personality and performance as Prime Minister. The political world rapidly filled with rumours of his moods.[3] Inordinately sensitive to criticism, particularly to charges of appeasement, he was determined that no future crisis should resemble the events of September 1938. In May 1955 'all looked set fair. Yet within six months there was turmoil within the party.'[4] By the autumn the economy was in the doldrums and Eden was increasingly under attack for his delay in reorganizing the Government and acting against inflation. Eden's honeymoon with his backbench critics ended abruptly in September 1955 with the bombshell of Czech arms sales to Egypt. The spectacle of Russia leap-frogging over the Northern Tier confirmed Conservatives' worst fears of the emptiness of Egypt's promise to maintain the Suez base in a high state of readiness. Persistent anti-British propaganda pumped out by Radio Cairo, against the background of mutiny in the Southern Sudan, further primed Tory anger,[5] and prompted some members of the Suez Group[6] to look at possible alternative allies in the Middle East. Amery shared the French politicians' view of the threat posed to Algeria by Egyptian nationalism, and was at the heart of moves behind the scenes to weld a Franco-British alliance in North Africa and the Middle East.[8] Amery was also central to Tory pressure on Macmillan when Foreign Secretary for a closer alliance with Israel, as a means to counter Nasser's influence, and because of Cyprus.[9] Britain's position in Cyprus was under attack from the Enosis campaign for union with Greece, and EOKA guerillas. Orchestrated by the Suez Group,[10] there were increasing calls for a clarification of Government policy and decisive action. It was argued that the arrival of Russia in the Middle East reinforced the need for Britain's continued presence in Cyprus to protect the region from Soviet incursion, to keep the peace within and to underpin Britain's role as the rightful guardian and arbiter in the Middle East, to defend vital supplies of oil, and to sustain her allies in the Gulf, as well as her communications with the Commonwealth. No one was immediately inclined to regard this as an incipient backbench revolt, but it represented a serious body of Conservative opinion, which extended far beyond the original Suez Group, which was increasingly restive and anxious.[11]

Conservatives were already alarmed[12] by Macmillan's commitment to self-determination for Cyprus[13] when the furore erupted over the failure of General Templar's[14] mission to persuade Jordan to adhere to the Baghdad Pact. The Suez Group had supported this attempt to pull Amman from Cairo's orbit,[15] as Britain's traditional predominance in Jordan was threatened by Arab nationalism fuelled by Radio Cairo. The blow to British prestige was attributed directly to Nasser and Eden's indecisiveness: Britain was being maligned and insulted by an upstart Egyptian. Any image of firm and competent handling of Middle Eastern affairs further dented by the political storm surrounding the export of surplus war stores to Egypt in January 1956. Tory dissatisfaction with the persistent lack of direction spilled over into the Conservative press,[16] and culminated in a scathing editorial in *The Daily Telegraph* lambasting Eden's half-measures and 'clumsy courtship of unfriendly and fickle Arab statesmen'.[17] Eden was cut to the quick, and resolved to strike back at his detractors.[18] Not unnaturally, he turned to the field of foreign affairs where 'he was absolutely the master'.[19]

Anthony Nutting later described the abrupt dismissal of General Sir John Glubb as commander of the Arab Legion by King Hussein on 1 March 1956 as the start of the whole Suez episode. Coming hard on the heels of Eden's domestic discomforts, such a set-back in a sphere where Eden was the acknowledged expert, was 'the last straw' for the Prime Minister.[20] The Suez Group were incandescent with rage. It fully shared Eden's view[21] that this was another stroke in Nasser's relentless campaign. This was a 'studied affront',[22] the most sinister event since the Czech arms deal, and since the Foreign Secretary was at that moment in Cairo, a 'calculated insult'.[23] Britain seemed to be 'marching with dreadful certainty' towards a clash over oil in the Middle East which was more likely than any other event to precipitate a third World War. The time for concession was past.[24] Eden must accept the challenge while the Communist position was still unconsolidated and vigorously demonstrate that there were points beyond which Britain would not be driven.

The reinforcement of British ground troops and the air force in Jordan, was merely the preliminary step in the Suez Group's recipe for containing the 'xenophobic upsurge'[25] and ensuring a revitalized British presence in the region. 'An all-out effort now, military, then economic and political' was needed;[26] France should do the same, or face the loss of Algeria. Britain should adopt a clear policy of unwavering support for her friends, deemed far more likely to earn the respect of 'neutralist' Arab nations, and counter the influence of Saudi Arabia and Egypt. Appeasement stood no chance of stemming the anti-British tide.[27]

Thanks largely to Amery's and Randolph Churchill's private lobbying of Butler and Macmillan,[28] a Cabinet meeting was rapidly convened to discuss the issue. Intent on maintaining the pressure on Eden, the next day two letters appeared in *The Times*[29] outlining the Suez Group's 'strong feelings and serious misgivings'.[30] Eden was pressed further in the Commons by Amery and Maitland demanding an emphatic reassertion of British interests in the area. There appeared an ineluctable correlation between the evacuation of the Suez base and the withdrawal from the Sudan – which had done nothing to secure Egyptian friendship for Britain – and Glubb's humiliating dismissal; significantly, Amery urged that in default of American cooperation, Britain should act for herself – a comment which revealed his knowledge of the outcome of Eden's recent visit to Washington.

For the time being, the critics were 'mainly content to make their views known and influence felt through the party's foreign affairs and defence committee rather than any independent action'[31] – a thinly veiled warning to the Whips. Disgusted by Eden's abysmal parliamentary performance on 7 March 1956, they stepped up their pressure through letters to the press, and the normal party channels, hotly disputing as a dangerous fallacy the argument that the Arab/Israeli conflict was to blame for Britain's humiliation.[32] Their demand for the restoration of Britain's position in Jordan was justified on the need to uphold the Baghdad Pact, to sustain Britain's allies in the Persian Gulf, and to maintain access to vital oil supplies.[33]

Eden too was incensed by Glubb's dismissal. He took parental pride in having created the Arab League,[34] and while he wrongly attributed the blame to Nasser, he correctly assessed the enormous blow to Britain's prestige. Significantly, Eden's main concern was that he would be jeered in the Chamber of the House.[35] With the Suez Group and at least half the national press insisting that 'a lost grip . . . had to be recovered', in the view of Nutting, this was enough to stampede Eden, a man relatively unaccustomed to harsh criticism.[36] Crucially, in the party committees the bulk of the Conservative party now endorsed the Suez Group's vigorous demands that action should be taken immediately to restore British prestige in the Middle East.[37] Eden was also under considerable pressure from his Cabinet colleagues for a dramatic reassertion of British might; the majority were in favour of withdrawing the remaining British staff from Jordan without notice. Fearful of driving Jordan further into Egypt's embrace, Eden cast round in his desperate need to flex British muscle to silence his vociferous critics; he initially toyed with the idea of reoccupying Suez,[38] but then decided on Cyprus to provide the check for the apparent slide, banishing Archbishop Makarios to the Seychelles on 10 March 1956.

The Suez Group and its sympathizers were jubilant.[39] Eden received a great ovation when he addressed the 1922 Committee and in the debate on Cyprus, when he asserted that Cyprus must be held to defend the oil of Arabia. Future opponents of Eden's Suez policy were concerned Eden's gesture to placate the Suez Group 'unleashed certain emotions in the party that were dangerous and which could easily recoil on him',[40] as he raised expectations that henceforth whenever Britain was slighted he would take resolute action. From this moment Eden became convinced that his role was to be 'that of a strong man who was going to speak up for England and for the Empire, for this is what the Tory party in the country really wanted, and in a sense he was perfectly right, they did want it'.[41]

The immediate result of the Glubb episode was a toughening of British policy everywhere in the Middle East and East Mediterranean.[42] 'We and the Americans really gave up hope of Nasser and began to look around for means of destroying him.'[43] Eden made overtures of friendship to Israel and France, ended his objections to French secret arms sales to Israel[44] and lent support to France's policy of suppression in Algeria. The Suez Group welcomed this shift to an anti-Nasser policy; the inner core gave considerable thought to the chances of a Wafdist counter-revolution supported by dissident Egyptian officers which, they were assured by their Egyptian intelligence sources, would look more kindly upon Britain:

> Even if (a) Restoration (government) ultimately proved a disappointment a good deal might still have been gained. The Nasser myth would have been broken, a communist *coup* forestalled and the immediate threat to the Baghdad Pact removed. At best, therefore, Restoration would seem to offer a chance of getting off to a fresh start in Anglo-Egyptian relations and at worst a means of paralysing a country which, under its present rulers is a real danger to our vital interests.[45]

Glubb's dismissal exacerbated the general mood of apprehension that had built up over Eden's leadership. His government was struggling in more than mid-term doldrums. After disappointing results in four by-elections in February 1956, the dramatic drop in the Conservative vote at the Tonbridge by-election on 7 June delivered a further blow. The party was restive with Cyprus providing a rallying point for those profoundly concerned at the erosion of Britain's pre-eminence in the Middle East. Significantly, the issue had attracted far wider backbench support than the 1954 Suez Group rebellion. Eden's political future – given that he had 'virtually railroaded' the evacuation strategy through Churchill's cabinet in 1954[46] – became inextricably linked with Egypt's continued observance of the spirit of the 1954 treaty. The embattled Eden had no choice but to respond forcefully to Nasser's decision to nationalize the Suez Canal Company on 26 July 1956.

THE SUEZ GROUP

The Suez Group felt Nasser's action vindicated its stand that withdrawal from Suez would lead to a rapid decline of British influence in the region.[47] Before Parliament rose for the summer recess, it became the most vociferous section of the party, a combination of an atavistic surge of the past (Suez as the fulcrum of the Empire) and a hard-headed and sober response[48] to the threat to Britain's position in the Middle East and vital access to oil.[49] Nasser's act posed a calamitous precedent for British investment overseas. He should be made to restore the Suez Canal Company to its former rights – indeed, most people did not see it as 'nationalization', just plain theft.[50]

Thereafter the Suez Group's moves were those of a three-pronged attack: to create and maintain a political atmosphere that would deny Eden a diplomatic solution that did not ensure the permanent removal of the Canal from Egyptian control by an international body and Nasser's abject humiliation;[51] given that the Anglo-French invasion force would not be ready until mid-September, to rally domestic support for the use of force if necessary, and to forge an alliance in the Middle East that would effectively halt Russian direct encroachment and check Moscow's stooges in Damascus and Cairo.

Once Parliament had risen for the summer, the Suez Group used the correspondence columns in the press, and speeches in the constituencies to maintain its pressure upon the Government to deny Nasser 'unfettered control of the Canal.'[52] The

Suez Group's principal arguments were emotional ones. While not all went as far as Hinchingbrooke's argument that the Suez Canal was an integral part of Britain,[53] the Canal's strategic importance to Britain, her Empire and Commonwealth, was thought to give Britain inalienable rights. There was an acute awareness if Nasser 'got away with it', his stock would rise inordinately,[54] and the situation in the Middle East would become extremely dangerous. Britain's ally, Nuri-es-Said of Iraq would be more vulnerable, as would Israel. There should be no negotiation with Nasser until the decree had been revoked: he had deliberately 'sown discord between Britain and the Arab world', and had already delighted in flouting, whenever convenient to himself, free passage of the Canal in defiance of the 1888 Convention. The economic sanctions (freezing Egypt's sterling reserves and blocking the Suez Canal Company's assets) were insufficient – the example of Europe's failure to bring Mussolini to heel after the Abyssinian war was cited. While it was the Government's duty to determine exactly what these stronger measures should be,[55] armed force, in this case, was fully justified. In the absence of a UNO police force, 'Britain and France with or without America should present an ultimatum to Egypt with a time limit attached to it'[56] to 'teach Nasser and any other aspiring dictator that crime does not pay'.[57]

Bolstered by its contacts with French politicians, who saw this as their chance to confront Nasser,[58] the Suez Group was intent on preventing any capitulation to transatlantic pressure.[59] It was well aware that the American administration in a Presidential election year could not tolerate anything which might lead to war, let alone defend Britain's oil interests and her lifeline with the Empire. However, the Suez Group had no doubts that Britain could and should act independently in her traditional sphere of influence.[60] 'It is really a question of whether the Government has the necessary willpower.'[61]

Kenneth Love suggests that 'the rebels had no official standing and little organization'.[62] This is inaccurate. The Suez Group was united by a firm sense of purpose, held regular closed meetings, and many of its members occupied key positions within the backbench structure of the party. 'It was not just what they might do, it was what they *were* doing! They effectively converted the Prime Minister to their point of view.'[63] The Suez Group MPs were no longer seen as political pariahs, indulged for their eccentricity and outdated view of the world. The faction had now grown well beyond its original number to approximately 100 strong (out of a total of 345 Conservative MPs). The new adherents 'did not necessarily respond to some of the Suez Group's vibrations, but felt in terms of defence they were right'.[64]

Thus the Suez Group's views had acquired a remarkable reverberation.[65] The danger Nasser posed was felt to be greater by 'middle and older generations,[66] the inheritors of an imperial sense of military geography and an experience of a Middle East in which Britain held positions of power and influence' – a sense that Nasser was upsetting the natural order of things. There remained a residue of their guilt in accepting the appeasement of dictators in the 1930s which spurred some pre-war MPs into a determination not to countenance appeasement again in any form. Younger Tories, influenced by their war service,[67] shared the sense of the critical danger Nasser posed to the West, and to Britain and her imperial possessions in particular. 'After Suez, we became the party',[68] may seem an exaggeration, but to a very great extent the Suez Group had educated the party to accept that something now *had* to be done.[69] There was widespread support for resolute action,[70] and apart from *The Manchester Guardian*,[71] the national press was united in its indignation at Nasser's 'grab'.

Although the Suez Group was unable to keep 'bellicosity on the boil' during the summer recess, the cumulative effect of its political sabre rattling raised Conservative backbench expectations of a rapid and humiliating diplomatic defeat for Nasser.[72] Although the extent to which Eden was bent on a vengeful war from the outset is disputed,[73] Eden too was determined that Nasser should be humiliated as publicly as possible. Although Eden's first statement on the Suez question in the House was measured, he soon appeared to be swept up by the hue and cry.[74] Selwyn Lloyd had privately sought the Suez Group's endorsement of his 'extremely strong statement' before his address to the Foreign Affairs Committee on 31 July 1956.[75] The enthusiastic backbench reception of this belligerent message was of crucial importance in the hardening of Eden's rhetoric.[76] Thereafter Eden certainly gave the impression that he was determined to 'have a go at Nasser' to achieve a swift and crushing victory.[77]

The Suez Group's behaviour prevented the party from cooling down sufficiently to let Eden climb back down to a position which gave him more room to manoeuvre.[78] As Eden had little contact with his backbenchers, either before or after the crisis erupted, '[this] distance strengthened the influence of our dissident group'.[79] By the end of August some political insiders thought the Prime Minister would listen to calmer counsels and might succeed in finessing his belligerent supporters.[80] But the pressure was mounting on Eden to avoid any suggestion that he might be compelled to negotiate for a long time.[81] There was mounting restiveness among the reservists whose morale was plummeting; and impatience in sections of the press and Conservative party was hardening, with calls for immediate action and renewed talk of indecision at the top.[82] Amery was actively hawking the slogan: 'Either Nasser or Eden must go before October'.[83]

The strain on the Prime Minister was beginning to tell.[84] Faced with the prospect of protracted negotiations which might not achieve the desired end, or one that could be sold to the party as a triumph for Britain, by the end of August Eden was pressing the Cabinet for an immediate decision on the use of force if Nasser refused to accept the internationalization of the Canal.[85]

The Suez Group were confident at the beginning of September that the Government was 'still firm', much encouraged by the landing of French troops in Cyprus and Selwyn Lloyd's private assurance to Hinchingbrooke of Eden's intention to 'go through with it'.[86] 'All the same... [Eden] will need more nerve than he has shown hitherto if he is to act in what is by now rather cold blood.'[87] The Suez Group still regarded getting rid of Nasser of equal importance to getting a satisfactory solution to the Canal problem, underwritten by an Anglo-French force permanently stationed in the Zone – and were frankly sceptical of America's reliability. Much to Amery's amusement, 'the Foreign Office have suddenly discovered they have no friends among the anti-Nasser forces and have accordingly come, slightly cap in hand, to me of all people to help'. Amery put them in touch with the opposition in Cairo.[88] He undoubtedly knew MI6 had concluded assassinating Nasser would make him a martyr; instead it was hoped an Anglo-French military operation against Nasser would arouse so much popular discontent that dissident Egyptian officers and politicians could seize power. With Britain and France in charge of the Canal and a new Egyptian government, the prospects of 'a new plan' for the Canal looked rosy.[89]

The Suez Group's hopes were soon 'belied by events'.[90] The failure of the Menzies' mission[91] was not followed by the desired British action against Nasser; instead there were renewed cross-party demands[92] for Britain to take the dispute to the Security Council. The Suez Group was firmly opposed to this[93] and was already discussing an amendment for the Party Conference 'should we need one'.[94] At the short emergency session of Parliament in September its initial pleasure over the Suez Canal Users Association[95] (SCUA) as the opportunity for 'an incident... of sufficient size to justify dramatic action'[96] with America's backing, rapidly gave way to open disgust.[97] With SCUA rendered bankrupt, there were renewed calls for recourse to the UNO, an organization for which the Suez Group had scant respect.[98] It was convinced that any claim by the UNO to superior moral authority was nullified by the membership of nations who openly flouted international convention. The consequence would undoubtedly be a Russian veto[99] – whereupon Britain would be faced either with not acting at all, or acting in default of a Security Council mandate, which would contravene international law.

The Suez Group made its opposition plain in the 1922 Committee, fearing the matter would become bogged down in a mire of legal language and irresolution. But it lost this round.[100] Faced with the pressure from the 'wet' wing of the party, Eden 'failed to give leadership' and agreed to take the matter to the Security Council. Little could be done to promote a belligerent policy before the party conference.[101] 'The military plan has apparently been changed and no effective action can be taken for several weeks; 4–5 weeks is the figure I heard today... I hear the Jordanians are already asking us to withdraw from air bases there. I also had an indication from the French side that they are beginning to despair. If the rot sets in in Paris, it will spread very quickly.'[102]

'The general malaise which followed the abortive September debate fuelled Eden's difficulties with the backbenches who felt he had lost his touch.'[103] The pretexts for military force seemed to be slipping away. Contrary to all expectations,

Egyptian pilots clearly could run the Canal. Nasser appeared to be getting away with his theft. The Government was on the defensive in foreign and domestic policy, with the party restless and impatient, and widely reported to be so,[104] while the Labour party was 'in buoyant spirits' under its newly elected leader, Hugh Gaitskell. The clear undercurrent at the Llandudno party conference was that unless the Government could pursue policies that were 'distinctly Conservative',[105] Labour was going to win the next election.[106] Therefore Conservative unity was of vital importance.[107]

The Suez Group was determined to act to prevent the issue going 'off the boil'. In defiance of the Chief Whip,[108] Waterhouse and Amery, ably abetted by Angus Maude, drew up an addendum which 'put teeth' into the original anodyne resolution in the foreign policy debate, put forward by crypto-members of the Suez Group.[109] This addendum which was accepted (in itself an extraordinary occurrence) immediately,[110] pledged support for a solution 'designed to ensure international control of the canal in accordance with the proposals of the London Conference'. In the debate Waterhouse's robust message that at all costs and by all means Nasser's aggression must be resisted and defeated met with his audience's wholehearted approval. Amery's explicit warning to Eden received an equally enthusiastic reception: 'If the discussions at the Security Council do not bring Nasser to his senses, then I believe the process of negotiation will be exhausted.' Any further compromise would mean surrender. 'We must go forward with American approval if we can get it, without it if they withhold it, and against their wishes if need be.' The debate was televised which provided a further fillip for the Suez Group's cause.

The Suez Group's concerted effort at Llandudno was crucial in Eden's later decision to use force. While the party conference was proceeding, the Foreign Secretary was negotiating in New York with the Egyptian Foreign Minister; and Selwyn Lloyd, whose own instinct was for a diplomatic solution,[111] was optimistic about the prospect of a negotiated settlement.[112] Eden, who remained convinced in the very last resort action would be necessary,[113] was increasingly fearful that Britain's position was being eroded.[114] Egypt appeared confident the crisis was 'burnt out'; therefore it was imperative that 'we should not be inveigled away in negotiations with the fundamentals to which we have held all along'.[115] Above all, he was insistent that Britain 'should not be parted from the French'.[116]

The Cabinet plainly hoped to regain the initiative from the Suez Group which was riding on the crest of the wave. Butler and Lennox-Boyd were closely involved in the Chief Whip's frantic manoeuvres to reduce the impact of the Suez Group's addendum.[117] Whatever the later debate over Nutting's integrity, his speech[118] 'left little, if anything for the Suez Group to say against the Government'.[119] However, this proved a high-risk approach as the audience's support of the Suez Group's strident rhetoric from the platform created the fear in the minds of many in the Cabinet that if the Government did not act on the brave words uttered by ministers at the conference, these would be shown up as 'rhetorical verbiage'.[120] Eden did nothing to defuse the charged atmosphere at Llandudno. The Prime Minister, who had just risen from his sick bed, wound up the conference on 13 October 1956 with a pugnacious speech.[121] To tremendous applause, he echoed Nutting's commitment that the Government meant business and 'will stand firm . . . I have always said force is the last resort, but it cannot be excluded'. The day after the end of the conference, Eden received a deputation from General Challe and Acting Foreign Minister, Albert Gazier.

The importance of the French Government's links with the Suez Group cannot be exaggerated. The French feared Eden would weaken and not seek the desired confrontation with Nasser[122] by no later than the end of October,[123] leaving France isolated;[124] talking to the Americans was a waste of time as 'they will never authorize any action likely to provoke the fall of Nasser at any rate until after the US presidential elections'.[125] Throughout the crisis Guy Mollet, the French Prime Minister, maintained contact with Amery who was also aware of the Franco-Israeli contacts[126] and had long kept in very close touch with the Israeli Ambassador in London.[127] Just before the conference Mollet urged Amery to keep up the pressure on Eden at the party conference 'as it may be our last chance to fuel the fire'.[128]

Therefore it was a question of national and international pressure working in close communion on Eden whose judgment was affected by the strain of overwork, ill-health, and a highly strung temperament.[129] Eden's own beliefs would have made him more susceptible to the Suez Group's arguments. He was personally less inclined than Churchill to work to secure American cooperation in all areas;[130] Dulles' behaviour over SCUA in September 1956 had revived the antipathy between Eden and the American Secretary of State which had developed at the Geneva conference on Indo-China in 1954.[131] Like the Suez Group,[132] Eden was concerned at the extent of Soviet infiltration in the Middle East, and believed that there was an alternative government to Nasser.[133] And the pressure on Eden for a tough stance was strong: from the Suez Group; from Mollet and Pineau; from Clarissa Eden, who was 'eager that Eden should assert himself against the calumnies of Conservative newspapers and drawing rooms that he was a man of straw'; and from the pressure of his memories of the First and Second World Wars.[134] Given the 'rocky autumn',[135] the bumpy spring and the warning of the Tonbridge by-election, it was inevitable the Prime Minister should be concerned about the reception of his actions on the benches behind him, quite apart from his own hyper-sensitivity to criticism. Eden's leadership of the party was not yet seriously in question, but he would not have been human if he had remained impervious to the rip current of opinion within the party. The rebels' role at the party conference was all-important in re-injecting steam into public debate when the issue was 'going cold'[136] and in demonstrating that the party as a whole would not accept anything that smacked of retreat.

The Suez Group had also bolstered the Chancellor's resolve at a critical time. In a private conversation with his son-in-law at the end of August,[137] Macmillan expressed reservations about the wisdom of an alliance with Israel[138] and was upbraided by an irate Amery. The Chancellor's renewed determination to confront Nasser rendered him deaf to the crucial hints he received in Washington that his optimism of ultimate American benevolent neutrality was wildly misplaced.[139] In the view of his biographer, Alistair Horne, the effect of Macmillan's conviction[140] that 'Ike would lie doggo' can hardly be exaggerated.[141] Macmillan threatened to resign in September unless the Government played its hand 'to the end'. The feverish Eden had just returned from Paris where the French government was agitating for immediate action, and the Chancellor's hawkish views enjoyed the support of a third of the backbench party.

Macmillan was also a rival for the premiership. Eden had 'a very deep distrust of Macmillan' and their rivalry, especially since 1953, had been a very important factor in their relationship.[142] The ill-disguised menace of the Suez Group for Eden[143] was that it would not have to look far for a satisfactory replacement. It was recognized in political circles that should Macmillan put himself at the Suez Group's head he would pose a potentially lethal threat to Eden's authority in Cabinet; thus Macmillan did not need to take any such crude action. This could not fail to influence Eden's assessment of the options open to him.

By 16 October Eden had opted for war; his supremacy in Cabinet on foreign policy matters was of critical importance[144] for there were doubters in the Cabinet.[145] Despite Selwyn Lloyd's encouraging telegrams, Eden was faced with the stark prospect of undoubtedly protracted and possibly inconclusive negotiations; weighing very heavily in the scales was his knowledge, gained first hand at Llandudno, that his party as a whole would not accept a less vigorous policy. Indeed, the party conference probably appeared to confer a mandate for military action against Egypt, which the Cabinet had been most reluctant to seek in Parliament.[146] To the increasingly ill Prime Minister, the French plan seemed miraculously to cut the Gordian knot.

Mollet, the French Premier, assured Amery a week or two before the invasion 'it is going to be alright. We are going ahead. America will be intolerable but if we see it through, not only will Britain and France benefit: If we can win against America and Russia, I will make a good European of your Anthony Eden yet!'[147] Amery's lingering doubts over Eden's resolve[148] were jubilantly dispelled by the news of the Anglo-French ultimatum. Fears that Britain's standing in the Middle East had been weakened to the point that Jordan might demand an immediate revision of the Anglo-Jordanian treaty and Britain's withdrawal from bases there, her ally, Nuri, murdered or even revolution in Khartoum,[149] were forgotten. 'The Suez Group's policy is at last accepted. Here is our great chance to restore our position in the Middle East and build for the future.'[150] Britain and France in possession of the Canal would be able to make satisfactory terms for both the future regime of the Canal, and the establishment of an international, or better still, an Anglo-French base to police the area and prevent future hostilities between Israel and Egypt.[151]

Eden's announcement received most Conservatives' hearty endorsement.[152] Immediately before the Israeli attack on Egypt, there had been Conservative fears that the Tripartite Declaration could result in Britain fighting Jordan in a future Middle Eastern conflict (which appeared imminent), or even with Egypt against Iraq;[153] Britain was now fighting the 'right' war. 'Eden was striking a blow for world order. Nasser had to be checked – it was important for the whole trading world and the continued threats to the new state of Israel were intolerable.'[154] Many, who were fed up with the humiliations, had little time for niceties: 'We asked ourselves, when was the last time the Egyptian Army won an engagement? It was the second act of Aïda.'[155] And resolutions of support for Eden's policy were flooding into Conservative Central Office.[156]

Conservative MPs rapidly discovered the military operation held a cross-party appeal in their constituencies:[157] 'their jingoism was coloured by a general feeling, a hangover from the last War, that the Egyptians should be thumped regularly.'[158] Others attributed constituency support to more of a visceral reaction – 'Our boys are in danger' – rather than a thinking response.[159] The widespread antipathy to Dulles reinforced this further: 'Anything which simultaneously hit Nasser for six, and Dulles for six, must be good.'[160]

Whatever their private doubts about the morality of the venture,[161] Tories were scornful of Labour's arguments: letting 'things rip until the UNO could intervene' was seen as both unrealistic and impractical, whereas Britain and France had the base and all the necessary equipment.[162] However, the sceptics questioned the aims of the military operation; if it was just to secure the Canal, they doubted whether Nasser would necessarily fall – which would in turn reproduce all the old problems which had led to the 1954 agreement. 'If, on the other hand, the objective was to topple Nasser, this could only [be] achieved by a direct onslaught on Cairo and Alexandria'[163] – an argument with which both the Suez and Anti-Suez MPs agreed.[164]

MPs on all sides were well aware that continued political

support for Eden was dependent upon a quick and overwhelming success against Egypt.[165] The initially strong Conservative support eroded when it was realized just how long the military operation would take.[166] The lack of information was immensely frustrating. It rapidly became apparent to the backbenchers that even a sizeable proportion of the Government were equally in the dark.[167] All the signs were that Eden was running a very personal policy,[168] although this was not in fact the case.[169]

All wanted a rapid conclusion to the crisis.[170] '90% of the party were ex-services'[171] and the incompetence was baffling.[172] The vocal support of the Suez Group and its sympathizers and the growing impatience of the French government (who had given up all concern with appearances and wanted to launch an attack on the Canal with open Israeli support) could not match the heavy artillery trained upon the beleaguered Eden. He was under mounting pressure now to stop from all sides – from the White House, in the United Nations, from the Commonwealth, from Labour MPs whose sustained vitriolic attack on the Prime Minister created tumultuous scenes in the House, and from within his own party.

The Suez Group were aghast at the cease-fire on 6 November, a 'fiasco not through lack of power, but lack of guts. Eden [had] left the war unfinished to satisfy his pacific critics.'[173] 'Another 48 hours and we would ... have toppled Nasser and seen the emergence of a new [pro-Western] Egyptian regime ... [This] would have offered a new treaty over the Canal and the whole question of the base would have been up for discussion again.'[174] Indeed most Tories were first stunned and then infuriated by Eden's capitulation.[175] Having had the audacity to take such a terrific gamble, and having withstood the venom of the Labour party, Eden had then not had the courage to see the venture through.[176] For the Suez Group, Eden's abrupt departure to Jamaica on 23 November 1956 sealed his fate.

It had not occurred to the Suez Group that America would throw a spanner in the works. Perhaps their inside knowledge of MI6's liaison with the CIA in the *coup* which ousted Mossadeq had lulled them into a mistaken belief that America accepted the legitimacy of force, whereas America, hypocritically, drew a distinction between covert and overt action.[177] They certainly thought Jewish domestic pressure would muzzle America,[178] and Amery was undoubtedly aware of his father-in-law's conviction of American benevolent neutrality. There had been no thought that Britain would, or could, be constrained in the Middle East.[179]

The Suez Group continued to meet[180] and prepare its strategy. Having concluded that 'while America regarded Britain as a major ally in Europe against the threat of Soviet expansion, they were equally concerned to destroy the British Commonwealth and Empire' and break British predominance in the Middle East, these MPs became increasingly anti-American, even to the extent of 'informal contacts with Russian representatives, to try to persuade Moscow that a British and French presence in the Middle East was preferable to an American take-over of these areas'.[181] Now intent on keeping British troops on the Canal, either independently or as part of the UNO force, the critics' clamour was for British provision for clearing the Canal, an international settlement of the Canal dispute and a resolution of the Arab/Israeli conflict.[182]

Having 'hi-jacked' the Prime Minister, the Suez Group now appeared to do the same to the party.[183] 'We agreed with the Suez Group that the humiliation of being "seen off" by the Egyptians was appalling.'[184] Most Tories felt cheated by Washington,[185] even those who had harboured doubts about military intervention;[186] despite warnings in the press,[187] the majority had thought that the Americans would be 'benevolent neutrals'[188] in the Anglo-French action. The Whips' initial fears of embittered Conservatives abstaining in the crucial vote of confidence on 8 November 1956 did not materialize, but press speculation of a revolt grew as the Suez Group tapped Tory disgust at Washington's policy.[189]

It was the prospect of an ignominious unconditional withdrawal which 'really excited the hostility of the Tory party... Many of them were quite ready to see the UNO come to Suez ... the difficulty was that the force was not strong, was not ready; it was not really competent and would come in very slowly.'[190] Nor were there guarantees 'that the Suez Canal will be cleared and maintained as an international waterway'.[191] The rumours that 'Ike' was threatening Eden with economic sanctions, and the 'hint of military sanctions'[192] were enough to convince excitable Conservatives, already apoplectic at American behaviour in the UNO, of Washington's iniquity.[193]

'The ruling emotions of Tory backbenchers are an amalgam

of all the emotions that make the worst counsellors – hurt national pride, a desire for party unity by those MPs who never wanted Britain to go in in the first place, but who are now more inclined to agree with the militants that there was more danger in getting out precipitously and the desperate urge of the militants to prove the military operation was in some way a success.'[194] With the party in this mood, no political observer would predict what sort of compromise the Government might be able to sell its disgruntled supporters.

Faced with American obduracy and threatened with schism on its backbenches, the Cabinet careered through November 1956 as 'the driver of a fast car, with no eyes except for the next bend in the road'.[195] The influence of the Suez Group on the content of government policy was negligible. Despite the backbench tumult, it became increasingly clear that the Cabinet had little choice but to withdraw.[196] Britain was hoist on its own petard: having gone in ostensibly to separate the combatants, London could not change its stance now. Ministers came to the conclusion that Britain must capitulate to American demands.[197] 'To sit at Port Said with a UNO force and a blocked canal in front of you and the threat of oil sanctions behind you seems a high price to pay for the smiles of the Suez Group.'[198] The most the Cabinet could offer its backbenchers was an assurance about the competence of the UNO force to discharge its tasks and the prospect of a very early start on clearing the canal along its whole length – the sop was to be the British naval task force under UNO direction. Butler and his colleagues were relying upon backbench political hardheadedness and devoutly hoped that the rebels would not make life any more difficult by withholding their support. In the end, a British contribution to the UNO force clearing the Canal was denied and there were no arrangements to settle the Arab/Israeli conflict nor to secure an international settlement for the Canal dispute. Nasser seemed to have triumphed.

However, the influence of the Suez Group on the Government's *presentation* of policy was considerable. In his rearguard action against unremitting American pressure for a complete British withdrawal, Butler was obliged to tread extremely carefully. At one point Julian Ridsdale stressed to Robert Allan, Eden's PPS, 'For God's sake, don't let's fall out with the Americans', whereupon Allan pointed to Waterhouse and said, 'We have to take care of these people first'.[199] Heath, the Chief Whip, also consulted the Suez Group for recommendations for the replacement of Boyle as Economic Secretary and to discover whether Derek Walker-Smith had its support; Ian Harvey, who had supported the Suez venture, was promoted to Parliamentary Secretary to the Ministry of Supply.

The Cabinet was acutely aware that 'there would be an outburst of public indignation against the Government if there were anything that smacked of a "scuttle"' from Egypt before the objectives of the original intervention had been reasonably achieved,[200] which would 'seriously weaken the Government'.[201] The Suez Group stalwarts, bolstered by reports from Wafdist sources which suggested, 'If we hold on Nasser may crack',[202] were warning Heath that they would feel compelled to resign the party whip if there was any withdrawal of British troops before the Canal had been cleared *and* international control of the Canal established.[203] Outspoken constituency support for the rebels' stance[204] removed much of the Whips' clout.

The danger of mutiny grew, as 112 Conservatives signed a critical EDM deploring the UNO resolution and the attitude of America. The sponsors had deliberately drafted the motion to attract the widest possible support to increase its impact on the Government.[205] The list comprised approximately one third of the Government's supporters:[206] both the Suez Group and 'the larger body of members who represent moderate opinion within the party'.[207] This EDM and press reports that approximately 70 MPs were seriously considering withdrawing their support[208] lent credence to Maude's threat of a massive Conservative revolt[209] if Britain was 'humiliated, betrayed by her friends abroad, forced to crawl to the Americans for every drop of oil,' while Nasser triumphed.[210] The Government's future seemed at stake.[211]

Determined to 'expose the smallest possible flank for criticism',[212] the Cabinet decided that the interim statement to the House on 29 November should be one of fact, not policy. 'If the immediate Parliamentary situation could be held in this way',[213] a more detailed statement of policy could be deferred until Monday 3 December, offering the opportunity for further approaches to the UN Secretary General and America for more definite undertakings[214] – 'so as to strengthen the case for presentation to Conservative opinion here'.[215] 'The

Government must be able to demonstrate that they had secured ... the most positive assurances about clearance of the Canal which it was practicable to obtain in the present circumstances, and their policy in the UNO had been designed to protect vital interests of Britain in the Middle East as these were interpreted by a large section of Conservative supporters.'[216]

This turmoil within the Conservative party, whipped up by the Suez Group, worked to Butler's temporary advantage in his efforts to avoid a specific date for withdrawal.[217] Washington was so alarmed at the outburst of feeling which seemed to threaten the survival of the Conservative Government (it was particularly loath to see a Labour government as Aneurin Bevan had just been appointed Shadow Foreign Secretary), that Eisenhower offered assurances of American oil and loans, and of 'America's intention to work towards clearing the Canal and the need to proceed to a final settlement of the problems of the area as speedily as possible'[218] to sweeten the announcement of withdrawal, instead of waiting until Britain's physical departure.[219]

Following the 'bitter pill' of the announcement of withdrawal on 3 December 1956, there was febrile press speculation of a possible rebellion with estimates of the number of rebels ranging wildly from approximately 20[220] to between 40–50.[221] Thanks to the herculean efforts of Heath, with the invaluable support of John Morrison, Chairman of the 1922 Committee, and other party grandees (Anthony Hurd, Sir Guy Lloyd, and Legge-Bourke),[222] the Suez Group's threatened schism did not materialize. 'The majority ... held firm between the critics of the whole adventure and the critics of the cease-fire.'[223] The high profile of the Suez Group was not to everyone's taste; there was a feeling that these MPs 'were carrying things to extremes. They were a very self-conscious, publicity-seeking crowd, who loved pontificating at press conferences and giving interviews.'[224] Hinchingbrooke was forgiven everything, but some saw in such people as Paul Williams and John Biggs-Davison 'too much of glint of satisfaction in their eye as they were tearing the party to pieces. And the press were loving it.'[225]

Opposition jeers at Conservative discomfort served to bring the party closer together.[226] A large-scale backbench revolt would only serve to wreck the Government, letting in Labour. Although die-hard Conservatives felt that a small majority in the forthcoming division would 'hasten the reconstruction of the Government, which they would welcome under a new Prime Minister',[227] the prevailing Tory mood remained that there was no feasible alternative to withdrawal;[228] the only sensible way forward was for the Conservative backbenchers to back their leaders in pressing for effective UNO action.[229] Heath reached a deal with the rebels[230] and only 15 abstained in the vital division,[231] well aware that by the time the vote was taken their demonstration would not have serious consequences for the Government.[232] Once the division was over, 'parliamentary tension expired like a punctured balloon'.[233]

The political reverberations from the Suez débâcle continued. Eden resigned as Prime Minister on 9 January 1957 on the grounds of ill-health and the 'influence of the . . . Suez Group and those sharing their views' on the choice of Macmillan as Eden's successor was clear.[234] Macmillan himself was extremely dubious that his government would last more than six weeks:[235] the breaches in the Conservative party needed to be healed, the alliance with America re-established, the problems of Suez and Cyprus resolved, as well as the economic situation addressed and the lessons of Suez applied in terms of defence.[236] In March 1957 the Government also had to face the threat of devastating strikes throughout industry[237] and the inevitable by-elections, some of which were worse than others.

Initially the political speculation was that the 'old guard of the party will be encouraged and fortified to try and turn their rear guard action into an offensive one.' Their existence could not be denied, nor their persistence ignored.[238] However, over the next five months Macmillan proceeded consistently to reverse his Suez policy – 'while saying just as consistently that he [was] doing precisely the opposite'.[239] The Suez Group lost a forceful and energetic advocate when Amery joined the Government in January; and the faction's nominal leader, Waterhouse was no longer in a rebellious mood.

The two-day parliamentary inquest on the Suez operation in March revealed the enduring backbench anxieties and frustration,[240] but was deemed 'a poor parody of its predecessors'.[241] Lord Salisbury's resignation on 29 March 1957 over the Government's decision to release Archbishop Makarios[242] was first seen as a problem that would tear the party apart as he had been a vital prop to Macmillan's premiership.[243] But despite the profound feelings aroused over Cyprus[244] on top of 'the other discontents', the much feared internal Conservative split never materialized.[245] Macmillan's growing dominance of his party obscured Salisbury's decision;[246] Salisbury had chosen an issue on which no strong public opinion was aroused[247] as most Conservatives believed the security forces had established their ascendancy over EOKA and regained the initiative; nor did Salisbury set himself at the head of the Suez rebels.[248]

Lacking a powerful leader, the dissidents' attempts to prevent Britain's capitulation to Nasser through frequent impassioned pleas in the party committees,[249] interventions in debate,[250] letters to the press,[251] critical EDMs[252] and constituency speeches[253] could not ward off the realities of Britain's position. Despite determined efforts to avoid the immense blow to British prestige that would come with conceding canal dues should be paid to the Egyptian government,[254] faced with the breakdown of the voluntary boycott once the Canal was open to larger vessels, on 13 May the government advised British ships to use the Suez Canal.

Although the Suez Group had no impact upon the direction of policy, its continued existence and the wider support its views enjoyed within the party did affect the presentation of government policy: Macmillan paid assiduous attention to presenting this humiliating retreat in the best possible light[255] and to the timing of the announcement[256] to defuse the anticipated backbench outcry.[257] This deliberate drawn out approach[258] and emphasis that 'the circumstances had been too strong' for Britain[259] paid off, aided by the positive responses to Thorneycroft's Budget, the Defence White paper in early April (with its frank dependence on the nuclear deterrent)[260] and the announcement of the successful detonation of Britain's H-bomb. Only Hinchingbrooke, Lawrence Turner, Sir Victor Raikes, Angus Maude, John Biggs-Davison, Paul Williams, Anthony Fell and Patrick Maitland resigned the party Whip in protest at the 'complete scuttle'.[261] While some political observers interpreted these defections as a set-back to the Conservative party's reviving fortunes,[262] this was not the case. Macmillan was more than satisfied with the Government's majority of 49 in what amounted to a vote of confidence in the Government on 16 May;[263] six Conservatives abstained[264] while others, such as Waterhouse, who sympathized with the rebels voted with the Government. The overwhelming majority of Conservatives were determined to 'let bygones be bygones'.[265]

There was no official witch-hunt[266] – undoubtedly to assuage the feelings of those opponents of his Suez policy who remained within the party[267] and because Macmillan had no desire to disaffiliate the rebels for fear of byelections.[268] This small die-hard band, nicknamed 'The Bedford Group',[269] continued to meet to push for a resolute foreign policy. Crucially it lacked a leader of real stature;[270] thus it had no impact whatsoever on British policy in the Middle East.[271] Putting on a brave face with the announcement that they were heartened by the 'continuing trend of events which [went] a long way to halt the decline in British prestige, power and influence',[272] five Independent Conservatives reapplied for the party Whip on 28 June 1958,[273] concluding eight months of secret negotiations.[274] Thus ended 'a small but brave political adventure'.[275]

THE ANTI-SUEZ GROUP

In July 1956 even those Conservatives who were to be the most ardent opponents of military intervention, initially deplored Nasser's action – that 'impetuous expropriation', which ignored proper safeguards and did not offer prompt, adequate and effective compensation.[276] Decided second thoughts soon appeared on Conservative backbenches[277] as cooler heads came to the conclusion that Eden had missed his chance. 'If we had possessed the requisite force of the right type to take action within a matter of hours after Nasser had seized the Canal, all would have been well. There is only one rule and it is a golden rule that should govern any action in the Middle East: it must be quick and it must be successful.'[278]

Conservative misgivings remained subdued until after the failure of the Menzies mission; as *The Economist* pointed out, 'No Tory wanted to sound pacific if the Government happened to be bellicose' while no backbencher could hurt 'his conscience or his personal prospects in the party by urging the Government towards stronger action'. There was nothing to be gained in the constituencies by openly denouncing the Suez Group's rhetoric. Although Eden was very reluctant to take the matter to the Security Council,[279] he was aware of a 'general feeling that it would not be right to resort to military force without further conversations' including a referral to the UNO.[280] Salisbury was urging Eden that under the UNO Charter, Britain could not resort to force unless the matter had been referred to the UNO.[281] The Cabinet was conscious that if matters did lead to war, and a war that entailed bombing, this could alienate a large section of Tory voters who held liberal views on foreign affairs.[282]

The Cabinet was very conscious of the growing division in political opinion over the use of force,[283] and accordingly was extremely reluctant to recall Parliament.

> If we are likely to have unhappily to proceed to extremes, a debate in Parliament is going to put us in an impossible position. Yet in such circumstances and before action of the utmost gravity is taken, it will surely be very difficult to maintain the position that Parliament has no right to be consulted at all ... In a situation such as this we should certainly not want to disclose our intentions and plans.[284] It would be highly embarrassing to invite Parliament to approve a proposal to launch a military operation against Egypt ... In both World Wars the Government acted in response to aggression then invited Parliament to endorse [its action].[285]

Conservative opposition to the use of force against Egypt before recourse to the UNO[286] reached a peak in the short parliamentary session on 12th/13th September 1956. With misgivings about the progress of negotiations, and alarmed by the influence of the Suez Group, the 'Heald Group'[287] (as it was dubbed by some newspapers) began to coalesce. When Dulles' 'bombshell' effectively torpedoed SCUA,[288] backbench pressure mounted on Eden to refer the matter to the Security Council; although the French government was opposed to this,[289] the Cabinet knew that the Commonwealth was in favour of this move.[290] Eden faced a critical meeting of the 1922 Committee on 13th September 1956 held immediately before the resumption of the Commons debate on SCUA. Feelings were running high, and the rift between the supporters of recourse to the Security Council and the 'blood and thunder boys'[291] came out into the open. The whole mood of the party had changed from July: those in favour of taking the matter to the UNO were in a majority, and 'were not at all pleased with the Government's attitude'. Well aware that the Security Council would prove ineffective, these MPs appreciated that to say so in advance would alienate opinion at home and abroad. 'No one except France agrees we should [go to war against the wishes of the Opposition] ... If we went to war in defiance of our allies, we should do terrible harm to all our alliances [NATO, SEATO and the Commonwealth]'; it would wreck any chance of making the UNO an effective force if Britain defied its rulings. There was a classic opportunity to demonstrate economic pressure could be more effective than military action.[292]

Heald and Nigel Nicolson insisted that any action against Egypt (which Tories had concluded was now merely a matter of time) must be taken only after a referral to the Security Council; and unless Eden gave such an undertaking they were prepared to abstain in the division lobby that evening. The Whips understood that approximately 23 other Members supported this view. As the debate resumed in the Chamber amid confusion on the Government benches,[293] Heald made another impressive contribution that commanded a 'wide measure of agreement on both sides of the House'.[294] This backbench pressure was decisive in persuading Eden to take the matter to the UNO,[295] despite the Suez Group's and Washington's opposition.[296] This gesture also appeared to strengthen Britain's hand in any future confrontation with Nasser since the Russians would undoubtedly use their veto (hence Dulles' opposition).

Over the next six weeks, from their private soundings within the party and contacts with the Cabinet,[297] the Anti-Suez Group MPs were increasingly worried about the direction of government policy. The overwhelming impression they gained was 'the Suez Group are driving [Eden] into a corner, from which the only escape is either a humiliating climb-down or ... war'.[298] Nicolson believed that Eden was 'only too anxious to hear a more moderate voice raised within the party' but he feared, at best, 'it will mean a row like Munich'.[299] This impression was reinforced by the reaction of the audience at the Llandudno party conference to William Yates' lone stand against a belligerent policy. In a spirited speech Yates declared British policy in the Middle East was driving pan-Arab nationalism into the arms of communism. Amid cries of 'Shame', he demanded to know why had Britain not passed the matter to the Security Council, and charged that the British and French governments were intended to 'screw out a new agreement from Egypt under threat of war'.[300] When Parliament returned, Yates was greeted by loud Opposition cheers when he rose to speak in the Chamber.

A week later Israel attacked Egypt. The Anti-Suez Group saw Eden's decision to intervene with the French as the triumph of the Suez Group. These Conservatives felt the diplomatic options had not been exhausted and the six principles thrashed out between Selwyn Lloyd and Fawzi in New York had offered a real chance of a peaceful and honourable settlement. While they had no liking for Nasser, it seemed insanity to have attacked him 'when for the first time in his career he appears to have been wronged, instead of being the wrongdoer'.[301]

> The political aims appeared incomprehensible. The argument that Britain had gone in to separate the combatants? The thing was a nonsense... I remember the night Israel invaded. I was doing *The Week in Westminster* – it was a quiet week and not many were around. When I saw this story coming over the tape, I went with Hinch to the Library and together we got out maps of Lower Egypt. We both agreed that if we were going to intervene we had to take Alex and Cairo – these were vital to control Lower Egypt. The Canal was a side-show. The question was 'What do we do then?' Install a puppet government? How long do we stay? How do we get out? There we disagreed. I was arguing we should do nothing and let Israel get on with it... Hinch and I were both agreed about one thing – we saw it as a political operation not a military one. It was back to Clausewitz: war as an extension of politics.[302]

Over the week Price became progressively more unhappy. He and others were deeply distressed at the split with Washington and the talk in the military that 'you could not trust America'.[303] The stupidity of acting without American support was seen as 'suicidal',[304] particularly so close to an American election. 'It put an intolerable strain on the American alliance.'[305] The military intervention had disrupted British oil supplies crucial to NATO defence and Britain's sustained economic growth. Appalled at the damage to Britain's international position, they were mortified by the spectacle of British bombing. The proffered reasons for British intervention (the protection of British lives and property, and to stop the fighting) appeared specious. British lives were in greater danger because of British action; it could not be argued that it was intended to keep the Canal open for British shipping since the first action had been to order British shipping to stay 1 000 miles clear of the Canal; and it was odd, to say the least, to intervene against the military interests of the victim.[306]

Given the post-war emphasis on respect for international law, the whole reason for intervention in Korea, the violation of the UNO Charter, particularly by one whose public reputation had been built upon the myth of championing respect for international law and the League of Nations, appeared cynical in the extreme. The Anti-Suez Group were in an extraordinarily invidious position in the eyes of their constituents. Most were members of the UNO Association and were occasionally invited to address their local branches, yet they represented a government who defied the Charter.[307] While these MPs recognized the UNO's limitations, they still believed that it represented a force for international political stability. Their opinion that Britain was in breach of the UNO Charter found an undercurrent of support among the Tory barrister MPs. To flout openly the UNO's dictums was to threaten a return to the uncertainties of the 1930s.

Deeply disillusioned that a man of Eden's reputed integrity could act in so underhand a fashion, they had private confirmation of the extent of Eden's collusion with Israel.[308] This would merely serve to unite Arab feeling, which was already inflamed against France and would cause irrevocable damage to British interests in the rest of the Arab world. The Anti-Suez rebels were prevented by discretion from telling their detractors, like the Bournemouth Tories, that Eden and Selwyn Lloyd had lied to the House.[309]

They were also horrified that the Suez expedition coincided with Russian intervention in Hungary,[310] since it denied Britain (and France) any moral authority in seeking to restrain the Soviet Union. To risk war with the country divided seemed politically suicidal and morally indefensible. Similarly, there was deep disquiet that the Commonwealth had not been advised nor consulted. Not only was Britain at odds with her former Dominions; the public division within the Commonwealth itself threatened to rend the organization in two. MPs were fearful that although fundamental goodwill could restore the damage to relations with the old White Dominions, the position with the Asian member countries was very different.

Indeed, many Conservatives who had backed Eden's claim that Britain was entitled to use force in the last resort were shocked by the obvious collusion with France to use the Israeli attack.[311] Israel was seen by these Tories as a dangerous ally[312] who 'would exploit the situation for her own purposes and we were mugs to get involved';[313] they also seriously questioned the wisdom of launching a military venture when the country was so clearly deeply divided. It was keenly appreciated that the recent World War could not have been won without the wholehearted support of the British people. The big shock came with the news that Britain's first military action had been to drop bombs. As the Cabinet had foreseen,[314] 'for many it revived unpleasant memories'.[315]

There was considerable concern where all this would lead; it was all very well to give Nasser a bloody nose, but it would reproduce all the old problems of the Canal Zone which had led to the 1954 agreement.[316] If Eden's aim was really to topple Nasser, this could have only been done by a direct onslaught on Cairo and Alexandria – which was not a practical proposition in 1956 – or by allowing Israel to advance to the east bank of the Canal, and there were great doubts whether this was logistically possible.

These critics were in a fearful dilemma: how to make their views known forcefully enough without risking the appearance of being disloyal to their leader. Any open criticism would imply that Eden's reasons for military intervention were false and hypocritical – tantamount to treachery to adoring Conservatives in the country. They were also confronted with the very real abilities of Heath, who was an extremely persuasive Chief Whip; and the trenchant views of their constituency parties – indeed any outright opposition raised the very real spectre of deselection.[317] During the first weekend anxious private meetings were held under the direction of Heald and Elliot. It was decided to make their views known through private channels. 'Most seriously consider what they should do and came unanimously to the conclusion they must tell the

Whips privately of their strong feelings, but support the Government in the lobby for the sake of our troops'[318] as 'it is not very easy to risk your life when you know that even the Government's own party believe you should never have been asked to do so'.[319] 'Some could see that things were shaping up for a national disaster, but felt duty bound to support the Government.'[320]

Gaitskell's apparent vacillation and the manner and brutality of Labour's attack and contempt for parliamentary order closed Tory ranks. There was widespread Tory disgust at Gaitskell's appeal (repeated in his broadcast on 4 November 1956) for Tory waverers to take action. It served to rally support to Eden's banner;[321] in Nigel Nicolson's view, Gaitskell clearly did not understand the Conservative party and its bond of personal loyalty to its leader. While the 'ferocious atmosphere in the House did decide doubters to support Eden',[322] as the week progressed the continuing spectacle of 'a particularly bloody prize fight'[323] daunted the stoutest heart.

The Anti-Suez Group's position became increasingly difficult with Nutting's resignation as Minister of State at the Foreign Office (made public on 4 November 1956), because they had previously declined to criticize Eden personally. Nutting's resignation was a very personal attack, and was closely followed by that of Boyle from his position as Economic Secretary to the Treasury, with his reputation of being the only one at the Treasury who had a real grasp of economic matters.[324] Admittedly, neither of these two ministers held Cabinet portfolios. However, Nutting's resignation was an enormous embarrassment for the Government.[325] But whereas the departure of one of the men most closely involved in Middle Eastern policy strengthened some people's doubts on the morality and wisdom of the military venture, to many others the spectacle of Eden being stabbed in the back by his protégé seemed positively Roman.[326] 'Thanks for Nutting' ran the popular political quip.

Despite the tensions within the party, until the announcement of the cease-fire on 6 November 1956, the Tory ranks were still closed,[327] a tribute to Heath's skill. The Anti-Suez MPs were very slow to organize themselves, but gradually did so 'as the dragging international failure brought them into the open'.[328] Under the direction of Alexander Spearman and emboldened by the knowledge of Monckton's unhappiness and James Stuart's support, the group began to take shape; after two meetings at Spearman's flat at 32 Queen Anne's Gate sixteen Conservatives[329] signed a protest letter to the Prime Minister,[330] demanding a halt to the military operation, the withdrawal of British troops and for the matter to be put before the UNO.[331]

The influence of the Anti-Suez Group in the week before the cease-fire announcement was more passive than active, but it did have a bearing upon the Cabinet's decision to halt the military operation. The Whips' Office was acutely aware that the Government did not enjoy a massive majority, and of the likely impact of a public split in the British ruling party upon international and Egyptian opinion. Given the circumstances, even the threat of 20 abstaining became critical.[332] Although in retrospect it is possible to see the pressure from Washington, the UNO and the Commonwealth as the major factors in the Cabinet's decision, the rumour around Westminster[333] was that Eden had been told that 30 Tories would vote against the Government unless a cease-fire was ordered in the very near future. Certainly the threat of open revolt from so many Conservatives would have constituted vital pressure. Eden himself denied that either reports of this dissident minority,[334] or reports of contacts between one or two Tories and the Opposition leaders played any part in the Cabinet's decision to call a halt. But he conceded that 'all were in our minds in varying degrees'.[335]

Certainly in the turmoil of the time, the Anti-Suez Group's influence appeared to be decisive. In a political crisis when events moved and changed at bewildering speed, fact had little part to play, particularly as the whole affair appeared to be shrouded in such secrecy and intrigue. The very rumour of 'weak sisters' threatening to pull the rug out from underneath Eden was enough to condemn the Anti-Suez Tories in the eyes of their diehard colleagues, who regarded their dissent as typical of the 'soft underbelly of the party' that had been responsible for Munich. Rumours of contacts with Labour MPs firmly branded the Anti-Suez Group as 'quislings';[336] these MPs rapidly joined America and the UNO in the demonology of the Suez Group and their sympathizers.[337] In reality, 'largely by informal personal communication to parliamentary leaders, the Anti-Suez Group did add its pressure to the international forces seeking to stop Eden's military intervention... They were helped by several factors: a powerful moderate group within the Cabinet; a general uneasiness among a wider section of Tories and perhaps the haunting memory in the Prime Minister's mind of how Chamberlain had fallen.'[338] 'Eden could have dealt with America if he had had a united party; and could have dealt with a divided party with Washington's support.'[339] But he had neither.

The Anti-Suez Group certainly claimed no public credit for influencing Eden. But their private belief was that once their protest had been lodged 'which they believed had achieved its objective',[340] theirs was a constructive influence in rescuing Britain from her diplomatic isolation. They saw no profit in continuing their protest.[341] Under Spearman's leadership, a nucleus of about a dozen MPs was hopeful of salvaging something from the wreckage. The Anti-Suez Group prepared another letter to Eden, calling on the Government to place troops in Suez under the UNO.[342] Two further meetings followed, which led to the submission of two more joint letters to the Government. The Anti-Suez Group certainly recognized the danger to the Government from the Suez rebels as:

> the bulk of the ... party realize that the operation has been a disastrous flop and as usual in such circumstances, they are looking round for a scapegoat. They have found one in America which is now their central target rather than Mr Gaitskell and the Tory 'traitors'. The Government is in an awful hole: if they withdraw their troops at once, they cannot survive the diplomatic humiliation and the anger of their backbenchers. If they stay, we shall seriously risk the imposition of a form of economic sanctions on us by the USA.[343]

The Anti-Suez Group's determination to improve Anglo-American relations received a severe battering during November. Disillusioned with Washington's unyielding policy, Ridsdale and Sharples signed the critical EDM at the end of the month. The fact that 'the whole Conservative party [was] on the side of the Suez rebels'[344] was one of the great difficulties of the Anti-Suez Group's position, for it rendered these MPs' 'opposition' as displeasing as Gaitskell's stance. 'This will not prevent us from flying our flag bravely in the breezes of committees. But little is to be gained by bringing down on our heads publicly the rage of the entire Conservative party inside and outside Parliament ... [but] the time may soon come when we must make another public demonstration of support for the moderate policy.'[345]

Older Tories, who were profoundly concerned at the possibility of lasting damage to the NATO alliance, were spurred into action by Grimston's critical EDM. On 28 November 1956 a group, 'including several former ministers and a number of members who have criticized the Government's Middle East policy in public', tabled a motion urging the Government to do all in its power to restore active cooperation with the American administration. Elliot, the principal sponsor,[346] had been very active in the committee rooms and behind the scenes to temper the mood of the party, 'in the way a very senior Privy Counsellor could most helpfully act'.[347] He had just led an all-party parliamentary delegation to the NATO Parliamentary Conference in Paris, where he and others had had the opportunity to discuss the frayed state of Anglo-American relations with members of Congress. The message they had received was that in spite of the strains, NATO must be maintained. Members of Congress appeared to have a better appreciation of British motives and problems in the Middle East than the Washington Administration. The thought was encouraging that 'greater attention would be paid to this more understanding approach'[348] when Congress met in January.

The EDM was a reflection of the public and private grave backbench misgivings about Britain's policy of intervention. The sponsors deplored any further fanning of the virulent anti-American feeling, since it was a fundamental requirement of British foreign policy that Anglo-American relations should be maintained on as close an understanding as possible. This motion was designed as a demonstration to Washington, where very close attention was being paid to Tory internal strains, of enduring Conservative good-will towards America – Conservative backbench feeling was running so high that the sponsors had considerable difficulty in getting even 30 signatures[349] – and to convince Butler and his colleagues that there was influential backbench support for 'the most vigorous action by the Government to do their part in restoring the traditional ties of cooperation and friendship with the US and Commonwealth alike'.[350]

This voice of moderation and expediency was most welcome to Butler and his Cabinet colleagues in their battle with the Suez rebels. After the announcement of withdrawal, the Anti-Suez Group's efforts to improve the glacial state of Anglo-American relations were aided by an unofficial grouping of Conservatives with American connections who set about trying to improve relations with America.[351] These MPs offered considerable support to Macmillan's efforts when Prime Minister to rebuild the Anglo-American 'special relationship' after January 1957.

Transient pressures are difficult to measure precisely at this distance since so much of the Suez Group's and the Anti-Suez Group's lobbying was done in informal private conversations, and in the party committee meetings, the minutes of which make scanty reading. But the Suez Group and the Anti-Suez Group were not inconsiderable factors in the decisions of the day; their influence was discernible at the time, both to political players and observers who 'did see the Suez Group as goading Eden on in the crisis'.[352] But there was nothing the Suez Group could do to sustain Britain's presence in Suez nor resist the inexorable pressure to use the Suez Canal again once the waterway had been cleared. Although the Anti-Suez Group's preference for diplomacy did not restrain Eden from colluding with the French and Israelis, the Group as a manifestation of the wider undercurrent of acute dismay within the party was an important factor in the Cabinet's decision to halt the military operation, and a welcome support to the embattled Cabinet in the aftermath of the débâcle.

In marked contrast to the staunch support from their local constituency associations which bolstered the outspoken critics of withdrawal from Port Said in November and December 1956,[353] those who had publicly criticized Eden's policy of military intervention rapidly found themselves in difficulties with their local parties. Of the eight Anti-Suez Group MPs who abstained in November 1956, only Boothby and Edward Boyle survived politically unscathed;[354] Boyle joined Macmillan's government as Under Secretary at the Minister of Education, part of the Prime Minister's deliberate balancing act to heal the Conservative schism. Unlike the official tolerant treatment meted out the eight Independent Conservatives after May 1957, 'no broad and kindly hints were dropped from official quarters when Frank Medlicott and Nigel Nicolson were fighting to keep their seats'.[355] As *The Spectator* commented, 'The Tories never mind revolts on the right, since they know perfectly well such demonstrations are the inevitable concomitant of progress: a number of members can always be relied upon to mistake progress and sanity for bloody revolution. But revolts on the left can be dangerous, as the only successful one they have had this century demonstrated fairly conclusively to the late Neville Chamberlain. For at the eastern gate the lone and level sands stretch far away; but at the western portal stands the enemy, hungry for rapine, loot and office.'[356] As matters transpired, despite the 'spectacular ebb and flow' of Tory fortunes since May 1955, the Conservatives won the 1959 election with an increased majority of 100 – on the strength of the Government's economic policy. Suez was forgotten.[357]

11 Conclusion

In the 1940s and 1950s the House of Commons was the main forum for airing political issues that today would be churned over on the television and radio. Although Conservative backbenchers could not affect the flow of events, their ability to influence the climate of debate and contribution to setting the limits of acceptable policy was considerable – hence the significance of a possible Tory split and the leverage dissident Conservatives could give a Cabinet minister.[1]

There was no Conservative pressure group on Europe comparable to the Suez Group.[2] Those Conservatives who supported European integration formed a loose affiliation of about 60 MPs, motivated primarily by a desire for security against a resurgence of Franco-German antagonism and to provide a bulwark against the advance of Soviet Russia in Western Europe. In their view, Western Europe must be seen to earn American financial and military support. For some Conservative Europeanists, underlying this sentiment was also a thread of anti-American feeling; while they did not endorse 'Third Force' arguments (that Western Europe could form an independent bloc between the two superpowers), British leadership of Western Europe offered the attraction of bolstering Britain's position at 'the top table'. The emerging European institutions should be directed according to British interests to offset American encouragement for West European federation.

In marked contrast to the Suez Group, the Conservative Europeanists in opposition enjoyed considerable success, despite their individualist approach, slender parliamentary numbers, an overwhelming Labour parliamentary majority and Bevin's outright antagonism, backed by the Cabinet. The strength of this Conservative tendency lay in the support of highly respected and influential MPs, above all in the unrivalled advantage conferred by Churchill's advocacy and the attention his views commanded. Indeed, as former prime minister and world statesman, Churchill constituted a pressure group in himself. The influence of the Conservative Europeanists was also enhanced by the unusual cross-party enthusiasm for Churchill's crusade, their membership of external organizations, and above all, the stage later provided by the Council of Europe.

Despite Bevin's determination to ignore moves towards European integration not initiated by governments, he was obliged to yield to a considerable degree to the momentum generated by Churchill and Sandys' invaluable work behind the scenes, ably supported by Churchill's 'private army', and to accede to the creation of a Consultative Assembly of the Council of Europe. The Conservative delegates at Strasbourg scored again against Labour, both in the manner in which they dominated the proceedings, and in Churchill's determination to secure West German participation. They contributed to the transformation of the Council of Europe from an intergovernment debating forum (envisaged by Bevin) into the venue for discussion of political integration. Thanks to Churchill's initiative, the idea of a European Army gained currency and credibility in 1950, as it seemed to offer a solution to Western Europe's need for manpower while avoiding the nightmare of a revived, rearmed West Germany free to play the West off against Russia in her quest for reunification.

As Continental federalists set the pace of the debate, backed by the Conservative Europeanists who were frustrated by Labour's apparent dilatory approach to Continental developments, there developed a two-track approach to European integration. As Bevin and the Foreign Office made no attempt to regain the initiative from their opponents to ensure that moves towards Europe were not travelling in parallel, public debate on political integration was concentrated on the Council of Europe, rather than developing the available machinery of the Brussels Treaty; similarly, discussion on economic integration with Europe was distracting from the work of the OEEC, the intergovernmental organization preferred by Bevin, the Foreign Office, Eden and the Conservative Sceptics.

There were important limits to the Conservative Europeanists' influence in opposition. Bevin's hostility ensured that any success was piecemeal; indeed, Churchill's campaign reinforced Bevin's determination to pursue an Atlantic, intergovernmental approach. Wider Conservative support was lacking, beyond general agreement that 'better relations with Europe were a good idea'.[3] Very early on senior Tories were noting the profound backbench doubts of the wisdom of Churchill's activities. Although the Conservative Europeanists strove hard to convince their colleagues that the causes of Empire and Europe were complementary – seen in their work at the Westminster Economic Conference of April 1949 – they were not aided by confused and sometimes contradictory statements on Britain's role in a united Europe.

Eden's resistance to the lure of Europe was of considerable importance, coming from the other recognized Conservative foreign policy expert. In the Sceptics' view, the Europeanists were placing excessive emphasis on Britain's relations with Europe, and paid insufficient attention to Britain's global position, and above all her responsibilities to her Commonwealth and Empire. This was underlined by a residue of animosity towards the French. To most Tories, France appeared a power of the second rank, who owed her permanent seat on the Security Council to Britain's insistence, not to her own efforts in the recent War. The continuing political instability in Paris (and Rome) did nothing to enhance the appeal of European integration. There was also irritation that West Germany was looking to France for her international rehabilitation, rather than Britain, together with disdain for what was seen as the emotional appeal of Churchill's campaign to excitable Continentals. Most Conservatives shared Eden's opinion that the whole 'Europe thing' was insubstantial, while a small section of the Tory party carried this scepticism to the extreme of opposing European federation with or without Britain.

Conservative debate was concentrated in private in the party committees as the electoral advantage of seeming to offer a positive response to Continental developments, compared to Labour's apparent resistance, outweighed the desire to stymie emerging ideas of European federation. As the Conservatives moved closer to power, considerations of the actual electoral wisdom of Europe weighed heavily in the scales. The Schuman Plan caused a crisis of conscience for many Tories who had previously been vaguely pro-European and fermented the backbench debate about the direction in which the supranationalism of the French was leading; the sceptics recognized the validity of Attlee's argument that it would be sharp diplomatic practice to join the Paris discussions, only then to pull out, and stayed quiet. Severely handicapped by the British Government's determined aloofness from the Paris talks (and hostility towards any Conservative lobbying in the Council of Europe) and their own party's indifference to their confederal proposal, Macmillan and Eccles' attempts to bridge the growing gap between the Continental federalists and the British position stood little chance of success. This, combined with the determination in Paris to see Schuman's proposal come to fruition, meant the Macmillan-Eccles plan sank with little trace; the plan's contribution to the final shape of the ECSC was a small consolation.

The indication that by mid-1950 Europe was no longer looking to Britain's lead does not seem to have percolated through to the bulk of the Conservative party. In all the arguments surrounding Labour's refusal to attend the Paris discussions, no Conservative addressed the fundamental point that British participation was not acceptable to the French without the prior acceptance of the principle of supranationality. There seems to have remained the conviction in one part of the party that the French did not have the political courage to proceed in discussions with the West Germans without Britain's backing; and if the French did go ahead without Britain, that the talks were doomed to failure.

Despite high hopes, the Conservative Europeanists failed to follow up their success in opposition once Churchill returned to Downing Street. This appears a contradiction, given the mighty authority of Churchill and the manner in which he embodied the spirit of Europe and the presence of pro-Europeans in the government and Cabinet. However, in the early 1950s the Conservative Europeanists who strove to educate their party faced overwhelming odds. By 1951 the whole question of European integration had become inextricably entangled with the explosive issue of German rearmament, and the EDC had become the chosen vehicle. No Europeanist possessed any enthusiasm for British participation in such a clumsy organization. The differences between the Conservative and Labour parties on European integration had become those of emphasis and tone, not substance. In addition, the Europeanists were faced with the loss of Churchill's leadership and support; the growing animosity of leading Continental politicians, such as Spaak and Monnet, who had been rudely disillusioned over

Conservative policy on Europe; their cause was emasculated by the effective muzzling of senior pro-European Conservatives by the demands of ministerial office; and the powerful distraction of the internal Conservative debate over imperial preference. The active Europeanists formed neither a coherent nor a sizeable group in Parliament, and none was a leading politician. Crucial public and media support was lacking, and the 'bumpy first 18 months'[4] of Churchill's peace-time administration enhanced a general Conservative desire not to rock the boat. The visceral Conservative backbench desire to stand aloof from the Continent continued to act as a powerful brake on their backbench colleagues who urged using the Council of Europe to counter the development of Little Europe and Britain's consequent exclusion. To the bulk of the party, the Council of Europe 'was like an engine without a gear-box'[5] and merely duplicated the functions of existing European institutions (WEU, the OEEC and the ECSC).[6] The demise of the EDC in July 1954 reinforced the sceptics' views of the inefficacy of the Continentals.

The supremacy of Eden in Cabinet, backed by key civil servants and compounded by Foreign Office jealousy of any free-enterprise efforts in Strasbourg, meant there was little hope for the few Conservatives who advocated a different approach. Eden did not see the need, nor did ministers at the Foreign Office see Europe as on the political agenda.[7] The Eden Plan proved a temporary aberration. As far as the Foreign Secretary and the mainstream of the party were concerned, intergovernmental moves towards European cooperation were proceeding most satisfactorily, seen in the reform of NATO in the spring of 1952, the expansion of West European Union in October 1954 and British association with the ECSC (signed 23 December 1954). Association, not participation, remained the name of the game.

It was not until the 1955 election, which saw the advent of another political generation, with different political experiences and connections, that attitudes towards Europe began to shift within the body of the party, aided by the defeat of imperial preference at the party conference in 1954. Only then was the Conservative party as a whole was prepared to consider closer links with Britain, the Commonwealth and Empire, and Europe, reflected in the growing backbench support for

Macmillan's and Thorneycroft's moves to develop a European free trade area in the summer of 1956. The Europeanists were responsible in part for this re-education: in the 1950s, key Conservative supporters of Europe had concentrated much of their efforts on the form economic integration of Britain and Europe could take. Thus they contributed towards laying the foundations in 1951–54 of the later EFTA bloc, through the Economic Committee at the Council of Europe, the British Committee of ELEC, and conferences of the European Movement.

Although, as in 1950, the Conservative Europeanists were singularly unsuccessful in pressing the Government to participate in the negotiations for a common market in 1956, hoping that Britain could thereby ward off the creation of an exclusive economic bloc, by this point more and more Conservatives were coming to the conclusion that Europe was something which could not be ignored. It was not going to go away.[8] Whitehall officials remained convinced the *rélance* would fail, but in 1956 – unlike 1950 – the British Government 'was ready to take an initiative of its own, to forestall a continental trading bloc'.[9]

For Conservative backbenchers the Macmillan government's decision to pursue a free trade area which excluded the Commonwealth proved the opening skirmish in the enduring bitter intraparty struggle over Europe. And, just as in 1903–11 in the internecine struggle over Tariff Reform, the present Tory convulsions over Europe amount to a clash of rival ideologies – 'between progressive Conservatives and those whose attitudes favour the *status quo*'[10] – while the position of the neutrals becomes progressively more difficult. The Major government's slim majority gives these rebels a powerful weapon and the events of November 1993 revealed that, unlike the Suez Group in 1954 and 1956, the current Conservative Europhobes are prepared to bring their Government down.[11] For the party which prides itself on being the party of political pragmatism, all depends upon the gravity of the split over Europe (which conveniently overshadows the mirror schism within the Labour party on the issue) and the electoral damage it inflicts upon the party. In 1906 the Conservatives were consigned to the Opposition benches for 9 years,[12] and did not form a majority government until 1922.

THE SUEZ GROUP

The formative experiences of the Suez Group were in opposition: the Palestine crisis, Britain's humiliation at Abadan, and Anglo-Egyptian relations prior to the Cairo government's unilateral abrogation of the Anglo-Egyptian treaty of 1936. The backbench storm over the proposed Anglo-Egyptian agreement on the Sudan proved the catalyst for this backbench faction determined to fight what it had come to regard as Eden's appeasement of Egypt, and the threat posed to Britain's rightful, pre-eminent position in the Middle East by Arab nationalism and American policy. In a sense, the formation of the Suez Group was an admission by its members that informal influence had failed. The rebels concluded overt pressure offered a greater chance of success as party managers could not ignore the cumulative effect of backbench criticism on the political atmosphere.[13]

The Suez Group was a Conservative phenomenon. It represented a clearly identifiable faction within the party. It possessed a named leader, held organized regular meetings attended by invitation only, and enjoyed considerable support in the Conservative national press (contacts which it also ruthlessly manipulated) and within the country at large, articulated through constituency associations. This exercise of influence was very public. No less important was the influence the Suez Group exercised behind the scenes. Although many political commentators placed the Suez Group on the fringe of the party – an 'irritant minority'[14] – their positions on the official and unofficial party committees placed these men and their beliefs far more centrally within the pattern of the party than has been appreciated. Thus members of the Suez Group were not necessarily the negligible men some writers would have one believe.

The Suez Group vehemently opposed first a specific treaty (which in itself was unusual), and thereafter sought to promote a more hard-line approach to British relations in the Middle East and, specifically, towards Egypt. This was a policy of confrontation. The Suez Group's adherents possessed a coherent philosophy related to Britain's position and role in world affairs. Significantly, this faction's activities did not extend into domestic affairs; many of its members held progressive liberal views on social and fiscal policy, and capital punishment. In this sense they were the heirs to Social Imperialism.

The Suez Group, in the inchoate form it took when the Conservatives were in opposition (the Palestine and Abadan crises), failed to win the day. It also lost the battles over the Sudan and the Suez Base Agreement; this was a paradox for, in addition to the sympathy it commanded within the party outside its immediate number, the Suez Group enjoyed Churchill's tacit support. Lord Amery's comment, 'When Churchill accepted what Eden wanted, the Suez Group lost a lot of influence,' reveals its true factional strength as a backbench cabal manipulated by the Prime Minister to his own advantage against his Foreign Secretary in Cabinet.

Although he privately dismissed the Suez Group as 'men of Munich and one or two younger right-wing Tories',[15] throughout the course of his dealings with Egypt and his battles with Churchill in Cabinet, Eden was obliged to pay assiduous attention to the presentation of his policy, to the extent of giving private briefings to the Suez Group. The rebels exercised a discernible brake on Eden's pursuit of an agreement with Egypt, not least through the prevailing attitudes towards backbench dissent. In the 1950s there was a greater independence of thought – as Churchill once commented, 'A tame Tory is no Tory at all.'[16] – and the management of the Conservative party was more tolerant[17] than it is today. The very fact that dissent was not stamped on but was aired in public, gave it greater influence on public debate. Admittedly, the feeling that the party could afford some dissent was encouraged by the 'friendly wind that is blowing in economic and general affairs'[18], and by the far more critical Bevanite division within the Labour ranks. In 1954 the Government's difficulties over the future of the Canal Zone base were greatly aggravated by their irresolution in two other politically emotive matters: MPs' salaries and the Crichel Down affair. In both these cases 'backbench pressure ... played a decisive part in the Government's change of heart', whetting backbenchers' appetites for assertions of parliamentary authority.[19]

The views of their contemporaries vary on the actual influence exercised by the Suez Group MPs in 1953 and 1954. At ministerial level, Lord Aldington credits them with 'little actual influence, but they had to be taken into account and handled in debate'.[20] Churchill's own views on the manner in which an Anglo-Egyptian agreement should be concluded, as well as the final treaty's terms, augmented their impact. In the opinion of the mainstream backbenchers, the Suez Group 'certainly slowed things down: Eden was always looking over his shoulder at Suez Group objections, always asking would this or that be acceptable to the Suez Group'.[21] 'They had a substance because they appealed to a gut feeling in the Tory party and country. A lot more people wished they could have agreed publicly with their attitude. They mattered.'[22] Their opponents, the Anti-Suez Group, certainly felt Eden had failed 'the most searching test of leadership' in his failure 'to resist swimming with the tide'.[23]

And in their own estimation? Some former MPs are inclined to be somewhat flippant: 'I don't know whether we had any decisive influence, but we certainly gave them a run for their money!'[24] Others take a more measured view: 'We had considerable influence as long as Churchill was resisting Eden. When he accepted what Eden wanted, we lost a lot of influence.'[25] Although, by July 1954, the Government was not in danger of defeat on the issue of the Suez Canal base, the topic had been 'a long continuing headache for them'.[26]

Despite their best efforts and favourable circumstances, the Suez Group failed to carry their party up to 1954. It was hampered by the public perception of the calibre of its membership and its leadership.[27] Although its members included several ex-ministers, Privy Councillors, holders of important backbench posts, several very able and ambitious young MPs and respected older members, it appeared that the Group was comprised of predominantly yesterday's men.[28] This was in marked contrast to the Conservative Europeanists in opposition, many of whom were indeed the party 'heavyweights'. Therefore overall the Suez Group was not the sum of its parts. The limits of the influence of the Suez Group also reflected the shift in the party since the 1930s. Both Captain Waterhouse and Assheton would certainly have wielded great power within the pre-war Conservative party. Their power in the 1950s was more strictly circumscribed, partly because of the strengthening since 1945 of the power of Conservative Central Office over the Conservative Unionist Associations.[29] The effect was a strengthening of the party leadership at Westminster. In addition, in 1953–54 the Suez Group did not secure wider support in the Cabinet. Churchill was supported by Maxwell Fyfe and Monckton, but other members of the Cabinet (Salisbury, Macmillan and Sandys) whom one might have expected to have condoned their campaign, either supported Eden or were silent. In particular, Macmillan was noticeable in his reticence; he did, of course, discuss the issue with his son-in-law, giving the advice: 'Don't assert, ask questions!'[30] Part of the problem was the great divide between those in government and those on the backbenches;[31] another was Eden's undeniable authority in foreign affairs.

The Suez Group sought to revive the imperial traditions of the Tory party of old,[32] but the mood and character of the party had also altered since the War. By the mid-1950s the Conservative party at Westminster was far more a party of 'the professional middle-class', with the temper of this class. It was thus less susceptible to appeals to the doctrines and traditions of Empire; the rebels did not strike a contemporary chord among their younger colleagues, although their cause did possess a important visceral appeal to the party in the country. 'Having so many young MPs also dampened radical fervour. Many of them were too hungry for preferment to want to sacrifice their chances on the altar of rebellion.'[33] Here the importance of a competent 1922 Chairman was shown; Derek Walker-Smith worked closely with the Conservative Chief Whip, Patrick Buchan-Hepburn, which helped channel backbench opinion. The Churchill government's small majority increased potential backbench influence, but also raised the fear of bringing the Government down and forcing a general election. Therefore powerful forces militated against 'rocking the boat' too much.

Paradoxically, the Suez Group appeared much more influential under Eden when he became Prime Minister, even though Eden was seen as the architect of the detested Anglo-Egyptian treaty of 1954. 'The seed was sown',[34] with backbench concern over the future of Cyprus providing the fuel for the continuation of the Suez Group. Domestic setbacks, dissatisfaction with Eden's premiership and Glubb Pasha's abrupt dismissal saw the Suez Group evolve into the faction that seized the ear of the party in July 1956. And importantly, by July 1956 Eden was on probation with an increasing number of his backbenchers.

Convinced that the Egyptian leader was increasingly under communist influence and posed the greatest threat to British interests in the Middle East, the Suez Group were determined to see Nasser crushed – by swift diplomacy if possible, by force if need be; it was hoped that this would provoke a counter-revolution in Cairo, and the subsequent reopening of the question of a British garrison at Suez. Its influence became critical in the Suez crisis when larger sections of the party concurred with the Suez Group's arguments of the need for a vigorous reassertion of Britain's position in the Middle East.

In the Suez crisis Eden was not pulled along passively in the wake of the Suez Group's rhetoric; but nor did the Suez Group follow in Eden's slipstream as he headed for confrontation with Nasser.[35] In Sir Anthony Nutting's opinion, Eden all along wanted 'to have a fight with Nasser' because of his sense of personal betrayal, but this was not necessarily a physical fight; Eden certainly wanted Nasser to be humiliated, and as publicly as possible. The weight of the Suez Group upon the Prime Minister was considerable. Not only was Eden as Prime Minister peculiarly sensitive to the Suez Group's opposition in a manner which he had never revealed as Foreign Secretary;[36] the Suez Group also limited the options open to Eden. It 'had to be taken account of... Eden had to tread warily because the Suez Group might well be able to start a fire burning in the party.'[37] Concern over his standing in the party, and his party's chances in the next election could not but feed Eden's fears of being thought indecisive in a crisis, particularly as he was now 'wearing the robes of Churchill' – as his wife repeatedly reminded him.[38] With this came the corresponding feeling he had to make a mark on his supporters.

The Suez Group, both actively and passively, influenced the Prime Minister, by fanning criticism to which the Prime Minister was extraordinarily sensitive[39], and as a support and a weapon in Macmillan's arsenal, helping to reinforce the expectation that America would tacitly condone any British military action. The party conference at Llandudno was crucial in Eden's decision to collude with the French and Israelis. Any possibility of a short, sharp diplomatic triumph over Egypt appeared to be receding into the mists of the UNO. Thanks to the Suez Group, it was brought home to Eden and his Cabinet colleagues that the party in the country would not tolerate anything less than a vigorous assertion of Britain's power. To intensify this, and knowing that Eden was adamant Britain must not be divided from the French, the Suez Group was able to coordinate its pressure with the French government which was equally determined to see Nasser crushed. 'The Suez Group could not have done any more than they did. They effectively converted the Prime Minister to their point of view.'[40] 'If it had not been for the Suez Group, Eden would have hesitated for a long time before he undertook such a dangerous manoeuvre.'[41]

After the Cabinet's decision to launch the military operation, in Lord Aldington's view, the Suez Group did provide 'an extremely useful safety valve with the Conservative party on a major venture that had not been discussed and was kept close to the Prime Minister's chest'.[42] But the support of the Suez Group was insufficient to encourage Eden to press ahead with military action in the face of the international outcry. Although its opposition to withdrawal could not withstand the realities of Britain's isolation, the outcry the Suez Group orchestrated in November and early December 1956 forced the Cabinet to 'play for time'[43] and pay assiduous attention to the presentation of policy.

Was the Suez Group right in its argument that any retreat from Britain's position in the Middle East would have disastrous results? The alternative thesis was Eden's policy of phased withdrawal, and dependence on the Baghdad Pact. Both sides correctly assessed the problem as a political one, but both arguments were based on a fallacy. Egypt saw Britain as an occupying power and regarded the Canal Zone base as theirs by right. Although Eden was correct in his appreciation of the need to remove the irritant from Anglo-Egyptian relations, he was mistaken in his hopes of the future benefits that would accrue from this, and in his belief in the future efficacy of the Baghdad Pact.[44] The profound animosity harboured by Arab nations towards Britain[45] as the perpetrator of the state of Israel was all-embracing; there was no appreciation of British attempts to take a middle line. By permitting the existence of the Tel Aviv government Britain was supporting the enemy. On the other hand, the Suez Group's arguments of the need to stay in Suez to sustain British prestige were based on the assumption that if Britain sat tight, eventually either Cairo would see reason, or a more amenable government would replace the Neguib-Nasser regime. Legge-Bourke might have reasonably argued in 1956 that the nationalization of the Suez Canal Company was the logical outcome of Britain's withdrawal from the Canal Zone base, but in the Middle East in the 1950s Britain was damned if she did, and damned if she did not.

THE ANTI-SUEZ GROUP

In stark contrast to the Europeanist tendency within the party and the Suez Group, this group had a short history. Although only six Anti-Suez Conservatives were prepared to criticize the Government openly by abstaining in the crucial vote of confidence, the Chief Whip estimated between 20 and 30 Tories shared their deep unhappiness.[46] In all, they represented an amorphous pressure group, whose defiance gave expression to general unease within the party. In the main they were traditional Tories, who were anti-Left, that is, anti-Socialist – not that this necessarily made them 'right wing'. Their small number and disparate outlooks and personalities, together with their mixture of ages and backgrounds hardly merit the description 'group', even if they appeared to have an organizer in Alexander Spearman.

The nascent Anti-Suez Group was influential in pressing the Cabinet to refer the dispute to the UNO in September 1956 in the face of international opposition from the Americans and French, and domestic pressure from the Suez Group. However, this expressed preference for diplomacy provided an insufficient brake on Eden in his decision to collude with the French and Israelis to launch a punitive war against Nasser. As Julian Amery commented to Anthony Nutting following the latter's resignation, 'You are accused of deserting your leader; it was a case of your leader deserting you'.[47]

While the Anti-Suez MPs' links with Labour MPs strengthened their resolve, there was never any question nor desire to coordinate their opposition to Eden's Suez policy with the Labour party to vote the Government down.[48] When the ceasefire was announced on 6 November, none of the Anti-Suez Group publicly claimed credit for influencing the Cabinet's decision. The widespread speculation that Eden had done so

Conclusion 235

because of Butler and 40 'weak sisters', was misplaced but it was not wholly wide of the mark. In that the Anti-Suez Group represented wider Conservative anxiety over the wisdom and morality of military intervention, Eden acknowledged that the Anti-Suez Group was a factor in the Cabinet's decision to halt the military operation.[49] After the cease-fire, the Anti-Suez Group helped to off-set the rabid anti-American feeling that swept the party in November 1956 and exercised a minor but beneficial influence in the work to repair the damage to Britain's international relations.

Rebel factions were usually temporary *ad hoc* arrangements, but of the above three groupings, only the Anti-Suez Group conforms to the stereotype. Each fared very differently: both the Conservative Europeanists and the Suez Group aroused the ire of their peers, but the supreme anger of the party was saved for the Anti-Suez Group.

While Britain's standing in the Middle East after the War is now only a memory, little has changed in Conservative attitudes towards Europe in nearly fifty years – the 'antis' have merely become more vocal. Indeed, the modern day anti-Maastricht rebels are the true heirs of the Suez Group. There continues a visceral reluctance to join Europe, a hang-over of the post-war notion that doing so would drag Britain down. Those who would have Britain pull out of Europe conveniently forget the power of Empire that formerly sustained this country, while to portray European federation as the resurrected ghost of Hitler's grand design is a travesty: on these grounds Britain has no hope of reconciling herself with the future until the generation that fought or grew up in the Second World War has passed. Britain still suffers sadly from her former great power status: the delusion persists[50] (together with the not unnatural desire to 'have our cake and eat it'), with the paradoxical loss of national self-confidence that followed the unravelling of empire.

Notes

Notes to Chapter 1

1. I have used the term 'Conservative backbenchers' to describe the entire Conservative party in opposition, and those behind the Treasury bench once Churchill returned to No. 10 Downing Street in October 1951.
2. Gilbert Longden (secretary) memorandum to Charles Mott-Radclyffe, chairman of the Foreign Affairs Committee, Foreign Affairs Committee minutes, undated.1.56. The Conservative Party Archives at the Bodleian Library, Oxford.
3. Lord Thorneycroft interview with author.
4. Sir Cranley Onslow MP, chairman of the 1922 Committee 1984–92, interview with author.
5. For an excellent discussion of the role of the Whips, see Philip Norton: *Conservative Dissidents: Dissent within the Parliamentary Conservative Party 1970–74* (Maurice Temple Smith, London 1978), pp. 163–175.
6. The Whips' contact with backbenchers was three-fold: through the area whip, backbench committee whip and personal acquaintance.
7. The Chief Whip's Office.
8. Michael Dobbs: *To Play The King* (HarperCollins, London 1992).
9. Francis Pym, Chief Whip in Edward Heath's government (1970–74), quoted in Norton: *Conservative Dissidents*, p. 163.
10. See Donald Watt: *Personalities and Policies: Studies in the Formulation of British Foreign Policy in the Twentieth Century* (Longmans, London 1965), pp. 1–15. Personal affection for a fellow member, no matter how extraordinary his professed views, was very often accompanied by a greater tolerance for an aberrant opinion; conversely, deep-seated dislike would encourage dismissal of an argument: Sir Reginald Bennett interview with author.
11. For detailed discussion of the political *élite*, see Michael Charlton: *The Price of Victory* BBC (London 1983).
12. I have used this term to describe those Conservative MPs who favoured a more positive response to continental ideas of West European integration. This was not a contemporary term.
13. For important literature on the role of the Tory backbench MP, see Robert Jackson: *Rebels and Whips* (Macmillan, London 1968); Hugh Berrington: *Backbench Influence in the House of Commons 1945–55* (Pergamon, Oxford 1973); S.E. Finer, H. Berrington and D. Bartholomew: *Backbench Opinion in the House of Commons 1955–59* (Pergamon, Oxford 1961); Leon Epstein: *British Politics in the Suez Crisis* (Pall Mall Press, London 1964); see also Richard Leonard and Valentine Herman: *The Backbencher and Parliament* (Macmillan, London 1972); Philip Norton: *Dissension in the House of Commons 1945–74* (Macmillan, London 1975); Ronald Butt: *The Power of Parliament* (Constable, London 1967).
14. 213 MPs. In 1935, 429 Conservative MPs were elected.

15. Conservative Chief Whip 1944–48.
16. Conservative Chief Whip 1948–55.
17. The elevation of Edward Heath to the Whip's Office signalled a marked change, although at the time his friends all thought he had committed political suicide: Lord Carr interview with author.
18. John Baldock interview with author.
19. This persisted until the mid-1950s. See, for example, *Hansard* volume 548 (1956–7).
20. Sir Bernard Braine interview with author.
21. The Conservative 'Brigadier Group' was a creation of the press, inspired by the election in 1945 of a considerable number of former serving officers, of whom great things were expected. They included Otho Prior-Palmer, John Selwyn Lloyd, 'Toby' Low, Frank Medlicott, and after 1950, Enoch Powell. Their political views ranged widely, as did their preparedness to toe the party line.
22. For example, Ralph Rayner and Robert Boothby.
23. Paul Williams interview with author.
24. Sir Robert Cary interview with Anthony Seldon.
25. Lord Watkinson interview with author.
26. Lord Watkinson.
27. Morrison and Vere Harvey were not strictly 'knights of the shires' since they were ennobled as the Lords Margadale and Harvey respectively: Sir Cranley Onslow interview with author.
28. See Division on Suez Base Agreement, 29.7.54, *Hansard Official Report. Fifth Series. Parliamentary Debates. Commons* Volume 431 columns 820–822.
29. See Asa Briggs: *A History of Broadcasting in the United Kingdom: volume 4 Sound and Vision* (Oxford University Press 1979) pp. 605–12.
30. For example, Reginald Bevins: *The Greasy Pole* (Hodder & Stoughton, London 1965), p. 21.
31. £1200 per annum in 1950.
32. Sir John Astor interview with author.
33. Christopher Hollis: *Seven Ages: Their Exits and Their Entrances* (Heinemann, London 1974), p. 174.
34. Wilfred Sendall interview with author.
35. Sir John Astor interview with author.
36. John Baldock interview with author.
37. 'Ministers were very much more remote, more "godlike". One might see them in the Smoking Room' (Lord Watkinson interview with author), but given the general pattern of parliamentary attendance, this was the exception rather than the rule.
38. Sir Charles Mott-Radclyffe interview with author.
39. Lord Watkinson interview with author.
40. In the early 1950s Tories were incensed to discover that discussion within the 1922 and the Foreign Affairs Committees was being leaked to *The Daily Express* and the Opposition; they became so concerned that the committee rooms were searched for bugs. Sir Kenneth Thompson interview with Anthony Seldon.
41. Nigel Nicolson interview with author.

42. Lord Glendevon (then Lord John Hope) served on the 1922 executive between 1951–53: 'We used to see Winston every month or two. We did not mince our words, so much so that once he said, "Now, if you will forgive me, I will go and see my other Cabinet".' Lord Glendevon interview with author. Also see Thomas Iremonger letter, *The Times* 29.5.55; also Stanley Prescott letter, *The Times* 2.6.55.
43. Sir John Arbuthnot interview with Anthony Seldon.
44. Lord Glendevon interview with author.
45. The importance of the 1922 was the status conferred upon its officers and to a lesser extent the Committee's executive members. Most 1922 meetings were unimportant but this changed dramatically in time of crisis; more usually, trouble surfaced in backbench committees.
46. Mrs Goddard's table in the Members' Dining Room was a particular favourite. (Mrs Goddard was a portly waitress renowned for looking after senior backbenchers). Sir Peter Smithers letter to author.
47. See Richard Cockett: *Thinking the Unthinkable: Think-tanks and the Economic Counter-Revolution 1931–1983* (London 1995), pp. 68, 72–73; W.H. Greenleaf: *The British Political Tradition Volume II: The Ideological Heritage* (Metheun, London and New York, 1983), p. 307.
48. Hartmut Kopsch: *The Approach of the Conservative Party to Social Policy during the Second World War*, PhD thesis, London School of Economics, 1970; and see Cockett, p. 68.
49. Private information.
50. Private information.
51. Private information.
52. See Kopsch and Cockett.
53. Private information.
54. For example Donald McLachlan, *The Daily Telegraph*, 30.1.57.
55. 'Our fundamental rule was never to be seen talking willingly to a Whip, and above all the Chief Whip.' Sir Reginald Bennett interview with author.
56. Spurred by their frustration at the apparent continuation of the bankrupt policies in the 1930s, nine new young members in 1950 published their coherent social philosophy in the pamphlet *One Nation*, which had a considerable impact on the Conservative party conference later that year; the founder members were Iain Macleod, Enoch Powell, Angus Maude, John Rodgers, Gilbert Longden, Cuthbert Alport, Robert Carr, Edward Heath and Richard Fort. Powell and Macleod, together with Reginald Maudling, were former members of the Conservative Research Department, the powerhouse of the revitalized Conservative party under RAB Butler in the late 1940s; however, their opinions on British foreign policy varied widely, despite their affinity on domestic policy.
57. Sir Geoffrey Cox interview with author.
58. *The Times*, 22.4.55.
59. Lord Healey and Sir Cranley Onslow interviews with author.
60. See Thomas Braddock letter to Ronald MacKay, 1.4.48, R.W. Mackay papers, BPLES archive, London School of Economics.
61. For definition of a tendency, see John Barnes: *Ideology and Factions*

(p. 344) in Anthony Seldon and Stuart Ball eds: *Conservative Century: The Conservative Party Since 1900* (Oxford University Press, 1994).
62. For definition of a faction, see Richard Rose: *Parties, Factions and Tendencies in Britain, Political Studies* 21 (1964) pp. 33–46.
63. Lord Aldington interview with author.
64. Public backbench hostility towards the US and UNO in the aftermath of the Suez crisis soon receded without any change in Government policy.
65. Patrick Buchan-Hepburn to James Stuart 22.9.56, Lord Hailes papers, The Churchill Archives Centre, Churchill College, Cambridge.
66. Wilfred Sendall interview with author.
67. *The Way of the World* by John Congreve.
68. *Truth* 15.10.54.

Notes to Chapter 2

1. Sir Peter Smithers correspondence with author.
2. Lord Amery interview with author.
3. Sir Peter Smithers correspondence with author.
4. Lord Eccles interview with author.
5. The United Europe Movement (UEM – founded 1947), the European League for Economic Cooperation (ELEC – founded 1946) and the Council of Europe (founded 1949).
6. Lord Amery interview with author.
7. Sandys was out of Parliament from 1945 until February 1950, when he was returned for Streatham. He is included on the basis of his relationship with Churchill and his position in the European Movement.
8. See Appendix I for the list of names.
9. John Hay interview with author.
10. David Maxwell Fyfe, Peter Thorneycroft, David Eccles, Sir Peter MacDonald and Peter Roberts. William Teeling, George Ward, James Hutchison, Sir Cuthbert Headlam, Hugh Fraser, Edward Keeling, Lady Tweedsmuir and Lord Willoughby de Eresby also took a particularly active interest.
11. They strongly resisted British participation in a European customs union which did not permit the continuation of imperial preference. See Hutchison 22.1.48, *HC Deb.* 446.475.
12. MacDonald 22.1.48, *HC Deb.* 446.488.
13. See Appendix I for list of names.
14. John Hay correspondence with author.
15. Harold Macmillan: *Tides of Fortune 1945–55* (London 1969), p. 155.
16. John Colville: *The Churchillians* (London 1981), p. 208.
17. In 1939 as President of the New Commonwealth Society (an organization which was crucial to early support for European union) he called for a supranational peacekeeping force for Europe; in 1940 as part of a desperate attempt to shore up crumbling French morale following the French army's shattering defeat by Hitler's troops, he proposed an indissoluble union between France and Britain with a common

parliament. Between 1940 and 1942 he dwelt several times upon the idea of unifying Europe under a Council with powers to enforce its decisions. Walter Lipgens: *A History of European Union* (Oxford 1982); and Lipgens ed.: *Documents on the History of European Integration* Vol. II. *Plans for European Union in Britain and in Exile 1939–45*, pp. 229–233.
18. In Brussels 16.11.45 and the Hague 8.5.46.
19. Colville: *The Churchillians*, p. 208.
20. See Macmillan p. 159.
21. Boothby, in Alan Thompson: *The Day Before Yesterday* (London, 1971), p. 88.
22. Seen in the stress placed in the UEM's original declaration upon the whole of Europe, and the formation and activities of the UEM's East European committee.
23. See Macmillan, p. 159.
24. Lynn Ungoed-Thomas, 17.11.49, *HC Deb.* 469.2305.
25. Boothby, in Thompson, p. 88.
26. Sir Christopher Soames interview with Anthony Seldon.
27. Colville: *The Churchillians*, p. 208.
28. Lord Fraser of Kilmorack interview with author.
29. Colville: *The Churchillians*, p. 208.
30. President of the Pan-European Union, which he founded in 1923, and which held regular congresses, and founder of European Parliamentary Union (1947).
31. Lord Amery interview with author.
32. Leo Amery diary entry 19.9.46, in John Barnes ed.: *The Empire at Bay – The Leo Amery Diaries 1929–45* (Hutchinson, 1988), p. 1060.
33. See Leo Amery to Churchill 20.9.46, Sir Winston Churchill papers, The Churchill Archives Centre, Churchill College, Cambridge.
34. See Amery to Churchill 24.7.46, Churchill papers.
35. Lord Amery interview with author.
36. See Leo Amery diary 30.9.46, quoted in Barnes ed., p. 1060.
37. Sir Peter Smithers correspondence with author.
38. Lord Amery interview with author.
39. Sir Peter Smithers correspondence with author.
40. Amery to Churchill 12.11.45, quoted in Barnes ed., p. 1059.
41. See Amery to Sandys 20.9.46, forwarded by Sandys to Churchill 1.10.46, Churchill papers.
42. Amery to Churchill, 12.11.45, quoted in Barnes ed., p. 1059.
43. Barnes' transcript of Sandys Ms: Churchill to Sandys 25.6.46 and 29.6.46.
44. Lord Deedes interview with author.
45. Barnes' transcript of Sandys Ms.
46. Lord Amery interview with author.
47. John Pinder and Richard Mayne: *Federal Union*, p. 94; see *Truth* 15.10.54.
48. Barnes' transcript of Sandys Ms.
49. Lord Amery interview with author; Macmillan, p. 157; Boothby, p. 216; *Truth* 15.10.54.
50. Succeeded his father as Marquis of Salisbury in 1947.
51. Robert Rhodes James: *Churchill – A Study In Failure* (London 1970), p. 335.

52. Lord Amery interview with author.
53. Lord Orr-Ewing interview with author.
54. Lord Amery interview with author.
55. *Truth* 15.10.54.
56. See Pinder and Mayne, p. 94.
57. Sandys to Churchill 23.12.46, Churchill papers.
58. This was the founding conference for the European Union of Federalists and the Movement for World Government.
59. Retinger was a remarkable, somewhat enigmatic man. A former personal aide to General Sikorski during the Second World War and passionate European federalist, Retinger later became the first Secretary General of the International Committee, renamed in 1948 the European Movement. See Joseph Pomian ed.: *Joseph Retinger: Memoirs of an Eminence Grise* (London 1972).
60. Pomian ed., p. 215.
61. *Truth* 15.10.54.
62. In 1927 he had helped write a book entitled *Industry and the State*, which touched on the subject, with Macmillan and Loder.
63. Robert Boothby: *Recollections of a Rebel* (London 1978), p. 216.
64. See 4.6.46 *HC Deb.* 423.1944–1954; and 19.6.47 *HC Deb.* 438.2311–18.
65. Sir Reginald Bennett interview with author.
66. Robert Rhodes James: *Bob Boothby* (London 1991), pp. 337–8.
67. Dr Stuart Ball transcript of Sir Cuthbert Headlam Ms: Sir Cuthbert Headlam diary 2.9.47.
68. Sir Reginald Bennett interview with author.
69. See *Within the Fringe* (London 1967), p. 104.
70. Sir Godfrey Nicholson interview with author.
71. See *Industry and the State* (1927).
72. John Hay correspondence with author.
73. Alistair Horne: *Macmillan 1894–1956* (London 1988), p. 314.
74. Ivone Kirkpatrick shared this terror. Sir John Ward interview with Anthony Seldon.
75. The Soviet-German treaty of 1922 that marked Weimar Germany's escape from post-war diplomatic isolation.
76. Horne, p. 314.
77. Lord Eccles interview with author.
78. See the Earl of Kilmuir: *Political Adventure* (London 1964), p. 176.
79. Sir Hugh Lucas Tooth interview with Anthony Seldon.
80. Philip Goodhart: *The 1922* (London 1973), p. 126.
81. Sir Kenneth Thompson interview with Anthony Seldon.
82. Lord Garner interview with Anthony Seldon.
83. Ursula Branston interview with author.
84. Sir Kenneth Thompson interview with Anthony Seldon.
85. Reginald Bevins: *The Greasy Pole* (London 1965), p. 30.
86. Lord Eccles interview with author.
87. 22.1.48, *HC Deb.* 446.448.
88. Barnes' transcript of Sandys Ms: De Rougemont Diary 28.8.47.
89. Churchill, 23.1.48 *HC Deb.* 446.548–561.

90. Jeremy Moon: *European Integration in British Politics 1950–63* (London 1985), p. 86.
91. Boothby, p. 217.
92. See Aidan Crawley, 17.11.49, *HC Deb.* 469.2236–43.
93. 22.1.48, *HC Deb.* 446.553.
94. Aidan Crawley, 5.5.48, *HC Deb.* 450.1297.
95. 57 signed the EDM calling for a political union and trading area, whereas by February 1949 the more restrained EDM was supported by 61 Conservatives and included many from the wider circle.
96. Walter Lipgens ed.: *Documents on the History of European Integration*, p. 240. One of the few to consider European integration, Quintin Hogg, had concluded the idea was impractical: see Quintin Hogg in *The Spectator* 1943 and *Making Peace* (London 1945), quoted in Lipgens, p. 240.
97. Lord Colyton interview with author.
98. 39 Tories (from 133 MPs) supported the establishment of a 'European federation within the framework of the UNO' in January 1947. 62 Conservatives initially supported Mackay's European Parliamentary Union. R.W. Mackay papers, BPLES archive, London School of Economics.
99. Moon, p. 86.
100. John Hay correspondence with author.
101. Lord Amery interview with author.
102. Lord Amery interview with author.
103. 15.5.47 *HC Deb.* 437.1743 and 19.6.47 *HC Deb.* 438.2238.
104. 19.6.47, *HC Deb.* 438.2238.
105. Lord Fraser interview with author.
106. Sir Frank Bishop interview for *The Day Before Yesterday*.
107. Sir Evelyn Shuckburgh interview with Anthony Seldon.
108. Lord Fraser interview with author.
109. Sir Ashley Clarke interview with Anthony Seldon.
110. Sir Frank Roberts and Sir Ashley Clarke interviews with Anthony Seldon.
111. Lord Strang interview with Anthony Seldon.
112. Sir Frank Roberts interview with Anthony Seldon.
113. Lord Amery interview with author.
114. Kilmuir, p. 177.
115. Eden was particularly suspicious of Macmillan and Butler. Dr Stuart Ball transcript of Sir Cuthbert Headlam Ms: Sir Cuthbert Headlam diary entry 2.8.47.
116. Lord Butler interview with Anthony Seldon.
117. Lord Clitheroe interview with Anthony Seldon.
118. Lord Amery interview with author.
119. Sandys to Churchill 27.4.47, Churchill papers. Eden sent his apologies.
120. Lord Amery interview with author. The received wisdom was that he had resigned from Chamberlain's Cabinet in 1938 on principle but some political insiders thought that this had been more for reasons of style than substance.
121. 22.10.46, *HC Deb.* 427.1523.
122. Sir Evelyn Shuckburgh diary entry February 1949, quoted in Michael

Charlton, *The Price of Victory*, p. 79, reporting on a meeting between Butler and Hector MacNeil (Minister of State at the Foreign Office).
123. Kilmuir, p. 186.
124. John Hay correspondence with author.
125. Sir Peter Smithers correspondence with author.
126. Lord Amery and Somerset de Chair interviews with author.
127. Stuart, pp. 146–7.
128. Macmillan, p. 287.
129. Lord Glendevon interview with author.
130. 22.1.48, *HC Deb.* 446.418–429.
131. Attlee, 23.1.48, *HC Deb.* 446.615.
132. See Sandys to Churchill 27.4.47, Churchill papers.
133. Sandys to Churchill, 17.4.47, quoted in Martin Gilbert: *Never Despair* (London 1988), p. 321.
134. Sir Richard Body interview with author.
135. See Appendix I for list.
136. Legge-Bourke, FAC 5.5.54.
137. The first meeting of the Consultative Assembly of the Council of Europe was in August 1949.
138. See Sir Herbert Williams, *HC Deb.* 480.1458 and Legge-Bourke *HC Deb.* 480.1479, 13.11.50.
139. Sir Richard Body interview with author.
140. Lord Glendevon interview with author.
141. Sir Peter Smithers correspondence with author.
142. 'A Grand Whig!' Enoch Powell interview with author.
143. Sir Peter Smithers correspondence with author.
144. 47 Conservatives voted against Bretton Woods, and 74 against the second motion, despite an Opposition two-line whip instructing MPs to abstain. This vote is not an infallible litmus test of Tory attitudes towards Europe as Boothby, Hollis, Nutting, Thorneycroft, Moore, Savory and Teeling also had voted against the party whip.
145. Max Aitken, Beverley Baxter, Eric Gandar-Dower, Harry Legge-Bourke, Anthony Marlowe, Arthur Marsden and Sir John Mellor.
146. Lord Amery interview with author.
147. Sir Peter Smithers correspondence with author.
148. Sir Peter Smithers.
149. Sir Peter Smithers.
150. Sir Peter Smithers.
151. Sir Peter Smithers.
152. John Hay correspondence with author.
153. Lord Amery interview with author.

Notes to Chapter 3

1. See 22.1.48, *HC Deb.* 446.383–409.
2. Bevin Cabinet paper, drafted by Gladwyn Jebb 4.1.48 and 5.1.48, quoted in Michael Charlton: *The Price of Victory*, p. 54.
3. Lord Gladwyn in Charlton, p. 55.

4. Nutting *HC Deb.* 446.409–413 and Mott-Radclyffe *HC Deb.* 446.497–502, 22.1.48.
5. The Earl of Kilmuir: *Political Adventure*, pp. 174–5.
6. Lord Gladwyn in Charlton, p. 57.
7. Lord Gladwyn in Charlton, p. 56.
8. See Lord Gladwyn in Charlton, p. 56.
9. Harold Macmillan: *Tides of Fortune*, p. 156.
10. In which Churchill's UEM committee cooperated with the French Council for United Europe, chaired by M. Herriot; the Economic League for European Cooperation, based in Brussels under M. van Zeeland; the European Union of Federalists, whose chairman was Brugmans, a Dutchman, and the Nouvelles Equipes Internationales, composed of Christian Democrats. Kilmuir, p. 174.
11. Ronald Mackay to William Ross, Labour MP, 1.4.48, Mackay papers.
12. 16.3.48–27.4.48.
13. *The Economist* was surprised the 'old fashioned Tory' Sir Cuthbert Headlam had signed.
14. Wavell Wakefield, Ian Orr-Ewing, Ernest Taylor, Viscountess Davidson, Stanley Reed and Frank Sanderson.
15. Arthur Vere Harvey, Douglas Dodds-Parker, Edward Carson, David Gammans and Walter Fletcher.
16. Charles Mott-Radclyffe, Tufton Beamish, A.R. Low, Jocelyn Lucas and Vere Harvey.
17. Thorneycroft, FAC 21.4.48.
18. FAC 21.4.48.
19. Thomas Braddock to Ronald Mackay 1.4.48, Mackay papers.
20. See all-party group minutes 21.4.48, Mackay papers.
21. FAC 14.4.48 and Butler, FAC 21.4.48.
22. *HC Deb.* 450.1270–1392.
23. *HC.Deb.* 446.548–561 23.1.48.
24. *HC Deb.* 450.1371–1382.
25. Ronald Mackay to William Ross 1.4.48, Mackay papers.
26. 22.1.48, *HC Deb.* 446.423 and 5.5.48, *HC Deb.* 450.1270–1280.
27. 22.1.48, *HC Deb.* 446.423.
28. See FAC 14.4.48.
29. Macmillan, p. 159.
30. Pickthorn, FAC 21.4.48.
31. Pickthorn.
32. Author's italics.
33. Author's italics.
34. FAC 14.4.48.
35. Lord Colyton interview with author.
36. Lord Colyton.
37. See FAC 14.4.48.
38. Lord Colyton interview with author.
39. 28 sitting Conservative MPs, 7 Conservative candidates and Leo Amery.
40. Lord Eccles interview with author.
41. Macmillan, p. 161.
42. Lord Amery interview with author.

Notes

43. John Hay correspondence with author.
44. John Hay.
45. Kilmuir, p. 175.
46. Kilmuir, p. 175.
47. Lord Gladwyn in Charlton, p. 57.
48. John Pomian ed.: *Memoirs of an Eminence Grise*, pp. 222–3.
49. In the eyes of some Conservatives, no less significant was the decision ('though the papers made little of it') to promote the East European exiles from observers to full delegates: 'It shows that the movement is intended not just as a strategic bridgehead for the United States, but to serve the political and moral idea of Europe itself'. Julian Amery to John Biggs-Davison 20.5.48, Sir John Biggs-Davison papers, House of Lords Archives.
50. See Mackay papers 23.7.48.
51. Macmillan, p. 163.
52. Lord Fraser interview with author.
53. In July 1948 during a speech to the annual meeting of the Western Area in Exeter, Sir Herbert Williams, went as far as to describe the Conservative leaders as 'Colorado Beetles' for their endorsement of Western Union, the economic aspects of which risked splitting the party from top to bottom. Williams was sternly reprimanded by Lord Woolton, the Party Chairman, and nearly lost his chairmanship of the National Executive. Lord Woolton letter to Churchill, 19.6.48, Lord Woolton papers, The Bodleian Library, Oxford.
54. Sandys to Churchill 27.7.48, Churchill to Sandys 31.7.48, and Sandys to Churchill 6.8.48, Churchill papers.
55. See FAC 3.6.48.
56. Manningham-Buller, FAC 3.6.48.
57. Roberts, FAC 3.6.48.
58. Butler, FAC 3.6.48.
59. Pickthorn, FAC 3.6.48.
60. John Hay; see also Pomian ed., p. 220; PRO FO 371/73095 Mason to Jebb 23.2.48.
61. Sir Roderick Barclay in Charlton, p. 78.
62. Sir Roderick Barclay in Charlton, p. 75.
63. PRO FO 371/73095 Bevin circular 039. 22.3.48.
64. PRO PREM 8/986 Christopher Mayhew to Hugh Dalton 15.11.48.
65. PRO FO 371/73095 Mason to Gladwyn Jebb 23.2.48.
66. PRO FO 371/73096 Tomkins (Foreign Office) to Helsby (Prime Minister's office), 28.7.48.
67. Sir Roderick Barclay in Charlton, p. 75.
68. PRO FO 371/73096 Attlee to Bevin 28.7.48, reporting on a meeting between Churchill and Attlee. Attlee and Bevin were particularly concerned about the impact of such suggestions on the European Recovery Programme, orchestrated through the inter-governmental OEEC.
69. PRO CAB 134/232 minute by L. Rowan of conversation between Cripps and Paul Hoffman 28.7.48, quoted in Kenneth Morgan: *Labour in Power 1945–51* (Clarendon Press, Oxford 1984), p. 391.
70. Morgan, p. 391.

71. Macmillan, pp. 158–60; see also Healey in Charlton, p. 120; PREM 8/986 exchange of letters between Churchill and Attlee, 4.11.48, 6.11.48 and 11.11.48.
72. PRO FO 371/17808 C. Crowe 26.2.48; R.W.B. Clarke to R. Makins, 1.3.48; PRO FO 371/73095 Gladwyn Jebb note 5.6.48.
73. PRO FO 371/73095 Z 4416/4416/72 Gladwyn Jebb memo to Sir Orme Sargent 24.2.48.
74. Lord Gladwyn in Charlton, p. 57.
75. Charlton, p. 63.
76. PRO PREM 8/986 Christopher Mayhew (signed for Ernest Bevin) to Hugh Dalton 15.11.48; and Christopher Mayhew in Charlton, p. 77.
77. PRO FO 371/73101 B. Pollock, British Ambassador in Brussels, to Ivone Kirkpatrick 5.8.48; PRO FO 371/73097 McAlpine to Ivone Kirkpatrick 19.8.48; FO 371/73098 Kirkpatrick to Bevin, 2.10.48.
78. PRO FO 371/73096 Attlee to Bevin, on meeting with Churchill 28.7.48; Sandys to Bevin 21.7.48 and 4.8.48; and Christopher Mayhew in Charlton, p. 76.
79. PRO FO 371/73095 W. Beckett to G. Jebb 15.6.48; and PRO FO 371/73101 Kirkpatrick to Inverchapel 13.12.48.
80. Bevin to Mayhew, repeated by Christopher Mayhew in Charlton, p. 77.
81. The Labour Government's distaste for a European parliamentary assembly was made plain by the choice of the arch-sceptic Hugh Dalton to lead the British delegation; the choice of Dalton drew strong Conservative criticism. (see *The Manchester Guardian* 25.11.48.) Bevin's trenchant opposition to 'any grand constitution' for Europe was pungently expressed at the meeting of the Consultative Council in Paris in October (PRO FO 371/73098 Extract of meeting of the Consultative Council 25.10.48).
82. Barnes' transcript of Sandys Ms: Lord Layton to Sandys 13.5.48.
83. Layton to Sandys 13.5.48.
84. PRO FO 371/73101 Kirkpatrick to Inverchapel 13.12.48.
85. PRO CAB 134/232 28.7.48, quoted in Morgan, p. 391.
86. Paul Henri Spaak: *The Continuing Battle – Memoirs of a European 1936–1966* (Weidenfeld & Nicolson, London 1971), p. 196.
87. Charlton, p. 65.
88. Sir Anthony Nutting interview with David Elstein for *The Day Before Yesterday*.
89. Lord Sherfield in Charlton, p. 59.
90. Lord Sherfield in Charlton, p. 59.
91. Charlton, p. 65.
92. Lord Gladwyn in Charlton, p. 56.
93. Lord Sherfield in Charlton, p. 58.
94. Lord Gladwyn in Charlton, p. 56.
95. Lord Sherfield in Charlton, p. 59.
96. PRO FO 371/79212 Z 67/1071/72 Bevin to Paris Embassy 30.12.48.
97. In mid-1949, the Tories led the polls with 46%, compared to Labour's 40%.
98. Sir Evelyn Shuckburgh in Charlton, p. 79.
99. Lord Carr and Lord Glendevon interviews with author.

100. MacDonald letter, *The Times* 29.9.48.
101. Lord Amery interview with author.
102. Sir Arnold Gridley, Patrick Hannon, Brendan Bracken, Robert Grimston, Victor Raikes, Duncan McCallum, Colonel Ponsonby, Sir Thomas Moore and Roland Robinson.
103. Macmillan, p. 163.
104. Sir Peter Smithers correspondence with author. Peter Smithers, who was at the time prospective Conservative candidate for Winchester, acted as Secretary to the group preparing a British position.
105. Sir Peter Smithers.
106. Ironically, British officials were initially very reluctant to agree to the proposal for the Charter of Human Rights (PRO FO 371/73095 Jebb 5.6.48) which it was feared would duplicate the UN Bill of Human Rights; Britain only agreed to the creation of the Court of Human Rights in the firm belief that it would never pronounce judgement contrary to British interests. Sir Geoffrey Cox interview with author. Nor did Whitehall regard the proposal for a European supreme court as at all practical. (PRO FO 371/73095 W. Beckett to Jebb 15.6.48).
107. E.g. Macmillan, Hugh Fraser, Headlam and Foster, 21.7.49, *HC Deb.* 467.1570–1689.
108. Macmillan, p. 159.
109. Kilmuir, p. 178.
110. Lord Eccles interview with author.
111. Macmillan, p. 175.
112. Macmillan, p. 159.
113. Spaak, pp. 208–209.
114. Kilmuir, p. 178.
115. Anthony Nutting: *Europe Will Not Wait* (London 1960), p. 26.
116. Macmillan, p. 165 and p. 176.
117. West Germany was not formally in existence until November 1949.
118. Macmillan, p. 175.
119. Macmillan, p. 176.
120. Kilmuir, p. 179.
121. Bevin, 17.11.49, *HC Deb.* 469.2209.
122. Lord Eccles interview with author.
123. Herbert Morrison: *An Autobiography* (London 1960), p. 279.
124. See Morrison, p. 279.
125. See Bevin, 17.11.49, *HC Deb.* 469.2208.
126. Morgan, p. 237.
127. John Pinder and Richard Mayne: *Federal Union*, p. 103.
128. See Eccles' suggestion that delegates to the Council of Europe should be aware of the Foreign Affairs Committee's views, FAC 6.7.49.
129. Kilmuir, p. 177.
130. Lord Glendevon interview with author.
131. See Manningham-Buller, FAC 3.6.48; and Pickthorn and Stanley, FAC 1.11.49.
132. Barnes' transcript of Sandys Ms: Gridley to Sandys 4.10.49.
133. See Aidan Crawley, 17.11.49, *HC Deb.* 469.2236.
134. Crawley, 17.11.49, *HC Deb.* 469.2235–6.

135. Barnes' transcript of Sandys Ms: Sandys to Macmillan 26.9.49.
136. Sandys was replaced as Chairman of the European Movement in the summer of 1950 by Paul-Henri Spaak. Opinion is divided on whether Sandys was ousted (Retinger, the European Movement's Secretary General, claimed it was a federalist *coup*) or whether he had intended to step down following his return to Parliament in February 1950. The result was certainly a swing to federalism within the European Movement, something Sandys had always fought hard to contain.
137. FAC 1.11.49.
138. notably Macmillan. See Alistair Horne, *Macmillan 1894–1956*, p. 314.
139. Stanley, FAC 1.11.49.
140. Stanley, FAC 1.11.49.
141. Pickthorn, FAC 1.11.49.
142. Stanley, FAC 1.11.49.
143. Earl Winterton, FAC 1.11.49.
144. See Conservative Consultative Committee minutes 2.11.49, The Conservative Party Archives, The Bodleian Library.
145. Hugh Dalton: *High Tide and After. Memoirs* (London 1962) p. 335.
146. Butler, FAC 1.11.49.
147. Butler, FAC 1.11.49.
148. Macmillan, FAC 1.11.49.
149. Macmillan, 17.11.49, *HC Deb.* 469.2323.
150. Macmillan.
151. Eccles, FAC 1.11.49.
152. Stanley, FAC 1.11.49.
153. Sir William Hayter interview with Anthony Seldon.
154. Lord Gladwyn in Charlton, p. 57.
155. Business of the House 27.10.49, 3.11.49 and 10.11.49.
156. Bevin, 17.11.49, *HC Deb.* 469.2208.
157. Moon, p. 86.

Notes to Chapter 4

1. Lord Watkinson interview with author.
2. Hopkinson, a former career diplomat and head of the Conservative Parliamentary Secretariat, had been a keen European since the War when he had been much influenced by Monnet's ideas.
3. Macmillan article, *The Manchester Despatch* 11.10.49, quoted in Alistair Horne: *Macmillan 1894–1956*, p. 321.
4. 28.3.50, *HC Deb.* 473.262.
5. 28.3.50, *HC Deb.* 473.196.
6. Jeremy Moon: *European Integration in British Politics 1950–63*, p. 87.
7. See also Nigel Davies maiden speech, 28.3.50, *HC Deb.* 473.269–273.
8. 9.12.48, *HC Deb.* 459.589–594.
9. 23.3.49 *HC Deb.* 463.384–5.
10. Jean Monnet was head of the French reconstruction plan. This proposal was the result of the failure of Britain and France to agree on the future of the Ruhr industries since the War; it was based on ideas

which had been circulating in Paris for some time. See Lord Plowden, Lord Roberthall and Etienne Hirsch in Michael Charlton: *The Price of Victory*, pp. 82–8.
11. Speech in Edinburgh, reported in *The Times* 20.5.50.
12. Churchill, 27.6.50, *HC Deb.* 476.2141.
13. Lord Cherwell, *House of Lords Official Report. 5th Series. Parliamentary Debates. Lords* volume 168 columns 1219–1226.
14. Cherwell.
15. Sir Peter Smithers correspondence with author.
16. Sir Peter Smithers.
17. Sir Peter Smithers.
18. Somerset de Chair letter, *The Times* 24.6.50.
19. de Chair.
20. Aubrey Jones interview with author. Aubrey Jones worked as an assistant to Sir Andrew Duncan (the independent Chairman of the British Iron and Steel Federation) and then as Deputy Director before his election to Parliament in 1950. Jones wrote an article in *The Bulletin* (of The British Iron and Steel Federation) expressing his opposition. Ironically, Jones came to support the Messina process in the late 1950s.
21. Aubrey Jones.
22. Somerset de Chair letter, *The Times* 24.6.50.
23. de Chair.
24. Lord Watkinson interview with author.
25. Harold Macmillan: *Tides of Fortune*, p. 192.
26. Macmillan, p. 192.
27. Macmillan, p. 192.
28. Macmillan, p. 192.
29. Macmillan, p. 188.
30. Macmillan, p. 189.
31. Julian Amery was also the driving force of the Suez Group. See Chapter 6 for a discussion of his background.
32. British Committee of ELEC letter, *The Times* 22.5.50.
33. *The Times* 1.6.50.
34. *The Times* 2.6.50.
35. Etienne Hirsch, p. 88 and Lord Sherfield, p. 93 in Charlton.
36. Eccles, *The Times* 6.6.50.
37. Sir Anthony Nutting interview with author.
38. *The Times*, 16.6.50.
39. Macmillan, pp. 193–5.
40. Macmillan, p. 194.
41. Macmillan, p. 195.
42. 20.6.50, quoted in Horne, p. 320.
43. Macmillan, p. 196.
44. Foreign Affairs Committee brief 13.6.50.
45. FAC brief 13.6.50.
46. *The Madras Mail* 7.5.50.
47. *The Times*, 26.6.50.
48. Somerset de Chair letter, *The Times* 24.6.50.
49. de Chair.

50. de Chair.
51. *The Times* 26.6.50.
52. See *The Observer* 2.7.50.
53. *The News Chronicle* 1.7.50.
54. Macmillan, p. 196.
55. Lord Wilson in Charlton, p. 109.
56. P.A. Lobby Correspondent in *The Cambridge News* and others 27.7.50.
57. Since the end of May the Attlee government had survived from division to division only with the support of the Bevanites.
58. Harry Legge-Bourke, Stephen McAdden, John Mellor, Gerald Nabarro, Enoch Powell and Arthur Vere Harvey.
59. *The Statist* 1.7.50.
60. Legge-Bourke, quoted in Andrew Roth: *Enoch Powell: Tory Tribune* (London 1970), p. 68.
61. For example, *The Guardian, The News Chronicle, The Financial Times, The Daily Mirror, The Daily Herald* on 27.6.50, as well as the provincial newspapers.
62. *The Peterborough Citizen* 30.6.50.
63. *The Observer* 2.7.50.
64. Powell had an interview with Patrick Buchan-Hepburn on the following Monday after the Schuman Plan vote, in which the Chief Whip intimated that Powell would not be included in the first Tory administration after the War. With his Conservative Research Department background, Powell reasonably expected to join the junior ranks of a future Conservative government. Enoch Powell interview with author.
65. For example, *The Times, The Edinburgh Evening News, The Daily Graphic, The Daily Express, The Guardian, The News Chronicle.*
66. For example, *Truth* 30.6.50 and *The Statist* 1.7.50.
67. Westminster Review, in *The Egypt Gazette* 5.7.50.
68. PRO CAB 128/17 CM(50) 34th CC 2.6.50.
69. Lord Gordon-Walker in Charlton, p. 111.
70. PRO PREM 8/1428 Cripps to Bevin 1.7.50.
71. Charlton, p. 120; PREM 8/1428 note by Shinwell 11.5.50, Annex I and II by Chiefs of Staff.
72. Lord Gordon-Walker in Charlton, p. 111.
73. Lord Sherfield in Charlton, p. 122.
74. Michael Cullis in Charlton, p. 118.
75. Macmillan, p. 201.
76. Macmillan, p. 201.
77. FAC brief 18.9.50.
78. Macmillan, p. 202.
79. Taken from Macmillan, pp. 202–3.
80. Macmillan, p. 203.
81. Charlton, p. 89.
82. Macmillan, p. 209.
83. 15.11.50 *HL Deb.* 169.336–37.
84. *The Daily Express* 24.9.50.
85. Macmillan, p. 210.
86. See Birkenhead 15.11.50, *HL.Deb.* 169.336–7.

87. Macmillan, p. 212.
88. 28.3.50, *HC Deb.* 473.191.
89. *HC Deb.* 473.218–223.
90. 28.3.50, *HC Deb.* 473.316.
91. 28.3.50, *HC Deb.* 473.324.
92. Churchill to Macmillan, quoted in Macmillan, pp. 218–219.
93. Anthony Nutting: *Europe Will Not Wait*, p. 37.
94. Lord Sherfield interview with Anthony Seldon.
95. 13.11.50, *HC Deb.* 480.1415.
96. Sandys to Bidault, the French President, 9.2.51, Biggs-Davison papers.
97. Horne, p. 322.
98. 13.11.50, *HC Deb.* 480.1458 and 480.1483.
99. Martin Gilbert: *Never Despair*, p. 575.
100. Butler, 1.11.50, *HC Deb.* 480.166.
101. Julian Amery to Biggs-Davison 17.1.51, Biggs-Davison papers.
102. Wilson in Charlton, p. 110.
103. Attlee, 13.6.51, *HC Deb.* 488.2298.
104. Sir Christopher Soames interview with Anthony Seldon.
105. Taken from Horne, p. 321.

Notes to Chapter 5

1. Hay and Rodgers became Parliamentary Private Secretaries to Thorneycroft and Eccles; Kerr became Macmillan's PPS when the latter was appointed Minister of Defence in 1954.
2. Robert Boothby, *Recollections of a Rebel*, p. 219.
3. Sir David Maxwell Fyfe, Robert Boothby, Julian Amery, Tufton Beamish, James Harden, Christopher Hollis, Charles Mott-Radclyffe and Lady Tweedsmuir.
4. Lord Amery interview with author.
5. In 1950 British troops were active in Egypt, Malaya and Korea.
6. Boothby, quoted in *The Times*, 20.11.51.
7. Lord Amery interview with author.
8. Sir Robert Rhodes James interview; see Anthony Nutting, *Europe Will Not Wait*, p. 40.
9. At a press conference following the NATO meeting, Eden suggested that while Britain would not supply formations to the European army, she might be able to take part in other ways: *The Times* 29.11.51.
10. Lord Amery interview with author.
11. Ursula Branston interview with author.
12. Lord Amery interview with author; and see Boothby, p. 221.
13. Boothby in Alan Thompson, *The Day Before Yesterday*, p. 104.
14. See Churchill's reply to the Conservative delegates to the Consultative Assembly, PREM 11/153 quoted in Richard Lamb: *The Failure of The Eden Government* (Sidgwick & Jackson 1987), p. 64.
15. See Lamb pp. 64–65. John Young: 'Churchill's "No" to Europe: The Rejection of European Union by Churchill's post-war Government 1951–52', *Historical Journal* 28,4. 1985, pp. 923–937.

16. See Robert Rhodes James: *Bob Boothby*, p. 364; John Foster interview with Anthony Seldon.
17. Lord Colyton interview with author.
18. Lord Amery interview with author. On 11.12.51 the Belgian 'Father of Europe' Paul-Henri Spaak resigned as President of the Council of Europe, in part as a dramatic protest against British policy.
19. Roberts and Hope, FAC 5.5.54.
20. See John Pinder and Richard Mayne: *Federal Union*.
21. Amery article, *The Daily Telegraph* 9.6.52.
22. FAC 7.7.54.
23. Longden, FAC 5.5.54.
24. Lord Thomas interview with author.
25. Sir Peter Smithers correspondence with author.
26. Lord Glendevon interview with author.
27. FAC 29.10.52.
28. FAC 29.10.52.
29. Smithers, FAC 17.5.53.
30. Amery to Biggs-Davison 7.12.51, Biggs-Davison papers.
31. *The Manchester Guardian* 1.2.52.
32. Amery to Biggs-Davison 7.12.51, Biggs-Davison papers.
33. Lord Amery interview with author.
34. See Young: 'Churchill's "No" to Europe', pp. 931–934.
35. See Smithers, FAC 1.7.53.
36. FAC 7.7.54.
37. FAC 1.7.53.
38. Legge-Bourke, FAC 5.5.54.
39. Legge-Bourke, FAC 5.5.54.
40. Amery, quoted in *The Times* 8.10.54.
41. Smithers, FAC 23.11.54.
42. See Smithers, FAC 10.11.54.
43. Britain joined the ECSC as an associated member on 21.12.54.
44. FAC 23.11.54.
45. *The Times* 29.11.51.
46. *The Times* 29.11.51.
47. The 'lowly' level (Lord Colyton) of those ministers appointed to lead the British delegation manifestly demonstrated his poor opinion of the Strasbourg Assembly.
48. Boothby, quoted in *The Times* 7.1.52.
49. Ursula Branston interview with author.
50. Sir Peter Smithers correspondence with author.
51. Lord Glendevon interview with author.
52. Amery article, *The Daily Telegraph* 9.6.52; Nutting: *Europe*, p. 144. For more detailed analysis of the Eden Plan, see John Young: The Schuman Plan and British Association; in John Young ed.: *The Foreign Policy of Churchill's Peacetime Administration* (Leicester 1988) pp. 109–134.
53. Amery, *The Daily Telegraph* 30.9.52.
54. *The Times* 24.9.52.
55. Nutting, FAC 29.10.51.
56. Amery to Biggs-Davison 27.11.52, Biggs-Davison papers.

57. Lord Thorneycroft interview with author.
58. *The Daily Telegraph* 24.9.52.
59. Amery, FAC 9.7.52.
60. See Nutting: *Europe*, pp. 44–45; Paul-Henri Spaak: *The Continuing Battle*, p. 226; and Young in Young ed., pp. 115–116.
61. Sir Peter Smithers correspondence with author.
62. See *The Daily Telegraph* 12.5.53.
63. Nutting at Strasbourg, reported in *The Daily Telegraph* 9.5.53.
64. *The Daily Telegraph* 12.5.53.
65. Boothby to Juliet Rhys-Williams, 23.9.53, Lady Rhys-Williams papers.
66. John Hay correspondence with author.
67. Leo Amery letter, *The Times* 1.1.52.
68. Juliet Rhys Williams letter, *The Times* 19.10.53.
69. *The Times* 5.12.51.
70. Julian Amery profile in *The Queen*, 14.7.54.
71. Boothby letter, *The Times* 21.2.52.
72. Hollis letter, *The Times* 2.1.52.
73. FAC 9.7.52.
74. John Biggs-Davison: *The Walls of Europe* (London 1962), p. 66.
75. Biggs-Davison, p. 66.
76. Edward Beddington-Behrens letter, *The Times* 8.5.53.
77. Boothby, p. 223.
78. Biggs-Davison, p. 66.
79. *The Times* 9.2.53.
80. *The Times* 9.2.53.
81. Notes on European Movement Second Economic Conference (30.1.54), Biggs-Davison papers.
82. Ursula Branston interview with author.
83. Cyril Osborne letter, *The Times* 4.1.52.
84. John Tilney letter, *The Times* 23.2.52.
85. Tilney letter, *The Times* 9.12.52.
86. Tilney letter, *The Times* 4.1.52.
87. See 'Friends of Atlantic Union letters', *The Times* 25.9.51 and 9.7.52. The group included Edwin Leather, Longden, Tilney, Alfred Bossom and Nigel Nicolson.
88. Ursula Branston interview with author.
89. Boothby in Thompson, p. 104.
90. Lord Carr interview with author.
91. Viscount Muirshiel (formerly Jack Maclay) interview, BOAPAH, BPLES.
92. Lord Glendevon interview with author.
93. Colville in Thompson, p. 104; Lord Soames interview with Anthony Seldon.
94. Lord Carr interview with author; Sir Anthony Nutting interview with David Elstein for *The Day Before Yesterday*.
95. See Young: 'Churchill's "No" to Europe', pp. 930–31
96. Sir Anthony Nutting interview with David Elstein for *The Day Before Yesterday*.
97. Sir Anthony Nutting interview with author.
98. See Boothby in Thompson, p. 104.

99. Lord Amery interview with author.
100. Lord Carr interview with author.
101. Lord Glendevon interview with author.
102. Sir Peter Smithers correspondence with author.
103. Sir Peter Smithers.
104. Sir Peter Smithers.
105. Sir Anthony Nutting interview with author.
106. Sir Anthony Nutting interview with David Elstein for *The Day Before Yesterday*.
107. Ursula Branston interview with author.
108. Lord Tranmire interview with Anthony Seldon; Lord Thorneycroft interview with author.
109. Sir Peter Smithers correspondence with author.
110. Sir Frank Roberts interview with Anthony Seldon. Under Eden, Britain did not stand wholly aloof from the Six's attempts to create a European federation. For example, British policy towards the ECSC (continuing Labour's policy) concentrated on the issue of 'association'. See Young in Young ed. pp. 109–134. See also the excellent collection of documents by Roger Buller ed.: *Documents of British Foreign Policy Overseas* Seres II, Vol. II. *The Schuman Plan, The Council of Europe and West European Integration, 1950-2* (1986).
111. Lord Carr interview with author.
112. Ursula Branston interview with author.
113. Ursula Branston; see also *The Times* 1.9.50, quoted in Hugh Dalton: *High Tide and After*, p. 336.
114. Evelyn Shuckburgh: *Descent to Suez*, p. 18.
115. Lord Carr interview with author.
116. Lord Glendevon interview with author.
117. Lord Glendevon.
118. Lord Thorneycroft interview with Anthony Seldon.
119. Lord Glendevon interview with author.
120. Sir Eric Bertoud interview with Anthony Seldon.
121. See Charlton, p. 59; Sir Eric Bertoud interview with Anthony Seldon. Makins also had an American wife, but this was a minor factor.
122. Lord Boyle interview, BOAPAH, BPLES.
123. Sir John Ward interview with Anthony Seldon.
124. Lord Rhyl interview with Anthony Seldon.
125. Thorneycroft was also encouraged by his friend, Lady Rhys-Williams, Honorary Secretary of the United Europe Movement 1947–58 and Chairman, 1958–64. Anthony Seldon: *Churchill's Indian Summer. The Conservative Government 1951-55* (Hodder & Stoughton), p. 414.
126. Sir Anthony Nutting interview with author.
127. Butler in Thompson, p. 104.
128. Lord Thorneycroft interview with author.
129. Lord Amery interview with author.
130. Lord Duncan-Sandys interview with Anthony Seldon. Macmillan was the brief exception. As the former first chairman of the Central and East European commission of the European Movement. Macmillan had given the opening speech at the first conference of exiled Euro-

pean leaders in London on 22.1.52. With his son in law's help, he also prepared a brief for cabinet.: See footnote 132.
131. Lord Thorneycroft interview with author.
132. See Young: 'Churchill's "No" to Europe'.
133. He was badly burned in a fire on a train outside the Nancy tunnel just before Christmas. Lord Colyton correspondence with author. As the new leader of the Conservative delegation to Strasbourg, Hopkinson had written to Churchill reporting continental bitterness over Britain's refusal to join a European Army. Hopkinson to Churchill 13.12.51. *Documents on British Policy Overseas*, Series Two, Volume One, 1950, 1952, HMSO, 1985, quoted in Lamb p. 64.
134. John Foster interview with Anthony Seldon.
135. PRO CAB 128/24 CC(52)30 13.3.52.
136. Private information.
137. Viscount Muirshiel interview, BOAPAH, BPLES.
138. See Sir Herbert Williams letter, *The Times* 1.12.51.
139. Ursula Branston interview with author.
140. Lord Glendevon interview with author.
141. Lord Glendevon.
142. Lord Glendevon.
143. Ursula Branston interview with author.
144. John Hay correspondence with author.
145. *The Times* 17.5.51.
146. See Geoffrey De Freitas, 2.7.53, *HC Deb.* 517.585.
147. Sir Gilbert Longden interview with author.
148. John Hay correspondence with author.
149. Nigel Nicolson interview with author.
150. Nigel Nicolson.
151. John Hay correspondence with author.
152. John Hay.
153. Sir Robin Chichester-Clark interview with author.
154. John Hay correspondence with author.
155. Sir Robin Chichester-Clark interview with author.
156. Mott-Radclyffe was one such delegate 'who came from a much earlier school of thought (and who) was too much a cynic to really believe we Europeans knew what we were talking about.' Sir Peter Smithers correspondence with author.
157. John Hay correspondence with author.
158. Ursula Branston interview with author.
159. Ursula Branston.
160. Lord Thorneycroft and Sir Peter Smithers interviews with author.
161. Boothby letter, *The Times* 21.2.52.
162. Approximately 30 Conservatives signed an EDM urging the Government to remove where possible obstacles to the establishment of imperial preference: see *The Daily Telegraph* 10.4.52.
163. See Hugh Berrington: *Backbench Opinion in the House of Commons 1945–55*, p. 172.
164. Biggs-Davison article, *The Tablet* 16.7.51.
165. Lord Glendevon interview with author.

166. Sir Peter Smithers correspondence with author.
167. Sir Peter Smithers.
168. Private information.
169. David Renton, 4.7.55, *HC Deb.* 542.*69.*
170. See Smithers 27.7.55, *HC Deb.* 544.*160.*
171. John Hay correspondence with author.
172. Rippon had been in local government in the late 1940s, and 'had started organizing linking European councillors and local government – the forerunner of town twinning'. Sir Richard Body interview with author.
173. Unusually for a Conservative, Maddan was a federalist. He was involved in the Europe Youth Movement in the early 1950s, and by 1956 was Deputy Chairman of Federal Union's Council.
174. Sir Richard Body interview with author.
175. Sir Peter Smithers correspondence with author.
176. Sir Peter Smithers.
177. Lord Tranmire interview with Anthony Seldon.
178. Nigel Fisher: *Macmillan* (London 1982), pp. 151–2.
179. Ursula Branston interview with author.
180. Ursula Branston.
181. Lord Tranmire interview with Anthony Seldon.
182. Lord Tranmire.
183. Lord Tranmire. Butler presided over the Cabinet's Economic Policy Committee meeting on 11 November 1955 which decided Britain could not participate. Unfortunately at two meetings between Butler and Spaak and Dr Johan Beyen in November 1955, Butler gave his visitors the erroneous impression that Britain was thinking of joining the proposed Common Market. This had unfortunate repercussions as 'Spaak and Beyen felt Butler had misled them'. See Lamb, pp. 74–76.
184. Sir Peter Smithers correspondence with author.
185. Macmillan, FAC 30.11.55.
186. Thorneycroft and Macmillan, FAC 14.3.56.
187. Lord Glendevon interview with author.
188. Sir Peter Smithers correspondence with author.
189. Boothby, Smithers and Maclay, FAC 14.3.56.
190. Boothby, 19.6.56, *HC Deb.* 554.1207.
191. Lord Rippon interview with author.
192. Robert Mathew letter, *The Times* 13.7.56.
193. Mathew.
194. Rippon was by now Sandys' PPS – which 'demonstrates the greater latitude permitted to a PPS in the mid-1950s'. Lord Rippon interview with author.
195. Joseph, Harold Steward and the Liberal MP, Arthur Holt were co-sponsors. This EDM was signed by 89 Tory and Liberal MPs (62 Labour MPs signed a similar EDM).
196. Mathew letter, *The Times* 13.7.56.
197. Mathew; Boothby, 19.6.56, *HC Deb.* 554.1207 and 5.7.56 *HC Deb.* 554.1673–74.
198. Mathew.

Notes 257

199. Rippon letter, *The Times* 3.10.56.
200. Lord Rippon; Lord Eccles recalling Sir Roger Makins' reaction. Lord Eccles interview with author.
201. Sir Robin Chichester-Clark interview with author.
202. EDM No. 101: Common Market: Western Europe. *Orders of the Day and Notice of Motions.* 1955–56 No. 188 Vol. 5 4747.
203. Lord Rippon interview with author.
204. Hugh Berrington: *Backbench Opinion in the House of Commons 1955–59*, p. 90 and pp. 117–119.
205. Rippon letter, *The Times* 3.10.56.
206. Shuckburgh, p. 361.
207. The new Expanding the Commonwealth Group (born of the defeat of imperial preference the previous year) published a pamphlet during the conference suggesting foreign countries 'accepting the fundamental principles upon which the Commonwealth is founded' might be permitted to become members. 'A free association of Commonwealth communities comprised the seeds of a world system for which the middle powers are craving,' in a world threatened by partition between America and Russia: *The Times* 4.10.56.
208. Alistair Horne: *Macmillan 1894–1956*, p. 386.
209. Macmillan had not received Cabinet approval for this. See Alec Cairncross ed.: *The Robert Hall Diaries.*
210. See Rippon letter, *The Times* 3.10.56, and Richard Hornby, 26.11.56, *HC Deb.* 561.84–88. When the House met to discuss the issue on 26.11.56, there was a certain 'unreality' about the debate given the distraction of Suez. As Harold Macmillan commented, the House found it 'difficult to deal with one great issue at a time'. Macmillan *Riding the Storm, 1956–59*, p. 88.
211. Maurice Macmillan maiden speech, 26.11.56, *HC Deb.* 561.70–74.
212. Lord Rippon interview with author.
213. Conservative Research Department paper, 26.10.56, summarizing Conservative Finance Committee meeting 23.10.56, The Conservative Party Archives, The Bodleian Library.
214. Legge-Bourke letter, *The Times* 25.9.56.
215. See Hornby, *HC Deb.* 561.84–88; in August 1956 Thorneycroft requested a meeting with Legge-Bourke to reassure him about the horticulture position under the EFTA proposals; there were three main factors: Canada favoured free trade; only a very small number of countries wished to include agriculture in the new European set-up; and there was no question of overseas territories being brought into the EEC or EFTA. Sir Harry Legge-Bourke papers, Brotherton Library, University of Leeds.
216. CRD summary 26.10.56.
217. CRD summary.
218. Lord Rippon interview with author.
219. Sir Peter Smithers correspondence with author.
220. CRD summary 26.10.56.
221. Pinder and Mayne, p. 147.
222. Lord Rippon interview with author.

223. See Hay, Ramsden and Lindsay letter, *The Times* 28.11.56; Lord Rippon.
224. Smithers, FAC 14.11.56.
225. Smithers and Braine, FAC 14.11.56.
226. CRD summary of Consultative Assembly general political debate 8–11.1.57, The Conservative Party Archives.
227. Guy Mollet in conversation with Julian Amery, Lord Amery interview with author.
228. Lord Amery.
229. Lord Rippon interview with author.
230. See Legge Bourke amendments to EDMs of 7.56 and 12.56, signed by Alan Green and Captain Orr; and by Vere Harvey, Lucas, Biggs-Davison, Paul Williams, McAdden, Hirst, Page and – surprisingly – Beamish.
231. Lord Rippon interview with author.
232. Lord Rippon. The Cabinet decided on 20.11.56 to 'embark on negotiations with the Six and other European countries for agreement for adherence to Plan G.' Richard Lamb: *The Macmillan Years 1957–63. The Emerging Truth*, p. 109.
233. Now Chancellor of the Exchequer. Indeed, the principal members of the Cabinet were all ex-members of ELEC and were still in friendly contact. See Juliet Rhys-Williams private letter, 31.1.57, Lady Rhys-Williams papers.
234. *The Times* 15.1.57.
235. Lord Gladwyn interview with Anthony Seldon. The Government White paper on the Free Trade Area was published on 8.2.57.
236. Lord Boyle interview with John Barnes for *The Day Before Yesterday*; CRD 2/42/7 Extracts from speech by Sir David Eccles, Economic Secretary, 9.3.57, The Conservative Parch Archives, The Bodleian Library; PRO CAB 129/87 C.(57)106 Thorneycroft note to Cabinet 30.4.57. The British Government's insistence that agriculture should be excluded from the scheme had already caused considerable tension in the OEEC working group (*The Economist* 16.3.57). At the OEEC meeting in February Britain had found herself in a minority of one as Thorneycroft argued agriculture must be excluded from any new customs arrangement. The Six had refused to slow down the process of establishing a European customs union, but agreed to continue negotiations for a wider free trade area parallel to the EEC. The European Economic Community officially came into being on 1 January 1958.
237. *The Economist* 23.3.57.
238. Undated memo on the Common Market and the Free Trade Area, and memo by Alan Green 17.7.57, Sir Harry Legge-Bourke papers, Brotherton Library, University of Leeds.
239. PRO CAB 128/31 CC29(57) 3.4.57.
240. David Ormsby-Gore FAC 29.5.57.
241. PRO CAB 129/87 C.(57)106 Peter Thorneycroft note to Cabinet 30.4.57.
242. PRO CAB 128/31 CC(57)37 2.5.57.
243. Nora Beloff: 'Towards Free Trade?': *The Observer* 3.2.57.
244. Nora Beloff, *The Observer*, 3.2.57; Selwyn Lloyd address to FAC 1.8.57.
245. See Edward Heath to Michael Fraser, Director of the Conservative

Research Department, 6.3.57, The Conservative Party Archives, The Bodleian Library; Reginald Maudling: *Memoirs* (Sidgwick & Jackson 1978), p. 67.
246. D Dear, CRD, to Philip Bell MP, 30.4.57, CRD 2/42/7, The Conservative Party Archives, The Bodleian Library.
247. *The Economist* 17.7.57.
248. A free trade area consisting of the Six and the surrounding eleven West European countries; the proposal collapsed in December 1958.
249. The European Free Trade Association was created by the Stockholm Convention of 1 January 1960, and included Britain, Denmark, Norway, Sweden, Switzerland, Austria and Portgual. See Lamb: *The Macmillan Years* for a discussion of the EFTA negotiations.
250. CRD pamphlet *Some Reflections on British Foreign Policy*, written by Ursula Branston. March 1959.
251. Wilfred Sendall interview with author.

Notes to Chapter 6

1. Lord Thorneycroft interview with Anthony Seldon.
2. Lord Amery interview with author.
3. Lord Fraser interview with author.
4. *The Times* 15.6.54.
5. *The Times* 10.4.52.
6. *The Times* 10.4.52.
7. Harold Watkinson: *Turning Points*, p. 33.
8. See Gomme-Duncan, FAC 25.2.53.
9. See *The Times* 15.6.54.
10. During the Suez crisis Eden's policy of military intervention did receive unlikely support from the Labour MPs Emanuel Shinwell and Stanley Evans.
11. See Appendix II for membership of the Suez Group and the 'crypto'-Suez Group.
12. Lord Amery interview with author.
13. Sir Gilbert Longden interview with author.
14. John Baldock interview with author.
15. Private information.
16. Private information.
17. Sir Anthony Nutting interview with author.
18. Sir Godfrey Nicholson interview with author.
19. Sir Kenneth Thompson interview with Anthony Seldon.
20. Former Inspector General and head of the British Advisory Military Mission to the Iraq army 1938–41.
21. *The Daily Telegraph* 11.7.53.
22. *The Daily Telegraph* 11.7.53.
23. For example, he was chairman of the Zambezi Exploring Company and the Rhodesia-Katanga Company.
24. *The Observer* 20.12.53.
25. Lord Amery; Legge-Bourke, 16.5.57, *HC Deb.* 570.629–630; Julian

Amery: 'The Suez Group: a Retrospective on Suez' in Selwyn Troen and Moshe Shemesh ed.: *The Suez-Sinai Crisis 1956* (London 1990), pp. 110–126.
26. Sir Kenneth Thompson interview with Anthony Seldon.
27. Private information.
28. Andrew Roth: *Enoch Powell – Tory Tribune* (MacDonald 1970), p. 114.
29. Paul Williams interview with author.
30. Michael Foot, in *The Daily Herald* 14.11.52.
31. Sir Reginald Bennett interview with author.
32. Hinchingbrooke letter, *The Times* 2.7.51.
33. Letter, *The Times* 2.7.51.
34. Hinchingbrooke constituency speech, reported in *The Southern Times* 6.4.51.
35. Private information.
36. *The Spectator* 17.10.52.
37. See *The Daily Mirror* 6.8.52.
38. *The Times* 10.10.52.
39. Sir Richard Body interview with author.
40. Sir Kenneth Thompson interview with Anthony Seldon.
41. Letter, *The Times* 20.7.54.
42. Roth: *Powell*, p. 99; also Legge-Bourke, 16.5.57, HC Deb. 570.629–630.
43. Paul Williams interview with author.
44. Author's conversation with Captain William Legge-Bourke, Sir Harry Legge-Bourke's son.
45. Roth: *Powell*, p. 99.
46. Amery's close personal friend and war-time colleague.
47. Until he withdrew in July 1954.
48. Sir Douglas Dodds-Parker interview with author.
49. Richard Law and Austen Hudson were also excluded, together with Walter Elliot, a former Minister for Agriculture, Secretary of State for Scotland, and Health.
50. *The Sunday Express* 20.12.53.
51. *The Sunday Express* 20.12.53.
52. Leo Amery to Waterhouse, 30.9.53, Captain Charles Waterhouse papers.
53. Waterhouse, Julian Amery, Assheton, Robert Grimston, Holland-Martin, Hinchingbrooke, Lloyd, Morrison, Powell, Ian Horobin, Fitzroy Maclean, Sir Charles Williams and Legge-Bourke. Waterhouse papers.
54. Lord Amery interview with author.
55. Paul Williams interview with author.
56. Lord Amery interview with author.
57. Amery, in Troen and Shemesh ed., p. 111.
58. Amery in Troen and Shemesh ed., p. 111.
59. Lord Lauderdale interview with author.
60. Lord Lauderdale interview with author.
61. Lord Amery interview with author.
62. Arthur Gavshon interview with author.
63. See Amery to Biggs-Davison 8.11.53, Biggs-Davison papers.
64. For example, Amery to Biggs-Davison 8.11.53, Biggs-Davison papers.
65. Amery to Biggs-Davison 8.11.53, Biggs-Davison papers.

66. Arthur Gavshon interview with author.
67. Arthur Gavshon.
68. Amery, in Troen and Shemesh ed., p. 111.
69. Room J was usually used. Waterhouse papers.
70. Sir Douglas Dodds-Parker interview with author.
71. See Scott Lucas: *Divided We Stand: Britain, the US and the Suez Crisis* (London 1991), p. 101 and pp. 193–4.
72. Enoch Powell interview with author.
73. Amery, in Troen and Shemesh ed., p. 112.
74. Peter Smithers, FAC 8.2.56.
75. Amery, Williams and Glover, FAC 8.2.56.
76. Amery, FAC 8.2.56.
77. Maitland, FAC 8.2.56.
78. Anthony Nutting: *No End of a Lesson*, p. 36.
79. John Baldock interview with author.
80. Nutting: *No End of A Lesson*.
81. Sir Kenneth Thompson and Sir Hubert Ashton interviews with Anthony Seldon.
82. Sir Charles Mott-Radclyffe interview with author.
83. Duncan, Morrison, Darling, Powell, Legge-Bourke and Hinchingbrooke.
84. Sir Anthony Kershaw, Sir Richard Body, Sir Frederick Corfield interviews with author.
85. Private information.
86. Lord Killearn, another vociferous critic of Eden's determination to negotiate with Nasser, was also a member of the Council.
87. Crossbencher, *The Sunday Express* 4.7.54.
88. Hugh Berrington: *Backbench Opinion in the House of Commons 1955–59*, p. 110.
89. Leon Epstein: *British Politics in the Suez Crisis*, p. 51.
90. Biggs-Davison letter, *The Spectator* 21.2.63.
91. Maitland, Amery, Fitzroy Maclean, 'Billy' McLean, Montgomery Hyde and Captain Henry Kerby.
92. In the Abadan crisis Somerset de Chair was able to use confidential information about the supply of military spares and jets to Egypt, gleaned from his friendship with the South African chargé d'affaires in Israel, to attack the Labour Government, much to their horror: Somerset de Chair interview with author.
93. *The Times* 8.12.56.
94. Confirmed by Aubrey Jones and Sir Gilbert Longden interviews with author.
95. Lord Orr-Ewing interview with author.
96. Lord Orr-Ewing.
97. Lord Orr-Ewing.
98. Amery, in Troen and Shemesh ed., p. 111.
99. For example, Biggs-Davison letter, *The Spectator* 21.2.63.
100. Amery to Biggs-Davison 17.1.45, Biggs-Davison papers.
101. Enoch Powell interview with author.
102. Ironically, this was also Ernest Bevin's wish.
103. Biggs-Davison to Amery 13.11.45, Biggs-Davison papers.

104. Amery to Biggs-Davison 22.5.47, Biggs-Davison papers.
105. Hinchingbrooke in *The Sidcup, Eltham and Kentish Times* 7.3.52.
106. Paul Williams to Kenneth Black, his constituency chairman, 12.9.56, Paul Williams papers.
107. Paul Williams constituency speech, reported in *The Times* 1.12.56.
108. FAC 8.2.56.
109. Enoch Powell interview with author.
110. Hinchingbrooke, reported in *The Dorset Daily Echo* 5.10.51.
111. Lord Amery interview with author.
112. See Butler, 5.5.48, *HC Deb.* 450.1128.
113. Butler.
114. Aubrey Jones interview with author.
115. Lord Amery interview with author.
116. Amery to Biggs-Davison 29.5.48, Biggs-Davison papers.
117. Legge-Bourke letter, *The Daily Telegraph* 11.7.51.
118. Paul Williams to Kenneth Black 2.5.57, Williams papers.
119. Hinchingbrooke MES-C 23.4.56; Fraser and Paul Williams, FAC 18.4.56.
120. Conservative Chief Whip 1948–55.
121. Sir Richard Thompson interview with author.
122. Private information. After his elevation to the Whips' Office Richard Brooman-White's war-time experience in the intelligence services undoubtedly stood him in good stead with Amery, Neil McLean, Fitzroy Maclean and Hyde.
123. Sir Richard Thompson interview with author.
124. *The Daily Sketch* 15.12.53.
125. The deposition of the Kabaka of Uganda.
126. *The Daily Sketch* 15.12.53.
127. *The Daily Telegraph* 29.7.54.
128. Sir Richard Thompson interview with author.
129. Private information.
130. See Appendix II.
131. 13 Conservatives were 'paired or absent because sickness or because they were abroad' in this critical vote of confidence (*The Times* 9.11.56); of these Beamish, Bossom, Mathew, and Nield were probably uneasy about Eden's policy, either because of their American connexions or their barrister training.
132. Nigel Nicolson in Alan Thompson: *The Day Before Yesterday*, p. 141.
133. *The Economist* 10.11.56.
134. Boothby had advocated arms to Israel to counterbalance the Soviet decision to provide military equipment to Egypt through Czechoslovakia.
135. Epstein, pp. 97–122.
136. Sir Alec Spearman interview with Anthony Seldon.
137. Astor's brothers, Lord Astor and David Astor (editor of *The Observer*), also opposed Eden's Suez policy.
138. Boothby was the best known of the Anti-Suez Group rebels because of his television appearances. Keith Kyle: *Suez* (London 1991), p. 429.
139. Private information.
140. Paul Williams interview with author.
141. Nigel Nicolson interview with author.

142. Nigel Nicolson.
143. Sir John Astor interview with author.
144. *The Observer*, 18.11.56, confirmed by Sir John Astor.
145. Enoch Powell interview with author.
146. Price had been educated at Yale, Astor had an American mother, Keith Joseph an American wife, and Boothby had travelled extensively in the USA. See Eldon Griffiths: ' "Yanks at Westminster": Our Friends in Commons', *Newsweek Magazine* 3.2.58.
147. One Suez Group MP called Astor a 'degenerate' to his face, and never spoke to him again. Private information.
148. See Epstein: *British Politics in the Suez Crisis*, pp. 95–122, and Keith Kyle: *Suez* (Weidenfeld & Nicolson 1992) for an analysis of the fortunes of the Anti-Suez Group.
149. Brian Inglis, *The Irish Press* 7.1.57.
150. Inglis.

Notes to Chapter 7

1. Evelyn Shuckburgh: *Descent to Suez*, p. 109.
2. Julian Amery speech at the Margate party conference, 9.10.53, reported in *The Times* 10.10.53.
3. Churchill, 23.10.46, HC Deb. 428.1681.
4. See Ralph Glyn, HC Deb. 433.1971–5 and Brigadier Peto, HC Deb. 433.1975–8, 25.2.47.
5. For example, Edward Keeling HC Deb. 426.1290–1 and Colonel Ponsonby HC Deb. 426.1304–6, 1.8.46; Pickthorn, 23.1.48, HC Deb. 446.542.
6. Douglas Dodds-Parker, 4.5.48, HC Deb. 450.1169; Pickthorn, 1.8.46, HC Deb. 426.1271–9.
7. 1.8.46 HC Deb. 426.1252.
8. See Brendan Bracken to Legge-Bourke, 9.7.46 and John Maitland to Legge-Bourke 10.7.46, Sir Harry Legge-Bourke papers, Brotherton Library, University of Leeds.
9. For example, Churchill, *HC Deb.* 459.716 and Boothby, *HC Deb.* 459.785, 10.12.48.
10. FAC 3.3.48.
11. Fitzroy Maclean, 9.12.48 HC Deb. 459.657.
12. Legge-Bourke 10.12.48. HC Deb. 459.758.
13. Peto, 25.2.47, HC Deb. 433.1975–8.
14. Paul Williams interview with author. Earl Winterton (Conservative MP for Horsham 1904–18, Horsham and Worthing 1918–40, and Horsham 1940–51) had served with Lawrence in the First World War.
15. As Colonial Secretary, Churchill had drafted the 1922 White Paper clarifying the British Government's commitment to the creation of a Jewish national homeland, without prejudice to the rights of the indigenous Arab population.
16. See Churchill, 1.8.46, HC Deb. 426.1246–1257.
17. Churchill, 23.10.46, HC Deb. 427.1681.

18. Robert Rhodes James: *Bob Boothby*, p. 336.
19. See 31.7.46–1.8.46, *HC Deb.* 426.957–1075, and 426.1232–1317.
20. See Churchill, 1.8.46, *HC Deb.* 426.1249, referring to the 1941 pro-German revolt in Iraq.
21. Pickthorn, 1.8.46, *HC Deb.* 426.1272.
22. Sir Robert Rhodes James interview with author.
23. Rhodes James: *Boothby*, p. 335.
24. Brigadier Mackeson, 3.3.47, *HC Deb.* 434.37; General Jeffreys, 25.2.47, *HC Deb.* 433.1957–1960.
25. Beamish, 19.3.48, *HC Deb.* 448.2522–3.
26. Manningham-Buller, 25.2.47, *HC Deb.* 433.1993.
27. See Boothby, 10.12.48, *HC Deb.* 459.787.
28. Gammans, 23.10.46, *HC Deb.* 427.1709–10.
29. Churchill, 10.12.48, *HC Deb.* 459.715.
30. Churchill, 1.8.46, *HC Deb.* 426.1253.
31. Beamish, 19.3.48, *HC Deb.* 448.2523; Pickthorn, 9.12.48, *HC Deb.* 459.635, and Legge-Bourke, 10.12.48, *HC Deb.* 459.761; Boothby, 10.12.48, *HC Deb.* 459.787.
32. Macmillan, quoted in Alistair Horne: *Macmillan 1894–1956*, p. 145.
33. 1.8.46, *HC Deb.* 426.1253.
34. Stanley, 25.2.47, *HC Deb.* 433.1923.
35. Gammans, 23.10.46, *HC Deb.* 427.1708.
36. Stanley, 25.2.47, *HC Deb.* 433.1923.
37. See Stanley, 25.2.47, *HC Deb.* 433.1926–7; and Head, 4.5.48, *HC Deb.* 450.1160.
38. Legge-Bourke, 10.12.48, *HC Deb.* 459.758.
39. See Butler, 4.5.48, *HC Deb.* 450.1121–1133.
40. Quoted in John Barnes ed.: *The Leo Amery Diaries*, p. 362.
41. See Alan Bullock: *Ernest Bevin Foreign Secretary 1945–51* (Oxford University Press 1985) for a detailed study of Bevin's Palestine policy.
42. See Beamish 4.5.48, *HC.Deb.* 450.1210; Churchill 10.12.48, *HC.Deb.* 459.716.
43. Harold Macmillan: *Tides of Fortune*, p. 149.
44. Beamish, 4.5.48, *HC Deb.* 450.1210. Churchill was the exception: during the War he had asked Lord Wavell his opinion as to which side was the stronger in Palestine, and had received the unhesitating reply that if both sides were left to themselves the Jews would win. Churchill, 10.12.48, *HC Deb.* 450.716.
45. Beamish, 21.7.49, *HC Deb.* 467.1634.
46. Legge-Bourke, 10.12.48, *HC Deb.* 459.759.
47. Boothby, 10.12.48, *HC Deb.* 459.787 and letter, *The Times* 3.1.49.
48. Churchill, 10.12.48, *HC Deb.* 459.717.
49. On 26.1.49.
50. *The Times* 27.1.49.
51. Although Amery and Biggs-Davison both took a more progressive view of the necessity of Indian independence, they concurred with their Suez Group colleagues that a line should be drawn thereafter.
52. Legge-Bourke, 10.12.48, *HC Deb.* 459.759.
53. See Beamish, 21.7.49, *HC Deb.* 467.1633.

54. Churchill, 1.8.46, *HC Deb.* 426.1256.
55. FAC 4.5.46.
56. FAC 4.5.46.
57. Churchill, 23.10.46, *HC Deb.* 427.1681.
58. Mott-Radclyffe, *HC Deb.* 481.1194 and de Chair, *HC Deb.* 481.1229, 29.11.50.
59. Geoffrey Lloyd, 29.3.50, *HC Deb.* 473.514.
60. Beamish, 21.7.49, *HC Deb.* 454.1641.
61. See Eden, 21.6.51, *HC Deb.* 489.748.
62. See Eden, 28.3.50, *HC Deb.* 473.310; Arbuthnot, 19.5.50, *HC Deb.* 475.1510.
63. See Low, 21.7.49, *HC Deb.* 467.1645.
64. See de Chair, 28.3.50, *HC Deb.* 473.295.
65. Reginald Bevins: *The Greasy Pole*, p. 37.
66. See Fitzroy Maclean, 9.12.48, *HC Deb.* 459.657; Reginald Bennett, 14.9.50, *HC Deb.* 478.1313.
67. Mott-Radclyffe, 29.11.50, *HC Deb.* 481.1194.
68. Earl Winterton, 13.9.50, *HC Deb.* 478.1178; Dunglass, 28.3.50, *HC Deb.* 473.302.
69. Head, 12.2.51, *HC Deb.* 484.152.
70. See Amery, 30.7.51, *HC Deb.* 491.1023.
71. de Chair, 29.11.50, *HC Deb.* 481.1229-30.
72. de Chair, 29.11.50, *HC Deb.* 481.1229.
73. de Chair, *HC Deb.* 481.1234.
74. Amery, 30.7.51, *HC Deb.* 491.1024-5.
75. Amery, 30.7.51, *HC Deb.* 491.1024-5.
76. For example, de Chair, 29.11.50, *HC Deb.* 481.1233-4.
77. Amery, 30.7.51, *HC Deb.* 491.1025.
78. Earl Winterton, *HC Deb.* 478.1178 and Hinchingbrooke, *HC Deb.* 478.1198, 13.9.50; Amery, 30.7.51, *HC Deb.* 491.1024.
79. de Chair, 29.11.50, *HC Deb.* 481.1234.
80. Gammans and Richard Ryder, FAC 25.4.51.
81. See de Chair, 29.11.50, *HC Deb.* 481.1231.
82. Oliver Crossthwaite-Eyre, 14.6.50, *HC Deb.* 476.191.
83. See de Chair, 28.3.50, *HC Deb.* 473.295.
84. John Arbuthnot, 19.5.50, *HC Deb.* 475.1510.
85. Amery, supported by Geoffrey Lloyd, 10.7.50, *HC Deb.* 477.954-5.
86. Hugh Fraser, 19.4.50, *HC Deb.* 474.114.
87. For example, Arbuthnot, 19.5.50, *HC Deb.* 475.1510.
88. 12.9.50, *HC Deb.* 478.980-1.
89. 14.9.50, *HC Deb.* 478.1377.
90. de Chair, William Bennett, Gammans and Nigel Fisher, 20.11.50, *HC Deb.* 482.33; Low, de Chair and Edward Keeling, 29.11.50, *HC Deb.* 481.1151-4.
91. Mott-Radclyffe, 29.11.50, *HC Deb.* 481.1193.
92. Eden, 22.11.50, *HC Deb.* 481.341 and 23.11.50, *HC Deb.* 481.512-3; Churchill, 22.11.50, *HC Deb.* 481.344; 23.11.50, *HC Deb.* 481.515 and 29.11.50, *HC Deb.* 481.1153-4.
93. See adjournment debate, 22.11.50, *HC Deb.* 481.424-468.

94. Amery and Geoffrey Lloyd, 10.7.50, *HC Deb.* 477.954–5.
95. Mott-Radclyffe, 20.3.51, *HC Deb.* 485.2358.
96. *The Times* 21.3.51.
97. See Eden, 21.6.51, *HC Deb.* 489.747–54; and see Churchill campaign speech, reported in *The Times* 2.10.51.
98. Eden, 19.6.51, *HC Deb.* 489.239–241.
99. Vere Harvey, 18.4.51, *HC Deb.* 486.1818.
100. Hugh Berrington: *Backbench Opinion in the House of Commons 1945–55*, p. 171.
101. About 200 Tory MPs attended the 1922 Committee meeting which discussed Persia on 28.6.51.
102. See de Chair, Mott-Radclyffe, and Eden, 21.6.51, *HC Deb.* 489.746–833.
103. *The Times* 21.6.51.
104. de Chair, Sir Herbert Williams and Captain Waterhouse.
105. Amery, Maude and Powell.
106. Lord Amery interview with author.
107. At one point Amery, Fitzroy Maclean, Head and Cranborne, along with about six other concerned MPs, called on Churchill and urged him to take a vigorous line. Lord Amery.
108. Lord Carr interview with author.
109. Lord Carr, and see Churchill, 30.7.51, *HC Deb.* 491.978–995.
110. Eden letter to *The Daily Telegraph*, quoted in David Carlton: *Anthony Eden* (London 1981), p. 289.
111. 21.6.51, *HC Deb.* 489.752–3.
112. Robert Rhodes James: *Anthony Eden* (London 1986), p. 337.
113. Edward Wakefield, 21.6.51, *HC Deb.* 489.791.
114. Richard Thompson, 21.6.51, *HC Deb.* 489.807–8.
115. Edward Wakefield, 21.6.51, *HC Deb.* 489.792.
116. Rhodes James: *Eden*, p. 337.
117. 89 names were added to the list on the Order paper on 11.6.51.
118. Lord Amery interview with author.
119. Somerset de Chair interview with author.
120. Lord Amery interview with author.
121. *The Times* 2.5.51.
122. Legge-Bourke letter, *The Daily Telegraph* 11.7.51.
123. Amery, 30.7.51, *HC Deb.* 491.1019.
124. Somerset de Chair interview with author.
125. For example, Rayner, 16.7.51, *HC Deb.* 490.842.
126. See de Chair letter, *The Times* 19.6.51.
127. on 21.6.51.
128. Sandys, 21.6.51 *HC.Deb.* 489.759–60.
129. Fitzroy Maclean, 30.7.51, *HC Deb.* 491.1035.
130. de Chair letter, *The Times* 19.6.51.
131. *The Times* 21.5.51; Crossman, 21.6.51, *HC Deb.* 489.776.
132. *The Times*.
133. Legge-Bourke letter, *The Daily Telegraph* 11.7.51; Fitzroy Maclean, 30.7.51, *HC Deb.* 491.1039.
134. de Chair letter, *The Times* 31.6.51.
135. See de Chair letter, *The Times* 19.6.51.

Notes   267

136. Amery, 30.7.51, *HC Deb.* 491.1024–5.
137. de Chair letter, *The Times* 31.6.51.
138. Amery, 30.7.51, *HC Deb.* 491.1024–5.
139. 30.7.51, *HC Deb.* 491.1037–38.
140. Fitzroy Maclean, 30.7.51, *HC Deb.* 491.1042.
141. Somerset de Chair interview with author.
142. de Chair, 20.6.51, *HC Deb.* 489.526.
143. Legge-Bourke letter, *The Daily Telegraph* 11.7.51.
144. *The Times* 21.6.51.
145. On 7.6.51.
146. 5.7.51, reported in *The Times* 7.7.51. After an irate Eden had telephoned Salisbury, the latter wrote a lengthy letter to Churchill, apologizing for the acute embarrassment his views caused and offering to step down as Conservative leader in the House of Lords. See Lord Salisbury to Churchill 6.7.51, Churchill papers.
147. 21.6.51 *HC Deb.* 489.770; see 1922 Committee, 28.6.51, FAC 28.6.51. Dunglass seems an unexpected recruit, as a former PPS to Chamberlain, supporter of the Munich settlement and of Chamberlain in 1940.
148. 21.6.51, *HC Deb.* 489.763–65.
149. See Head letter, *The Times* 11.7.51. .
150. Head letter, *The Times* 11.7.51.
151. Butler, FAC 12.7.51; and see 1922 Committee, 28.7.51.
152. Sponsored by Fitzroy Maclean, Amery, Viscount Cranborne, Christopher Soames, Captain Ryder and Richard Fort, it was signed by Michael Astor, John Baker White, Tufton Beamish, Reginald Bennett, Eric Bullus, Albert Cooper, Viscountess Davidson, Nigel Fisher, Hugh Fraser, John Hare, Reader Harris, Edward Keeling, Gilbert Longden, Douglas Marshall, David Ormsby-Gore, Peter Smithers, Lady Tweedsmuir, Fletcher Vane, Captain Charles Waterhouse, Sir Herbert Williams, Geoffrey Wilson and Richard Wood. EDM No. 78. *Orders of the Day and Notices of Motions* (1951) Vol. 4. No. 122.
153. *Backbench Opinion in the House of Commons 1945–55*, p. 172.
154. Somerset de Chair interview with author.
155. Waterhouse, Amery, Hugh Fraser, Marshall, Fitzroy Maclean and Reader Harris. Ormsby-Gore and Fisher remained firmly sympathetic.
156. 'As Churchill's PPS, he was superb, much more intelligent, reactive, with a degree of sensibility which his earlier impression had totally belied.' Lord Carr interview with author.
157. Lord Carr.
158. Ormsby-Gore and Fitzroy Maclean in the 1922 Committee, 12.7.51, supported by a 'considerable majority of MPs' at the 1922 Committee, 26.7.50.
159. *The Times* 6.7.51.
160. Maxwell Fyfe weekend speech 7–8.7.51.
161. Churchill, 30.7.51, *HC Deb.* 491.994–5.
162. *The Times* 7.7.51.
163. 22.10.51.
164. See Attlee 30.7.51, *HC Deb.* 491.1072; Lord Chancellor's statement 31.7.51, reported in *The Times* 1.8.51.

165. See Fitzroy Maclean letter, *The Times* 26.9.51.
166. David Butler: *The British General Election of 1951* (Macmillan, London 1952), p. 117.
167. Maxwell Fyfe constituency speech, reported in *The Times* 22.8.51.
168. Henry Hopkinson constituency speech, *The Times* 9.9.51.
169. Sir John Coulson interview with Anthony Seldon.
170. Lord Amery interview with author.
171. Fitzroy Maclean, 30.7.51, *HC Deb.* 491.1040–1.
172. King Abdullah was assassinated on 19.7.51.
173. Amery, 30.7.51, *HC Deb.* 491.1021–2.

Notes to Chapter 8

1. Enoch Powell interview with author.
2. Sir Richard Thompson interview with author.
3. Sir Anthony Eden: *Full Circle* (Cassell, London 1960), p. 247.
4. See Tom Driberg, *The Daily Express* 13.4.52.
5. He did not enjoy the position as clear favourite (over Butler and Macmillan) until 1954, his *annus mirabilis*.
6. See John Grigg: 'The Crippled Giant', *Encounter*, April 1977, Vol. 48, pp. 9–16.
7. Sir Evelyn Shuckburgh interview with Anthony Seldon.
8. Lord Selwyn-Lloyd interview with John Barnes for *The Day Before Yesterday*.
9. See Eden, FAC 8.1.53.
10. Such as Amery, Kerby, Hyde, all of whom were to become members of the Suez Group.
11. Eden, FAC 8.1.53.
12. Lord Glendevon interview with author.
13. See Grigg: 'The Crippled Giant'.
14. Mott-Radclyffe letter, *The Times* 19.2.52.
15. Anthony Adamthwaite: 'Eden, the Foreign Office and the Making of Foreign Policy', *International Affairs* 1988 No. 64 No. 2, pp. 241–259.
16. Adamthwaite.
17. Nutting, 20.11.51, *HC Deb.* 494.232.
18. For example, Legge-Bourke, 19.11.51, *HC Deb.* 494.128.
19. Aubrey Jones interview with author.
20. Confirmed by *The Times* 5.8.52.
21. 1922 Committee minutes, 21.2.52.
22. PRO PREM 11/91, quoted in Ritchie Ovendale: 'Egypt and the Suez Base Agreement', in John Young ed.: *The Foreign Policy of Churchill's Peacetime Administration* 1951–55 (Leicester 1988), p. 138.
23. See John Colville: *The Fringes of Power – Downing Street Diaries 1939–55*, p. 645.
24. See Churchill address to Congress, 17.1.52, reported in *The Times* 18.1.52.
25. Eden, 15.11.51, *HC Deb.* 493.1176–8.
26. FAC 7.5.46, and Churchill, 1.8.46, *HC Deb.* 426.1256.

Notes 269

27. See Fitzroy Maclean, 7.5.52, *HC Deb.* 500.354.
28. Julian Amery: 'The Suez Group', in Selwyn Troen and Moshe Shemesh ed.: *The Suez-Sinai Crisis*, p. 113.
29. Edward Wakefield, FAC 30.4.52.
30. *The Times* 12.5.52.
31. Wm Roger Louis: 'The Tragedy of the Anglo-Egyptian Settlement of 1954', in Wm R Louis ed: *Suez 1956 – the Crisis and its Consequences* (Oxford 1989), p. 51.
32. Dodds-Parker, FAC 28.1.53.
33. Waterhouse, 5.3.53, *HC Deb.* 512.593.
34. Harold Macmillan: *Tides of Fortune*, p. 658.
35. Sir Richard Thompson interview with author.
36. Savory, FAC 10.2.53.
37. Assheton, 12.2.53, *HC Deb.* 512.608–9.
38. Sir Douglas Dodds-Parker interview with author.
39. Reflected in Waterhouse's question, 17.2.53, *HC Deb.* 511.1067.
40. Eden, 12.2.53, *HC Deb.* 511.610.
41. See Waterhouse, 12.2.53, *HC Deb.* 511.609 and 17.2.53, *HC Deb.* 511.1067.
42. Waterhouse 17.2.53.
43. Malcolm McCorquodale, FAC 28.1.53.
44. Wakefield, FAC 30.4.52; Dodds-Parker, FAC 10.2.53.
45. Paul Williams interview with author.
46. Amery, FAC 10.2.53.
47. This formed part of the Bevin-Sidky agreement of 1946: *The Times* 4.1.52.
48. See *The Times* 5.8.52.
49. FAC 10.2.53.
50. Waterhouse and Harmar Nicholls, FAC 10.2.53.
51. See Eden diary 9.2.53, Lord Avon papers, University of Birmingham.
52. FAC 10.12.52.
53. FAC 28.1.53.
54. Sir Anthony Nutting interview with author.
55. See Eden diary 22.12.53, Avon papers.
56. Evelyn Shuckburgh: *Descent to Suez*, p. 77.
57. Sir Anthony Nutting interview with author; Shuckburgh, p. 75.
58. *The Bristol Evening Post* 20.2.53.
59. Sir Richard Thompson interview with author; *The Bristol Evening Post*.
60. Sir Richard Thompson.
61. Shuckburgh, pp. 74–5.
62. PRO PREM 11/392, quoted in Ritchie Ovendale in Young ed.: *The Foreign Policy of Churchill's Peacetime Administration*.
63. Sir Anthony Nutting interview with author.
64. At Eden's suggestion, Waterhouse met Sir James Bowker, head of Egyptian affairs at the Foreign Office, and Nutting on 2.2.53; Waterhouse to Eden 11.2.53., Waterhouse papers.
65. Patrick Buchan-Hepburn to Anthony Eden 11.2.53, Avon papers.
66. *The Bristol Evening Post* 20.2.53.
67. FAC 10.2.53.
68. *The Bristol Evening Post* 20.2.53.

69. *The Bristol Evening Post* 20.2.53.
70. PRO CAB 128/26 CC(53)9 11.2.53.
71. Sir Anthony Nutting interview with author.
72. Sir Richard Thompson interview with author.
73. Eden, p. 247.
74. *The Bristol Evening Post* 20.2.53.
75. *The Bristol Evening Post* 20.2.53.
76. Sir Anthony Nutting interview with author.
77. Sir Anthony Nutting interview with author.
78. PRO CAB 128/26 CC(53)10 11.2.53.
79. *The Times* 13.2.53.
80. Waterhouse, 17.2.53, *HC Deb.* 511.1067; Waterhouse FAC 25.2.53; Waterhouse letter to Eden 2.3.53, Waterhouse papers; Fitzroy Maclean and others, FAC 22.4.53.
81. Lord Amery interview with author.
82. Crossbencher, *The Sunday Express* 22.2.53.
83. Jocelyn Simon writing in 'The Week in Westminster', *The Evening Gazette* 14.2.53.

Notes to Chapter 9

1. Lord Selwyn-Lloyd interview with John Barnes for *The Day Before Yesterday*.
2. Eden to Waterhouse 24.6.54, Waterhouse papers.
3. PRO FO 371/102766/JE1052/134 Dodds-Parker personal notes after visit to Egypt 7–16.10.53.
4. Dodds-Parker, FAC 21.10.53.
5. Mott-Radclyffe memo to the Foreign Office, quoted in *Foreign Body in the Eye*, (London 1975), pp. 213–221; Spearman, FAC 25.11.53.
6. Mott-Radclyffe, pp. 213–221; Alport, FAC 30.6.54.
7. Dodds-Parker, FAC 21.10.53.
8. Otho Prior-Palmer, FAC 2.12.53.
9. *The Times* 17.12.53.
10. See Mott-Radcliffe memo, *Foreign Body*, pp. 213–221.
11. See Mott-Radclyffe, pp. 213–221.
12. Prior-Palmer, 1922 Committee, 3.12.53.
13. Derek Marks, *The Daily Express* 16.12.53.
14. Lambton to Waterhouse undated.12.54, Waterhouse papers.
15. 17.12.53, *HC Deb.* 522.623.
16. Lord Lambton was a controversial politician who once called Lord Woolton, the Chairman of the Party, a liar in the 1922 Committee – much to the outrage of his colleagues. Sir Kenneth Thompson interview with Anthony Seldon.
17. Fitzroy Maclean, FAC 22.4.53; Guy Lloyd, FAC 2.12.53.
18. Holland-Martin, Waterhouse and others letter, *The Times* 13.5.53.
19. Waterhouse press statement, *The Times* 16.12.53; Hinchingbrooke, in *The Dorset Daily Echo* 1.11.53.
20. Suez Group to Eden 17.6.54, Waterhouse papers.

21. Amery to Waterhouse 16.2.54, Waterhouse papers.
22. Anthony Fell letter, *The Times* 29.7.54; James Duncan to Churchill 15.7.54, Waterhouse papers.
23. Waterhouse to Eden 17.6.54, Waterhouse papers.
24. *The Daily Telegraph* 18.6.54; Patrick Maitland letter, *The Daily Telegraph* 7.7.54; Suez Group to Eden 17.6.54, Waterhouse papers.
25. Maitland letter, *The Daily Telegraph* 7.7.54.
26. See Hankey *et al* letter, *The Times* 24.9.53; see Legge-Bourke letter, *The Times* 12.11.53.
27. Maitland letter, *The Daily Telegraph* 17.7.54.
28. PRO PREM 11/636 Hankey to Salisbury and Eden 7.2.53.
29. Powell, 5.11.53, *HC Deb.* 432.344.
30. *The Times* 10.7.54.
31. Legge-Bourke letter, *The Times* 6.5.53.
32. Lord Amery interview with author.
33. Mott-Radclyffe, pp. 213–221.
34. See *The Times* 29.6.53.
35. Lord Amery interview with author.
36. Julian Amery: 'The Suez Group: A Retrospective on Suez', in Selwyn Troen and Moshe Shemesh ed.: *The Suez-Sinai Crisis*, p. 112.
37. Amery, 5.11.53, *HC Deb.* 432.379; Powell, 5.11.53, *HC Deb.* 432.345–6.
38. Legge-Bourke speech at Downham Market, *The Sunday Express* 13.12.53 and widely reported elsewhere.
39. Legge-Bourke, 17.2.54, *HC Deb.* 523.1966.
40. Assheton, FAC 2.12.53.
41. Fell letter, *The Times* 29.7.54; James Duncan to Churchill 15.7.54, Waterhouse papers.
42. PRO PREM 11/635 Suez Group letter to Churchill 22.4.53.
43. Waterhouse press statement, *The Times* 16.12.53; Leo Amery letter, *The Times* 30.9.53; Julian Amery to Waterhouse 16.2.54; Hinchingbrooke to Waterhouse 4.3.54, Waterhouse papers.
44. Fell letter, *The Times* 29.7.54.
45. Powell, *Truth* 5.3.54, quoted in Patrick Cosgrave: *The Lives of Enoch Powell* (London 1989), p. 130; and Leo Amery letter, *The Times* 20.2.53.
46. Leo Amery letter, *The Times* 25.9.53.
47. Hinchingbrooke, FAC 30.6.54.
48. See the Lords Rennell, Hankey, Vansittart and Killearn, 17.12.53, *HL Deb.* 185.189–258.
49. Leo Amery letter, *The Times* 30.9.53.
50. PRO PREM 11/636 Hankey to Churchill 25.11.53.
51. Hankey to Churchill; Suez Group to Eden 17.6.54; Sir Herbert Williams to Buchan-Hepburn 16.7.54, Waterhouse papers.
52. Paul Williams interview with author.
53. See Powell, 5.11.53, *HC Deb.* 520.342–349.
54. Beresford Craddock, FAC 3.3.54.
55. PRO PREM 11/636 Hankey to Churchill 4.6.54.
56. PRO PREM 11/636 Hankey to Churchill 4.6.54.
57. Leo Amery letter, *The Times* 20.2.53.
58. Leo Amery letter, *The Times* 20.2.53.

59. Leo Amery letter, *The Times* 20.2.53.
60. See Leo Amery letter, *The Times* 25.9.53.
61. Leo Amery to Biggs-Davison 23.10.53, Biggs-Davison papers.
62. Draft press release drawn up by Julian Amery, in Amery to Biggs-Davison 8.11.53, Biggs-Davison papers.
63. William Rees Davies, 11.3.54, *HC Deb.* 524.2595; Julian Amery letter to Eden, 18.3.53, quoted in Wm R Louis: 'The Tragedy of the Anglo-Egyptian Settlement of 1954' in Roger Louis & Roger Owen ed.: *The Suez Crisis and its Consequences*, p. 59.
64. Hankey was still on the board of the Suez Canal Company, and took his directorship seriously. See Stephen Roskill: *Hankey, Man of Secrets* (London 1974).
65. See PRO FO 371/102766 Leo Amery to Churchill 7.10.53, signed by 13 peers, including Hailsham, Cromer and Simon.
66. Lord Aldington interview with author.
67. Sir Richard Thompson interview with author.
68. Amery in Troen and Shemesh ed., p. 111.
69. Paul Williams interview with author.
70. Paul Williams.
71. Enoch Powell interview with author; see John Barnes ed.: *The Leo Amery Diaries*, p. 1064.
72. *The Times* 10.3.54.
73. In February 1954 Mrs Barbara Castle sponsored an EDM, deploring the Government's handling of the Anglo-Egyptian negotiations; this was deliberately amended to exclude the words 'and urges that the withdrawal of our troops and equipment should begin forthwith'.
74. Amery to Waterhouse 16.3.54, Waterhouse papers.
75. *The Economist* 7.8.54.
76. See Louis in Louis ed., p. 53.
77. Louis in Louis ed., p. 53.
78. Paul Williams and Arthur Gavshon interviews with author.
79. Paul Williams; see also Suez Group letter to Churchill 22.4.53, Waterhouse papers.
80. Lord Amery interview with author.
81. See Suez Group to Churchill 22.4.43, Waterhouse papers.
82. Jane Portal in conversation with Evelyn Shuckburgh: *Descent to Suez*, p. 141.
83. Denis Healey, 5.11.53, *HC Deb.* 520.423; Barbara Castle, 11.3.54, *HC Deb.* 524.2510.
84. Lord Amery interview with author.
85. Churchill wanted American cooperation to set up a joint command in the Middle East. Harold Macmillan: *Tides of Fortune*, p. 501 and Shuckburgh, p. 77.
86. Shuckburgh, p. 75.
87. Ursula Branston interview with author.
88. Shuckburgh, p. 86.
89. Macmillan, p. 502.
90. PRO FO 371/102806 Amery to Eden 18.3.53, quoted in Louis in Louis ed., p. 59.

Notes

91. PRO PREM 11/635 Suez Group to Churchill 22.4.53.
92. FAC 25.2.53.
93. PRO PREM 11/635 Mott-Radclyffe to Buchan-Hepburn 22.4.53.
94. PRO PREM 11/635 Buchan-Hepburn to Churchill 24.4.53.
95. Buchan-Hepburn to Churchill.
96. FAC 29.4.53.
97. 11.5.53, *HC Deb.* 515.885–889.
98. Waterhouse note 11.5.53, Waterhouse papers.
99. Legge-Bourke, FAC 6.5.53, referring to *The Times* and *The Daily Telegraph*; Fitzroy Maclean and Legge-Bourke, FAC 17.5.53.
100. Fitzroy Maclean, FAC 1.7.53.
101. 22.1.53.
102. PRO FO 371/102766 JE1052/137 Ledward memo: 'Lord Hankey and the Suez Canal' undated.
103. PRO FO 371/102766 22.7.53.
104. See PRO FO 371/102766.
105. *The Times* 29.7.53.
106. *The Gloucestershire Echo* 17.11.53.
107. Louis in Louis ed., p. 61.
108. The Suez Group could 'only conclude that [Churchill] has found it necessary to shift his ground greatly to our disadvantage.' Waterhouse to Leo Amery 1.10.53, Waterhouse papers.
109. The Lords Hankey, Vansittart, Killearn and Rennell letter, *The Times* 24.9.53; and from Leo Amery letter, *The Times* 25.9.53.
110. For example, *The Times* 9.10.53; *The Daily Telegraph* 9.10.53.
111. PRO FO 371/102826 minute by Salisbury 9.9.53, quoted in Louis ed., p. 60.
112. Paul Williams interview with author.
113. *The Gloucestershire Echo* 17.11.53.
114. *The Gloucestershire Echo.*
115. *The Daily Herald* 26.10.53.
116. *The Gloucestershire Echo* 17.11.53.
117. *The Gloucestershire Echo.*
118. John Colville: *The Fringes of Power,* pp. 679–80.
119. Paul Williams interview with author.
120. PRO CAB 128/26.CC(58)53 15.11.53.
121. PRO CAB 128/26.CC(58)53 15.11.53.
122. Waterhouse to Leo Amery 15.10.53, Waterhouse papers.
123. Derek Marks, *The Daily Express* 16.12.54.
124. PRO FO 371/1026766 Leo Amery to Churchill 7.10.53; Paul Williams; and *The Times* 17.12.53.
125. *The Economist* 9.12.53.
126. Eden to Waterhouse 20.10.53, Waterhouse papers.
127. When pressed by the agitated Chief Whip to attend to this committee meeting to support Eden against the Suez Group, Churchill agreed very reluctantly, adding 'You see, I'm not on "our" side'. Leo Amery diary entry 22.11.53 in John Barnes ed., p. 1064.
128. PRO PREM 11/635 Buchan-Hepburn to Churchill 24.10.53.
129. Healey, 5.11.53, *HC Deb.* 520.423.

130. *The Gloucestershire Echo* 17.11.53; PRO PREM 11/635 Suez Group (27 signatures) to Churchill 22.10.53; Suez Group and Hankey letters to Churchill 25.11.53.
131. Powell, *HC Deb.* 520.342–349 and Amery, *HC Deb.* 520.369–380, 5.11.53.
132. For example, *The Morning Advertiser* 3.11.53; *The Sunday Despatch* 8.11.53; *The Birmingham Post* 10.11.53.
133. *The Birmingham Post* 12.11.53.
134. See Reginald Bevins: *The Greasy Pole*, p. 39.
135. For example, Maclay and Elliot, FAC 16.12.53.
136. Godfrey Nicholson, FAC 16.12.53.
137. PRO PREM 11/635 Buchan-Hepburn to Churchill 24.10.53.
138. Buchan-Hepburn to Churchill.
139. See Eden's lengthy written reply to Prior-Palmer, 13.11.53, *HC Deb.* 102.*102–104*.
140. Marks, *The Daily Express* 16.11.53.
141. PRO PREM 11/636 Hankey to Churchill 25.11.53.
142. See PRO PREM 11/635 Waterhouse to Churchill 25.11.53.
143. *The News of the World* 13.12.53.
144. *The Daily Express* 16.12.53.
145. Waterhouse to Churchill 25.11.53, Waterhouse papers.
146. FAC 25.11.53 and 2.12.53.
147. PRO PREM 11/635 Minister of State to Eden, telegram 105 3.12.53; Marks, *The Daily Express* 9.12.53 and 16.12.53.
148. PRO FO 371/102766 Killearn notice of Parliamentary Question 15.12.53.
149. PRO FO 371/10276611 Leward 12.12.53, and Shuckburgh to O'Regan 12.12.53.
150. PRO PREM 11/635 Foreign Office to Bermuda telegram 105 3.12.53.
151. Foreign Office to Bermuda; *The Daily Telegraph* 16.12.53.
152. Foreign Office to Bermuda.
153. PRO CAB 128/26 CC(53)79 14.12.53.
154. Foreign Office to Bermuda telegram 3.12.53.
155. Assheton, Waterhouse, Charles Williams, Maclay, McCorquodale and Spens.
156. Foreign Office to Bermuda.
157. *The Birmingham Post* 2.12.53.
158. *The Times* 16.12.53; see *The Daily Telegraph* 16.12.53; *The News of the World* 13.12.53.
159. Marks, *The Daily Express* 9.12.53.
160. Marks.
161. *The Daily Express*, 16.11.54.
162. Eden to Churchill 12.12.53 Top Secret, PM/53/342 AP/20/16, Avon papers.
163. Shuckburgh, p. 118.
164. *The Times* 14.12.53.
165. PRO CAB 128/26 CC(53)79 15.12.53; PRO PREM 11/635 Buchan-Hepburn to Churchill 15.12.53.
166. PRO PREM 11/635 Eden to Churchill 14.12.53.
167. PRO CAB 128/26.CC.(53)79 14.12.53.

168. PRO PREM 11/635 Buchan-Hepburn to Churchill 14.12.43.
169. Buchan-Hepburn to Churchill; At Eden's prompting, Montgomery also spent two hours with Waterhouse. Montgomery to Eden, 18.12.53, AP/20/16, Avon papers.
170. PRO CAB 128/26 CC(53)79 14.12.53.
171. Alexander was accompanied at this meeting by Butler, Selwyn Lloyd, Lord Reading and Head. FAC 16.12.53.
172. Derek Marks, *The Daily Express* 9.12.53.
173. *The Daily Telegraph* 18.6.54.
174. Diary, *Time and Tide* 19.12.53.
175. *Time and Tide.*
176. *The Yorkshire Post* 17.12.53.
177. PRO CAB 128/26 CC(53)79 14.12.53.
178. PRO PREM 11/699 T.310/53 Churchill to Eisenhower 19.12.53. Eden agreed Washington's position over Egypt was becoming increasingly unhelpful: Eden to Churchill 21.12.53, AP/20/16 PM/53/347, Avon papers.
179. Proposed in Cabinet 9.12.53: Shuckburgh, p. 118.
180. PRO PREM 11/635 Churchill to Eden 14.12.53.
181. *The Guardian* 17.12.53.
182. PRO FO 371/102766 Ledward 12.12.53 and Lord Reading *HL Deb.* 185.68 15.12.53. Lord Reading refused to commit the Government to a debate before entering into Heads of Agreement.
183. *The Times* 18.12.53.
184. *The Times* 18.12.53.
185. PRO PREM 11/635 Whips' note from conversation with (unspecified – but probably Patrick Maitland) member of the Suez Group 18.12.53.
186. Whips' note.
187. See *The Times* 18.12.53.
188. *The Times.*
189. Amery to Waterhouse 23.2.54, Waterhouse papers.
190. *The Daily Telegraph* 26.1.54; *The Sheffield Telegraph* 3.3.54.
191. Army Estimates Debate 3.3.54 *HC Deb.* 524.2450–2828.
192. Powell article in *New Commonwealth* 4.1.54, quoted in Cosgrave, pp. 130–1.
193. Maitland, 3.2.54, *HC Deb.* 523.364.
194. See *The Daily Telegraph*, 26.1.54, *The Sheffield Telegraph* 3.3.54; Maitland, Paul Williams, Bromley-Davenport and Waterhouse, 17.2.54, *HC Deb.* 523.1960–1963.
195. *The Sheffield Telegraph* 3.3.54.
196. Powell article, *Truth*; Nabarro, 1.3.54, *HC Deb.* 524.827.
197. Maitland, 3.2.54, *HC Deb.* 523.364.
198. Suez Group meeting 15.3.56, Waterhouse papers.
199. Amery to Waterhouse 19.3.54, Waterhouse papers.
200. Shuckburgh, p. 125.
201. Scott Lucas: *Divided We Stand: Britain, the US and the Suez Crisis*, p. 30.
202. Macmillan, pp. 502–3.
203. Shuckburgh, p. 125.
204. Shuckburgh, p. 125.

205. Shuckburgh, p. 137.
206. Shuckburgh, p. 148.
207. Shuckburgh, p. 141.
208. Waterhouse to Amery 23.3.54, Waterhouse papers.
209. before the Suez Group's letter was sent to the Chief Whip.
210. Waterhouse to Amery 23.3.54, Waterhouse papers.
211. PRO CAB 129/66 CC(54)74 25.2.54, Memorandum by Chiefs of Staff, 'Egypt', quoted in Louis in Louis ed., p. 64 and p. 66; Scott Lucas, p. 31.
212. PRO FO 371/110819/V1193/8 Eden minute 12.1.54, quoted in Scott Lucas, p. 31.
213. 'Suez and Why We Must Stay': Waterhouse article, *The Daily Telegraph* 5.7.54.
214. Powell, *The Times*, 25.6.54; Hankey, Vansittart, Killearn and Rennell, *The Times* 10.7.54.
215. 23.6.54.
216. Waterhouse to Eden 17.6.54, Waterhouse papers.
217. *The Daily Telegraph* 18.6.54.
218. PRO PREM 11/635 Waterhouse to Churchill 9.7.54.
219. See Crossbencher, *The Sunday Express* 4.7.54.
220. Suez Group to Eden 17.6.54, Waterhouse papers.
221. See FAC 30.6.54.
222. Crossbencher, *The Sunday Express* 4.7.54.
223. FAC 12.7.54.
224. See Walter Fletcher letter, *The Times* 21.6.54.
225. See Eden to Waterhouse 24.6.54, Waterhouse papers.
226. See Amery vs Legge-Bourke, FAC 26.5.54; Patrick Maitland letter, *The Daily Telegraph* 7.7.54.
227. Eden to Waterhouse 24.6.54, Waterhouse papers.
228. *The Times* 14.7.54.
229. PRO PREM 11/635 Waterhouse note of meeting: Waterhouse to Buchan-Hepburn 13.7.54.
230. See PRO PREM 11/702 CAB CC(54)43 22.6.54 and CC(54)47 2.7.54.
231. Ovendale in John Young ed.: *The Foreign Policy of Churchill's Peace time Administration*, p. 146.
232. PRO PREM 11/699 and PREM 11/702.
233. See Shuckburgh, pp. 137–9; Eden, pp. 257–9; Selwyn Lloyd, *Suez 1956* (New York 1978), pp. 14–23.
234. Sir John Colville in conversation with Professor Donald Watt.
235. Macmillan, p. 505; Sir Richard Thompson interview with author.
236. Churchill had promised to step down as Prime Minister on 21 September, and then reneged. Sir John Colville interview with John Barnes for *The Day Before Yesterday*.
237. *The Daily Telegraph* 14.7.54.
238. Lord Amery interview with author.
239. Amery, FAC 30.6.54.
240. Waterhouse note of Suez Group meeting with Churchill 12.7.54, Waterhouse papers.

241. Amery to Waterhouse 4.8.54, Waterhouse papers; Enoch Powell interview with author.
242. Enoch Powell interview with author.
243. *The Times* 14.7.54.
244. See *The Daily Telegraph* 15.7.54 and 16.7.54.
245. Chairman of the Empire Economic Union and with a distinguished war record, he was the second Conservative that year to resign the party Whip; Sir John Mellor had resigned the party Whip over the issue of MPs' salaries.
246. Robert Jackson: *Rebels and Whips*, p. 112.
247. Paul Williams interview with author.
248. *The Times* 15.7.54.
249. Lord Amery interview with author.
250. *The Times* and *The Daily Telegraph* 15.7.54; *The Daily Telegraph* 30.7.54.
251. *The Daily Telegraph* 15.7.54.
252. Amery to Biggs-Davison 3.8.54, Biggs-Davison papers.
253. Amery to Biggs-Davison.
254. Lord Lauderdale interview with author.
255. Amery to Biggs-Davison 3.8.54, Biggs-Davison papers.
256. For example, *The Daily Mail* 3.9.54.
257. *The Daily Mail* 29.10.54; Amery to Waterhouse 20.10.54, Waterhouse papers.
258. *Crossbencher* 4.7.54; *The Daily Telegraph* 31.7.54; Amery to Waterhouse 20.10.54, Waterhouse papers. When the Suez Group reconvened in November 1954, Powell informed his colleagues that he would not be taking part in 'any nonsense' over Cyprus. Enoch Powell interview with author.
259. Legge-Bourke speech at The Empire Economic Union, *The Cambridge Times* 24.9.54.
260. *The Sunday Express* 1.8.54.
261. Correspondence in Waterhouse papers; see Geoffrey Wakeford, *The Daily Mail* 3.9.54.
262. Amery to Waterhouse 20.10.54, Waterhouse papers.
263. *The Times* 1.11.54.
264. For example, *The Daily Telegraph* 30.7.54.

Notes to Chapter 10

1. See Phillip Williams ed.: *The Diaries of Hugh Gaitskell 1945–56* (London 1983), p. 411; Godfrey Nicholson to Patrick Buchan-Hepburn, 7.12.55, Lord Hailes papers, The Churchill Archives Centre.
2. Maitland, FAC 9.11.55. The Whips were not complacent about the supposed 'comfortable' majority: See Martin Redmayne to Patrick Buchan-Hepburn 29.5.55, Hailes papers.
3. See Lord Moran: *Winston Churchill: The Struggle for Survival 1940–65* (London 1968).
4. Sir Edward Du Cann interview with author.

5. See Middle East Sub-Committee meetings May/June 1956, The Conservative Party Archives, The Bodleian Library.
6. Amery, Hinchingbrooke and Hugh Fraser all had close links with Israel: Arthur Gavshon interview with author.
7. Amery, who enjoyed excellent contacts in Egypt, was also in touch with a group of rebel Egyptian officers. Julian Amery: 'The Suez Group' in Selwyn Troen and Moshe Shemesh: *The Suez-Sinai Crisis 1956*, p. 121.
8. Roger Louis seminar on Eden, London School of Economics, 1992.
9. See Legge-Bourke, MES-C 23.4.56.
10. See *The Times* 28.6.56; Suez Group letters to Heath (20.6.54) and to Eden (28.6.54), Waterhouse papers.
11. 5.12.55, HC Deb. 547.32–156; FAC 27.6.56; FAC 4.7.56; and *The Times* 28.6.56.
12. *The Times* 16.12.55.
13. 5.12.55.
14. Chief of the Imperial General Staff.
15. See Randolph Churchill: *The Rise and Fall of Sir Anthony Eden* (London 1959) p. 223.
16. See Williams ed: *Gaitskell*, pp. 421–2; Reginald Bevins: *The Greasy Pole*, p. 37.
17. *The Daily Telegraph* 3.1.56.
18. Anthony Nutting: *No End of a Lesson*, pp. 25–26.
19. Robert Allan in Alan Thompson: *The Day Before Yesterday*, p. 122.
20. Nutting: *No End of a Lesson*, p. 27.
21. Nutting: *No End of a Lesson*, p. 27.
22. Waterhouse letter, *The Times* 5.3.56.
23. Waterhouse.
24. Waterhouse.
25. Stephen McAdden letter, *The Times* 7.3.56.
26. Waterhouse letter, *The Times* 5.3.56.
27. McAdden letter, *The Times* 7.3.56.
28. See Churchill, p. 225.
29. Amery and Waterhouse *The Times*, 5.3.56.
30. Churchill, p. 225.
31. *The Times* 6.3.56.
32. Amery and McAdden letters, *The Times* 7.3.56.
33. Amery, *The Times* 7.3.56.
34. Sir Anthony Nutting interview with David Elstein for *The Day Before Yesterday*.
35. Evelyn Shuckburgh: *Descent to Suez*, p. 340.
36. Nutting: *No End of a Lesson*, p. 32.
37. *The Times* 7.3.56.
38. Shuckburgh, p. 341.
39. *The Times* 13.3.56.
40. Sir Edward Boyle in Thompson, p. 125.
41. Nigel Nicolson in Thompson, p. 125.
42. Nutting: *No End of a Lesson*, p. 36.
43. Shuckburgh, p. 345.
44. Williams ed.: *Gaitskell*, p. 493.

45. Amery to Waterhouse 14.6.56, Waterhouse papers.
46. Sir John Colville interview with Anthony Howard: *RAB*, p. 228.
47. Amery, in Troen and Shemesh ed., pp. 116–117. In July 1954 Amery received an intelligence report from Egypt which warned that the present Egyptian regime had decided to nationalize the Canal if it stayed in power: Amery to Waterhouse 4.8.54, Waterhouse papers.
48. Paul Johnson: *The Suez War* (London 1957), pp. x–xi.
49. Amery letter, *The Times* 30.7.56.
50. Anthony Fell letter, *The Times* 2.8.56.
51. Waterhouse, MES-C 30.7.56.
52. Waterhouse letter, *The Times* 8.8.56.
53. Hinchingbrooke speech, reported in *The Dorset Daily Echo* 3.10.56.
54. Killearn letter, *The Times* 4.8.56.
55. Amery letter, *The Times* 30.7.56.
56. Hinchingbrooke, 2.8.56, *HC Deb.* 557.1640.
57. Fell letter, *The Times* 2.8.56; Donald McI. Johnson, Henry Kerby and Robert Crouch letter, *The Times* 18.9.56.
58. Amery to Waterhouse 3.8.56, Waterhouse papers.
59. Many feared an ignominious conclusion to the affair – see Harold Nicolson: *Diaries and Letters, 1945–62*, p. 306.
60. See Hinchingbrooke, 2.8.56, *HC Deb.* 557.1640; Hinchingbrooke, reported in *The Dorset Daily Echo* 27.9.56.
61. Amery to Waterhouse 3.8.56, Waterhouse papers.
62. *Suez: The Twice Fought War* (London 1969), p. 401.
63. Sir Anthony Nutting interview with author.
64. Sir David Price interview with author.
65. See Alfred Bossom letter, *The Times* 10.8.56.
66. Iverach MacDonald: *History of the Times 1939–1966* (London 1984), p. 260.
67. Sir David Price interview with author.
68. Lord Amery interview with author.
69. 120–130 MPs attended the MES-C on 30.7.56. 'Every speaker supported our general view. No one indicated dissent at all'. Waterhouse note 'Events Following Canal Seizure' 3.8.56, Waterhouse papers.
70. Sir Charles Mott-Radclyffe interview with author. At least five officers and members of the 1922 executive in 1956 were privately sympathetic to the Suez Group's views: Morrison, Charles Ian Orr-Ewing, Alan Green, Vere Harvey and Legge-Bourke.
71. 28.7.56.
72. *The Economist* 8.8.56 and 18.8.56.
73. Nutting vs Iverach MacDonald.
74. See Eden, 2.8.56, *HC Deb.* 557.1602–1608.
75. Lambton (Selwyn Lloyd's PPS)/Waterhouse conversation before FAC meeting. Waterhouse notes 3.8.56, Waterhouse papers.
76. The Prime Minister was initially 'much disturbed ... and thought Selwyn Lloyd had gone too far' Eden/Raikes conversation in the division lobby, 31.7.56: Waterhouse notes 3.8.56, Waterhouse papers. William Clark: *From Three Worlds* (London 1986), p. 167; Harold Nicolson: *Diaries*, pp. 306–7.

77. John Baldock interview with author.
78. *The Economist* 11.8.56.
79. Sir Richard Body interview with author.
80. Williams ed: *Gaitskell*, p. 587.
81. *The Economist* 18.8.56.
82. Robert Rhodes James: *Anthony Eden*, p. 510.
83. Williams ed: *Gaitskell*, p. 588.
84. Clark, p. 178. Eden's health was deteriorating: see diary entry 21.8.56, Avon papers.
85. Clark, p. 180.
86. Selwyn Lloyd warned that 'there would be some diplomatic diversions to gain time, which we must not misunderstand'. Hinchingbrooke to Waterhouse 28.8.56, Waterhouse papers.
87. Amery to Waterhouse 3.9.56, Waterhouse papers.
88. Amery to Waterhouse 3.9.56, Waterhouse papers.
89. Amery, in Scott Lucas, pp. 193–4.
90. Amery to Waterhouse 18.9.56, Waterhouse papers.
91. 3–9.9.56 to persuade Nasser to accept the proposals of the London Conference for the internationalization of the Canal.
92. PRO PREM 11/1123 Oliver Poole to Eden 29.8.56; Fraser to Poole 11.9.56.
93. Lawrence Turner to Biggs-Davison 7.9.56, Biggs-Davison papers; PRO PREM 11/1123 Poole to Eden 29.8.56.
94. Biggs-Davison to Amery 5.9.56, Biggs-Davison papers.
95. Proposed by Dulles on 10.9.56. Eden hoped to get 'serious negotiations' from SCUA: *The Backbench Diaries of Richard Crossman*, p. 514.
96. Paul Williams letter to his constituency chairman 2.9.56, Paul Williams papers.
97. Lord Amery interview with author.
98. PRO PREM 11/1123 Poole to Eden 29.8.56.
99. Turner to Biggs-Davison 7.9.56, Biggs-Davison papers.
100. Churchill, pp. 252–3.
101. Amery to Biggs-Davison 18.9.56, Biggs-Davison papers.
102. Amery to Waterhouse 18.9.56, Waterhouse papers.
103. Lord Watkinson interview with author.
104. For example, *The Economist* 29.9.56.
105. *The Times* 11.10.56.
106. *The Economist* 13.10.56.
107. *The Times* 11.10.56.
108. Lord Amery interview with author.
109. Churchill, pp. 260–1.
110. *The Times* 12.10.56.
111. Sir Anthony Nutting in Lamb: *The Failure of the Eden Government*, p. 228.
112. See PRO PREM 11/1102; Sir Anthony Nutting interview with David Elstein.
113. PRO PREM 11/1102 Eden to Selwyn Lloyd telegram T.440/56 7.10.56.
114. PRO PREM 11/1102 Eden to Selwyn Lloyd T.445/56 8.10.56.
115. Eden to Selwyn Lloyd 7.10.56.

116. PRO PREM 11/1102 Eden to Selwyn Lloyd telegrams 7.10.56 and 12.10.56.
117. Waterhouse notes on 'Suez Canal Comings and Goings at the Conservative Conference 16.10.56', Waterhouse papers.
118. Nutting delivered Salisbury's speech, the text of which was cleared by the Cabinet beforehand.
119. Nutting: *No End of a Lesson*, p. 82.
120. Selwyn Lloyd: *Suez 1956*, p. 191.
121. *The Times* 15.10.56.
122. See PRO PREM 11/1102 Eden to Lord Privy Seal T.415/56 27.9.56.
123. 'They allege the weather will preclude it later.' PRO PREM 11/1102 Eden telegram to Lord Privy Seal T.415/56 27.9.56.
124. The French-Israeli military operation was dependent upon British logistical support.
125. PRO PREM 11/1100 Sir Gladwyn Jebb telegram to Foreign Office No. 295, 9.9.56.
126. Lord Amery interview with author.
127. Arthur Gavshon interview with author.
128. Lord Amery interview with author; Richard Crossman remarked on the 'peculiar alignment of the Conservatives' real sense of entente cordiale with the Socialist M. Mollet', while the Labour party found itself broadly in accord with the Republican Dulles: *Diaries*, p. 577.
129. In Sir Evelyn Shuckburgh's view Eden's ill-health aggravated his nervousness and sensitivity. Sir Evelyn Shuckburgh interview with Anthony Seldon.
130. Witness his willingness to oppose American action in Guatemala in July 1954.
131. Lord Selwyn-Lloyd interview with John Barnes for *The Day Before Yesterday*.
132. Amery to Waterhouse 14.6.56, Waterhouse papers; Amery speech at Llandudno.
133. Scott Lucas, p. 101.
134. Hugh Thomas, *The Sunday Times* 4.9.66.
135. Sir Anthony Nutting interview with author.
136. Lord Amery interview with author.
137. Recorded in Amery's diary: Wm Roger Louis seminar on 'Eden and Suez', LSE, 1992.
138. Proposed to Eden by Macmillan in early August: Alistair Horne: *Macmillan 1894–1956*, pp. 400–401.
139. In the discussions with America the question of the use of force was never specifically addressed. Sir John Coulson and Lord Sherfield interviews with Anthony Seldon.
140. See PRO PREM 11/1102 Macmillan to Eden 26.9.56.
141. Horne, p. 422.
142. Lord Carr interview with author.
143. See Macmillan diary 13.9.56, in Horne, pp. 416–417.
144. No one dared to challenge Eden in Cabinet on a foreign policy decision as this was akin to blasphemy. On Tuesday 16th October Selwyn Lloyd returned from New York, confident that a reasonable deal could

be achieved, even if it was not everything Britain wished; Eden whisked the jet-lagged Foreign Secretary off to lunch, and then to Paris the same afternoon. Selwyn Lloyd later admitted that he was so exhausted in the Suez crisis that it had seemed easier to go along with Eden's plans rather than to oppose them. Lord Thorneycroft interview with Anthony Seldon; Sir Anthony Nutting interview with Alan Thompson and John Baldock interview with author.

145. Sir Anthony Nutting interview with David Elstein.
146. See PRO PREM 11/1099 Salisbury to Eden 9.8.56; CAB.CMCC(56)59 14.8.56 and Egypt Committee minutes 9.9.56. As the Cabinet realized (see note 285) in both World Wars Britain had responded to an act of aggression. In April 1982 Mrs Thatcher's decision to send the Task Force to retake the Falkland Islands from the invading Argentine forces was publicly endorsed by Michael Foot, the Labour Leader, with the benevolent neutrality of the Reagan administration. See Tony Benn: *The End of an Era. Diaries 1980–1990*, pp. 204–6.
147. Lord Amery interview with author.
148. Amery to Waterhouse 29.10.56, Waterhouse papers.
149. Amery to Waterhouse 29.10.56.
150. Amery diary entry 1.11.56, quoted in Louis seminar 'Eden and Suez', LSE, 1992.
151. Amery, in Troen and Shemesh ed., p. 121.
152. Harold Nicolson: *Diaries*, p. 312.
153. see Longden, FAC 29.11.56.
154. Sir Bernard Braine interview with author.
155. Sir Reginald Bennett interview with author.
156. Lord Amery interview with author.
157. Lord Orr-Ewing and Lord Amery interviews with author.
158. Sir Anthony Kershaw interview with author.
159. Lord Watkinson interview with author.
160. Nigel Nicolson in Thompson, p. 141.
161. Godfrey Nicholson, FAC 21.11.56.
162. Charles Mott-Radclyffe: *Foreign Body in the Eye*, p. 225.
163. Mott-Radclyffe, p. 224.
164. Sir David Price interview with author; Richard Crossman: *Diaries*, p. 541.
165. Sir Gilbert Longden interview with author; Christopher Hollis in *Punch* 7.11.56.
166. Sir Anthony Kershaw interview with author.
167. Mott-Radclyffe, p. 222.
168. *The Economist* 3.11.56.
169. See David Carlton: *Anthony Eden*, and Louis seminar, LSE.
170. Mott-Radclyffe, p. 222.
171. Sir Edward Du Cann interview with author.
172. Sir Anthony Kershaw interview with author.
173. Hinchingbrooke speech on BBC Northern Region February 1957, Hinchingbrooke papers.
174. Amery in Troen and Shemesh ed., pp. 120–121.

175. *The Economist* 8.11.56.
176. 'Churchill's comment: "I would never have dared..." was doing the rounds.' Sir Anthony Kershaw interview with author.
177. Diane Kunz: *The Economic Diplomacy of the Suez Crisis* (Raleigh 1991), p. 33.
178. See Churchill, p. 296.
179. See Amery's Llandudno speech, *The Times* 11.10.56.
180. Lord Amery interview with author.
181. Amery in Troen and Shemesh ed., p. 119.
182. Amery, FAC 7.11.56.
183. Sir Anthony Nutting interview with author.
184. Sir Reginald Bennett interview with author.
185. Sir Bernard Braine interview with author.
186. Sir Gilbert Longden interview with author.
187. See *The Economist* 11.8.56.
188. Robert Allan in Thompson, p. 145.
189. *The Economist* 10.11.56; see Peter Smithers letter, *The Times* 12.12.56, Frederick Bennett letter, *The Times* 14.12.56; FAC 14.11.56.
190. Butler in Thompson, p. 143.
191. *The Times*, reporting on FAC 21.11.56.
192. Biggs-Davison private letter 3.1.57, Biggs-Davison papers.
193. See *The Times* 29.11.56.
194. *The Economist* 24.11.56.
195. *The Times* editorial, 21.11.56.
196. PRO PREM 11/1107 CAB CC(56)92 29.11.56.
197. PRO PREM 11/1107 CAB CC(56)92 29.11.56.
198. Birch to Butler, quoted in Howard: *RAB*, p. 240.
199. Sir Julian Ridsdale interview with author.
200. *The Times* 22.11.56; PRO PREM 11/1107 CC(56)91 Minute 2 29.11.56.
201. CAB CC(56)91 Minute 2 29.11.56.
202. Amery to Waterhouse 26.11.56, Waterhouse papers.
203. Hinchingbrooke to Heath 20.11.56; Williams to Heath, Biggs-Davison to Lennox Boyd: 21.11.56, Biggs-Davison papers.
204. Lord Watkinson interview with author.
205. *The Times* editorial 29.11.56.
206. *The Daily Telegraph* 28.11.56; *The Times* 29.11.56.
207. *The Times* 28.11.56.
208. *The Economist* 24.11.56.
209. Constituency speech 21.11.56.
210. Rebels' weekend constituency speeches warned Britain could 'become the lackey of the US and the whipping boy of the UN' (Paul Williams), 'the 49th state' (Gerald Nabarro) and that if a decision to withdraw was taken by the Government, 'the Conservative party will be split from top to bottom' (Hinchingbrooke). See *The Times* 1.12.56.
211. *The Daily Mail* 1.12.56; *The Sunday Express* 2.12.56; see Hinchingbrooke, reported in *The Times* 1.12.56.
212. PRO PREM 11/1107 CAB CC(56)91 Minute 2 29.11.56.
213. CAB CC(56)91 Minute 2 29.11.56.

214. PRO PREM 11/1107 CAB CC(56)92 29.11.56.
215. PRO PREM 11/1107 Norman Brook telegram to Eden T.592/56 No. 64 30.11.56 and CAB CC(56)92 29.11.56.
216. PREM 11/1107 CC(56)91 Minute 2 29.11.56.
217. PRO PREM 11/1107 Foreign Office to Washington Telegram 5670 1.12.56; notes of Butler/Humphries conversation 2.12.56 and Butler/Aldrich conversation 3.12.56.
218. PRO PREM 11/1107 Note of Conversation: George Humphries to Butler 2.12.56.
219. Sherman Adams: *First Hand Report* (New York 1961), pp. 267–70; PRO PREM 11/1107 Foreign Office to Washington telegram No. 5612 29.11.56.
220. *The Sunday Express* 2.12.56.
221. *The Times* 4.12.56. With the current majority of 58, if a dozen Tories voted against the Government, it would survive comfortably, whereas if the larger number were to abstain it would be a much more serious matter: Sir Thomas Moore, 1922 Committee 6.12.56.
222. Sir Frederick Corfield interview with author. Ironically, both Lloyd and Legge-Bourke were former members of the Suez Group.
223. Peter Rawlinson: *A Price Too High* (1989), pp. 70–1.
224. Sir Reginald Bennett interview with author.
225. Sir Reginald Bennett.
226. *The Times* 4.12.56.
227. *The Times* 4.12.56; Amery was so incensed at American pressure that he approached Sandys (Minister of Housing and Local Government) urging him to consider resigning and leading a reconstructed Government. 'Duncan's reaction was sphinx-like.' Lord Amery correspondence with author.
228. See *The Daily Telegraph* 4.12.56.
229. See *The Economist* 15.12.56; *The Times* 6.12.56.
230. Andrew Roth: *Heath and Heathmen*, p. 111.
231. Four of the original number dropped out, but three unexpectedly joined: Julian Amery, John Biggs-Davison, Terence Clarke, Anthony Fell, Hinchingbrooke, Ian Horobin, Montgomery Hyde, Patrick Maitland, Angus Maude, Neil McLean, Gerald Nabarro, William Teeling, Lawrence Turner, Charles Waterhouse and Paul Williams.
232. *The Economist* 15.12.56; Waterhouse 5.12.56 HC Deb. 561.1302.
233. *The Economist* 15.12.56.
234. *The Times* 11.1.57; see *The Economist* 12.1.57. Butler's fate had been sealed at a 1922 meeting in November 1956, when he had given a lack-lustre speech in marked contrast to Macmillan who had delivered 'the speech the disappointed warriors on the backbenches wanted to hear'. Sir Anthony Kershaw interview with author.
235. Sir Frederick Bishop interview with Alan Thompson for *The Day Before Yesterday*; Harold Macmillan: *Riding the Storm*, p. 185. Macmillan did not see how his government could fail 'to take a toss at the [Suez] Canal hazard', which he repeatedly called 'the water jump'. See Macmillan, p. 231 and 263.
236. Macmillan, pp. 198–99.

237. Macmillan p. 211.
238. *The Times* 11.1.57.
239. *The Economist* 18.5.57.
240. *HC Deb.* 566.1318–1438.
241. *The Daily Telegraph* 15.3.57.
242. This was seen as the price of winning back American friendship at Bermuda: *The Daily Express* 20.4.57.
243. *The Daily Express* 30.3.57; *The Times* 1.4.57.
244. Sir Frederick Bishop interview with Alan Thompson for *The Day Before Yesterday*; *The Times* 1.4.57.
245. Sir Frederick Bishop; see *The Times* 1.4.57.
246. *The Economist* 6.4.57; Macmillan's ebullient parliamentary performance on his return from Bermuda overshadowed Salisbury's resignation: London Day by Day in *The Daily Telegraph* 2.4.57.
247. Macmillan diary note 29.3.57, p. 229; *The Daily Telegraph* 1.4.57 and 2.4.57. Salisbury implied to Lord Woolton that he had resigned because he had been told there was no chance of fundamental reform of the House of Lords: Lord Woolton note on Salisbury's resignation, Woolton papers, The Bodleian Library.
248. *The Daily Telegraph* 13.5.57.
249. See FAC 20.2.57, 27.2.57, 13.3.57, 27.3.57, 3.4.57, 17.4.57 and 7.5.57.
250. Waterhouse *HC Deb.* 566.1356.14.3.57.
251. John Eden letter, *The Times* 18.4.57.
252. *House of Commons Notice of Motions, Questions and Orders of the Day 1956–57* Vol. 3, No. 96, 17.4.57 (p. 2767) sponsored by Hinchingbrooke and signed by 31 MPs; and No. 63 (No.105) 9.5.57.
253. Hinchingbrooke constituency speech in Wareham, reported in *The Daily Express* 11.5.57.
254. PRO PREM 11/1786 CC(57) 3rd Conclusions Minute 3, 24.1.57; CAB 129/85C(57)6 29.1.57; CAB 128/31 (57)12 19.2.57; PRO CAB 128/31 (57)24 26.3.57.
255. PRO CAB 128/31 (57)29 and 30 3.4.57 and 8.4.57.
256. PRO CAB 128/31 (57)39 10.5.57; PREM 11/1786 Foreign Office telegram to Tokyo No. 187, 13.4.57; Macmillan to Menzies. The announcement of Britain's successful test of the H-bomb was announced before the debate. Macmillan, p. 236.
257. Macmillan, p. 231. Up to 30 Tories were expected to abstain, which with a majority of only 50, would be a 'serious, even fatal' blow to the Government: p. 236.
258. Macmillan, p. 231.
259. Selwyn Lloyd FAC 14.5.57.
260. See Crossman: *Diaries*, pp. 588–89.
261. Paul Williams diary note 13.5.57, Williams papers; Suez Group press statement, *The Times* 14.5.57. Lord Lambton also resigned as Selwyn Lloyd's PPS, but had not intention of joining the 8 rebels.
262. *The Yorkshire Post* 18.5.57.
263. *The Times* 17.5.57.
264. Greville Howard, Norman Pannell, Neil McLean, Lord Lambton, Montgomery Hyde and John Eden.

265. Sir Guy Lloyd FAC 14.5.57, reported in *The Daily Express* 15.5.57.
266. *The Sunday Times* 19.5.57; *The Economist* 18.5.57. Within a week the Prime Minister was publicly lunching with Sir Victor Raikes at the Carlton Club: *The Daily Express* 23.5.57.
267. See Neil McLean statement, reported in *The Times* 15.5.57.
268. Paul Williams diary note 20.5.57, Williams papers. Most of the rebels held very marginal seats: Maitland (majority 958); Fell (917); Williams (1775); Biggs-Davison (1875), McLean (966) and Pannell (1814). Despite the Prime Minister's resistance to 'disciplinary demands to put up rival candidates' (*Crossbencher* 29.12.57), Fell, Biggs-Davison and Williams came under severe threat from their constituency associations: *The Daily Express* 13.5.58.
269. The chosen venue was the Bedford pub in Pont Street, so no member could abuse a fellow rebel's telephone bill. Paul Williams interview with author.
270. *The Economist* 18.5.57 and 1.6.57.
271. Julian Amery acting as link with the Prime Minister. Williams papers.
272. Independent Conservative press statement 24.6.58. This small group had applauded the decision to despatch British troops to the Oman in August 1957, and to Aden and the Lebanon in the spring of 1958. They also approved the plan for self-government for Cyprus – overlooking their past call for the retention of British sovereignty in Cyprus: *The Daily Telegraph* 6.2.58.
273. Raikes and Maude resigned their seats: Raikes went to Southern Rhodesia, Maude to become editor of *The Sydney Morning Herald*. Patrick Maitland had rejoined the party in December 1957, to the fury of the others.
274. Paul Williams note of meeting with Oliver Poole 25.11.57; Hinchingbrooke letter to Macmillan 8.11.57. 'The Bo-Peep of the Whips' Office has been justified ... "Leave them alone and they will come home".' *The Daily Telegraph* 25.6.58.
275. *The Daily Express* 13.5.58.
276. Boothby, *The Times* 11.8.56; see Harold Nicolson: *Diaries*, pp. 306–7.
277. PRO PREM 11/1099 CAB CC(56)59 14.8.56 and PREM 11/1123 Poole to Eden 29.8.56; *The Economist* 18.8.56.
278. Mott-Radclyffe, p. 222.
279. PRO PREM 11/1100 Eden to Selwyn Lloyd M.191/56 26.8.56.
280. Poole to Eden 29.8.56.
281. PRO PREM 11/1100 Salisbury to Eden 27.8.56.
282. Clark, p. 144.
283. PRO PREM 11/1099 Salisbury to Eden 9.8.56.
284. Salisbury to Eden 9.8.56.
285. PRO PREM 11/1099 Egypt Committee minutes 9.9.56.
286. PRO PREM 11/1123 Michael Fraser to Oliver Poole 11.9.56, forwarded to Eden.
287. Named after Sir Lionel Heald, the popular and respected former Attorney General.
288. For the Cabinet the attraction of SCUA had been as a means to bring the issue as a head, with American backing: PRO PREM 11/1101 CAB

CC(56)64 11.9.56. SCUA also 'should satisfy your colleagues that we need not, for the time being, go to the UN': PRO PREM 11/1101 Brook to Eden 10.9.56.
289. See Eden diary 12.9.56, Avon papers.
290. PRO PREM 11/1101 CAB CC(56)64 11.9.56.
291. Harold Nicolson: *Diaries*, p. 309.
292. Nicolson private letter 21.9.56, Nicolson papers.
293. Rhodes James: *Eden*, p. 516.
294. *The Times* 14.9.56.
295. See Macmillan diary 13.9.56, quoted in Horne, p. 416.
296. PRO PREM 11/1101 CAB CC(56)64 11.9.56.
297. Private information.
298. Nicolson private letter 21.9.56, Nicolson papers.
299. Nicolson private letter 21.9.56, Nicolson papers.
300. Yates followed this speech with a long letter to *The Times*, again setting out his criticisms. *The Times* 18.10.56.
301. Nicolson private letter 1.11.56, Nicolson papers.
302. Sir David Price interview with author.
303. Sir David Price.
304. Lord Boyd-Carpenter interview with author.
305. Nicolson undated letter to constituent, Nicolson papers.
306. Nicolson private letter 1.11.56, Nicolson papers.
307. Nigel Nicolson interview with author.
308. From William Clark, Eden's Press Secretary; and from General Lyne, Chairman of the UNA. Nicolson private letter 6.2.57, Nicolson papers.
309. Nigel Nicolson interview with author.
310. Sir David Price interview with author.
311. *The Observer* 13.1.57.
312. Pickthorn MES-C 29.11.56.
313. Lord Watkinson interview with author.
314. See Clark, p. 179.
315. Private letter to *The Times* 3.11.56.
316. Sir Charles Mott-Radclyffe interview with author.
317. Nicolson private letter 10.11.56, Nicolson papers.
318. Nicolson reply to Balliol dons' telegram 2.11.56, Nicolson papers.
319. Nicolson to UN Students Association 2.11.56, Nicolson papers.
320. Private information.
321. See *The Times* 6.11.56.
322. Sir Anthony Kershaw interview with author.
323. Rawlinson, p. 61.
324. *The Economist* 10.11.56.
325. See Harold Nicolson: *Diaries*, p. 315.
326. Allan Noble interview with Anthony Seldon.
327. Rawlinson, p. 70.
328. *The Economist* 3.11.56.
329. Benn, p. 207.
330. Nicolson diary entry 5.11.56 in Harold Nicolson: *Diaries*, p. 317.
331. Nigel Nicolson interview with Alan Thompson for *The Day Before Yesterday*.

332. Harold Nicolson: *Diaries*, p. 315.
333. See Serge and Merry Bromberger: *Secrets of Suez* (London 1957).
334. Sir Anthony Eden: *Full Circle*, p. 557.
335. Eden, p. 557. See Benn: *Diaries* p. 207, for Peter Kirk's opinion.
336. Nicolson private letter 16.11.56, Nicolson papers.
337. See Amery, *HC Deb.* 561.889–90 3.12.56; Robert Crouch refused to open a bazaar in Nigel Nicolson's Bournemouth constituency: Nicolson private letter 9.11.56, Nicolson papers.
338. *The Economist* 17.11.56.
339. Private information.
340. *The Economist* 17.11.56. See also Benn: *Diaries*, p. 207.
341. Nicolson private letter 7.12.56, Nicolson papers.
342. Nicolson diary note 5.11.56, in Harold Nicolson: *Diaries*, p. 317.
343. Nicolson private letter 29.11.56, Nicolson papers.
344. Nicolson private letter 28.11.56, Nicolson papers.
345. Nicolson private letter 28.11.56.
346. The EDM's other sponsors included Heald, Sir Hugh Lucas-Tooth and Sir Edward Boyle.
347. Lord Boyle interview with John Barnes for *The Day Before Yesterday*.
348. *The Times* 29.11.56.
349. Lord Boyle interview with John Barnes for *The Day Before Yesterday*. It was signed by John Jacob Astor, Humphrey Atkins, Philip Bell, Richard Body, Alfred Bossom, Richard Conant, John Cordeaux, Frederick Corfield, Henry D'Avigdor Goldsmid, Edward Du Cann, John Harvey, Richard Hornby, Anthony Hurd, Keith Joseph, Anthony Kershaw, Peter Kirk, Frank Medlicott, Godfrey Nicholson, Nigel Nicolson, Sir Ian Orr-Ewing, David Price, William Shepherd, Jocelyn Simon, Alec Spearman, and Douglas Spencer-Nairn (5 later withdrew their names: Atkins, Corfield, Du Cann, Harvey and Kershaw. Body and Conant later signed Grimston's EDM.) *The Times*, 29.11.56.
350. *The Times* 29.11.56.
351. Eldon Griffiths: '"Yanks at Westminster": Our Friends in Commons', *Newsweek* 3.2.58.
352. Arthur Gavshon interview with author.
353. Patrick Maitland publicly complained of the Chief Whip's extraordinary attempts to exert pressure on his local agent and constituency party: *The Daily Herald* 8.12.56.
354. Leon Epstein: *British Politics in the Suez Crisis*, pp. 97–122; Kyle, pp. 489–91.
355. *The Observer* 19.5.57.
356. *The Spectator* 24.5.57.
357. Richard Lamb: *The Macmillan Years 1957–1963. The Emerging Truth*, pp. 59–60.

Notes to Chapter 11

1. Sir Geoffrey Cox interview with author.
2. Sir Anthony Nutting interview with author.

3. Lord Thomas interview with author.
4. Lord Fraser interview with author.
5. Sir Charles Mott-Radclyffe interview with author.
6. See Smithers, FAC 30.5.56.
7. Lord Glendevon interview with author.
8. Sir Edward Boyle interview, BOAPAH, BPLES.
9. John W Young: *Britain and European Unity 1945–1992*, (Macmillan 1993), p. 47.
10. Alan Ball: *British Political Parties* (Macmillan, 1981), p. 55.
11. The punishment of withdrawing the party Whip from Messrs Gill, Wilkinson, Shepherd, Budgen, Marlowe, Cartiss, Sir Teddy Taylor and Mrs Gorman was diminished by the spectacle of the Whips' invitation to them to rejoin, rather than at their own request. Sir Richard Body resigned the Whip – a reflection of his political vintage.
12. Between 1915–1922 the Conservatives and the Lloyd George Liberals constituted a coalition government.
13. See Richard Hornby: 'The Influence of the Backbencher: A Tory view', *Political Quarterly* Vol. 36, 1965, pp. 286–294.
14. *The Times* 7.10.54.
15. Sir Anthony Nutting interview with David Elstein for *The Day Before Yesterday*.
16. Quoted by Lord Lauderdale in interview with author.
17. Lord Carr interview with author.
18. *The Times* 7.10.54.
19. *The Times* 30.7.54.
20. Lord Aldington correspondence with author.
21. Sir Charles Mott-Radclyffe interview with author.
22. Lord Carr interview with author.
23. William Shepherd letter, *The Observer* 6.1.57.
24. Lord Lauderdale correspondence with author.
25. Lord Amery interview with author.
26. *The South Wales Argus* 24.7.54.
27. A Cummings cartoon in *Punch* on 21.7.54 depicted Waterhouse in a glass box, holding an umbrella and fuming, 'By Gad, Sir'. The box's label read, 'Vintage Tory'; the button underneath was marked 'Press for Sound'.
28. Lord Orr-Ewing interview with author.
29. *The Times*, 15.6.54.
30. Lord Amery interview with author.
31. Sir Anthony Nutting interview with author.
32. Richard Crossman described the Suez Group in July 1954 as the 'Keep Right Group', the exact counterpart to Bevanism. Just as the latter claimed to be the keepers of the Socialist conscience against those who were betraying it by compromise, so 'they are keeping the Conservative conscience. Both hate Butskellism for equal and opposite reasons – and can one blame the unfortunate Tea Room men who cannot make out what is really Conservatism and what is really Socialism, after a Conservative government signs the treaty with Russia and China against the will of America and evacuates Suez, policies which

were considered Bevanite by the right wing of the Labour party only twelve months ago?' Crossman: *Diaries*, p. 340.

33. Anthony Seldon: 'Churchill's Post-War Government' in Peter Hennessy ed.: *Ruling Performance*, p. 83.
34. Lord Amery interview with author.
35. See Robert Rhodes James: *Anthony Eden*, p. 456.
36. Sir Anthony Nutting interview with David Elstein for *The Day Before Yesterday*.
37. Lord Carr interview with author.
38. Sir Anthony Nutting interview with author.
39. Sir Anthony Nutting.
40. Sir Anthony Nutting.
41. Sir Anthony Kershaw interview with author.
42. Lord Aldington interview with author.
43. Alec Cairncross ed.: *The Robert Hall Diaries 1956–61* (London 1991), p. 79.
44. Shuckburgh feared Eden was using 'instruments that would break in our hands': Evelyn Shuckburgh: *Descent to Suez*, p. 326. The thorny problem of Egyptian/Iraqi rivalry for leadership of the Arab world gravely threatened British reliance upon Iraq.
45. Shuckburgh, pp. 311 and 314.
46. Private information.
47. Sir Anthony Nutting interview with author.
48. Lord Healey interview with author.
49. Sir Anthony Eden: *Full Circle*, p. 557.
50. See Roy Jenkins: *A Life at the Centre* (London 1981).

Appendix I

THE EUROPEANISTS

European 'enthusiasts'

Cuthbert Alport	(elected to Parliament 1950)
Julian Amery	(elected to Parliament 1950)
Tufton Beamish	
Richard Body	(elected to Parliament 1955)
Robert Boothby	
Sir Edward Boyle	(elected to Parliament 1950)
Richard Brooman-White	(elected to Parliament 1951)
Herbert Butcher (NL&C)	
Uvedale Corbett	(left Parliament 1951)
Frederick Corfield	(elected to Parliament 1955)
Viscountess Davidson	
Nigel Davies	(in Parliament 1950–51)
Lord Willoughby de Eresby	(left Parliament 1950)
Douglas Dodds-Parker	
David Eccles	
Walter Elliot	
Ian Orr-Ewing	
Walter Fletcher	(left Parliament 1955)
John Foster	
Hugh Fraser	
Connelly Gage (UU)	(left Parliament 1952)
David Gammans	
John Hay	(elected to Parliament 1950)
Sir Cuthbert Headlam	(left Parliament 1951)
Edward Heath	(elected to Parliament 1950)
James Henderson Stewart	
Viscount Hinchingbrooke	
Quintin Hogg	(left the House of Commons 1950)
Christopher Hollis	(left Parliament 1955)
Lord John Hope	
Henry Hopkinson	(elected to Parliament 1950)
John Hughes Hallett	(elected to Parliament 1951)
James Hutchison	
Montgomery Hyde	(elected to Parliament 1950)
Keith Joseph	(elected to Parliament 1956)
Edward Keeling	(died 1954)
Hamilton Kerr	(elected to Parliament 1950)
Peter Kirk	(elected to Parliament 1955)
Anthony Langford-Holt	
Richard Law	(left the House of Commons 1954)

Martin Lindsay
Gilbert Longden   (elected to Parliament 1950)
Jocelyn Lucas
Hugh Lucas-Tooth
Sir Peter MacDonald
John Maclay (NL&C)
Harold Macmillan
Martin Maddan   (elected to Parliament 1955)
Reginald Manningham-Buller
Sidney Marshall   (left Parliament 1954)
Robert Mathew   (elected to Parliament 1955)
David Maxwell Fyfe
Hugh Molson
Sir Thomas Moore
Godfrey Nicholson
Nigel Nicolson   (elected to Parliament 1952)
Basil Nield
Anthony Nutting
Christopher Peto
James Pitman
Oliver Poole
David Price   (elected to Parliament 1955)
David Price-White   (left Parliament 1950)
Otho Prior-Palmer
David Renton (NL&C)
Geoffrey Rippon   (elected to Parliament 1955)
Peter Roberts
John Rodgers   (elected to Parliament 1950)
Duncan Sandys   (elected to Parliament 1950)
Douglas Savory   (left Parliament 1955)
Jocelyn Simon
Walter Smiles (UU)   (left Parliament 1953)
Peter Smithers   (elected to Parliament 1950)
Alexander Spearman
Henry Spence
Ernest Taylor   (left Parliament 1950)
William Teeling
Peter Thorneycroft
Colin Thornton-Kemsley
John Tilney   (elected to Parliament 1950)
Lady Tweedsmuir
Arthur Vere Harvey
Sir Wavell Wakefield
George Ward
Gerald Williams   (left Parliament 1956)

Pro-Commonwealth MPs

Derick Heathcoat Amory
Brendan Bracken   (left Parliament 1952)

Appendix I

Alfred Bossom	
Norman Bower	(left Parliament 1951)
Malcolm Bullock	(left Parliament 1953)
Rupert de la Bère	(left Parliament 1955)
Edward Carson	(left Parliament 1953)
William Cuthbert	(left Parliament 1953)
William Darling	
Barnaby Drayson	
William Duthie	
Ian Fraser	
Sir Gifford Fox	(left Parliament 1950)
Thomas D Galbraith	(left the House of Commons 1955)
Ernest Gates	
Sir Arnold Gridley	(left the House of Commons 1955)
Patrick Hannon	(left Parliament 1950)
John Hare	
Frederick Harris	
Anthony Head	
John Henderson	
Sir Arthur Howard	(left Parliament 1950)
Sir John Kerr	(left Parliament 1950)
Neill Cooper-Key	
Alan Lennox-Boyd	
Geoffrey Lloyd	
John Selwyn Lloyd	
A.R. 'Toby' Low	
Duncan McCallum	
John Maitland	(left Parliament 1951)
Ernest Marples	
John Maude	(left Parliament 1951)
Frank Medlicott (NL)	
Charles Mott-Radclyffe	
Allan Noble	
Cyril Osborne	
Charles Ponsonby	(left Parliament 1950)
Stanley Prescott	(left Parliament 1951)
Victor Raikes	
David Robertson	
Roland Robinson	
Sir Stanley Reed	(left Parliament 1950)
Sir Frank Sanderson	(left Parliament 1950)
Sidney Shephard	(left Parliament 1950)
William Shepherd	
Edward Smith	(left Parliament 1950)
Oliver Stanley	(died 1950)
Malcolm Stoddart-Scott	
Henry Studholme	
Robert Thorp	(left Parliament 1951)
Derek Walker-Smith	
Mervyn Wheatley	(left Parliament 1951)

Christopher York (left Parliament 1954)
Sir Arthur Young (died 1950)

THE ANTI-EUROPEANISTS

Max Aitken (left Parliament 1950)
Beverley Baxter
Eric Gandar-Dower (left Parliament 1950)
Aian Green (elected to Parliament 1955)
Harry Legge-Bourke
Anthony Marlowe
Arthur Marsden (left Parliament 1950)
Sir John Mellor (left Parliament 1955)
Stephen McAdden
Captain Lawrence Orr (elected to Parliament 1951)
Kenneth Pickthorn
Enoch Powell (elected to Parliament 1950)
Gerald Nabarro (elected to Parliament 1950)
Roland Russell
Sir Herbert Williams (died 1954)
Waldron Smithers (left Parliament 1954)

List of Signatures of the Early Day Motion on Western Union (March 1948)

Tufton Beamish
Robert Boothby
Norman Bower
Malcolm Bullock
Frederick Burden
Edward Carson
Neill Cooper-Key
Uvedale Corbett
Viscountess Davidson
Lord Willoughby de
  Eresby
Douglas Dodds-Parker
David Eccles
Walter Fletcher
Connelly Gage (UU)
David Gammans
Sir Cuthbert Headlam
Derick Heathcoat
  Amory
Quintin Hogg
Christopher Hollis
Sir Arthur Howard
Hugh Fraser
James Hutchison
Jocelyn Lucas
Edward Keeling
Anthony Langford-
  Holt
Martin Lindsay
A.R. ('Toby') Low
Hugh Lucas-Tooth
Sir Peter MacDonald
John Maitland
Sidney Marshall
John Maude
Frank Medlicott
  (NL&C)
Charles Mott-
  Radclyffe
Godfrey Nicholson
Basil Nield
Allan Noble
Ian Orr-Ewing
Christopher Peto
Oliver Poole
David Price-White
Sir Stanley Reed
David Renton (NL&C)
Peter Roberts
Sir Frank Sanderson
Walter Smiles (UU)
Alexander Spearman
Ernest Taylor
William Teeling
Peter Thorneycroft
Colin Thornton-
  Kemsley
Derek Walker-Smith
Arthur Vere Harvey
Sir Wavell Wakefield
George Ward
Gerald Williams

Appendix I

List of Signatures of the Early Day Motion on the European Consultative Assembly (February 1949)

Robert Boothby
Brendan Bracken
Uvedale Corbett
William Cuthbert
Viscountess Davidson
Lord Willoughby de Eresby
Barnaby Drayson
William Duthie
David Eccles
Hugh Fraser
David Gammans
Sir Arnold Gridley
Robert Grimston
Patrick Hannon
John Hare
Sir Cuthbert Headlam
Quintin Hogg
Christopher Hollis
James Hutchison
Lancelot Joynson-Hicks
Norman Hulbert
Edward Keeling
Martin Lindsay
Hugh Lucas-Tooth
Jocelyn Lucas
Duncan McCallum
Hugh Molson
Sir Peter MacDonald
Frank Medlicott
Sir Thomas Moore
Charles Mott-Radclyffe
Basil Nield
Ian Orr-Ewing
Charles Ponsonby
Otho Prior-Palmer
Victor Raikes
Peter Roberts
Roland Robinson
Douglas Savory (UU)
Malcolm Stoddart-Scott
Ernest Taylor
William Teeling
Peter Thorneycroft
Robert Thorp
Lady Tweedsmuir
Arthur Vere Harvey
Derek Walker-Smith
George Ward
Gerald Williams

Appendix II

MEMBERSHIP OF THE SUEZ GROUP

*Voted against the Heads of Agreement in July 1954

Julian Amery*
Ralph Assheton* (Privy Counsellor)   (left Parliament 1955)
Peter Baker   (left Parliament 1954)
Philip Bell   (left group in July 1954)
John Biggs-Davison   (elected to Parliament 1955)
Richard Body   (elected to Parliament 1955)
Walter Bromley-Davenport
Frederick Burden
Terence Clarke
Robert Crouch*
Will 'Y' Darling*
Patrick Donner*   (left Parliament 1955)
James Duncan*
Anthony Fell
Fergus Graham*
Alan Green   (elected to Parliament 1955)
Sir Robert Grimston*
John Hall
Frederick Harris
Reader Harris
William Hicks Beach
Viscount Hingchingbrooke*
Christopher Holland-Martin*
Ian Horobin*
Montgomery Hyde* (UU)
Captain Kerby*   (elected to Parliament 1954)
Hamilton Kerr*
Harry Legge-Bourke*
Guy Lloyd*
Fitzroy Maclean   (left group in July 1954)
Neil ('Billy') McLean   (elected to Parliament December 1954)
Patrick Maitland*
Douglas Marshall   (left group in February 1954)
Angus Maude*
Ray Mawby   (elected to Parliament 1955)
John Mellor   (left Parliament in 1955)
John Morrison   (left group in 1955)
Gerald Nabarro*

Appendix II 297

Captain Orr (UU)   (elected to Parliament 1955)
James Pitman*
Enoch Powell*   (left group in November 1954)
Ralph Rayner
William Rees Davies*
Douglas Savory (UU)   (left Parliament in 1955)
William Teeling*
Captain Charles Waterhouse*   (Privy Counsellor)
Sir Herbert Williams   (died July 1954)
Sir Charles Williams*   (Privy Counsellor)
Paul Williams*   (elected to Parliament May 1953)

Sympathizers (The 'crypto-Suez Group')

Sir Peter Agnew
Sir William Anstruther-Gray
Commander Eric Bullus
Beresford Craddock
Lord Cranborne   (left Parliament February 1954)
Petre Crowder
Douglas Dodds-Parker   (joined the Government in November 1953)
Edward Du Cann   (elected to Parliament 1956)
John Eden   (elected to Parliament February 1954)
Nigel Fisher
Walter Fletcher   (left Parliament 1955)
Richard Fort
Douglas Glover
Alan Gomme-Duncan
John Howard   (elected to Parliament 1955)
Greville Howard
Eric Johnson
Edwin Leather
Jocelyn Lucas
John ('Jacko') Macleod
Stephen Maydon
Sir Thomas Moore
David Ormsby-Gore
Charles Ian Orr-Ewing
Norman Pannell
John Peyton
Sir Victor Raikes
Ronald Russell
Christopher Soames
Colin Thornton-Kemsley
John Tilney
Arthur Vere Harvey
Patrick Wall

MEMBERSHIP OF THE ANTI-SUEZ GROUP

*Abstained on in the vote of confidence on 8.11.56; Banks resigned the party Whip on 8.11.56 in protest against Eden's Suez policy.

Jakie Astor*
Cyril Banks*
Philip Bell
Robert Boothby*
Edward Boyle*
Henry D'Avigdor Goldsmid
Walter Elliot
John Foster
Harry Hylton-Foster
Sir Lionel Heald
Richard Hornby
Keith Joseph
Peter Kirk
Hugh Lucas-Tooth
Maurice Macmillan
Robert Mathew
Frank Medlicott*
Nigel Nicolson*
Basil Nield
Anthony Nutting*
David Price
Julian Ridsdale
William Shepherd
Jocelyn Simon
Alexander Spearman
William Yates*

Bibliography

PRIMARY SOURCES

Parliamentary Debates (Hansard), Fifth Series, House of Commons Official Reports, 1946–1957
Public Records Office, Kew
Orders of the Day and Notice of Motions, The British Library
The Times Guide to the House of Commons, 1945, 1950, 1951 and 1955
Who Was Who, 1951–1960, 1971–1980, 1980–1990 and *Who's Who*, annually

Newspapers and Periodicals

The Daily Telegraph, Cuttings Library
The Economist
The Times
The Daily Express
The Observer

Private Papers

Lord Avon, Birmingham University Library
Lord Boyle, Brotherton Library, University of Leeds
Lord Butler, Trinity College, Cambridge
Sir John Biggs-Davison, House of Lords archives
Sir Winston Churchill, Churchill Archives Centre, Churchill College, Cambridge
Lord Hailes, Churchill Archives Centre, Churchill College, Cambridge
Lord Hinchingbrooke (private collection)
Sir Harry Legge-Bourke, Brotherton Library, University of Leeds (and private collection)
Gilbert Longden papers (South–West Herts Conservative and Unionist Association topical commentaries)
R.W. Mackay papers, BLPES archives, London School of Economics
Nigel Nicolson (private collection)
Lady Rhys Williams, BLPES archives, London School of Economics
Captain Charles Waterhouse (private collection)
Paul Williams (private collection)
Lord Woolton, The Bodleian Library, Oxford

The Conservative Party Archives
(The Bodleian Library, Oxford)

Minutes of the Conservative Party Foreign Affairs Committee
Conservative Research Department briefs

Minutes of the Conservative 1922 Committee
Conservative Consultative Committee 1945–51
Advisory Committee on Policy and Political Education
Conservative Finance Committee briefs
Conservative Inter-committee minutes, 1949

Transcripts of Interviews in the British Oral Archive of Political and Administrative History, London School of Economics
Lord Carr
Sir Edward Boyle
Viscount Muirshiel

Transcripts of Interviews with Anthony Seldon
Sir Hugh Lucas-Tooth
Sir Kenneth Thompson
Lord Garner
Sir John Arbuthnot
Sir John Ward
Sir Evelyn Shuckburgh
Sir Ashley Clarke
Sir Frank Roberts
Lord Strang
Lord Butler
Lord Clitheroe
Sir William Hayter
Lord Sherfield
Sir Christopher Soames
John Foster
Lord Tranmire
Lord Thorneycroft
Sir Eric Bertoud
Lord Rhyl
Lord Duncan-Sandys
Lord Gladwyn
Sir Hubert Ashton
Sir John Coulson
Allan Noble

Transcripts of Interviews for The Day Before Yesterday
Sir Anthony Nutting
Lord Selwyn-Lloyd
Sir Frederick Bishop
Lord Boyle

Correspondence with author
Sir Peter Smithers
John Hay

Published Memoirs and Diaries
Dean Acheson: *Present at the Creation.* (Norton, New York 1969)
Sherman Adams: *First Hand Report.* (New York 1961)
John Barnes and David Nicholson eds.: *The Empire at Bay: The Leo Amery Diaries 1929–45.* (Hutchinson, London 1988)
George Ball: *The Past has Another Pattern. Memoirs.* (Norton, New York 1973)
Edward Beddington Behrens: *Look Back Look Forward.* (London 1963)
Tony Benn: *Years of Hope. Diaries, Papers and Letters 1940–1962* (ed. by Ruth Winstone) (Hutchinson, London 1994)
Reginald Bevins: *The Greasy Pole: A Personal Account of the Realities of British Politics.* (Hodder & Stoughton, London 1965)
Robert Boothby: *I Fight to Live.* (Gollancz, London 1947)
Robert Boothby: *My Yesterday Your Tomorrow.* (Hutchinson, London 1962)
Robert Boothby: *Recollections of a Rebel.* (Hutchinson, London 1978)
John Boyd-Carpenter: *Way of Life.* (Sidgwick & Jackson, London 1980)

Bibliography

R.A. Butler: *The Art of the Possible: The Memoirs of Lord Butler.* (Hamilton, London 1971)
Alec Cairncross ed.: *The Robert Hall Diaries 1954–61.* (Unwin Hyman, London 1991)
William Clark: *From Three Worlds. Memoirs.* (Sidgwick & Jackson, London 1986)
Aidan Crawley: *Leap Before You Look: A Memoir.* (Collins, London 1988)
Sir John Colville: *The Fringes of Power: The Downing Street Diaries 1939–1955.* (Hodder & Stoughton, London 1985)
Hugh Dalton: *High Tide and After: Memoirs 1945–60.* (Muller, London 1962)
Douglas Dodds-Parker: *Political Eunuch.* (Springwood Books, Ascot 1986)
Sir Anthony Eden: *Full Circle.* (Cassell, London 1960)
Paul Einzig: *In the Centre of Things.* (Hutchinson, London 1960)
Ian Gilmour: *The Body Politic.* (Hutchinson, London 1969)
Lord Hailsham: *A Sparrow's Flight. Memoirs.* (Collins, London 1990)
Sir George Harvie Watt: *Most of My Life.* (Springwood Books, London 1980)
Denis Healey: *The Time of My Life.* (Michael Joseph, London 1989)
Christopher Hollis: *Seven Ages: Their Exits and Their Entrances.* (Heinemann, London 1974)
Roy Jenkins: *A Life at the Centre* (London 1981)
The Earl of Kilmuir: *Political Adventure.* (London 1964)
Selwyn Lloyd: *Suez 1956.* (Cape, New York 1978)
Harold Macmillan: *Tides of Fortune 1945–55.* (Macmillan, London 1969)
Harold Macmillan: *Riding the Storm 1956–59.* (Macmillan, London 1971)
Reginald Maudling: *Memoirs* (Sidgwick & Jackson, London 1978)
Janet Morgan ed.: *The Backbench Diaries of Richard Crossman.* (Hamilton, London 1981)
Lord Morrison of Lambeth: *An Autobiography.* (Odhams Press, London 1960)
Charles Mott-Radclyffe: *Foreign Body in the Eye: A Memoir of the Foreign Service New and Old.* (Lee Cooper, London 1975)
Harold Nicolson: *Diaries & Letters 1945–62,* edited by Nigel Nicolson. (London 1968)
Nigel Nicolson: *People & Parliament.* (Weidenfeld & Nicolson, London 1958)
Anthony Nutting: *Europe Will Not Wait: A Warning and A Way Out.* (Hollis & Carter, London 1960)
Anthony Nutting: *No End of a Lesson: The Story of Suez.* (Constable, London 1967)
Peter Rawlinson: *A Price Too High.* (Weidenfeld & Nicolson, London 1989)
Evelyn Shuckburgh: *Descent to Suez, Diaries 1951–56.* ed. by John Charmley. (Weidenfeld & Nicolson, London 1986)
Paul-Henri Spaak: *The Continuing Battle – Memoirs of a European 1936–1966.* Translated from the French by Henry Fox. (Weidenfeld & Nicolson, London 1971)
James Stuart: *Within the Fringe – An Autobiography.* (Bodley Head, London 1967)
Sir William Teeling: *Corridors of Frustration.* (Johnson, London 1970)
Alan Thompson: *The Day before Yesterday (An Illustrated History of Britain from Attlee to Macmillan).* (Thames Television, London 1971)
Ian Trethowan: *Split Screen.* (Hamilton, London 1984)

Denis Walters: *Not Always With the Pack.* (Constable, London 1989)
Philip M. Williams ed.: *The Diaries of Hugh Gaitskell 1945–1956.* (Cape, London 1983)
Harold Watkinson: *Turning Points: A Record of Our Times.* (Michael Russell, Wilton 1986)
Edward, 6th Earl of Winterton: *Orders of the Day.* (Cassell, London 1953)
Frederick James Marquis (1st Earl of Woolton): *The Memoirs of the Rt Hon The Earl of Woolton.* (Cassell, London 1959)

SECONDARY SOURCES

Biographies

Walter Allen: *The Reluctant Politician: Derick Heathcoat Amery.* (Johnson, London 1958)
Stephen Ambrose: *Eisenhower: Soldier and President.* (Simon & Schuster, London 1991)
Lord Birkenhead: *Walter Monckton: The Life of Viscount Monkton of Brenchley.* (London 1969)
Alan Bullock: *Ernest Bevin – Foreign Secretary.* (Oxford University Press paperback, Oxford 1985)
John Campbell: *Edward Heath – A Biography.* (Jonathan Cape, London 1993)
David Carlton: *Anthony Eden.* (Allen & Unwin, London 1981)
Randolph Churchill: *The Rise and Fall of Sir Anthony Eden.* (MacGibbon & Kee, London 1959)
John Colville: *The Churchillians.* (Weidenfeld & Nicolson, London 1981)
Colin Coote: *Companion of Honour: The Story of Walter Elliot in Scotland and in Westminster.* (Collins, London 1965)
Patrick Cosgrave: *The Lives of Enoch Powell.* (Pan Books in association with The Bodley Head, London 1989)
John Dickie: *The Uncommon Commoner – A Study of Sir Alec Douglas-Home.* (Pall Mall Press, London 1964)
Tom Driberg: *Beaverbrook: A Study in Power and Frustration.* (Weidenfeld & Nicolson, London 1956)
Nigel Fisher: *Harold Macmillan.* (Weidenfeld & Nicolson, London 1982)
Martin Gilbert: *Winston S. Churchill, Vol. VIII. Never Despair: 1945–65.* (Heinemann, London 1988)
Townsend Hoopes: *The Devil & John Foster Dulles.* (Little, Brown, Boston 1974)
Alistair Horne: *Macmillan 1894–1956.* (Macmillan, Basingstoke 1988)
Anthony Howard: *RAB – The Life of R.A. Butler.* (Cape, London 1987)
David Hubback: *No Ordinary Press Baron A Live of Walter Layton* (Weidenfeld & Nicolson, London 1985)
George Hutchinson: *Edward Heath: A Personal and Political Biography.* (Longmans, London 1970)
Margaret Laing: *Edward Heath – Prime Minister.* (Sidgwick & Jackson, London 1972)

Charles Lysaght: *Brendan Bracken.* (Allen Lane, London 1979)
Roy Lewis: *Enoch Powell: Principles in Politics.* (Cassell, London 1979)
Donald McIntosh Johnson: *Ted Heath: A Latter Day Charlemagne: Europe, Slave or Free.* (Johnson, London 1971)
Frank McLynn: *Fitzroy Maclean.* (John Murray, London 1992)
Lord Moran: *Winston Churchill: The Struggle for Survival 1940–65: taken from the diaries of Lord Moran.* (Constable, London 1966)
John Pomian ed.: *Joseph Retinger: Memoirs of an Eminence Grise.* (London 1972)
Stephen Roskill: *Hankey, Man of Secrets Vol. III 1931–63.* (Collins, London 1974)
Robert Rhodes James: *Bob Boothby: A Portrait.* (Hodder & Stoughton, London 1991)
Robert Rhodes James: *Churchill, A Study in Failure 1900–39.* (Weidenfeld & Nicolson, London 1970)
Robert Rhodes James: *Anthony Eden.* (Weidenfeld & Nicolson, London 1986)
Andrew Roth: *Enoch Powell: Tory Tribune.* (London 1970)
Andrew Roth: *Heath and the Heathmen.* (MacDonald, London 1972)
Anthony Sampson: *Macmillan: A Study in Ambiguity.* (Routledge & K. Paul, London 1967)
Douglas Schoen: *Enoch Powell and the Powellites.* (Macmillan, London 1977)
D.R. Thorpe: *Selwyn Lloyd* (Cape, London 1989)
Alan Wood: *The True History of Lord Beaverbrook.* (Heinemann, London 1965)

Europe

Max Beloff: *Europe and the Europeans.* (Chatto & Windus, London 1957)
Nora Beloff: *The General Says No: Britain's Exclusion from Europe* (Penguin, 1963)
Nora Beloff: *Transit of Britain: A Report on Britain's Changing Role in the Post-War World* (Collins, London 1973)
John Biggs-Davison: *The Walls of Europe.* (Johnson, London 1962)
Miriam Camps: *Britain and the European Community 1955–63.* (Oxford University Press, Oxford 1964)
Michael Charlton: *The Price of Victory.* (Parkwest Publications Incorporated, London 1983)
Uwe Kitzinger: *Diplomacy and Persuasion: How Britain Joined the Common Market.* (Thames & Hudson, London 1973)
Walter Lipgens: *A History of European Union. Vol. 1: 1945–47.* (Clarendon Press, Oxford 1982)
Walter Lipgens: *Documents on the History of European Integration Vol. II. Plans for European Union in Britain and in Exile, 1939–45.* (Walter de Gruyter, Berlin 1986)
Jeremy Moon: *European Integration in British Politics 1950–63: A Study in Issue Change.* (Gower, Aldershot 1985)
Roger Morgan: *West European Politics Since 1945: The Shaping of the European Community.* (Batsford, London 1972)
Roger Morgan and Caroline Bray ed.: *Partners and Rivals in Western Europe: Britain, France and Germany.* (Gower, Aldershot 1986)

John Pinder & Richard Mayne: *Federal Union: The Pioneers – A History of Federal Union.* (Macmillan, Basingstoke 1990)
John W. Young: *Britain and European Unity, 1945–1992* (Macmillan, Basingstoke 1993)
John W. Young: *Britain, France and the Unity of Europe 1945–51.* (Leicester University Press, Leicester 1984)
Arnold J. Zurcher: *The Struggle to Unite Europe 1940–58.* (Greenwood Press, Westport, Connecticut 1958)

The Middle East

Russell Braddon: *Suez: The Splitting of a Nation.* (Collins, London 1973)
Serge and Merry Bromberger: *Secrets of Suez* (Pan, London 1957)
David Carlton: *Britain and the Suez Crisis.* (Basil Blackwell, Oxford 1988)
Michael Devereux: *The Formulation of British Defence Policy Towards the Middle East 1948–56.* (Macmillan in association with King's College, London: Basingstoke 1990)
Leon D. Epstein: *British Politics in the Suez Crisis.* (Pall Mall Press, London 1964)
Leon Epstein: *Britain – Uneasy Ally.* (University of Chicago Press, Chicago 1959)
Douglas A. Farnie: *East and West of Suez: the Suez Canal in History 1854–1956.* (Clarendon Press, Oxford 1969)
Herman Finer: *Dulles over Suez.* (Quadrangle Books, Chicago 1964)
Michael Foot & Mervyn Jones: *Guilty Men* (Gollancz, London 1957)
Mohamad Hassanein Heikal: *Nasser – The Cairo Documents.* (New English Library, London 1972)
Paul Johnson: *The Suez War.* (MacGibbon & Kee, London 1957)
Keith Kyle: *Suez.* (Weidenfeld & Nicolson, London 1991)
Diane Kunz: *The Economic Diplomacy of the Suez Crisis.* (University of North Carolina Press, Raleigh 1991)
Wm Roger Louis and Roger Owen eds.: *Suez – The Crisis and Its Consequences.* (Clarendon Press, Oxford 1989)
Kenneth Love: *Suez – the Twice Fought War.* (Longmans, London 1969)
W. Scott Lucas: *Divided We Stand: Britain, the US and the Suez Crisis.* (Hodder & Stoughton, London 1991)
Terance Robertson: *Crisis – the Inside Story of the Suez Conspiracy.* (Hutchinson, London 1965)
Selwyn Troen and Moshe Shemesh ed.: *The Suez-Sinai Crisis 1956: Retrospective and Reappraisal.* (Cass, London 1990)
T.E. Utley: *Not Guilty: The Conservative Reply* (McKibbon & Kee, London 1957)

British Politics

Alan Ball: *British Political Parties* (Macmillan, Basingstoke 1981)
Max Beloff & Gillian Peele: *The Government of the UK: Political Authority in a Changing Society.* (Weidenfeld & Nicolson, London 1980)

Bibliography

Hugh Berrington: *Backbench Opinion in the House of Commons 1945–55*. (Pergamon, Oxford 1973)
Harry Boardman: *The Glory of Parliament*. ed. by Francis Boyd. (New York undated)
Marjorie Bremner: *Analysis of British Parliamentary Thought Concerning the USA in the Post-war Period*. unpublished thesis. University of London 1950
David Butler: *The British General Election of 1951* (Macmillan, London 1952)
David Butler: *The British General Election of 1955* (Macmillan, London 1955)
David Butler and Gareth Butler: *British Political Facts 1900–94* (7th revised edition, Macmillan, Basingstoke 1994)
Ronald Butt: *The Power of Parliament*. (Constable, London 1967)
Richard Cockett: *Thinking the Unthinkable: Think-Tanks and the Economic Counter-Revolution 1931–1983*. (Fontana Press, an imprint of HarperCollins Publishers 1995)
S. Finer: *Anonymous Empire* (London, 1966 2nd edition)
S.E. Finer, H.B. Berrington, D.J. Bartholomew: *Backbench Opinion in the House of Commons 1955–59*. (Pergamon, Oxford 1961)
F.N. Forman: *Mastering British Politics*. (Macmillan, Basingstoke 1985)
Norman Gash, D. Southgate, D. Dilks, and J. Ramsden: *The Conservatives: A History from their Origins to 1965* ed. by Rt Hon Lord Butler KG PC CH. (Allen & Unwin, London 1977)
Philip Goodhart: *The 1922 – The Story of the Conservative Backbenchers' Parliamentary Committee*. (Macmillan, London 1973)
N.H. Greenleaf: *The British Political Tradition Volume II: The Ideological Heritage* (Metheun, London and New York 1983)
Peter Hennessy and Anthony Seldon ed.: *Ruling Performances: British Governments from Attlee to Thatcher* (Basil Blackwell, Oxford 1987)
John D. Hoffmann: *The Conservative Party in Opposition: 1945–51*. (MacGibbon & Kee, London 1964)
Robert J. Jackson: *Rebels & Whips. An Analysis of Dissention, Discipline and Cohesion in British Political Parties*. (Macmillan, London 1968)
Harmut Kopsch: *The Approach of the Conservative Party to Social Policy during the Second World War*. PhD thesis. London School of Economics 1970
Richard Lamb: *The Failure of the Eden Government*. (Sidgwick & Jackson, London 1987)
Richard Lamb: *The Macmillan Years 1957–1963. The Emerging Truth* (John Murray, London 1995)
Zig Layton-Henry ed.: *Conservative Party Politics*. (Macmillan, London 1980)
Richard Leonard & Valentine Herman: *The Backbencher & Parliament*. (Macmillan, London 1972)
Leslie Macfarlane: *Issues in British Politics Since 1945*. (Longman Group, London 1975)
John Mackintosh: *The Government and Politics of Britain*. (Hutchinson, London 1970)
Robert McKenzie: *British Political Parties*. (Heinemann, London 1955)
P.J. Madgwick: *Introduction to British Politics* (second edition, Hutchinson, London 1976)
Kenneth Morgan: *Labour in Power 1945–51* (Clarendon Press, Oxford 1984)
Philip Norton: *Dissension in the House of Commons 1945–74: Intra-party Dissent*

in the House of Commons' Division Lobbies 1945–74 (Macmillan, London 1975)
Philip Norton: *Conservative Dissidents: Dissent within the Parliamentary Conservative Party 1970–74* (Maurice Temple Smith, London, 1978)
Glyn Parry: *British Government* (revised edition). (Edward Arnold, London 1979)
Peter Richards: *The Backbenchers.* (Faber, London 1972)
Professor Richard Rose: *Do Parties Make a Difference?* (Macmillan, 1980)
Anthony Seldon: *Churchill's Indian Summer. The Conservative Government 1951–56.* (Hodder & Stoughton, London 1981)
Anthony Seldon and Stuart Ball eds.: *Conservative Century: The Conservative Party Since 1900* (Oxford University Press, 1994)
Alan Sked & Chris Cook: *Post-war Britain: A Political History.* (Harvester Press, Brighton 1979)
Parliamentary Reform 1933–1960. Cassell, for the Hansard Society

British Foreign Policy

Robert Blake: *The Decline of Power 1915–64* (Granada, London 1985)
Michael Dockrill & John W. Young: *British Foreign Policy 1945–56.* (Macmillan, Basingstoke 1988)
Joseph Frankel: *British Foreign Policy 1945–73.* (Oxford University Press for the Royal Institute for International Affairs, London 1975)
Paul Kennedy: *The Realities Behind Diplomacy: Background Influences on British External Policy 1865–1980.* (Fontana, London 1981)
H.G. Nicholas: *Britain & The United States.* (Chatto & Windus, London 1963)
Avi Shlaim, Peter Jones and Keith Sainsbury: *British Foreign Secretaries Since 1945.* (David & Charles, Newton Abbot 1977)
Donald Watt: *Personalities & Policies. Studies in the Formulation of British Foreign Policy in the Twentieth Century* (Longmans, London 1965)
C.M. Woodhouse: *British Foreign Policy Since the Second World War.* (Hutchinson, London 1961)
John W. Young ed.: *The Foreign Policy of Churchill's Peacetime Administration 1951–55.* (Leicester University Press, Leicester 1988)
John Zametica ed.: *British Officials and British Foreign Policy 1945–50.* (Leicester University Press, Leicester 1990)

General

Asa Briggs: *A History of Broadcasting in the United Kingdom: Volume 4: Sound and Vision* (Oxford University Press, 1979)
Trevor Lloyd: *Short Oxford History of the Modern World. Empire to Welfare State English History 1906–1985.* (3rd edition, Oxford University Press, Oxford 1986)
Iverack McDonald: *History of the Times 1939–1966. Struggles in War and Peace, Vol. V.* (Time Books, London 1984)
Manfred Michel: *German Rearmament as a Factor in Anglo-West German Relations 1949–55.* Unpublished PhD thesis, London School of Economics 1963

Keith Robbins: *The Eclipse of a Great Power 1870–1975.* (Longman, London 1983)

Articles

Anthony Adamthwaite: 'Eden, the Foreign Office and the Making of Foreign Policy, 1951–55'. *International Affairs,* Vol. 64. No. 2 Spring 1988

Richard Hornby: 'The Influence of the Backbench MP: The Tory View'. *Political Quarterly,* Vol. 36. July–Sept 1965

John Grigg: 'Churchill, the Crippled Giant'. *Encounter,* April 1977

Leon Epstein: 'The Politics of British Conservatism'. *American Political Science Review,* Vol. XLVIII 1954

Leon Epstein: 'British MPs and their Local Parties'. *American Political Science Review,* Vol. LIV 1960

Leon Epstein: 'Partisan Foreign Policy: Britain in the Suez Crisis'. *World Politics,* Vol. 12 (Jan 1960) p. 201–24

Eldon Griffiths: 'Yanks At Westminster: Our Friends in Commons'. *Newsweek,* 3.2.58

Nigel Nicolson: 'Long Life'. *The Spectator,* 7.11.92

Richard Rose: *British MPs: A Bite as well as a Bark?* Studies in Public Policy, No. 88 Glasgow: Centre for the Study of Public Policy, University of Strathclyde, 1982

Richard Rose: 'Parties, Factions & Tendencies in Britain', *Political Studies* 21 (1964) pp. 33–46

John Young: 'Churchill's "No" to Europe: The "Rejection" of European Union by Churchill's Post-War Government, 1951–1952'. *The Historical Journal,* 28, 4. (1985) pp. 923–937

Index

Biographical details of Members of Parliament can be found in Michael Stenton and Stephen Lees: *Who's Who of British Members of Parliament* volume IV: 1945–79 (Harvester Humanities Press, 1981).

Abadan (*see also* Anglo-Iranian Oil Company) 9, 107, 110, 128, 152–3, 167, 173, 229
Abadan crisis 141–50
  impact on Suez Group 142, 149
  interaction with Anglo-Egyptian relations 140
Abdullah, King 134, 150
Agnew, Sir Peter (MP for Camborne 1931–50; Worcester S. 1955–66) 297
Aitken, Max (MP for Holborn 1945–50) 30, 294
Alexander, Lord 179, 181
Algeria 189, 190, 192
All-party Parliamentary Committee 8
Allan, Robert (MP for Paddington S. 1951–66) 205
Alport, (later Lord) Cuthbert (MP for Colchester 1950–61) 291
Amery, Julian (later Lord) (MP for Preston 1950–66; Brighton Pavillion 1969–92) 16, 79, 127, 152, 173, 190–2, 229, 234, 291, 296
  Abadan crisis 143, 146–7
  alliance with Israel 137, 189, 200
  British Committee of ELEC 61
  contacts with French government 201
  driving force in Suez Group 110
  Eden Plan 84
  European economic integration 85–8
  Expanding the Commonwealth Group 120
  formation of Suez Group 113, 156–7, 177
  Macmillan's submission to Cabinet (Jan. 1952) 81
  hope for common European policy in Middle East 104
  intelligence contacts 196, 199
  joins government 208
  Llandudno party conference 198
  Margate party conference 176
  personality and political influence 110–1, 117–8
  Schuman Plan 61
  secretary to Suez Group 115, 116, 169
  Suez base agreement negotiations 181, 186
  Suez crisis 196, 199, 203
  views on Britain's global role 119
  West German rearmament 72, 81
Amery, Leo
  and Suez Group 115–6, 118, 172
  attitude to Europe 17, 50, 85, 88
  influence upon Churchill to adopt Europe 16
  suggested amendments to Sandys' draft resolution 40
Anglo-Iranian Oil Company 128, 144, 147–8
  nationalization 141
  Persian Parliament refuses to ratify Supplementary Agreement 140
Anstruther-Gray, Sir William (MP for N. Lanark 1931–45; Berwick & E. Lothian 1951–66) 297

Index

Anti-Suez Group 2, 8, 210–21, 230, 298
  American connections 220
  attitude to America 126, 213
  coalesces 211–2
  collusion 214
  contacts with Labour party 217, 234
  formation and composition 124–6
  growing concern at government policy 212
  Llandudno party conference 212–3
  military intervention in Suez crisis 213–6
  nationalization of Suez Canal Company 210
  open rebellion (Nov. 1956) 124, 234
  organization 216–7
  political influence 126–7, 217–8, 220, 234–5
  political difficulties post-Suez 220–1
  Suez Group 127, 218, 230
  support for government after ceasefire 220
  views 125–6
  wider support within party 125
ANZUS Pact (1950) 138
Arab League 191
Assheton, Ralph (later Lord Clitheroe) (MP for Rushcliffe 1934–45; City of London 1945–50; Blackburn W. 1950–55) 182, 296
  attitude to European integration 27
  critical EDM on Suez base agreement 178
  leadership of economic pressure group 7, 109
  leaves Suez Group 116
  membership of Suez Group 114
  political influence 114, 117, 230
  Sudan, the 163, 165

Astor, John Jacob ('Jakie') (MP for Plymouth 1950–55; Plymouth S. 1955–59) 124, 127, 298
Atlantic Union 10, 78, 85, 88–9, 98
Atom bomb 170, 184–5, 187, 209
Attlee, Clement (later Earl) (Prime Minister)
  Abadan crisis 146, 149
  attitude to European integration 28, 41, 48
  Schuman Plan 68, 224
  West German rearmament 75

Baghdad Pact 189, 233
Baker, Peter (MP for Norfolk S. 1950–54) 186, 296
Banks, Cyril (MP for Pudsey 1950–9) 126, 298
Baldwin, Stanley (Prime Minister) 109, 147
Balfour Declaration 129–31
Baxter, Beverley (MP for Middlesex, Wood Green 1935–50; Southgate 1950–64) 30, 294
Beamish, Tufton (later Lord Chelwood) (MP for Lewes 1945–74) 80, 291, 294
Beaverbrook, Lord 30, 40, 61, 68, 115
Bell, Philip (MP for Bolton E. 1951–60) 296, 298
  leaves Suez Group 116, 186
Benelux 33
Berlin crisis (1948–9) 26
Berlin Four-Power Conference (1954) 182
Bermuda conference (December 1953) 178, 179, 184
Bevan, Aneurin (Minister of Health; Minister of Labour & National Service) 4, 41, 207
Beveridge Report 6, 112
Bevin, Ernest (Foreign Secretary) 31, 38, 48, 68, 75, 222–3
  attempts to involve America in Palestine issue 133
  attitude to European integration 26, 28, 34, 36, 37, 41–3, 53

Bevin, Ernest – *continued*
  hostility to customs union 42
  opposition to West German rearmament 73
  Palestine conflict 132
  reaction to Congress at the Hague 40
  Schuman Plan 68
  Western Union speech (January 1948) 33
Biggs-Davison, John (MP for Chigwell 1955–74) 117–8, 152, 207, 209, 296
  Expanding the Commonwealth Group 120
  membership of Suez Group 114
  press briefings for Suez Group 115
Birkenhead, Lord 46, 71
Black, Cyril (MP for Wimbledon 1950–70) 80
Board of Trade 93
Body, Richard (MP for Billericay 1955–59; Holland with Boston 1966–) 99, 291, 296
Boothby, Robert (later Lord) (MP for Aberdeenshire E. 1924–58) 4, 21, 24, 26, 46, 51, 64, 71, 78–9, 88, 91, 291, 295, 298
  attitude to European integration 16, 19, 23, 85–6
  co-Vice President of all-party group 19
  concern at British exclusion from a common market 100
  concern at French supranationalism 55
  favours alliance with Israel 134, 137
  Consultative Assembly 47, 87
  influence upon Churchill to adopt Europe 16
  membership of Anti-Suez Group 124–7, 220
  opposes EDC 81
  Palestine conflict 131
  part of Churchill's personal clique on Europe 13
  personality and political influence 19–20
  resignation from European Movement 84
  Schuman Plan 61
  secretary to all-party parliamentary committee 19
  sponsors EDMs on Western Union 34, 36, 44
Bossom, Alfred (MP for Maidstone 1931–59) 293
Bower, Norman (MP for Harrow W. 1941–51) 293, 294
Boyle, Sir Edward Boyle (later Lord) (MP for Hansworth 1950–70) 80, 127, 206, 291, 298
  rejoins Macmillan's government 220
  replies for Government in Rippon's adjournment debate 100
  resignation 216
Bracken, Brendan (MP for Paddington N. 1929–45; Bournemouth E. & Christchurch 1945–52) 44, 292, 295
Braine, Bernard (MP for Billericay 1950–55; Essex S.E. 1955–92) 103
Branston, Ursula 65, 96
Bretherton, Russell 100
Bretton Woods 31, 86
Briand Plan 14
British Group of European Parliamentary Union (EPU) 22
  (*see also All party committee*)
Brown, Ernest (MP for Rugby 1923–4; Leith 1927–45) 24
Bromley-Davenport, Walter (MP for Cheshire Knutsford 1945–70) 118, 296
  leaves Suez Group 116, 186
Brooman-White, Richard (MP for Rutherglen 1951–64) 291

Brussels Treaty (1948)   33, 36, 71
Buchan-Hepburn, Patrick (later
    Lord Hailes) (MP for
    Liverpool, E. Toxteth
    1939–50; Beckenham 1950–7
    (Chief Whip; Minister of
    Works)   3, 27, 115, 179, 231
  Heads of Agreement debate
    (July 1954)   123
  Suez Group   122, 174–5, 177
Bullock, Malcolm (MP for
    Lancashire Waterloo 1923–50;
    Crosby 1950–53)   293, 294
Bullus, Eric (MP for Wembley
    North 1950–74)   297
Burden, Frederick (MP for
    Gillingham 1950–83)   186,
    294, 296
Burma   121
Butcher, Herbert (Nat. Lib.,
    Holland with Boston 1937–50;
    NL&C, Holland with Boston
    1950–66)   291
Butler, R.A. (RAB) (later Lord)
    (MP for Saffron Walden
    1929–64) (Chancellor of the
    Exchequer; Lord Privy Seal &
    Leader of the House)   7, 108,
    118, 162, 178, 183, 190, 235
  attitude to European integration
    27
  decision to withdraw Bretherton
    from Spaak Committee
    100
  need for clarification of party
    policy on Europe   40
  in charge in Eden's absence
    (Nov.–Dec. 1956)   205–7,
    220
  Llandudno party conference
    199

Caffrey, Jefferson (US Ambassador
    to Cairo)   157
Canada   10, 82, 89
Capital punishment   118, 124
Carson, Edward (MP for Isle of
    Thanet 1945–53)   45, 293,
    294

Ceylon   98, 121
Challe, Major General Maurice
    (Deputy (Air) to French Chief
    of General Staff)   199
Chamberlain, Neville (Prime
    Minister)   30, 126, 147, 151,
    218, 221
Charter of Human Rights   46, 48
Churchill, Winston (Con. MP for
    Oldham 1900–4; Lib. Oldham
    1904–6; Lib. Manchester N.W.
    1906–8; Dundee 1908–22;
    Con. Epping 1924–45;
    Woodford 1945–64) (Prime
    Minister)   4, 6, 8, 10, 12–3,
    50, 53, 71, 76, 78, 109, 115,
    147–9, 200, 222–5, 229–31
  Abadan crisis   142, 147–9
  adheres to Bevin's Europe policy
    106
  assumes control of Egypt policy
    174
  atom bomb   184–5, 187
  attitude to European integration
    13–6, 22–4, 37–8, 55, 58
  attitude to Neguib regime   156
  British links with America   15
  call for admission of West
    Germans to Council of
    Europe   47
  concedes defeat on Egypt policy
    184, 187
  Congress at the Hague   36–40
  Conservative confusion over
    attitude to Europe   30
  Consultative Assembly   46–8,
    73–4
  debate on Western Union (1948)
    36
  decision to lead United Europe
    Movement   14
  defeated on the Sudan
    agreement   163–4
  desire for Minister of European
    Affairs (1951)   91
  EDM on Western Union (1948)
    36
  encouragement of Suez Group
    157, 174

Index 313

Churchill, Winston – *continued*
  friction with Eden over
    succession 93, 152
  Fulton, Missouri speech 14
  hopes for summit 90, 168, 184
  impact of Europe campaign 33,
    42–3, 47–8, 53
  latitude given to backbenches in
    Opposition 107
  'Let Europe Arise' speech
    14–5, 49
  loss of interest in European
    integration 90–1
  Macmillan-Eccles Plan 70, 71
  Middle East Defence
    Organization 137
  negotiating Suez base agreement
    175–81, 182–3, 186
  opposition to Eden's Sudan
    policy 162–3
  opposition to Eden's Egypt
    policy 90, 151–2, 156, 162,
    173–4, 176, 180–2
  Palestine crisis 129, 130, 132,
    134
  persuades party to accept Heads
    of Agreement 183
  pre-war articles on Europe 14,
    16
  resignation 188
  Schuman Plan 57, 60, 62–5, 67
  stroke 175
  support for Bevin's foreign
    policy in general 75, 134
  supports calls for military
    sanctions against Egypt 139
  UEM inaugural meeting speech
    15, 18
  vetoes Sandys' draft resolution
    on Europe (1948) 40
  West German rearmament
    72–4, 76–7, 79
Churchill, Randolph 111, 190
Clarke, Terence (MP for
  Portsmouth W. 1950–66)
  186, 296
Commonwealth 9, 10, 12–3, 15–7,
  23, 28, 29, 31, 40, 42, 44,
  48–9, 56, 60, 62–3, 68, 70,
  75–6, 78, 80–1, 85–9, 94,
  97–8, 101–5, 110, 119–21,
  128, 136, 140, 143–5, 159–61
  169–70, 172, 187, 189, 224,
  226, 227
  attitude to European unity 52
  Amery urges contribution to
    West European defence 81
  EFTA 104, 105
  invitation to parliamentarians to
    Consultative Assembly 75
  Middle East defence 145
  Suez crisis 194, 203–4, 211,
    214–5, 217, 219
  Suez Group's view 120
Congress at the Hague 16, 19, 21,
  24, 27, 33–6, 38–9, 47, 57, 78
Conservative 1922 Committee 5,
  6, 28, 109, 117, 146, 156, 164,
  167, 177, 179–80, 192, 197,
  211
Conservative 5,000 Acre Club 7
Conservative Anti-Europeanists
  29–32, 51, 224, 294
  alliance with Conservative
    Europeanists 81–2, 152
  anti-American sentiment 30
  Bretton Woods and US loan
    (1945) 31
  attitude to Churchill 30
  attitude to Empire 31
  attitude to European integration
    12, 29–32, 224
  attitude to GATT 31
  attitude to Marshall Aid 31
  composition of group 13, 294
  political and economic
    differences 22
  rebellion on the Schuman Plan
    67
  support for Empire and
    Commonwealth 29
  West German rearmament 75
Conservative backbench pressure
  groups 2, 108, 151
  Anti-Suez Group *see separate
    entry*
  Conservative Europeanists
    see separate entry

Conservative backbench pressure groups – *continued*
  Conservative Anti-Europeanists *see separate entry*
  economic policy 7, 108
  fuel and power 7
  introduction of commercial television 7
  social policy (One Nation) 7
  Sudan, the 151, 157–65
  Suez Group *see separate entry*
  transport policy 7
Conservative Defence Committee 5, 110, 179, 185
  Army Sub-committee 183
Conservative Europeanists 2, 8, 76, 222–7, 230, 235, 291–4
  attitude to Messina process 100
  Conservative backbench indifference 95–6
  discussion on future of Ruhr industries 56
  desire for British leadership within Council of Europe 79, 83
  doubts about continental federalists 40, 43
  attitude to European economic integration 85–8
  attitude to European political integration 82–5
  Eden Plan 83
  EDMs on Western Union 36, 44
  favour economic bloc of Europe and 'Europe overseas' 85
  frustrated by Eden's Europe policy 83, 91
  hopes of shift in policy swiftly disillusioned 78
  impact at Consultative Assembly 46, 76
  impatience at Labour's policy 33
  influence on Brussels Treaty negotiations 33, 36
  invitation to Commonwealth parliamentarians to Consultative Assembly 75–6
  lack of ministerial support 94
  loss of Churchill's interest and support 79, 90
  Macmillan-Eccles Plan 69
  political influence 37, 48, 76, 84, 89, 106–7, 222–7
  Suez Group 120
  Atlantic Union 72, 88–9
  support for Sandys' efforts to create Council of Europe 39
  West German rearmament 73–8, 80–2
Conservative Europhobes (1990s) 227
Conservative Finance Committee 52
Conservative Foreign Affairs Committee 5, 52, 64, 87, 109, 114–5, 153, 161, 163, 174–5, 177, 179, 183, 195
  Middle East Sub-Committee 117
  Suez Group 116, 121
Conservative Government (*see also Churchill, Eden and Macmillan entries*)
  alarm at possible backbench revolt on Suez (1954) 183
  attempts to pacify Suez Group 179
  attitude to critical EDM on Suez base agreement 178
  Churchill's non-partisan emphasis 108
  continental federalists' hopes of shift of policy 78
  free trade area proposals 103–5
  managing withdrawal from Suez 205–7
  opposition to customs union 104
  reaction to Messina 99
Conservative Imperial Affairs Committee 22, 52
Conservative party
  Abadan crisis 141–9
  acceptance of Eden's arguments on Suez base 166–7
  and Suez Group 166–7

Conservative party – *continued*
　Anglo-Egyptian financial negotiations　140
　anti-American feeling in Suez crisis　204, 206–7, 219
　attitude to Egypt　135, 153–4
　backbench MPs and influence　1–2, 7, 222
　backbench concern at EURATOM proposals　100
　backbench committees (*see also individual committees*)　5–7
　calls for economic and military sanctions against Egypt　139, 141
　ceasefire　203
　Churchill's personal appeal on Suez base agreement　183–4
　Council of Europe　51, 195–7, 226
　critical of US policy in Palestine conflict　132
　criticism of Labour's Egypt policy　137, 139
　criticism of UNO in Palestine conflict　132
　criticism of Labour's Palestine policy　132–3
　desire for clarification of policy on Europe　40
　discontent over Churchill's leadership　152
　divisions on Egypt　154
　divisions on links between West Germany and Europe　55, 74
　divisions on Palestine conflict　129, 132
　divisions emerge over Abadan　143
　doubts crystallizing about Europe　37, 43, 49
　Eden's performance as Prime Minister　192, 197
　free trade area proposal　103, 105
　greater tendency to rebellion post-1951　107
　impact of 1950 and 1955 elections on attitudes to Europe　55, 99
　impact of Churchill's retirement　188
　impact of Suez crisis upon attitudes to Europe　103
　industrial policy statement (1947)　56
　interaction of Anglo-Egyptian and Anglo-Persian relations　140
　Jewish immigration into Palestine　129, 134
　leadership sensitivity to backbench opinion　7
　Macmillan's reversal of Suez policy　208–10
　majority endorse Eden's attitude to Europe　80, 81
　methods of selecting delegates to Strasbourg　96
　Middle East defence organization　171
　military intervention in Suez crisis　202–3
　NAAFI club　7
　nature and structure (1945–57)　2
　opposition to use of force　211–2
　opposition to military withdrawal from Suez　204–7
　political management　1
　press reports of divisions on Schuman Plan　65
　reaction to Makarios' banishment　192
　reaction to Glubb's dismissal　191
　revival of interest in Europe　98–106
　support for Bevin's foreign policy in general　134
　support for Suez Group's views　195
　threatened schism　206–7
　West European Union　82
　West German rearmanent　72–83

Conservative party conference 49
  Blackpool (1954) 186
  Llandudno (1956) 102, 232
  Margate (1953) 176
Conservative Research Department
  114, 118
  discussion on future of Ruhr
    industries 56
  Schuman Plan 65
Conservative Sceptics 223–4
  attitude to Churchill 27
  attitude to Empire and
    Commonwealth 29
  attitudes to European
    integration 12, 24, 27–9
  growing opposition to
    Conservative Europeanists
    51
  Schuman Plan 66
Cooper-Key, Neill (MP for Hastings
  1945–70) 293, 294
Coote, Colin (Managing Editor,
  *The Daily Telegraph & The
  Morning Post*) 115
Corbett, Uvedale (MP for Ludlow
  1945–51) 291, 294, 295
Corfield, Frederick (MP for
  Gloucester S. 1955–74) 99,
  291
Coudenhove-Kalergi, Count
  Richard
  leadership of pan-European
    movement 16
Council of Empire Economic
  Union 118
Council of Europe 46, 50, 52, 89,
  92, 223, 226
  Committee of Ministers 21, 48,
    53, 73
  Conservative Europeanists' desire
    for British leadership 79
  Consultative Assembly 46–8, 55,
    69–72, 73–4
  Economic Committee 82, 86,
    87, 227
  general low Conservative opinion
    95–7
  methods of selecting
    Conservative delegates 96

Schuman Plan 72
Strasbourg Plan 87, 88
Craddock, Beresford (MP for
  Spelthorne 1945–70) 120, 297
Cranborne, Lord (MP for
  Bournemouth W. 1950–54)
  143, 297
Crichel Down affair (1954) 185
Cripps, Stafford (President, Board
  of Trade; Minister, Economic
  Affairs; Chancellor of the
  Exchequer) 68
  hostility to customs union 42
  hostility to European integration
    41
  Schuman Plan 68
Crookshank, Harry (later Viscount)
  (MP for Gainsborough
  1924–56) (Minister of Health;
  Lord Privy Seal & Leader of
  the House) 27, 178
  approached by Sandys to support
    Churchill's nascent
    movement 18
Crouch, Robert (MP for Dorset N.
  1950–7) 296
Crowder, Petre (MP for Ruislip
  Northwood 1950–74;
  Hillingdon-Ruislip-Northwood
  1974–9) 297
Crypto-Suez Group 109, 198, 297
Cyprus 9, 116, 128, 161, 169, 171,
  177, 185, 191–3, 196, 208–9,
  231
  continuation of Suez Group
    116, 187–9
Cuthbert, William (MP for Rye
  1945–50) 293, 295
Czechoslovakia
  arms sales to Egypt 188–9, 190
  Communist *coup* (Feb. 1948) 34

Davies, Clement (Liberal leader)
  supports Conservative pressure
    on Schuman Plan 64
D'Avigdor Goldsmid, Henry (MP
  for Walsall N. 1950–74) 298
  membership of Anti-Suez Group
    124

Index

Dalton, Hugh (Chancellor of the Exchequer; Chancellor of Duchy of Lancaster; Minister of Town & Country Planning)
  hostility to European integration 41
Darling, William (Will 'Y') (MP for Edinburgh S. 1945–57) 4, 181, 293, 296
Davidson, Viscountess (MP for Hemel Hempstead 1937–59) 147, 291, 294, 295
Davies, Nigel (MP for Epping 1950–51) 291
De Chair, Somerset (MP for Norfolk S.W. 1935–45; Paddington S. 1950–51) 137
Defence White Paper (Feb. 1957) 105
de la Bère, Rupert (MP for Worcester 1935–55) 293
Dodds-Parker, Douglas (MP for Banbury 1945–59; Cheltenham 1964–74) 158, 183, 291, 294, 297
Donner, Patrick (MP for Islington W. 1931–35; Basingstoke 1935–55) 116, 296
Drayson, Barnaby (MP for Skipton 1945–79) 293, 295
Du Cann, Edward (MP for Taunton 1956–87) 297
Dugdale, Sir Thomas (later Lord Crathorne) (MP for Richmond 1929–59) 185
Dulles, John Foster (US Secretary of State) 200, 202, 211–2
Duncan, James (MP for S. Angus 1950–64) 296
Dunglass, Lord (later Earl of Home; Sir Alec Douglas-Home, then Lord Home of the Hirsel) (MP for S. Lanark 1931–50; Lanark 1950–51; Kinross & W. Perthshire 1963–74)
  Abadan crisis 146
Duthie, William (MP for Banff 1945–64) 293, 295

Eccles, David (later Viscount) (MP for Chippenham 1943–64) (Minister of Works; Minister for Education) 21, 46, 51, 71, 225, 291, 294, 295
  attitude to European integration 22, 56
  attitude to West Germany 56
  British Committee of ELEC 21, 61
  Consultative Assembly 47
  discussions on future of Ruhr industries 57
  Macmillan-Eccles Plan 69–72
  political influence 21
  Schuman Plan 60–2
  support for GATT 23
Eden, Anthony (later Earl of Avon) (MP for Warwick & Leamington 1924–57) (Foreign Secretary; Prime Minister) 40, 52, 71, 108–9, 115, 123–4, 168, 176–81, 183, 187, 226
  Abadan crisis 142–3, 146, 148–9
  Anglo-Egyptian financial negotiations 140
  attempts to pacify Suez Group 177–9, 183
  attends Congress at the Hague 38
  attitude to European integration 25–7, 29, 37, 79, 83, 91, 224, 226
  attitude to Messina process 99–100
  attitude to Neguib regime 156
  attitude to calls for military sanctions against Egypt 139
  attitude to Churchill's Europe campaign 25–6, 48
  attitude to Suez Canal Zone base 166
  banishment of Makarios 192
  cease-fire decision 217
  Churchill's hopes for summit with Russia 184
  Conservative critics 18, 26, 35, 151–2

Eden, Anthony – *continued*
  continues Bevin's Atlantic
    approach 80, 106
  decision to use force in Suez
    crisis 125, 198–9, 201, 203,
    213, 215
  decision to withdraw Bretherton
    from Spaak Committee 100
  departure to Jamaica 203
  determination for crushing
    victory over Nasser 195
  determined support of EDC 81
  economic cooperation with
    Europe 25, 56, 63, 82
  Eden Plan 83–4, 93, 226
  Egypt policy 110, 154, 171, 178,
    180, 182, 229
  endorsement of Bevin's
    approach to Europe 37, 43
  friction with Churchill over
    succession 152
  friction with Churchill over
    Egypt 156–7, 162, 181–2
  hostility to Conservative
    Europeanists 26, 92
  illness (April–Oct. 1953) 174
  impact of personality 25, 92,
    182, 188
  Llandudno party conference
    199
  Macmillan-Eccles Plan 70, 71, 90
  Middle East defence organization
    171
  opposition to Sudan policy 151,
    157–65
  Palestine 130, 133–4
  performance as Prime Minister
    188, 190
  policy towards Persia (1951–54)
    153
  political cost of the Sudan
    agreement 151, 165
  political implications of
    succession 152
  reaction to Glubb's dismissal
    191
  reluctance to refer Suez crisis to
    UNO 210–1
  resignation 106, 208

Schuman Plan 63
sensitivity to political standing
  26
speech in Rome (Nov. 1951)
  79
Strasbourg Plan (1951) 87
Suez crisis 210, 212, 214–6,
  218, 231–5
West European Union (Oct. 1954)
  82
West German rearmament 72,
  74, 81
Eden, Clarissa 200
Eden, John (MP for Bournemouth
  W. 1954–63) 127, 297
Eden Plan 83, 93, 226
EDM
  Abadan crisis (7 June 1951) 143
  Abadan crisis (21 June 1951)
    146–7
  Anglo-American cooperation
    (Nov. 1956) 219
  Messina talks (July 1956) 100
  Suez Canal Zone base agreement
    (Dec. 1953) 115, 117
  West European unity (Dec. 1956)
    103
  Western Union (March 1948)
    19, 34–8, 294
  Western Union (Feb. 1949) 44,
    295
  UNO and USA (Nov. 1956)
    206, 218
Egypt (*see also Nasser and Neguib
  entries*) 9, 113, 115–6, 123,
    125–6, 128–9, 134, 228, 229,
    232, 233
  Abadan 140, 143, 144, 147, 149
  American pressure for Britain to
    reach settlement 171, 182,
    184
  Anglo-Egyptian relations and the
    Sudan 157–65
  Anglo-Egyptian financial
    negotiations 140, 153
  Anglo-Egyptian relations
    (1948–51) 131, 135–41
  Anglo-Egyptian relations
    (1951–53) 151–7

Egypt – *continued*
  attacks on British troops in
    Canal Zone 154, 181
  British sales of military
    equipment 141, 189
  call for British withdrawal from
    Canal base 139
  demands revision of 1936 treaty
    129, 131
  friction between Churchill and
    Eden 152
  negotiating Suez base agreement
    166–87
  overthrow of King Farouk 113,
    156, 158
  Sudan, the 157, 168, 177, 178,
    182
  Suez crisis 188–91, 193, 194, 198,
    199, 201–3, 203, 206, 211–3
  unilateral abrogation of 1936
    treaty 153
Eisenhower, Dwight (US President)
  180, 200, 204, 207
Elliot, Walter (MP for Lanark
  1918–23; Kelvingrove 1924–45;
  Combined Scottish Universities
  1946–50; Kelvingrove 1950–8)
  124–5, 215, 219, 291, 298
  approached by Sandys to support
    Churchill's nascent
    movement 18, 21
  Munich crisis 126
  Palestine conflict 130
  political influence 21
  views in Suez crisis 124
EURATOM 100, 105
European Army 223
  (*see also European Defence
  Community*)
European Coal and Steel Community
  (*see also Schuman Plan*) 32,
  45, 55, 57–63, 65–6, 68–9, 76,
  79, 83–4, 89, 226
European Court 48
European Defence Community (*see
  also West German rearmament*)
  74, 79–82, 83, 225, 226
  defeated on procedural vote in
    French Assembly 82

European Economic Community
  102, 105, 106
European Free Trade Area (EFTA)
  227
  EFTA of the Seven 105
  EFTA of the Seventeen 105
  government commitment to
    policy 104
  majority of Conservatives support
    102
European League for Economic
  Cooperation (ELEC)
  British Committee 57, 61, 79,
    86, 227
  Westminster Conference (1949)
    45, 57
  Commonwealth-Empire
    conferences (1951) 87
  monetary conference (Brussels
    1953) 88
European Movement (*see also
  International Committee of the
  Movements for European Unity*)
  45, 58
  economic conference (London
    1954) 88
European Payments Union (EPU)
  86, 87
European Political Community
  (*see also European Defence
  Community*) 79
European Recovery Programme
  (*see also Marshall Aid*)
  dependence on Middle Eastern
    oil 136
Expanding the Commonwealth
  Group 120

Fawzi, Mahmoud (Egyptian Foreign
  Minister) 213
Federal Union 12, 80
  representatives on Churchill's
    United Europe Committee
    19
  survey of attitudes towards free
    trade area 103
Fell, Anthony (MP for Yarmouth
  1951–66; 1970–83) 186, 209,
  296

320 Index

Fisher, Nigel (MP for Hitchin 1950–5; Surbiton 1955–74) 297
Fletcher, Walter (MP for Bury & Radcliffe 1945–55) 45, 291, 294, 297
Foreign Office 79, 106, 223, 226
  attitude to European integration 25, 41, 42
  attitude to Messina process 100
  Council of Europe 84, 226
  determination to combat US isolationism 42
  influence on Europe policy 91, 93
  Schuman Plan 58
  Sudan, the 158, 160
Fort, Richard (MP for Clitheroe 1950–9) 297
Foster, John (MP for Chester, Northwich 1945–74) 46, 51, 80, 291, 298
Fox, Sir Gifford (MP for Henley 1932–50) 293
France 13, 25, 32, 41, 51, 52, 56, 62, 65, 80, 82, 88, 95, 100, 104, 137, 143, 145, 154, 175, 215, 224
  government contacts with Suez Group 199
  Suez crisis 189, 190, 192, 194, 196, 197, 199–200, 201, 202, 204, 211–2, 214, 232–4
Fraser, Hugh (MP for Stone 1945–50; Stafford & Stone 1950–83) 80, 117, 291, 294, 295
Fraser, Ian (MP for St Pancras N. 1924–37; Morecambe & Lonsdale 1940–58) 293

Gage, Connolly (UU MP for Belfast S. 1945–52) 291, 294
Gaitskell, Hugh (Chancellor of the Exchequer; Leader of the Labour party) 198, 216, 218
Galbraith, Thomas Dunlop (later Lord Strathclyde) (MP for Glasgow Pollok 1940–55) 293

Gammans, David (MP for Hornsey 1941–57) 291, 294, 295
Gandar-Dower, Eric (MP for Caithness & Sunderland 1945–50) 294
Gates, Ernest (MP for Middleton & Prestwick 1940–51) 293
General Agreement on Trade and Tariffs (GATT) 23, 31, 97
Gazier, Albert (French Minister for Social Affairs) 199
General Election
  (February 1950) 55, 141
  (May 1955) 99, 188, 226
  (October 1951) 148, 107
  (October 1959) 221
Geneva conference (1954) 183, 200
Glover, Douglas (MP for Ormskirk 1953–70) 297
Glubb, General Sir John Glubb ('Glubb Pasha') (Chief of Staff, Arab Legion) 128, 191, 192, 231
  dismissal 190
Gomme-Duncan, Alan (MP for Perth & E. Perthshire 1945–59) 297
Graham, Fergus (MP for Cumberland N. 1926–35; Darlington 1951–9) 296
Greece 145
Green, Alan (MP for Preston S. 1955–64; 1970–4) 296
Gridley, Sir Arnold (later Lord) (MP for Stockport S. 1935–55) 44, 293, 295
  urges Sandys to modify resolution on Europe (1949) 49–50
Grimston, Sir Robert (later Lord) (MP for Westbury 1931–64) 167, 295, 296
Gstaad conference (1947) 19

Haifa 129, 136, 139, 140
Hall, John (MP for Wycombe 1952–78) 185, 296
Hankey, Lord (formerly Sir Maurice) 172, 175

Hankey, Robin   175
Hannon, Patrick (MP for Birmingham Molesley 1921–50)   44, 293, 295
Hare, John (later Viscount Blakenham) (MP for Woodbridge 1945–50; Sudbury & Woodbridge 1950–63)   293, 295
Harris, Frederick (MP for Croydon N. 1948–55; Croydon N.W. 1955–74)   186, 293, 296
Harris, Reader (MP for Heston & Isleworth 1950–70)   80, 118, 186, 296
Harvey, Ian (MP for Harrow E. 1950–8)   206
Hay, John (MP for Henley 1950–74)   80, 291
Head, Anthony (later Viscount) (MP for Carshalton 1945–60)   183, 293
   Abadan crisis   143, 146
Headlam, Sir Cuthbert (MP for Barnard Castle 1924–29; 1931–35; Newcastle-upon-Tyne N. 1940–51)   291, 294, 295
Heald, Sir Lionel (MP for Chertsey 1950–70) (Attorney General)   212, 215, 298
   September 1956 speech   125
   views in Suez crisis   124
Heath, Edward (MP for Bexley 1950–74; Bexley & Sidcup 1974–) (Chief Whip)   96, 106, 291
   Suez crisis   198–9, 206–8, 215–6
Heathcoat Amory, Derick (later Viscount Amory) (MP for Tiverton 1945–60)   292, 294
Henderson, John (MP for Cathcart 1946–64)   293
Henderson Stewart, James (MP for Fife E. 1933–61)   130, 291
Hicks Beach, William (MP for Cheltenham 1950–64)   185, 296

Hinchingbrooke, Viscount (later Victor Montagu) (MP for Dorset S. 1941–62)   118, 127, 177, 194, 196, 207, 209, 213, 291, 296
   chairman of Transport Committee   7, 117
   chairman of Middle East Sub-Committee   117
   co-founder of Tory Reform Group   22
   Expanding the Commonwealth Group   120
   leadership of transport policy pressure group   7
   opposition to rearmament   112
   part of moves to oust Churchill   112
   personality and political influence   111
   vice-chairman of Foreign Affairs Committee   117
Hogg, Quintin (later Viscount Hailsham) (MP for Oxford 1938–51)   291, 294, 295
Holland-Martin, Christopher (MP for Ludlow 1951–60)   296
   joint Treasurer of the Conservative party   117
   political influence   114
Hollis, Christopher (MP for Devizes 1945–55)   86, 291, 294, 295
Hope, Lord John (later Lord Glendevon) (MP for Midlothian & Peebles 1945–50; Pentlands 1950–64)   80, 85, 93, 94, 291
Hopkinson, Henry (later Lord Colyton) (MP for Taunton 1950–6)   94, 108, 291
Hornby, Richard (MP for Tonbridge 1956–74)   298
Horobin, Ian (MP for Southwark 1931–5; Oldham E. 1951–59)   296
House of Commons
   nature and structure   2–4

Howard, Sir Arthur (MP for Westminster, St. Georges 1945–50) 293, 294
Howard, Greville (NL&C MP for St Ives 1950–66) 297
Howard, John (MP for Southampton Test 1955–64) 297
Hughes Hallett, John (MP for Croydon 1951–5; Croydon N.E. 1955–64) 80, 291
Hulbert, Norman (MP for Stockport 1935–50; Stockport N. 1950–64) 295
Hurd, Anthony (later Lord) (MP for Newbury 1945–64) 4, 207
Hussein, King 190
Hutchison, James (MP for Glasgow Central 1945–50; Scotstoun 1950–59) 291, 294, 295
Hyde, Montgomery (UU MP for Belfast N. 1950–59) 118, 119, 291, 296
Hylton-Foster, Harry (MP for York 1950–65) 298

Imperial Preference 8–9, 11, 13, 16–7, 22, 29–31, 35, 49–50, 52, 56, 62, 70, 79, 85–6, 97–8, 102, 106, 107–9, 112, 120, 123, 131, 134, 138, 147, 155–6, 158, 168, 172, 226, 231
Independent Conservatives 210
India 23, 44, 52, 98, 121, 129, 134, 145, 169, 173
Indian Army 169
Interlaken conference (1948) 43
International Committee of the Movements for European Unity (*see also* European Movement) (*post* Feb. 1949) 34, 39, 58
Iraq (*see also* Nuries-Said*) 128, 129, 131, 136, 144–5, 169, 183, 194, 202
Israel (*see also* Palestine) 126, 133–5, 137, 145, 166–8, 179, 182, 189, 192, 232–3
  Suez crisis 194, 199, 200, 202, 213–5
Italy 32, 45, 51

Johnson, Eric (MP for Blackley 1951–64) 297
Jordan 128, 134, 150, 169, 183, 185, 188–91, 197, 201, 202
Joseph, Keith (later Lord) (MP for Leeds N.E. 1956–87) 99, 124, 291, 298
Joyson-Hicks, Lancelot (later Viscount Brentford) (MP for Chichester 1942–58) 295

Keeling, Edward (MP for Twickenham 1935–54) 291, 294, 295
Kenya 160
Kerby, Captain Henry (MP for Arundel & Shoreham 1954–71) 119, 181, 296
Kerr, Sir John (MP for Scottish Universities 1935–50) 293
Kerr, Hamilton (MP for Oldham 1935–45; Cambridge 1950–66) 80, 114, 291, 296
Killearn, Lord 113, 172
Kirk, Peter (MP for Gravesend 1955–64; Saffron Walden 1965–74) 99, 291, 298
Kohl, Chancellor Helmut 10
Korean War 67–8, 72–3, 122, 137–8, 149, 214

Labour Government (*see also* Attlee and Bevin entries) 76, 107
  Anglo-Egyptian financial negotiations 140
  attitude to Conservative Europeanists 40, 48, 52
  Congress at the Hague 40
  decision to withdraw AIOC personnel from Abadan 148
  determination to dilute supranational idea 41
  hostility to Council of Europe 72, 76
  inability to settle problem of Arab/Israeli animosity 136
  negotiating the Brussels Treaty (1948) 33

Labour Government – *continued*
  opens question of British withdrawal from Suez base 135
  Palestine conflict 129, 132–3
  reluctance to debate EDM on Western Union 35
  sales of military equipment to Egypt 141
  Schuman Plan 57, 59, 66, 68
  West German rearmament 75
Labour party 198
  attitude to European integration 13
  attitude to Churchill's leadership of UEM 15, 24
  Congress at the Hague 38
  divisions on Palestine 133
  influence upon Conservative opinion 8
  National Executive Committee 19, 22, 24, 31, 36, 63
  Suez Canal Zone treaty 175, 185
  Suez crisis 202–3, 207, 216
  Suez Group 173, 176
  support for EDMs on Western Union 35, 44
  West German rearmament 72
Lambton, Lord (MP for Berwick-on-Tweed 1951–73) 167
Lancaster, Colonel Claude (MP for Fylde 1938–50; S. Fylde 1950–70)
  leadership of fuel and power pressure group 7
Langford-Holt, Anthony (MP for Shrewsbury 1945–84) 291, 294
Law, Richard (later Lord Coleraine) (MP for Kingston-upon-Hull 1931–45; Kensington S. 1945–50; Kingston-upon-Hull, Haltonprice 1950–4) 291
Lawrence, T.E. 130
Leather, Edwin (later Lord) (MP for Somerset N. 1950–64) 297
Lee, Frank (Permanent Under Secretary, Board of Trade) 93

Legge-Bourke, Major Harry (MP for Isle of Ely 1945–73) 4, 71, 75, 111, 117–9, 165, 207, 234, 294, 296
  attitude to EDC 75
  applies for restoration of Whip 186
  contemptuous gesture to Morrison 144
  opposition to Sudan settlement 163
  personality and political influence 112
  rebellion on Schuman Plan 68
  resigns party Whip (1954) 113, 185
  stance during Suez crisis 113
Lennox-Boyd, Alan (later Viscount Boyd) (MP for Mid-Bedfordshire 1931–60) (Minister of State, Colonial Office; Secretary of State for the Colonies) 293
Llandudno party conference 199
Lindsay, Martin (MP for Solihull 1945–64) 292, 294, 295
Lloyd, Geoffrey (later Lord Geoffrey-Lloyd) (MP for Birmingham, Ladywood 1931–45; Birmingham, Kings Norton 1950–5; Sutton Coalfield 1955–74) (Minister of Fuel and Power) 293
  approached by Sandys to join Churchill's nascent movement 18
Lloyd, Major Guy (MP for E. Renfrewshire 1940–59) 4, 114, 207, 296
Longden, Gilbert (MP for Hertfordshire S.W. 1950–74) 80, 85, 292
Low, A.R. 'Toby' (later Lord Aldington) (MP for Blackpool N. 1945–62) 229, 233, 293, 294
Lucas, Jocelyn (MP for Portsmouth South 1939–66) 186, 292, 294, 295, 297

Lucas-Tooth, Hugh (MP for Isle of Ely 1924–29; Hendon S. 1945–70)   292, 294, 295, 298
Lyttleton, Oliver (later Viscount Chandos) (MP for Aldershot 1940–54)   27, 70

MacDonald, Sir Peter (MP for Isle of Wight 1924–59)   292, 294
  attitude to European integration   22
  involvement in British Group of EPU   22
  political influence   22
  preparatory work for debate on Western Union   36
  sponsors EDMs on Western Union   34, 44
  support for imperial preference   22
Mackay, Ronald ('Kim') (Labour MP for Hull N.W. 1945–50; Reading 1950–1)
  founder of British Group of EPU   22
Maclay, Jack (later Viscount Muirshiel) (MP for Montrose Burghs 1940–50; W. Renfrewshire 1950–64)   80, 292
Maclean, Fitzroy (MP for Lancaster 1941–59; Bute & N. Ayrshire 1959–74)   114, 147, 296
  leaves Suez Group   116, 186
  opposition to Sudanese self-government   159
  sponsors EDM on Abadan (7 June 1951)   143
  sponsors EDM on Abadan (21 June 1951)   146
  views on Middle East Defence   145
Macleod, John (MP for Ross & Cromarty 1945–64)   297
Macmillan, Harold (MP for Stockton-on-Tees 1924–29; 1931–45; Bromley 1945–64) (Minister of Housing & Local Government; Minister of Defence; Foreign Secretary; Chancellor of the Exchequer; Prime Minister)   78, 108, 114–5, 190, 210, 225, 227, 231, 232, 292
  alliance with Israel   189, 200
  attitude to European integration   18, 20–1, 32, 55–6
  British Committee of ELEC   20
  Chairman of UEM's East European Committee   20
  Consultative Assembly   46–7, 69–72
  determination to confront Nasser   200
  discussions on future of Ruhr industries   57
  draft submission to Cabinet (Jan. 1952)   81, 94
  European Movement conference (Brussels 1949)   45
  fears of resurgent West Germany   56, 61
  Foreign Secretary   99
  free trade area proposals   102–6
  Macmillan-Eccles Plan   69–72, 76
  Palestine conflict   130
  part of Churchill's personal clique on Europe   13
  political influence   20, 50
  reverses Suez policy when Prime Minister   208–9
  self-determination for Cyprus   189
  Schuman Plan   60–1, 63–4
  Suez crisis   200–1
  UEM's General Committee   20
  West German rearmament   75
Macmillan, Maurice (MP for Halifax 1955–64)   298
Macmillan-Eccles Plan   69–72, 76, 225
Maddan, Martin (MP for Hitchin 1955–64; Hove 1965–73)   99, 103, 292
Maitland, Donald   106
Maitland, John (MP for Horncastle 1945–66)   293, 294

Maitland, Patrick (later Earl of Lauderdale) (MP for Lanark 1951–59)   117, 121, 191, 209, 296
 chairman of Expanding the Commonwealth Group   120
 membership of Suez Group   113
 opposition to Sudanese self-government   159
 Suez Group press relations   115
Major, John   11
Makarios, Archbishop   117
 banished to the Seychelles   192
 released   208
Makins, Robert (later Lord Sherfield)   69, 93
Malta   128, 169
Manningham-Buller, Reginald (later Lord Dilhorne) (MP for Daventry 1943–50; S. Northants 1950–62)   39, 292
Marks, Derek   115
Marlowe, Anthony (MP for Hove 1945–50)   30, 294
Marlowe, Thomas (former editor of *The Daily Mail*)   30
Marples, Ernest (later Lord) (MP for Wallasey 1945–74)   293
Marsden, Arthur (MP for Chertsey 1937–50)   294
Marshall Aid (*see also European Recovery Programme*)   23, 31, 56, 61, 65, 120
Marshall, Douglas (MP for Bodmin 1945–64)   296
Marshall, Sidney (MP for Sutton & Cheam 1945–54)   292, 294
Mathew, Robert (MP for Honiton 1955–66)   99, 292, 298
 sponsors EDM recommending British observer at Messina talks   100
Maude, Angus (later Lord) (MP for Ealing S. 1950–58; Stratford-on-Avon 1963–83)   117, 118, 206, 209, 296
 Expanding the Commonwealth Group   120

Llandudno party conference   198
 membership of Suez Group   113
Maude, John (MP for Exeter 1945–51)   293, 294
Mawby, Ray (MP for Totnes 1955–83)   296
Maxwell Fyfe, David (later Earl of Kilmuir) (MP for W. Derby 1935–54) (Home Secretary; Lord Chancellor)   46, 48, 78, 91, 231, 292
 attitude to European integration   21
 burdens of office   94
 Congress at the Hague   39
 Consultative Assembly   46, 78
 European Movement conference (Brussels 1949)   45
 membership of Churchill's committee   21
 relationship with Eden   21
 Strasbourg (Nov. 1951) speech   78
Maydon, Stephen (MP for Wells 1951–70)   297
McAdden, Stephen (MP for Southend E. 1950–79)   294
McCallum, Duncan (MP for Argyll 1940–58)   293, 295
McLean, Neil ('Billy') (MP for Inverness 1954–64)   296
 membership of Suez Group   114
 secretary to Middle East Sub-Committee   117
McNeil, Hector (Minister of State, Foreign Office)   145
Medlicott, Frank (Lib. Nat. MP for E. Norfolk 1939–50; NL&C Norfolk Central 1950–59)   124, 126, 221, 295, 296, 298
Mellor, John (MP for Tamworth 1935–45; Sutton Coalfield 1945–55)   30, 116, 294, 296
Menzies' mission   197, 210
Messina   98–101, 103, 104,
Middle East Defence Organization   137, 154, 156, 158, 171

Mollet, Guy (French Prime
    Minister)   104, 199–201
Molson, Hugh (later Lord) (MP
    for Doncaster 1931–39;
    Derbyshire High Peak
    1939–61)   292, 295
Monckton, Sir Walter (later
    Viscount) (MP for Bristol W.
    1951–7)   217, 231
Monnet, Jean   20, 57, 59, 84, 225
  hostility to Macmillan-Eccles
    Plan   70
  influence on Pleven Plan   72
Montreux conference (1947)   19
Moore, Sir Thomas (MP for Ayr
    Burghs 1925–50; Ayrshire &
    Bute 1950–64)   295, 297
Morrison, Herbert (later Lord)
    (Secretary of State, Home
    Affairs; Foreign Secretary)   53
  Schuman Plan   71
  Abadan crisis   142, 144, 146, 149
Morrison, John (later Lord
    Margadale) (MP for Salisbury
    1942–64)   4, 185, 207, 296
  political influence   117
Morrison, William ('Shakes') (later
    Viscount Dunrossil) (MP for
    Cirencester & Tewkesbury
    1929–59) (Speaker of the
    House)   27
Mossadeq, Dr (*see also* Abadan crisis
    and Persia)   141, 143–4, 148,
    153
  coup   153, 203
Mott-Radclyffe, Charles (MP for
    Windsor 1942–70)   4, 80, 293,
    294
Muggeridge, Malcolm (editor of
    Punch)   115
Munich crisis   122, 126, 212, 217
Mussolini, Benito   194

Nabarro, Gerald (MP for
    Kidderminster 1950–64;
    Worcestershire S. 1966–73)
    119, 294, 296
  leadership of fuel and power
    pressure group   7

Nahas Pasha   139, 152
Nasser, Gamal Abdul (Egyptian
    Prime Minister 1954–6 and
    President 1956–70) (*see also
    Egypt*)   144, 181, 187,
    197–200, 232–4
  nationalization of Suez Canal
    Company   194
  Suez crisis   188–96, 197–200,
    202, 203, 205, 206, 209, 210,
    212, 213, 215
Neguib, General Mohamed
    (Egyptian Prime Minister
    1952–54 and President
    1953–56)   156, 158, 159, 161,
    162, 174, 181
Nicholson, Godfrey (MP for
    Farnham 1937–66)   292, 294
Nicolson, General Sir Cameron
    (Commander-in-Chief, Middle
    East Land forces)   169
Nicolson, Nigel (MP for
    Bournemouth E. &
    Christchurch 1952–59)   80,
    85, 125–7, 212, 216, 221, 292,
    298
Nield, Basil (MP for Chester
    1940–56)   292, 294, 295, 298
Noble, Allan (MP for Chelsea
    1945–59)   44, 293, 294
North Atlantic Treaty Organization
    (NATO)   26, 71, 82, 88–9, 98,
    105, 145, 168, 226, 212, 213,
    219
Nuries-Said, General (Prime
    Minister of Iraq) (*see also Iraq*)
    194, 201
Nutting, Anthony (MP for Melton
    Mowbray 1945–56)   83, 93,
    127, 177–8, 183, 190–1, 232,
    234, 292, 298
  resignation   216
  Llandudno party conference
    speech   199

Organization for European
    Economic Cooperation
    (OEEC)   26, 39, 42, 65, 71,
    89, 100, 226

Ormsby-Gore, David (later Lord Harlech) (MP for Oswestry 1950–61) 143, 297
Orr, Captain Lawrence (UU MP for Down South 1950–74) 297
Orr-Ewing, Charles Ian (later Lord) (MP for Hendon 1950–70) 297
Orr-Ewing, Ian (MP for Weston-Super-Mare 1934–58) 291, 294, 295
Osborne, Cyril (MP for Lincolnshire, Louth 1945–69) 293

Pakistan 98, 121
Palestine (*see also Israel*) 9, 107, 113, 141, 144, 152, 167–9, 228–9
  1939 White Paper 130
  Arab revolt (1936) 131
  Britain surrenders Mandate 133
  Palestine crisis 128–35
Panama Canal 138, 145
Pannell, Norman (MP for Liverpool, Kirkdale 1955–64) 297
Persia (*see also Abadan crisis and Mossadeq*) 128, 135, 140, 142–8, 153, 184
  British policy (1951–54) 153
Peto, Christopher (MP for Devon N. 1945–55) 292, 294
Peyton, John (later Lord) (MP for Yeovil 1951–83) 297
Pflimlin Plan 86
Pickthorn, Kenneth (MP for Cambridge University 1935–50; Carlton 1950–66) 30, 294
Pineau, Christian (French Foreign Minister) 200
Pitman, James (MP for Bath 1945–64) 80, 127, 292, 297
Pleven Plan 72, 74–6, 78
Ponsonby, Charles (MP for Sevenoaks 1935–50) 293, 295
Poole, Oliver (MP for Oswestry 1945–50) (Chairman of the Party) 292, 294

Portal, Jane (Churchill's secretary) 174
Powell, Enoch (MP for Wolverhampton S.W. 1950–74; UU MP for South Down 1974–83) 118, 177, 294, 297
  leaves Suez Group 116
  membership of Suez Group 114
  rebellion on Schuman Plan 68
  secretary to Suez Group 116
Prescott, Stanley (MP for Lancaster, Darwen 1943–51) 293
Price, David (MP for Eastleigh 1955–92) 99, 127, 213, 292, 298
Price-White, David (MP for Carnarvon Boroughs 1945–50) 292, 294
Prior-Palmer, Otho (MP for Worthing 1945–64) 292, 295
Progress Trust 6–7, 112, 117, 163, 174

Radio Cairo 189
Raikes, Victor (MP for S.E. Essex 1931–45; Liverpool, Wavertree 1945–50; Liverpool, Garston 1950–57) 44, 209, 293, 295, 297
Rayner, Ralph (MP for Totnes 1935–55) 116, 119, 185, 297
Reed, Sir Stanley (MP for Aylesbury 1938–50) 293, 294
Rees Davies, William (MP for Isle of Thanet 1953–83) 119, 297
Rennell, Lord 172
Renton, David (later Lord) (Nat. Lib. for Huntingdonshire 1945–50; NL&C 1950–68; Con. 1968–79) 292, 294
Retinger, Joseph
  lobbying with Sandys for Congress at the Hague 19, 33
  work with Sandys to create Council of Europe 39
Rhodesia 9, 110

Ridsdale, Julian (Lib. Unionist MP for Harwich 1954–92)   205, 218, 298
Rippon, Geoffrey (later Lord Rippon) (MP for Norwich S. 1955–64; Hexham 1964–87)   104, 292
   moves adjournment debate on government policy towards Messina   100
   'main swing' of small pro-Europe group   99
   sponsor of Federal Union survey   103
   sponsors EDM calling for conference of West European nations   103
   sponsors EDM recommending British observer to Messina talks   100–1
Roberts, Peter (MP for Sheffield, Ecclesall 1945–50; C&L MP for Sheffield, Heeley 1950–66)   80, 292, 294, 295
   involvement in British Group of EPU   22
   preparatory work for debate on Western Union   36
   resignation from British Group of EPU   22
   sponsors EDM on Western Union (1949)   44
Robertson, David (MP for Streatham 1939–50; Caithness & Sunderland 1950–64)   293
Robinson, Roland (later Lord Martonmere) (MP for Widnes 1931–35; Blackpool 1935–45; Blackpool S. 1945–66)   293, 295
Rodgers, John (MP for Sevenoaks 1950–79)   99, 292
   sponsors EDM calling for conference of West European nations   103
   sponsors EDM recommending British observer at Messina talks   100

Ross, Sir Ronald (UU MP for Londonderry 1929–51)   46
Russell, Roland (MP for Wembley S. 1950–74)   120, 294, 297
Russia   104, 134, 197, 212
   intervention in Hungary   214
   possible intervention in Abadan crisis   143
   threat to Western defence in Middle East   120–1, 131, 137, 144, 145, 154, 167–8, 188–9, 193, 200–1
   threat to West European security   14, 58, 72–3, 80, 222–3

Salisbury, Lord (Lord President of the Council)   175, 177, 182, 211, 231
   approached to join Churchill's nascent Europe movement   18
   assumes control of Egypt negotiations   175
   attitude to European integration   27, 94
   attitude to Suez Group   176
   resignation   208–9
Sanderson, Sir Frank (MP for Lancashire, Darwen 1922–23; 1924–29; Ealing 1931–45; Ealing E. 1945–50)   293, 294
Sandys, Duncan (later Lord Duncan-Sandys) (MP for Lambeth, Norwood 1935–45; Streatham 1950–74)   10, 78, 108, 223, 231, 292
   Abadan crisis   146
   atomic bomb   170
   attitude to European integration   17, 23
   burdens of office   94
   Churchill wishes as Minister of European Affairs   91
   Council of Europe   39
   Consultative Assembly   47
   decisive role   18
   deliberately enlists continental federalists' support   18

Sandys, Duncan – *continued*
  draft resolution on Europe for
    party conference (1948) 39
  European Movement conference
    (Brussels 1949) 45
  Gstaad and Montreux
    conferences 19
  influence upon Churchill's
    decision to adopt Europe
    15–7
  International Committee of the
    Movements for European
    Unity 39, 42, 58
  International Committee for a
    United Europe 18
  party conference (1949) 49–50
  preparatory work for Congress at
    the Hague 19, 33–4
  part of Churchill's personal
    clique on Europe 13
  relationship with Eden 18
  sensitivity to Conservative unease
    28
  UEM inaugural meeting speech
    18
  working methods 18
  West German rearmament 73–4
Saudi Arabia 190
Savory, Professor Douglas (UU MP
  for Queen's University, Belfast
  1940–50; S. Antrim 1950–5)
  116, 186, 229, 295, 297
Schuman Plan (*see also European
  Coal and Steel Community
  (ECSC)*) 54, 56–69, 72, 76,
  79, 88, 113, 224
  Conservative divisions 58–60, 66
  Conservative rebellion 67–8
  impact on Conservative opinion
    of European integration 76
  Labour Government's refusal to
    attend Paris talks 29
  parliamentary debate 67
Selwyn Lloyd, John (later Lord
  Selwyn-Lloyd) (MP for Wirral
  1945–76) 91, 125, 175, 177,
  183, 293
  influenced by Suez Group 182
Sudan, the 161, 163

Suez crisis 195, 196, 198, 201,
  213, 214
Sharples, Richard (MP for Sutton
  & Cheam 1954–72) 218
Shephard, Sidney (MP for
  Nottinghamshire Newark
  1943–50) 293
Shepherd, William (MP for
  Cheshire, Bucklow 1945–50;
  Cheadle 1950–56) 293, 298
Shinwell, Emanuel (Minister of
  Fuel & Power; Minister of
  Defence) 149
Shuckburgh, Evelyn (Assistant
  Under Sec. (ME) FO) 102
Smiles, Walter (UU MP for Down
  N. 1945–53) 292, 293
Simon, Jocelyn (MP for
  Middlesborough W. 1951–62)
  292, 298
Smith, Edward (MP for Ashford
  1943–50) 293
Smithers, Peter (MP for
  Winchester 1950–64) 79, 85,
  292
  opposes EDC/EPC 81
Smithers, Waldron (MP for
  Chislehurst 1925–45;
  Orpington 1945–54) 294
Soames, Christopher (later Lord)
  (MP for Bedford 1950–66)
  147, 174, 182, 297
South East Asia Treaty
  Organization (SEATO) 212
Soviet Union (*see Russia*)
Spaak Committee 100
Spaak, Paul-Henri (Belgian Prime
  Minister and Foreign Minister)
  225
  nomination to Chairmanship of
    OEEC vetoed 42
  work with Sandys to create
    Council of Europe 39
Spearman, Alexander (MP for
  Scarborough & Witby 1941–66)
  124, 292, 294, 298
  views in Suez crisis 124
  directs Anti-Suez group 216–8,
    234

Index

Spence, Henry (MP for Central
    Aberdeenshire 1945–50;
    Aberdeenshire W. 1950–59)
    292
Spens, Sir Patrick (MP for Ashford
    1933–43; Kensington S.
    1950–9)   103
Stalin, Josef   168
Stanley, Oliver (MP for
    Westmoreland 1924–45;
    Bristol 1945–50)   24, 30, 293
  sponsors EDM on Abadan crisis
    143
  approached by Sandys to join
    Churchill's nascent
    movement   18
  attitude to European integration
    27
Sterling area   31, 42, 52, 55, 57,
    78, 86, 87, 89, 102, 119, 140,
    153, 170
Stoddart-Scott, Malcolm (MP for
    Pudsey & Otley 1945–50;
    Ripon 1950–73)   103, 293,
    295
Strasbourg Plan   87, 88
Stuart, James (later Viscount) (MP
    for Moray & Nairn 1923–79)
    (Opposition Chief Whip ;
    Secretary of State for
    Scotland)   3, 20, 27, 217
Studholme, Henry (MP for
    Tavistock 1942–66)   293
Suez Canal   140, 175, 198
  Anglo-Egyptian financial
    negotiations   140
  Egypt prevents passage of
    Israeli-bound cargo   136, 139
Suez Canal Company   128, 144,
    193, 194, 234
  nationalization   193, 234
Suez Canal Convention (1888)
    136, 139, 169, 194
Suez Canal Users Association
    (SCUA)   197, 200, 211
Suez Canal Zone base   115, 128,
    129, 142, 143, 151, 233
  Anglo-Egyptian Agreement (1954)
    113, 124, 184, 193, 229

Eden considers withdrawal   110
impact of Abadan crisis   149
military/strategic importance
    121, 135, 151
negotiating British withdrawal
    153, 154, 156, 161, 166–87
Suez Group   2, 8, 108–24, 126,
    222, 227, 228–34, 235, 296–7
  8 resign party Whip   209
  Abadan crisis   128, 142, 145,
    149, 151, 157
  age and political experience
    122
  Anti-Suez Group   127, 186, 217
  attitude to America   120–3, 132,
    138, 144, 145, 146, 171, 196,
    203, 204
  Anglo-Egyptian agreement on
    the Sudan   165
  anticipates Nasser's
    nationalization of Suez
    Canal Company   169
  arguments against withdrawal
    from Suez   167–72
  attitude to Egypt   137
  attitude of the Whips' Office
    122
  attitudes to Suez Canal Zone
    base   121, 138, 154
  Churchill's change of heart
    184, 187
  composition   109
  contacts with British Army   155
  contacts with French government
    194, 197, 199
  contacts with Russia   204
  contemplating resigning Whip
    206
  continuation   186–93
  critical EDM on Suez Canal
    Zone base agreement
    180
  decision to vote against Heads of
    Agreement   181
  departures   116
  Eden's stance in Abadan crisis
    143, 148
  Eden's performance as Prime
    Minister   189, 191

Index

Suez Group – *continued*
  emergence 141, 147
  encouraged by Churchill 157, 174
  Expanding the Commonwealth Group 120
  foreign policy views 119, 188, 190
  formation 107, 177
  formative experiences 128
  Glubb's dismissal 190–2
  government attempts to pacify 179
  influence upon Eden's decision to use force 198, 200
  influence on choice of Eden's successor 208
  intelligence contacts 153, 203
  interaction of events in British relations in Middle East 144
  Llandudno party conference 197–8
  Macmillan 201
  Middle East defence 145
  modus operandi 115, 173, 175, 176
  nationalization of Suez Canal Company 193–4
  opinion of Eden's Egypt policy 155, 172
  opportunity for political pressure 156
  opposition to UNO 121, 197, 211, 212
  Palestine crisis 134
  political influence 9, 117, 126, 147, 152, 174, 176, 182–3, 188, 192, 194–6, 200, 204–5, 207, 209, 220, 228
  preferred policy for Suez base 170–2
  Progress Trust 117
  reaction of Cabinet at Llandudno party conference 199
  rebellion 178–80, 185–6, 208
  reconstruction of government 208
  recruits (1955–56) 116
  Sudan, the 157–65, 178, 183
  Suez crisis 123, 193–212
  tool for Churchill 152, 156, 187
  Tripartite Declaration 137, 122, 138
  unlikely alliance with Conservative Europeanists 152
  unofficial alliance with peers 172
  welcomes shift to anti-Nasser policy 192
Swinton, Lord (Chancellor, Duchy of Lancaster & Minister of Materials; Secretary of State, Commonwealth Relations) 94
Sudan, The 9, 115, 124, 135, 139, 142, 143, 151–3, 166, 168, 174, 177, 182, 183, 189, 191, 201, 228, 229
  attempts to unite Egypt and the Sudan under Egyptian crown 139
  Cabinet considers draft agreement 163
  crucial Conservative 1922 Committee meeting 164
  impact of Abadan crisis 150
  impact on Suez Group 151, 157
  King Farouk's claim to sovereignty 153
  King Farouk's overthrow 158
  negotiating self-government 110, 157–65
Syria 193

Tariff Reform 9, 227
Taylor, Ernest (MP for Paddington S. 1930–50) 292, 294, 295
Teeling, William (MP for Brighton 1944–50; Brighton Pavillion 1950–69) 292, 294, 295
Templar, General (later FM) Sir Gerald (Chief of Imperial General Staff) 189

Thomas, Ivor (MP for Keighley 1942–50) 115
Thorneycroft, Peter (later Lord) (MP for Stafford 1938–45; Monmouth 1945–66) (President, Board of Trade; Chancellor) 78, 104, 106, 209, 227, 292, 294, 295
  British Committee of ELEC 22, 61
  co-founder of Tory Reform Group 22
  defeats imperial preference at 1954 party conference 97
  discussions on future of Ruhr industries 57
  free trade area proposals 102
  political influence 22
  President of the Board of Trade 93
  Schuman Plan 61
Thornton-Kemsley, Colin (MP for Kincardine & W. Aberdeenshire 1939–50; N. Angus & Mearns 1950–64) 291, 294, 297
Thorp, Robert (MP for Berwick on Tweed 1945–51) 293, 295
Tilney, John (MP for Liverpool, Wavetree 1950–70) 80, 85, 292, 297
Tory Reform Group 22, 111, 112
Treasury
  hostility to European integration 41, 53, 93
Treaty of Rome (March 1957) 104
Trieste 184
Tripartite Declaration (1950) 137, 138, 202
  and Suez Group 122
Truman, Harry (US President)
  attitude to Mossadeq 143
  influence of oil on Middle East policy 144
  susceptibility to domestic Zionist pressure 132
Turkey 134, 145, 154, 168, 182

Turner, Lawrence (MP for Oxford 1951–59) 209
Tweedsmuir, Lady (MP for Aberdeen S. 1946–66) 292, 295
  British Committee of ELEC 61
  discussions on future of Ruhr industries 57
  Schuman Plan 61

USSR (*see Russia*)
United Europe Committee 8, 17, 24, 27, 39
  United States 9, 10
  established January 1947 17
  membership 24
United Europe Movement 14, 28
United Nations Organization (UNO) 14, 121, 146, 148
  Palestine conflict 132, 133
  Suez crisis 194, 197, 202-204, 205, 207, 211, 212, 214, 217 232, 234
United States of America 15, 19, 23, 28, 31, 33, 36, 57, 69, 80, 82, 86, 89, 104, 134, 138, 143, 175, 222
  Anti-Suez Group 127, 217
  attitude to involvement in post-war Europe 14
  encouragement of Egypt in Anglo-Egyptian negotiations on Middle East defence 145, 154
  opposition to use of force in Abadan crisis 146, 148
  perceived threat to British interests 144
  pressure for Britain to reach settlement with Egypt 171, 182, 184
  pressure for West German rearmament 73
  recognises State of Israel 134
Sudan, the 157
Suez crisis 194, 196, 197, 199–201, 203–7, 212, 217, 218, 232, 234

United States of America – *continued*
  Suez Group 120–3, 132, 138, 144–6, 171, 196, 203–4
  support for Zionism 131
  Jewish domestic pressure 133, 203

Vansittart, Lord 172
Vere Harvey, Air Commadore Arthur (later Lord Harvey) (MP for Chester, Macclesfield 1945–71) 4, 292, 294, 295, 297
  rebellion on Schuman Plan 68

Wakefield, Edward (MP for Derbyshire W. 1950–62) 158
Wakefield, Sir Wavell (MP for Swindon 1935–45; St Marylebone 1945–63) 292, 294
Walker-Smith, Derek (later Lord Broxbourne) (MP for Hertford 1945–55; Hertford E. 1955–83) 156, 206, 231, 293, 294, 295
Wall, Patrick (MP for Hull, Haltemprice 1954–5; Haltemprice 1955–64) 297
Ward, George (later Viscount) (MP for Worcester 1945–60) 292, 294, 295
Waterhouse, Captain Charles (MP for Leicester S. 1934–45; Leicester N.E. 1950–57) 3, 16, 147, 151, 163, 165, 167, 179, 181, 186, 205, 208, 209, 230, 297
  Chairman of Defence Committee 110, 117, 185
  critical EDM on Suez base agreement 178
  formation of Suez Group 157, 177
  leadership of economic pressure group 7, 109, 110
  leadership of Suez Group 109, 115
  Llandudno party conference 198
  personality and political influence 109
Waterhouse, Major General Guy (former Head of British Advisory Military Mission to Iraq army) 109
West European Union 82, 89, 98, 226
West Germany 55–6, 74, 83, 88, 95, 105, 223, 224
  economic revival 56
  membership of Council of Europe 47–8
  perceived political instability 81
  problem of reunification 56
  rearmament 72–83, 186, 225–6
Western Union, Parliamentary debate (1948) 36
Wheatley, Mervyn (MP for E. Dorset 1945–50; Poole 1950–51) 293
Whips' Office 3
  Suez Group 122, 177–9, 185, 204
  Anti-Suez Group 217
Williams, Sir Charles (MP for Tavistock 1918–22; Torquay 1924–55) 127, 297
Williams, Gerald (MP for Tonbridge 1945–56) 292, 294, 295
Williams, Sir Herbert (MP for Reading 1924–9; Croydon S. 1932–45; Croydon E. 1950–54) 3, 40, 75, 111, 118, 147, 152, 186, 294, 297
Williams, Paul (MP for Sunderland S. 1953–64) 117, 207, 209, 297
  Expanding the Commonwealth Group 120
  membership of Suez Group 114
Willink, Henry (later Lord) (MP for Croydon N. 1940–48) 27

Willoughby de Eresby, Lord (later Earl of Ancaster) (MP for Rutland & Stamford 1933–50) 291, 294, 295
Woolton, Lord (Chairman of the Party)
  attitude to European integration 27
World Government 12, 23
  supporters enlisted by Sandys 19
Worsthorne, Peregrine 115

Yalta 9
Yates, William (MP for the Wrekin 1955–66) 126, 212-3, 298
York, Christopher (MP for Ripon 1939–50; Harrowgate 1950–54) 294
Young, Sir Arthur (MP for Glasgow, Patrick 1935–50; Glasgow Scotstoun 1950) 294